The series Lecture Notes in Bioinformatics (LNBI) was established in 2003 as a topical subseries of LNCS devoted to bioinformatics and computational biology.

The series publishes state-of-the-art research results at a high level. As with the LNCS mother series, the mission of the series is to serve the international R & D community by providing an invaluable service, mainly focused on the publication of conference and workshop proceedings and postproceedings.

Marcio Dorn · Fabricio Martins Lopes

Editors

Bioinformatics and Computational Biology

21st Brazilian Conference, X-Meeting 2025
João Pessoa, Brazil, June 3–6, 2025
Proceedings

 Springer

Editors
Marcio Dorn
Universidade Federal do Rio Grande do Sul
(UFRGS)
Porto Alegre, Brazil

Fabricio Martins Lopes
Universidade Tecnológica Federal do Paraná
(UTFPR)
Cornélio Procópio, Brazil

ISSN 0302-9743   ISSN 1611-3349 (electronic)
Lecture Notes in Bioinformatics
ISBN 978-3-032-09335-6   ISBN 978-3-032-09336-3 (eBook)
https://doi.org/10.1007/978-3-032-09336-3

LNCS Sublibrary: SL8 – Bioinformatics

Preface

The Brazilian Bioinformatics Conference: X-Meeting is an annual conference that, for the first time, publishes original, high-quality papers related to Bioinformatics and related fields, welcoming contributions on any aspect of theory as well as applications. X-Meeting has become a key research event, and one of the most important in Bioinformatics for the Brazilian community.

As has been the case for previous editions of the conference, X-Meeting 2025 hosted participants with the aim of promoting and disseminating ongoing research on Bioinformatics, as well as its applications in a number of diverse areas such as DNA and Genomics, RNA and Transcriptomics, Proteins and Proteomics, Database and Software Development, Phylogeny and Evolution, Systems Biology and Modeling, among others by considering applications in health, agriculture and microorganism and plants.

Moreover, X-Meeting 2025 was a forum for the scientific community to exchange research experience, to share new knowledge, and to increase the cooperation among research groups in Bioinformatics and related areas.

X-Meeting 2025 received 35 contributions. After a rigorous double-blind reviewing process, where at least 2 and in most cases 3 qualified reviewers reviewed each submission (94 reviews from 43 reviewers who spent significant time and effort in reviewing the papers), 16 papers were accepted, which is an acceptance rate of 45.71%.

The scientific quality of all the accepted papers was above the overall mean rating. The reviewers were chosen based on their expertise, ensuring that they came from different institutions. We would like to thank all the members of the Program Committee for their work, which we are sure contributed to improving the quality of the selected papers.

The conference was held from June 3–6, 2025, at the Centro Universitário — UNIESP — João Pessoa — Paraíba — Brazil and consisted of four days of papers, technical sessions, and keynotes.

X-Meeting 2025 was organized by the AB3C, the Brazilian Association of Bioinformatics and Computational Biology. We gratefully acknowledge the help of all members of the Steering Committee for their work in the organization of X-Meeting 2025, which allowed us to put together an excellent conference and proceedings.

We are especially grateful to the staff of Springer for their support and advice during the preparation of this LNBI volume. Special thanks are due to all authors who submitted to X-Meeting 2025, including those of papers that could not be accepted. Finally, we hope that these proceedings will be a useful reference for the Bioinformatics research community.

July 2025

Marcio Dorn
Fabricio Martins Lopes

Organization

General Chairs

Marcio Dorn	Universidade Federal do Rio Grande do Sul, Brazil
Fabricio Martins Lopes	Universidade Tecnológica Federal do Paraná, Brazil

Steering Committee

Marcelo Brandão	Universidade Estadual de Campinas, Brazil
Fabricio Martins Lopes	Universidade Tecnológica Federal do Paraná, Brazil
Nicole Scherer	Instituto Nacional de Câncer, Brazil
Ana Carolina Guimarães	Fundação Oswaldo Cruz (Fiocruz), Brazil
Helder Takashi Imoto Nakaya	Universidade de São Paulo, Brazil
Sávio Torres de Farias	Universidade Federal da Paraíba, Brazil

Program Committee

Alessandro M. Varani	Universidade Estadual Paulista Júlio de Mesquita Filho, Brazil
Alexandre Rossi Paschoal	Universidade Tecnológica Federal do Paraná, Brazil
Alexandre Francisco	Instituto de Engenharia de Sistemas e Computadores: Investigação e Desenvolvimento, Portugal
Ana C. Guimarães	Fundação Oswaldo Cruz (Fiocruz), Brazil
Ana C. Lima Camargo	Universidade Estadual de Campinas, Brazil
André Yoshiaki Kashiwabara	Universidade Tecnológica Federal do Paraná, Brazil
Artur T. L. Queiroz	Fundação Oswaldo Cruz (Fiocruz), Brazil
Carolina Saibro-Girardi	Universidade Federal de Ciências da Saúde de Porto Alegre, Brazil
Conrado Pedebos	Universidade Federal de Ciências da Saúde de Porto Alegre, Brazil

Cristiane B. D. Matielo	Universidade Federal do Rio Grande do Sul, Brazil
Daniela Megrian	Institut Pasteur, Uruguay
David C. Martins-Jr	Universidade Federal do ABC, Brazil
Deborah Antunes	Fundação Oswaldo Cruz (Fiocruz), Brazil
Diogo Antonio Tschoeke	Universidade Federal do Rio de Janeiro, Brazil
Dora Henriques	Instituto Politécnico de Bragança, Portugal
Douglas S. Domingues	Universidade de São Paulo, Brazil
Éderson S. M. Pinto	Universidade Federal do Rio Grande do Sul, Brazil
Elisangela A. S. Lizzi	Universidade Tecnológica Federal do Paraná, Brazil
Fabricio Silva	Fundação Oswaldo Cruz (Fiocruz), Brazil
Gabriela M. Breyer	Universidade Federal do Rio Grande do Sul, Brazil
Glaucia M. Bressan	Universidade Tecnológica Federal do Paraná, Brazil
Guilherme T. Valente	Hospital das Clínicas da Faculdade de Medicina de Botucatu (HCFMB), Brazil
Heitor S. Lopes	Universidade Tecnológica Federal do Paraná, Brazil
João Meidanis	Universidade Estadual de Campinas, Brazil
Jorge H. Fernandez	Universidade Estadual do Norte Fluminense Darcy Ribeiro, Brazil
Jose A. Molina Mora	Universidad de Costa Rica, Costa Rica
Juliano O. Silveira	Universidade Federal de Ciências da Saúde de Porto Alegre, Brazil
Liliane S. Oliveira	Empresa Brasileira de Pesquisa Agropecuária, Brazil
Lucas M. Carvalho	Universidade São Francisco, Brazil
Lucianna S. Santos	Institut Pasteur, Uruguay
Manuel Villalobos-Cid	Universidad de Santiago de Chile, Chile
Marcelo S. Reis	Universidade Estadual de Campinas, Brazil
Mauro A. A. Castro	Universidade Federal do Paraná, Brazil
Paulo Augusto Netz	Universidade Federal do Rio Grande do Sul, Brazil
Pedro H. Bugatti	Universidade Federal de São Carlos, Brazil
Priscila T. M. Saito	Universidade Federal de São Carlo, Brazil
Priscila Grynberg	Empresa Brasileira de Pesquisa Agropecuária, Brazil
Renato Tinos	Universidade de São Paulo, Brazil
Robson Francisco Carvalho	Universidade Estadual Paulista Júlio de Mesquita Filho, Brazil

Rocio L. B. R. Maidana	Fundação Oswaldo Cruz (Fiocruz), Brazil
Romain Guyot	French National Research Institute for Sustainable Development, France
Tetsu Sakamoto	Universidade Federal do Rio Grande do Norte, Brazil
Ulisses Nunes da Rocha	Nunes da RochaHelmholtz Centre for Environmental Research, Germany

Realization

Associação Brasileira de Bioinformática e Biologia Computacional (AB3C), Brazil

Contents

Detective Challenge: A Card-Game Approach to Teach Bioinformatics
and Gene Expression in High Schools 1
    Dayana K. Turquetti-Moraes, Gabriel Quintanilha-Peixoto,
    Ana Luiza Martins-Karl, and Thiago M. Venancio

Dissecting Structural Differences in Tumoral and Control Co-expression
Networks Through Centrality Measures 14
    Laura Galant Speggiorin, Thayne Woycinck Kowalski,
    and Mariana Recamonde-Mendoza

Diversity of Glycosyl Hydrolase Family 18 in Arthropods 30
    Lorrana Verdi Flores, Ana Beatriz Monteiro, Samanda López Peña,
    Renan Terassi Pinto, Khalid Haddi, and Luciano Vilela Paiva

Transcriptomic Profiling and Regulatory Network Reconstruction
Uncovers Central Genes in HTLV Infection Progression 45
    Laryssa Bandeira de Melo Silva, Gabriel Freitas Araújo,
    Patrícia Moura, and João Pacifico Bezerra Neto

Predicting Microsatellite Instability from Whole Slide Images Using
Texture Features 62
    Nilus Swanson, Mauro A. A. Castro, A. Gordon Robertson,
    Ilya Shmulevich, and Bahar Tercan

The Extended N-Terminal Domain of VPAC1 Isoform 2 Acts
as a Self-inhibitory Element: Insights from Molecular Dynamics
Simulations 74
    Matheus Henrique Reis, Deborah Antunes, Ingrid B. S. Martins,
    and Ernesto R. Caffarena

Using Machine Learning and Graph-Based Signatures to Evaluate Normal
and Decreased Function CYP2D6 Haplotypes 90
    Diego Mariano, Maria Carolina Puça, Yanka E. A. R. Salazar,
    Rafael Pereira Lemos, Giovana C. F. Maia, Lucas Moraes dos Santos,
    Tais Nobrega de Sousa, and Raquel Cardoso de Melo-Minardi

Immune Remodeling and Dysbiosis May Distinguish
the Microenvironments of Gastric Adenocarcinoma and Peritumoral Tissue   106
  Ronald Matheus da Silva Mourão, Juliana Barreto Albuquerque Pinto,
  Jéssica Manoelli Costa da Silva, Daniel de Souza Avelar da Costa,
  Valéria Cristiane Santos da Silva, Ana Karyssa Mendes Anaissi,
  Samia Demachki, Williams Fernandes Barra,
  Fabiano Cordeiro Moreira, and Paulo Pimentel de Assumpção

Viral Sequence Database Manager (VSDBM): A Distributed Framework
for Viral Genomic Analysis and Epitope Mapping   122
  Helton Fabio Santos de Araújo Junior, Tiago Feitosa Mota,
  José Írahe Kasprzykowski Gonçalves, Eduardo Rocha Fukutani,
  and Artur Trancoso Lopo de Queiroz

In Silico Assessment of Immune Cross Protection Between BCoV
and SARS-CoV-2   136
  Lana Bazan Peters Querne, Fernanda Zettel Bastos,
  Mikaela dos Anjos Adur, Vitória Luisa Cavalheiro,
  and Breno Castello Branco Beirão

Exploring the Therapeutic Potential of Flavonoids Present in Propolis
Against Colorectal Cancer Through a Network Pharmacology Approach   151
  Aline Cristina Felicio, Nicolly Clemente de Melo,
  and Lucas Miguel de Carvalho

BITSER: An Alignment-Free Approach for Feature Extraction
and Classification of Viral Genomes   166
  Lucas Costa Fuganti, Matheus Henrique Pimenta-Zanon,
  and Fabricio Martins Lopes

Towards Fast Binding Affinity Scoring in Protein–Protein Complexes
via Interatomic Contacts and Linear Regression   181
  Ana Luísa Araújo Bastos, Rafael Pereira Lemos,
  Diego Mariano, Camila A. O. Yamada, Milenna M. Pirovani,
  and Raquel Cardoso de Melo-Minardi

Characterization of the Terpene Synthase Gene Family and its Role
in Response to Water Deprivation in Stylosanthes scabra   192
  Ramon da Silva de Souza, Ana Luíza Trajano Mangueira de Melo,
  Manassés Daniel da Silva, Maria Luiza Carvalho Farias,
  Ana Maria Benko-Iseppon, and José Ribamar Costa Ferreira-Neto

Protein Dimension DB: A Unified Protein Repository for Representation
Learning and Functional Analysis 205
   Pitágoras de Azevedo Alves Sobrinho, Tetsu Sakamoto,
   and Wilfredo Blanco Figuerola

Forecasting Using SARIMAX Model and LSTM Approach for Arboviruses
Using Exogenous Climatic Variables in Predicting Dengue Incidence 214
   Claudia Stoeglehner Sahd, Elisângela Ap. da Silva Lizzi,
   Glaucia Maria Bressan, and Laurival Antonio Vilas-Boas

Author Index 227

Detective Challenge: A Card-Game Approach to Teach Bioinformatics and Gene Expression in High Schools

Dayana K. Turquetti-Moraes[1] , Gabriel Quintanilha-Peixoto[1] ,
Ana Luiza Martins-Karl[1,2] , and Thiago M. Venancio[1(✉)]

[1] Laboratório de Química e Função de Proteínas e Peptídeos, Centro de Biociências e Biotecnologia, Universidade Estadual do Norte Fluminense Darcy Ribeiro - UENF, Campos dos Goytacazes, RJ, Brazil
tmvenancio@uenf.br
[2] Laboratório Nacional de Computação Científica – LNCC, Petrópolis, RJ, Brazil

Abstract. This article presents an innovative educational activity based on the Soybean Expression Atlas (SEA). The current SEA version comprises over 5,000 publicly available RNA-seq samples from various soybean tissues, such as leaves, flowers, and seeds, providing detailed gene expression profiles for scientific and educational purposes. This powerful resource inspired us to develop a card game named *"Detective Challenge"*, designed to introduce high school students to gene expression principles using soybean as a model organism. The *Detective Challenge* bridges theoretical concepts with practical applications through a gamification approach. In the *Detective Challenge*, participants take on the role of "gene detectives", tasked with investigating the function of specific soybean genes by analyzing their expression patterns in SEA. By engaging with this real-world dataset, participants learn to formulate hypotheses about gene functions, expression patterns (such as tissue specificity), and key metrics, like TPM values. The activity fosters scientific curiosity, promotes active learning, and provides a hands-on introduction to molecular biology and genetics concepts. It also highlights the application of bioinformatics in educational settings, allowing students to work with computational tools and data analysis techniques commonly used in modern scientific research, which addresses a gap in educational tools. Ultimately, the goal is to popularize basic gene expression concepts in the classroom, encouraging students to engage with real scientific data and develop critical thinking skills.

Keywords: RNA-seq · Soybean Expression Atlas · Gamification

1 Introduction

Connecting theory with practice is essential in education and scientific outreach, particularly in complex fields such as genetics and molecular biology [11, 16]. Providing hands-on experiences with real data enables learners to apply theoretical concepts to tangible scenarios, promoting deeper understanding and better knowledge retention

M. Dorn and F. Martins Lopes (Eds.): X-Meeting 2025, LNBI 16037, pp. 1–13, 2026.
https://doi.org/10.1007/978-3-032-09336-3_1

[3]. Understanding gene expression is a complex topic for high school students. The regulation of gene expression involves intricate molecular mechanisms that determine when and where specific genes are activated, influencing plant growth, development, and environmental responses. However, due to the abstract nature of these processes and ever-evolving technologies, students often find difficulties in grasping fundamental concepts in this area [21].

In Brazil, even though high school curricula foresees basic aspects of DNA and gene function, the regulation of gene expression and transcriptomics remain largely under-explored, limiting students exposure to not only contemporary advances in the field, but also classic knowledge generated as early as the 1950s and 1960s [10, 14]. This education gap can impair comprehension and reduce engagement with modern biological concepts. A clear example of this was the COVID-19 pandemic, which highlighted the importance of omics and multi-omics approaches in SARS-CoV-2 research, including clinical studies, drug development, and vaccines. During this period, initiatives like the creation of the *GenomicNews* blog stood out by providing accessible and informative summaries, translating the complex world of omics sciences for the non-specialist public [4]. Furthermore, teachers often face challenges in translating complex transcriptomic data into accessible and interactive learning experiences, leading to a reliance on lecture-based instruction. Traditional teaching methods, which are predominantly teacher-centered, frequently lack student interaction, potentially hindering knowledge retention and conceptual understanding [17].

Active learning strategies have been widely recognized for their role in improving student engagement and knowledge acquisition [6, 24]. Educational approaches that incorporate real scientific data and problem-solving activities have been shown to enhance critical thinking and foster a deeper understanding of biological processes [19]. In this context, game-based learning represents an effective pedagogical strategy for making abstract scientific concepts more tangible. Games create immersive and interactive experiences that encourage students to apply theoretical knowledge to practical scenarios, thereby promoting motivation and meaningful learning [7, 20].

Among various game formats, inquiry-based challenges, in which students assume the role of investigators to solve scientific problems, have demonstrated particular effectiveness in science education. These activities not only promote active participation but also stimulate curiosity and logical reasoning [22]. In this context, we developed a card game named *"Detective Challenge"*, aimed at engaging students (especially high schoolers) in analyzing gene expression data from soybean plants, not only stimulating their curiosity but also enhancing critical thinking and problem-solving skills. The main objective of the *Detective Challenge* is to introduce learners to the concepts behind gene expression using soybean as a model organism. More specifically, the game enables learners to understand how the expression of specific genes influences plant traits while developing basic skills in analyzing RNA-seq data. By working with authentic datasets, learners might gain valuable insights into the scientific process, from formulating hypotheses to interpreting data.

Soybean (*Glycine max*) stands out as one of the most important crops worldwide, playing a crucial role in the food supply, feed, and industry due to its high protein and oil content [5]. It also plays a major role in the global economy, especially in Brazil, its top producer. Understanding the genetic basis of *G. max* through gene expression studies is essential for advancing sustainable agricultural practices and enhancing food security [1, 8]. The growing accumulation of soybean RNA-seq data in public repositories inspired the development of SEA v2, a comprehensive database featuring 5,481 RNA-seq samples that profile gene expression across various tissues, including leaves, flowers, and seeds [2]. This resource is central to the Detective Challenge. Through the challenge, participants explore how specific gene expression patterns influence plant phenotypes while acquiring fundamental biological skills. By working with real RNA-seq datasets, participants move from passive learning to active investigation, strengthening the connection between theoretical concepts and practical application. Our goal is to provide the participants with an engaging and intuitive way to explore transcriptomic data, deepening their understanding of gene expression in soybean. Supplementary materials are available at https://github.com/Dayana-Turquetti/Detective_Challenge_Supplementary.git.

2 Materials and Methods

2.1 Development of Soybean Expression Atlas

The increasing availability of soybean RNA-seq data in public repositories, combined with the computational challenges of processing raw sequencing data, motivated our group to develop the Soybean Expression Atlas [2, 13]. This platform provides transcript- and gene-level abundance matrices derived from 5,481 publicly available RNA-seq samples. All genomic data were based on the Wm82.a4.v1 assembly of the Glycine max genome. The reference transcriptome and transcript-to-gene mappings were retrieved from PLAZA Dicots 5.0 [23]. To estimate transcript- and gene-level abundance from raw sequencing data, our group developed an R package called bears (available at https://github.com/almeidasilvaf/bears), which integrates multiple RNA-seq analysis tools to process sequences available in the NCBI Sequence Read Archive (SRA) [18]. The latest version of the SEA v2 is available at https://soyatlas.venanciogroup.uenf.br/ (Fig. 1).

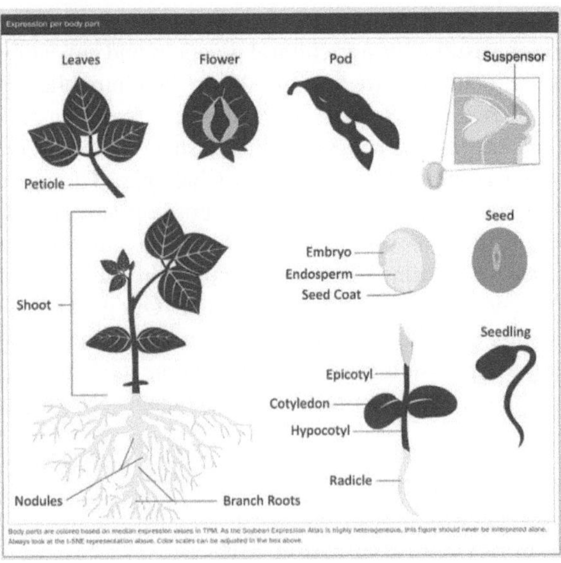

Fig. 1. Example of the Soybean Expression Atlas interface, displaying the expression of the gene Glyma.13G046200 across different soybean parts. Colors indicate expression levels in the respective tissues, with redder tones representing higher gene expression in that region.

2.2   Participants and Procedure

The activity is designed for students in their second and third years of high school, typically aged 15 to 17, and is conducted in public schools during a 1.5-h session. To assess the effectiveness of Detective Challenge, eight sessions were conducted in three public high schools in the State of Rio de Janeiro, Brazil, across two cities: Campos dos Goytacazes and Petrópolis, with a total of 119 participants in the period from October to November 2024 (Table 1). The participants were divided into 44 groups, averaging approximately three participants per group. Two participants completed the activity individually and were designated as groups 9 and 10, respectively. The session was structured around four main components: (i) an initial observational exercise, (ii) a conceptual introduction to soybean and gene expression, (iii) a collaborative problem-solving card game (*The Detective Challenge*), and (iv) a feedback questionnaire designed to assess both learning outcomes and participant satisfaction. Responses to the questionnaire constitute our primary source of results. Specifically, we analyzed the most frequently used terms participants employed to describe learned concepts, as well as whether each group accurately identified the function and expression pattern of their assigned gene. The translated questionnaire, along with the presentation slides (in Portuguese), are available at https://github.com/Dayana-Turquetti/Detective_Challenge_Supplementary.git.

Table 1. List of cities, schools, class years, dates, locations, and number of participants in each session.

City	School	Level	Date	Participants
Campos dos Goytacazes	VRB	2°	10/21/2024	12
		3°		22
	NP	3°	10/22/2024	50
Petrópolis	CEFET	3°	11/27/2024	12
		2°	11/28/2024	23

VRB: Colégio Estadual Visconde do Rio Branco, NP: Colégio Estadual Nilo Peçanha, CEFET: Centro Federal de Educação Tecnológica – UnEd Petrópolis.

2.3 Initial Exploration and Engagement

The activity started with an introduction from the instructors explaining the purpose of the session, emphasizing the investigative nature of the exercise. To capture participants' curiosity, each participant received a soybean seed and was encouraged to closely examine its physical traits, such as color, size, and texture. The instructor facilitated a discussion on their observations, highlighting the importance of careful analysis in scientific research. This exercise established a foundation for understanding that, beyond visible characteristics, the seed contains molecular features crucial for plant functioning and development. As part of this foundation, key molecular biology concepts were introduced, including DNA structure, the number of genes in soybean, and plant physiology. The instructors then introduced the main goal of the session: to uncover the hidden traits of the soybean seed through gene expression analysis using a card game. An example card is shown in Fig. 2, while the full set is available in the aforementioned GitHub repository. To reinforce the investigative approach, participants were encouraged to think like detectives and document their observations in preparation for the next phase of the activity.

Card Front   **Card Back**

Fig. 2. Card model used in the Detective Challenge game. The front of the card features an illustration with the Gene Expression Atlas logo and the game name. On the back, players find the gene identification, a tip about its potential function, and a reference to a publication that tested this function in vivo. The complete 24-card deck is available on GitHub.

2.4 Introduction to Gene Expression Atlas

Following the observational exercise, the instructor introduced the SEA, a tool developed using RNA-seq data from various soybean tissues, including leaves, flowers, and seeds (Fig. 1). To help participants grasp the concept of gene expression, an interactive demonstration using a ring light was performed: turning the light on and off illustrated the activation and suppression of gene expression, while adjusting the intensity represented varying levels of transcript abundance. Through this analogy, participants gained insight into how RNA-seq captures gene activity and how expression levels influence plant traits. The instructor then guided participants on how to navigate SEA, preparing them for the subsequent Detective Challenge.

2.5 Game Dynamics

In the final segment, students participated in the Detective Challenge. Participants were divided into groups and received a card with the identification (ID) of a soybean gene and a clue regarding its potential function (Fig. 2). Each group entered their assigned gene ID into the SEA to explore its expression profile across different tissues. SEA provided visual maps with color gradients (e.g. Figure 1) indicating expression levels (available at https://soyatlas.venanciogroup.uenf.br/), along with quantitative data on transcript abundance and tissue specificity (Tau index).

Participants analyzed the expression patterns of their assigned gene and formulated hypotheses about its potential function (Fig. 3). Through group discussions, they evaluated the collected data, refined their interpretations, and synthesized conclusions regarding gene roles in plant development and physiology. Finally, participants compiled their findings into an online questionnaire (available at: https://forms.gle/QMAdipaR3 jU2j5tSA), articulating their hypotheses and reinforcing their ability to apply scientific reasoning to real-world genomic data (available at GitHub).

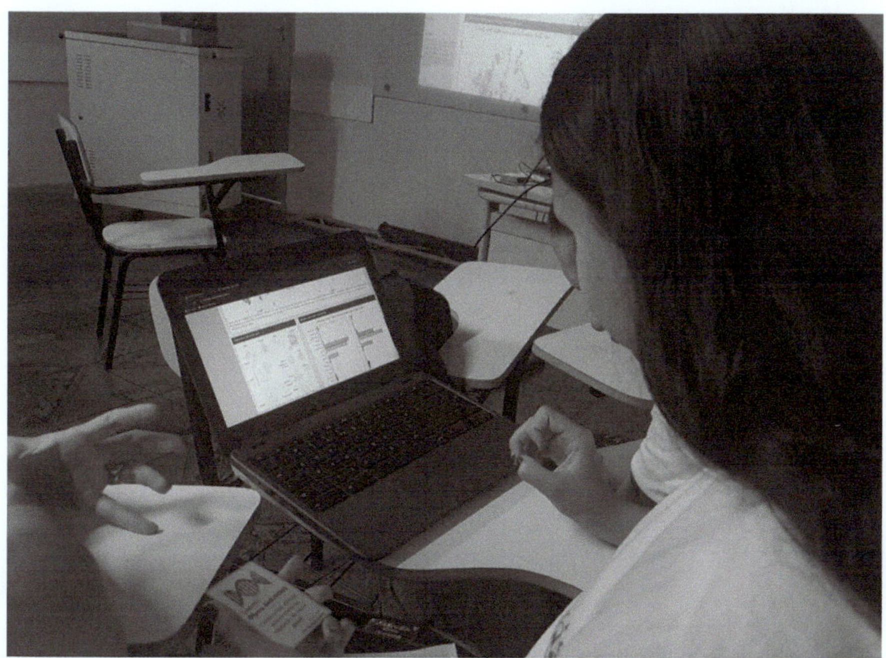

Fig. 3. Students participating in the Detective Challenge, exploring gene expression profiles using the expression atlas and analyzing tissue specificity with the provided materials.

3 Results and Discussion

3.1 Group Engagement, Learning Outcomes, and Previous Knowledge

The Detective Challenge activity proved to be highly engaging for participants, with 98% (43 out of 44 groups) reporting that they enjoyed the experience of being gene detectives for a day (Fig. 4, Fig. 5). When asked about their favorite aspects of the activity, participants highlighted a variety of elements that contributed to their enthusiasm. The most frequently mentioned points included the investigative nature of the task—often described as "being a detective" or "acting as a detective"—and the opportunity to explore gene function through interactive research. Many participants appreciated using SEA to solve the mystery and identify genes or their chromosomal positions.

Others emphasized the value of researching in groups, working with graphs, and navigating SEA to discover gene functions and plant characteristics. Several responses also pointed to the clarity and didactic quality of the instructors' explanations, the dynamic and interactive format of the activity, and the opportunity to learn more about plant biology and soybean reproduction in a hands-on way. A few groups simply stated that they enjoyed "everything" about the activity, underscoring its broad appeal. The most frequently mentioned terms related to participants' favorite parts of the activity are summarized in Fig. 4.

Fig. 4. The word cloud represents the most frequently mentioned words by participant groups when describing their favorite aspects of the Detective Challenge activity. Image generated on Wordcloud (available at: wordcloud.online/).

Additionally, when asked about what they learned from the activity, the groups reported gaining knowledge about investigative aspects, DNA, genes, and soybean genetics (Fig. 5). Participants demonstrated an understanding of a wide range of topics, including gene expression, chromosome structure, and the role of genes in plant development. Some participants mentioned learning that soybeans have more genes than humans, while others highlighted insights into the composition and classification of genes, as well as the function of specific plant parts. Responses also reflected an increased awareness of soybean biology, covering topics such as germination, plant anatomy, reproductive cycles, and the importance of the crop to the Brazilian economy. The use of SEA was especially appreciated as a tool to navigate and explore gene-related data. These findings suggest that integrating bioinformatics tools into interactive, inquiry-based activities can significantly enhance participants' understanding and retention of fundamental genetic concepts, while also promoting engagement with real-world scientific challenges.

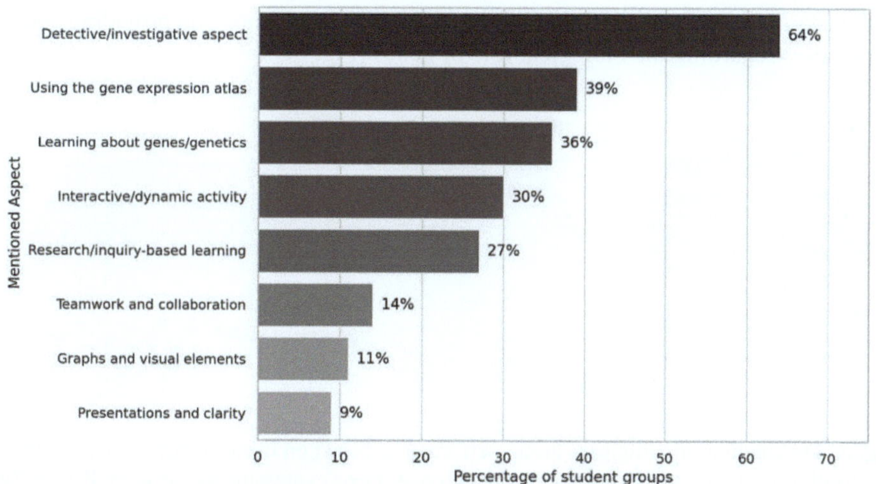

Fig. 5. Relative frequency of mentions of aspects learned from the activity (open-ended responses from 44 groups). Percentages represent the proportion of groups that mentioned each aspect. Since groups could mention multiple elements, the total sum exceeds 100%.

Notably, 50% of the groups (22 out of 44) reported having no prior knowledge of gene expression, highlighting the importance of introducing these concepts before engaging in more complex discussions. A playful introduction proved highly relevant in making these ideas more accessible and sparking participants' curiosity. Although half of the groups indicated unfamiliarity with the topic, the structured and engaging format of the activity enabled them to get a clear understanding of key concepts. It is worth noting that this question was asked at the end of the activity, which may have introduced a degree of bias, despite the instructors' emphasis that responses should reflect their knowledge before the activity. Nonetheless, this aligns with previous studies emphasizing the role of gamification and active learning in enhancing participant engagement in science education [12, 15]. The high level of participation observed suggests that this strategy was not only necessary but also successful in fostering interest and facilitating learning, particularly in topics that participants often find abstract or challenging.

3.2   Hypotheses About Gene Function from Gene Expression Pattern

Participant groups formulated hypotheses about gene function based on the data they gathered. Nearly 80% of the groups provided a satisfactory description of the gene expression site (Fig. 6A), and nearly 70% adequately described the function of the gene (Fig. 6B). More specifically, 20% of them (nine groups: 1, 2, 8, 14, 16, 30, 32, 37, and 38) correctly identified the plant part with the highest gene expression but presented inaccuracies in their hypotheses regarding its biological role. In contrast, 9% (four groups: 25, 29, 33, and 41) misidentified the gene expression site yet demonstrated an adequate understanding of the gene function. Approximately 11% (five groups: 5, 24, 26, 34, and 40) showed inconsistencies in both identifying the primary expression site and proposing the gene function. The remaining 59% (26 groups) performed well in both tasks, accurately determining the site of highest expression and providing coherent hypotheses regarding the biological role of genes (Fig. 6C).

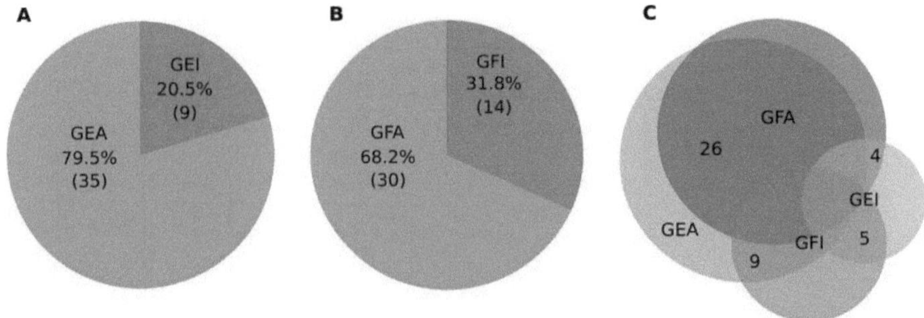

Fig. 6. Distribution of participant group performance based on the accuracy of gene expression localization and functional hypothesis formulation. **A.** Gene expression localization. **B.** Gene function. **C.** Venn diagram with group performance overlapping in both tasks. **GEA**: gene expression accurate, **GEI**: gene expression inaccurate, **GFA**: gene function accurate, **GFI**: gene function inaccurate. A Venn diagram was plotted with DeepVenn (available at deepvenn.com) [9].

These findings illustrate the participants' capacity to integrate biological knowledge with data interpretation, showcasing critical thinking and problem-solving skills. Notably, even when some groups misidentified either the plant part with predominant gene expression or the gene function, they were still able to engage meaningfully with the available data and construct plausible biological hypotheses. The ability to formulate hypotheses grounded in gene expression data suggests a developing proficiency in navigating bioinformatics tools and interpreting biological information through a computational lens. For instance, group 6 hypothesized, "It helps the plant withstand very high temperatures and drought, meaning they do not dry out easily and can survive longer without water, adapting better to these conditions".

These results indicate an emergent understanding of how gene expression correlates with physiological functions. Such engagement reflects a shift from rote memorization toward a more dynamic conceptualization of biological processes, as supported by educational research on inquiry-based learning. Encouraging participants to investigate gene function within real-world contexts—such as crop improvement and agricultural biotechnology—may further enhance their ability to apply genetic concepts critically and creatively.

3.3   Qualitative Feedback and Suggestions for Improvement

The qualitative feedback provided by the groups mainly consisted of suggestions to translate the website into Portuguese and to conduct the activity more frequently. However, the majority of responses did not offer specific suggestions. The suggestion to make the activity more frequent reflects a positive reception of the learning experience, indicating that participants found the activity beneficial and would appreciate more opportunities to engage with similar content.

From an educational perspective, this feedback highlights the need for greater accessibility and inclusivity in science learning resources. Language barriers can significantly impact comprehension, particularly in specialized fields such as genetics and bioinformatics. Moving forward, it might be useful to consider additional ways to enhance the accessibility of the materials, such as providing translations or supplementary resources in Portuguese to accommodate participants with different language proficiencies. Additionally, incorporating adaptive learning modules tailored to varying levels of prior knowledge could further support participant engagement and understanding.

Furthermore, future iterations of this activity could integrate collaborative elements, such as peer discussions and interdisciplinary connections to other scientific fields, to reinforce knowledge retention and application. Developing complementary resources, such as interactive tutorials or follow-up assignments that build upon the concepts explored in the Detective Challenge, may also contribute to long-term learning gains.

Overall, the results indicate that the Detective Challenge activity was highly effective in engaging participants, fostering scientific curiosity, and promoting foundational knowledge in genetics and bioinformatics. Refining and expanding upon this approach could serve as a model for integrating active learning strategies into science education more broadly.

4 Conclusion

This study demonstrates that the Detective Challenge activity is an effective tool for engaging students and improving their understanding of gene expression. By integrating hands-on, inquiry-based learning strategies, students actively interacted with bioinformatics tools, developed hypotheses, and critically analyzed gene function. The overwhelmingly positive reception and high participation rates reinforce the value of gamification in science education, particularly in making complex subjects like genetics more accessible and engaging.

The participants' ability to formulate hypotheses based on gene expression patterns highlights the strong link between data analysis and biological reasoning, emphasizing the importance of incorporating bioinformatics education into biology curricula. These findings align with research advocating for active learning approaches that enhance comprehension and long-term retention. Additionally, qualitative feedback suggests that increasing accessibility, such as providing translations and offering the activity more frequently, could further improve the learning experience.

Future iterations of the Detective Challenge could be expanded to include interdisciplinary connections and real-world applications, reinforcing the relevance of genetics and bioinformatics in broader scientific and societal contexts. Refining this approach may serve as a scalable model for student-centered science education, fostering curiosity, critical thinking, and a deeper understanding of genetic principles.

Acknowledgements. This work was supported by Fundação Carlos Chagas Filho de Amparo à Pesquisa do Estado do Rio de Janeiro (FAPERJ, grant number E-26/201.117/2022), Coordenação de Aperfeiçoamento de Pessoal de Nível Superior (CAPES), and Conselho Nacional de Desenvolvimento Científico e Tecnológico (CNPq, grant numbers 440221/2022-6 and 313024/2023-5).

Disclosure of Interests. The authors declare that they have no known competing financial interests or personal relationships that could have appeared to influence the work reported in this paper.

References

1. Aleem, M., et al.: Comprehensive RNA-seq analysis revealed molecular pathways and genes associated with drought tolerance in wild soybean (Glycine soja Sieb. and Zucc.). Physiol Plant. **172**(2), 707–732 (2021). https://doi.org/10.1111/ppl.13219
2. Almeida-Silva, F., et al.: The soybean expression atlas v2: a comprehensive database of over 5000 RNA-seq samples. Plant J. **116**(4), 1041–1051 (2023). https://doi.org/10.1111/tpj.16459
3. Apeadido, S., et al.: The impact of practical experiential learning on shaping high school students' attitudes towards biology. J. Sci. Educ. Res. **8**(2), 108–119 (2024). https://doi.org/10.21831/jser.v8i2.76369
4. Dávila, A.M.R.: Rethinking omics education in Brazil and South America: from genomics to multiomics and critical policy studies. OMICS **24**(7), 391–393 (2020). https://doi.org/10.1089/omi.2020.0064
5. Duan, Z., et al.: Genetic regulatory networks of soybean seed size, oil and protein contents. Front. Plant Sci. **14** (2023). https://doi.org/10.3389/fpls.2023.1160418
6. Freeman, S., et al.: Active learning increases student performance in science, engineering, and mathematics. Proc. Natl. Acad. Sci. **111**(23), 8410–8415 (2014). https://doi.org/10.1073/pnas.1319030111
7. Gutierrez, A.F.: Development and effectiveness of an educational card game as supplementary material in understanding selected topics in biology. LSE **13**(1), 76–82 (2014). https://doi.org/10.1187/cbe.13-05-0093
8. Hooker, J.C., et al.: Differential gene expression provides leads to environmentally regulated soybean seed protein content. Front. Plant Sci. **14** (2023). https://doi.org/10.3389/fpls.2023.1260393
9. Hulsen, T.: DeepVenn – a web application for the creation of area-proportional Venn diagrams using the deep learning framework Tensorflow.js (2022). http://arxiv.org/abs/2210.04597, https://doi.org/10.48550/arXiv.2210.04597
10. Jacob, F., Monod, J.: On the regulation of gene activity. Cold Spring Harb. Symp. Quant. Biol. **26**, 193–211 (1961). https://doi.org/10.1101/SQB.1961.026.01.024
11. Jenkinson, J.: Molecular biology meets the learning sciences: visualizations in education and outreach. J. Mol. Biol. **430**(21), 4013–4027 (2018). https://doi.org/10.1016/j.jmb.2018.08.020
12. Li, M., et al.: Examining the effectiveness of gamification as a tool promoting teaching and learning in educational settings: a meta-analysis. Front. Psychol. **14**, 1253549 (2023). https://doi.org/10.3389/fpsyg.2023.1253549
13. Machado, F.B., et al.: Systematic analysis of 1298 RNA-Seq samples and construction of a comprehensive soybean (Glycine max) expression atlas. Plant J. **103**(5), 1894–1909 (2020). https://doi.org/10.1111/tpj.14850
14. McClintock, B.: Chromosome organization and genic expression. Cold Spring Harb. Symp. Quant. Biol. **16**, 13–47 (1951). https://doi.org/10.1101/SQB.1951.016.01.004
15. Ratinho, E., Martins, C.: The role of gamified learning strategies in student's motivation in high school and higher education: a systematic review. Heliyon. **9**(8), e19033 (2023). https://doi.org/10.1016/j.heliyon.2023.e19033
16. Reydon, T.A., et al.: Genetics, genomics and society: the responsibilities of scientists for science communication and education. Pers. Med. **9**(6), 633–643 (2012). https://doi.org/10.2217/pme.12.69

17. Saira, N.Z.: A critical review on discussion and traditional teaching methods. Psychol. Educ. J. **58**(1), 1871–1886 (2021). https://doi.org/10.17762/pae.v58i1.1042
18. Sayers, E.W., et al.: Database resources of the national center for biotechnology information in 2023. Nucleic Acids Res. **51**(D1), D29–D38 (2023). https://doi.org/10.1093/nar/gkac1032
19. Schmaltz, R.M., et al.: Redefining critical thinking: teaching students to think like scientists. Front. Psychol. **8** (2017). https://doi.org/10.3389/fpsyg.2017.00459
20. Terrell, C.R., et al.: Game-based activities targeting visual literacy skills to increase understanding of biomolecule structure and function concepts in undergraduate biochemistry. Biochem. Mol. Biol. Educ. **49**(1), 94–107 (2021). https://doi.org/10.1002/bmb.21398
21. Tibell, L.A.E., Rundgren, C.-J.: Educational challenges of molecular life science: characteristics and implications for education and research. CBE Life Sci. Educ. **9**(1), 25–33 (2010). https://doi.org/10.1187/cbe.08-09-0055
22. Urdanivia Alarcon, D.A. et al.: Science and inquiry-based teaching and learning: a systematic review. Front. Educ. **8** (2023). https://doi.org/10.3389/feduc.2023.1170487
23. Van Bel, M. et al.: PLAZA 5.0: extending the scope and power of comparative and functional genomics in plants. Nucleic Acids Res. **50**(D1), D1468–D1474 (2022). https://doi.org/10.1093/nar/gkab1024
24. Williams, A.E., O'Dowd, D.K.: Seven practical strategies to add active learning to a science lecture. Neurosci. Lett. **743**, 135317 (2021). https://doi.org/10.1016/j.neulet.2020.135317

Dissecting Structural Differences in Tumoral and Control Co-expression Networks Through Centrality Measures

Laura Galant Speggiorin[1,2], Thayne Woycinck Kowalski[2,3,4], and Mariana Recamonde-Mendoza[1,2(✉)]

[1] Institute of Informatics, Universidade Federal do Rio Grande do Sul (UFRGS), Porto Alegre, RS, Brazil
{lgspeggiorin,mrmendoza}@inf.ufrgs.br
[2] Bioinformatics Core, Hospital de Clínicas de Porto Alegre (HCPA), Porto Alegre, RS, Brazil
tkowalski@hcpa.edu.br
[3] Graduate Program in Genetics and Molecular Biology, Genetics Department, Universidade Federal do Rio Grande do Sul (UFRGS), Porto Alegre, RS, Brazil
[4] Medical Genetics Service, Hospital de Clínicas de Porto Alegre (HCPA), Porto Alegre, RS, Brazil

Abstract. Gene co-expression networks provide a systems-level view of molecular alterations in diseases like cancer. While tumor and healthy tissues have been widely compared in network-based approaches, tumor-adjacent normal tissues (NAT) remain less explored, despite evidence of molecular alterations influenced by the tumor environment. Here, we constructed co-expression networks for tumor, NAT, and healthy tissues across four cancer types to investigate structural differences. Using uniformly processed transcriptomic data from TCGA and GTEx, we built weighted graphs and computed three centrality measures: weighted degree, betweenness, and clustering coefficient. Genes were classified into positive and negative classes based on prior disease association evidence. Statistical analyses showed significant differences in centrality distributions between networks and gene classes, particularly highlighting molecular distinctions in NAT samples. Functional enrichment of ranked gene lists further linked central genes to cancer-related pathways, and known driver genes displayed characteristic patterns across tissue types. Our findings support the observations that NAT samples are molecularly distinct from healthy tissues and reinforce the usefulness of centrality measures to capture structural signatures of cancer-related processes.

Keywords: co-expression networks · cancer genomics · node centralities · systematic comparison · systems biology

1 Introduction

Gene expression alterations play a central role in cancer development, affecting not only individual genes but also the interactions between them [22]. Traditional

M. Dorn and F. Martins Lopes (Eds.): X-Meeting 2025, LNBI 16037, pp. 14–29, 2026.
https://doi.org/10.1007/978-3-032-09336-3_2

approaches that focus on differential expression often overlook the complex relationships that emerge at the systems level. Network-based analyses provide a valuable framework to explore how genes coordinate and how these patterns are disrupted in disease [3]. Within networks, genes can assume distinct structural roles that impact biological processes. Centrality measures quantify these roles by assessing node importance, influence, and connectivity [20]. Metrics like weighted degree, betweenness, and clustering coefficient capture complementary aspects of network structure, deepening our understanding of how gene interactions are reorganized in cancer.

Cancer-associated genes often show distinct topological properties in biological networks, with system-level features offering insights into disease progression and prognosis [24]. Thus, centrality measures have been widely used to identify biologically informative genes in co-expression networks, especially in cancer studies [2,15]. However, many comparisons use tumor-adjacent tissue as controls, despite evidence that such tissues may already exhibit molecular changes due to the tumor environment [1]. While transcriptomic differences among tumor, tumor-adjacent, and healthy tissues have been detected [1], their structural and co-expression patterns are less explored.

In this study, we constructed gene co-expression networks separately for tumor tissues, tumor-adjacent normal tissues (NAT), and healthy tissues, considering four types of cancer. We calculated node centrality measures for each network and compared the structural properties of genes known to be associated with cancer to those not linked to any disease. The analysis included statistical evaluation of centrality differences, functional enrichment of ranked gene lists, and the investigation of centrality patterns among known cancer driver genes.

Our findings reveal significant structural distinctions between tumor, NAT, and healthy tissues, supporting the notion that tumor-adjacent tissues are molecularly distinct from true healthy controls. Moreover, the use of network centrality measures highlights specific genes and pathways that may contribute to the biological shifts occurring during tumorigenesis, providing new perspectives for understanding cancer biology.

This study offers a novel contribution by comparing tumor, healthy, and NAT tissues in a system-level approach. While the distinct molecular nature of NAT has been suggested in previous studies, the use of the combination of centrality measures, statistical methods and functional enrichment to compare three tissue types across four cancers provides a systematic and quantitative characterization of their structural differences. This analysis represents a significant step in understanding the cancer biology and the unique molecular profile of NAT.

2 Materials and Methods

This section presents the methodological details of our work. Gene expression data was processed to construct co-expression networks for different tissue types, from which centrality metrics were calculated, statistically analyzed, and functionally enriched, followed by a focused analysis on known cancer driver genes.

Table 1. Number of processed samples for each dataset and tissue.

	Breast	Lung	Prostate	Thyroid
Tumor	984	505	428	443
Normal	112	61	50	55
GTEx	91	315	108	320

2.1 Data Collection and Pre-processing

We collected gene expression data from the work of Qingguo Wang and colleagues [22], who proposed an approach for unifying cancer and normal RNA sequencing data from different sources. The authors developed a pipeline to obtain raw reads of RNA-seq samples from The Cancer Genome Atlas (TCGA) and the Genotype Tissue Expression (GTEx) project [12], realign them, evaluate the quality of the samples, quantify gene expression values, and then perform quantile normalization and correction for batch effects. The pipeline was originally applied to samples from 18 types of cancer from TCGA, using both normal and tumor tissues – where the "normal" samples in TCGA are taken from histologically normal tissue adjacent to the tumor site[1]. These were matched with GTEx samples obtained from corresponding tissue sites in individuals with no history of the related cancer. For this study, we selected four cancer types: breast invasive carcinoma, lung adenocarcinoma, prostate adenocarcinoma, and thyroid carcinoma, all of epithelial origin. The number of samples in each of the three datasets (tumor, adjacent normal, and GTEx normal), for each cancer type, can be seen in Table 1.

For each dataset, we kept only the gene expression values and their corresponding EntrezID, and applied a $\log 2(X+1)$ transformation. To remove genes with low variation in expression between groups, and therefore with low diagnostic value in this study, we filtered the data based on the Interquartile Range (IQR), keeping the top 75% most variable genes. Genes with an EntrezID of 0, which is not a valid identifier, were removed from the dataset. Additionally, genes with zero expression across all patients in at least one group were excluded, as their correlation could not be calculated in those cases.

2.2 Co-expression Networks

The following steps were applied individually to each cancer type. For each group of samples – tumor tissue, normal tissue adjacent to a tumor (NAT) and healthy tissue – a gene expression correlation matrix was created by calculating the absolute Pearson correlation between every pair of genes. Since every gene has a perfect correlation with itself, which is uninformative in the context of co-expression networks, the main diagonal of the matrix was set to zero. A second matrix was created to filter the correlation matrix based on the p-values adjusted using the false discovery rate (FDR) method. To guarantee only moderately

---

[1] https://figshare.com/articles/dataset/Data_record_3/5330593.

strong and statistically significant correlations were retained in the network, only gene pairs with a correlation greater than 0.6 [6] and a p-value less than 0.05 were kept in the correlation matrix.

Each matrix was then used as an adjacency matrix to create three undirected weighted graphs for each cancer type, where the vertices (i.e., nodes) represent genes and the edges represent the strength of the correlation between gene expression levels. Having a co-expression network for each group of samples, the genes that were not connected to any other gene in any of the three networks (genes that were not significantly correlated to any other gene in all of the groups) were removed from the three networks.

2.3   Node Centrality Measures

Considering each network as an undirected weighted graph G, where V is the set of vertices, E is the the set edges, and W the set of edge weights, we can define a graph as $G = \{V, E, W\}$. Based on this definition, three centrality measures were calculated for each gene in each co-expression network: weighted degree, betweenness and clustering coefficient.

Weighted Degree (or strength) is the total weight of a node's connections. It extends traditional degree centrality by summing the weights of all edges connected to a node, rather than simply counting the edges [4]. The strength of a node is calculated as follows, where S_i is the strength of a given node i, N_i is the set of neighbors of i, and $w_{i,j}$ is a weight of the edge $e_{i,j}$:

$$S_i = \sum_{j \in N_i} w_{i,j} \tag{1}$$

The strength is used normalized, by dividing the resulting value S_i by $n - 1$, n being the total number of vertices in the graph.

Betweenness measures the importance of a node based on the number of shortest paths between other nodes that pass through it [25]. Being a path-based method, it accounts for both direct and indirect influences of a node in the network [10]. The betweenness of a node i is given by:

$$B_i = \sum \frac{\delta_{k,j}(i)}{\delta_{k,j}}, i \neq k \neq j \tag{2}$$

where $\delta_{k,j}$ corresponds to the number of the shortest paths between nodes k and j and $\delta_{k,j}(i)$ is the number of those paths that pass through node i. Betweenness was normalized according to the equation below, where n is the number of vertices in the graph.

$$\frac{2 \times B_i}{(n \times n - 3 \times n + 2)} \tag{3}$$

Clustering coefficient reflects the tendency of a node to form clusters with its neighbors [25]. For weighted networks, the igraph package [8] calculates the clustering coefficient of a node i as:

$$CC_i^k = \frac{1}{S_i \times (k_i - 1)} \sum_{j,h} \frac{(w_{ij} + w_{ih})}{2} a_{ij} a_{ih} a_{jh} \tag{4}$$

where S_i is the strength of a node (Eq. 1), k_i is the node degree, w_{ij} and w_{ih} are the weights of the edges connecting i to j and h respectively, and n a_{ij}, a_{ih} and a_{jh} are elements of the adjacency matrix. Essentially, it measures the ratio of neighbors of a node that are also connected between themselves, considering the weight of the edges connecting them. As a ratio, it does not need normalization.

2.4   Genes Classification Based on Disease Association Evidence

To thoroughly analyze the relevance of comparing the extracted metrics between networks, the genes used in the analysis were divided into two classes: a positive class (POS), consisting of genes known to be associated with the respective diseases, and a negative class (NEG), comprising genes with no known association to any disease. The number of genes in each class can be visualized in Table 2.

The positive class includes a diverse set of genes previously linked to each selected cancer type. They were compiled from the DisGeNET database [17], the Network of Cancer Genes (NCG) version 6.0 [19] candidate cancer genes with strong support associated with "pancancer", Online Mendelian Inheritance in Man (OMIM), and GWAS data from the Phenotype-Genotype Integrator database compiled by Menche et al. [14], and the PubTator tool [23].

For DisGeNET, we used genes with a GDA score ≥ 0.3 – this score takes into account the quantity and type of reference. This cutoff guarantees either at least one curated source, or at least two other kinds of sources. The dataset that compiled OMIM and GWAS genes did not include any thyroid neoplasm data, so the Phenotype-Genotype Integrator [18] was used with a genome-wide significance cutoff of p-value $\leq 5 \times 10^{-8}$ (same used for the other diseases by the authors) to select an equivalent set of genes. PubTator is a tool that enhances the annotation of articles on PubMed using text mining techniques. We selected all the genes associated with each disease by at least 10 PubMed articles as a way to reduce the chance of weak or false associations. Duplicated genes were removed, and the Bioconductor package for Genome wide annotation for Human [7] was used to select only the human genes. The genes from this built set that were present in their respective networks were selected as the positive class set.

For the negative class, we compiled all the known cancer genes and all the candidate cancer genes with strong support identified by more than one mutational screening in the same primary site from NCG6, and every gene from

Table 2. Number of genes in each class for each tissue.

	Breast	Lung	Prostate	Thyroid
Positive class	1993	1997	1127	356
Negative class	9439	9859	10223	10175

OMIM associated with some disease [14], and then combined with the positive dataset. Every gene from this set that was found in the networks was removed, and the resulting genes, not associated to any disease by the datasets we used were defined in the negative class.

2.5   Statistical Analysis

To calculate the statistical significance of each metric between networks, between the positive class of each network, and between the negative class of each network, we used a Kruskal-Wallis rank sum test. To calculate the statistical significance of each metric between the positive and negative class of the same network, for all three networks, we used a two-sample Wilcoxon (aka 'Mann-Whitney') test. We considered statistically significant the tests which resulted in a p-value < 0.01.

2.6   Functional Enrichment Analysis

Functional enrichment analysis was conducted using a Gene set enrichment analysis (GSEA) [21] to identify which pathways found in KEGG [11] were enriched in each list of genes ranked by each metric for each network in each type of cancer investigated. The p-value reported by the enrichment analysis was adjusted using FDR [5], and those pathways with an adjusted p-value < 0.05 were considered significantly enriched.

3   Results

3.1   Networks and Centrality Measures

The number of nodes and edges in each of the resulting networks can be seen in Table 3. An interesting phenomenon observed in all four cancer types is that, with the same genes present in each of the three networks, the NAT networks consistently shows significantly more edges than the other two networks of the same tissue type. When compared to NAT, the number of connections in the

Table 3. Number of nodes and edges in each network.

		Breast	Lung	Prostate	Thyroid
Tumor	Nodes	12646	12478	12827	12178
	Edges	258760	950420	915433	193640
NAT	Nodes	12646	12478	12827	12178
	Edges	7391704	2546916	4019040	2065746
GTEx	Nodes	12646	12478	12827	12178
	Edges	3008177	911749	887870	772130

tumoral network varied from 3.5% in the Breast dataset to 37% in the Thyroid dataset. In the same manner, when compared to NAT, the GTEx network varies between 9% in the Thyroid data and 41% in the Breast data. This implies that gene expression levels in NAT networks are more correlated between themselves than in the other two types of samples.

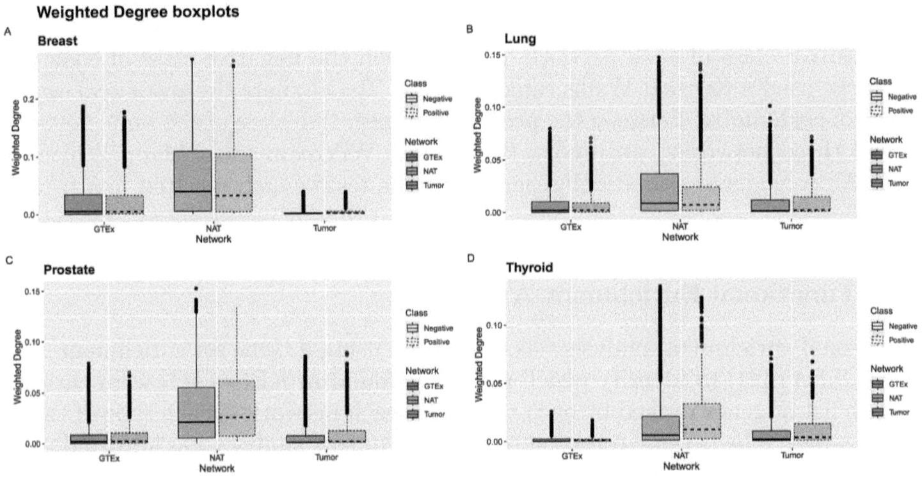

Fig. 1. Weighted degree of genes in each network, for each class.

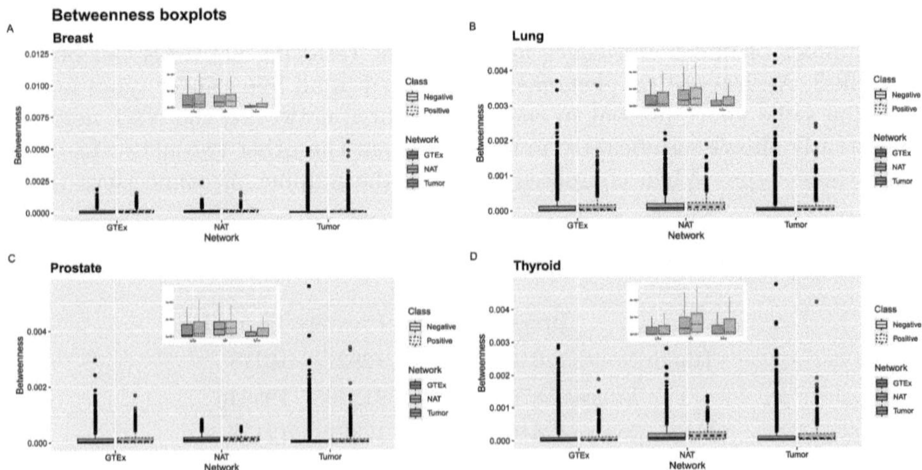

Fig. 2. Betweenness of genes in each network, for each class.

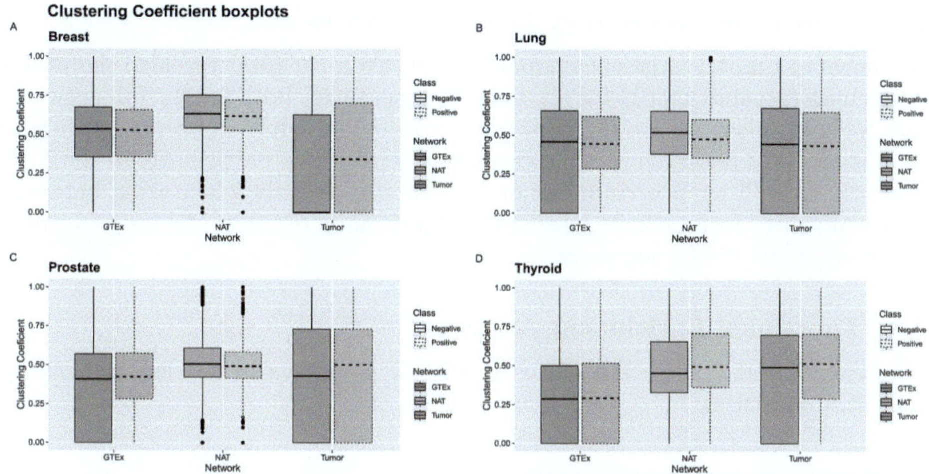

Fig. 3. Clustering coefficient of genes in each network, for each class.

This implication is further demonstrated by the distribution of centrality measures, as shown in Figs. 1, 2, and 3. In all four cancer types, NAT networks exhibited distinct centrality distributions compared to both tumor and healthy networks. Genes in the NAT networks generally displayed higher weighted degree and clustering coefficient values. Additionally, there were notable differences in the betweenness measure, with tumor networks exhibiting lower values compared to the control networks.

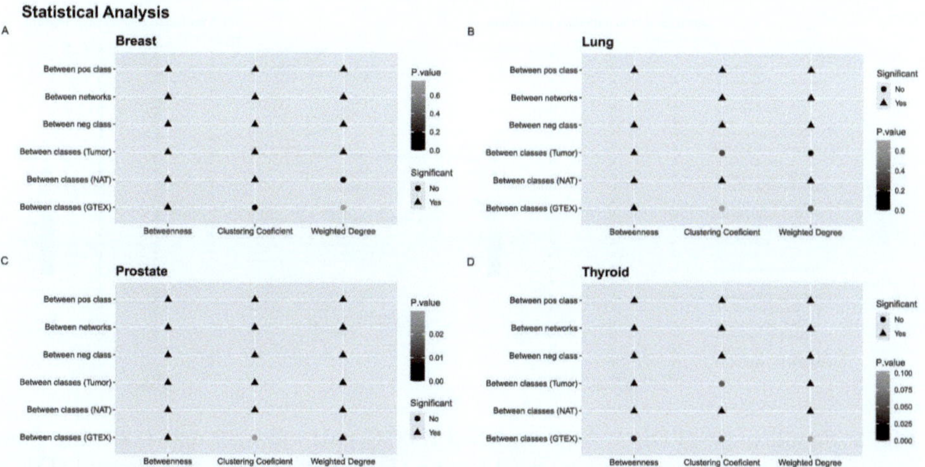

Fig. 4. Significance (p-value) of each metric between networks, between the classes of each network, and between positive and negative class of the same network for breast networks (**A**), lung networks (**B**), prostate networks (**C**), and thyroid networks (**D**).

3.2   Statistical Comparison Among Networks and Gene Classes

As shown in Fig. 4, statistical comparisons between networks revealed significant differences (p-value <0.01) for all centrality measures, both for the full networks and for each class separately. However, within individual networks, statistical significance was observed in some cases between classes, particularly in the NAT network, as well as in certain tumor networks, especially when using betweenness centrality. Interestingly, statistical significance between classes was rarely observed in the GTEx networks.

3.3   Functional Enrichment Analysis

Figures 5, 6 and 7 show the enriched KEGG pathways in the lists ranked by centrality measures.

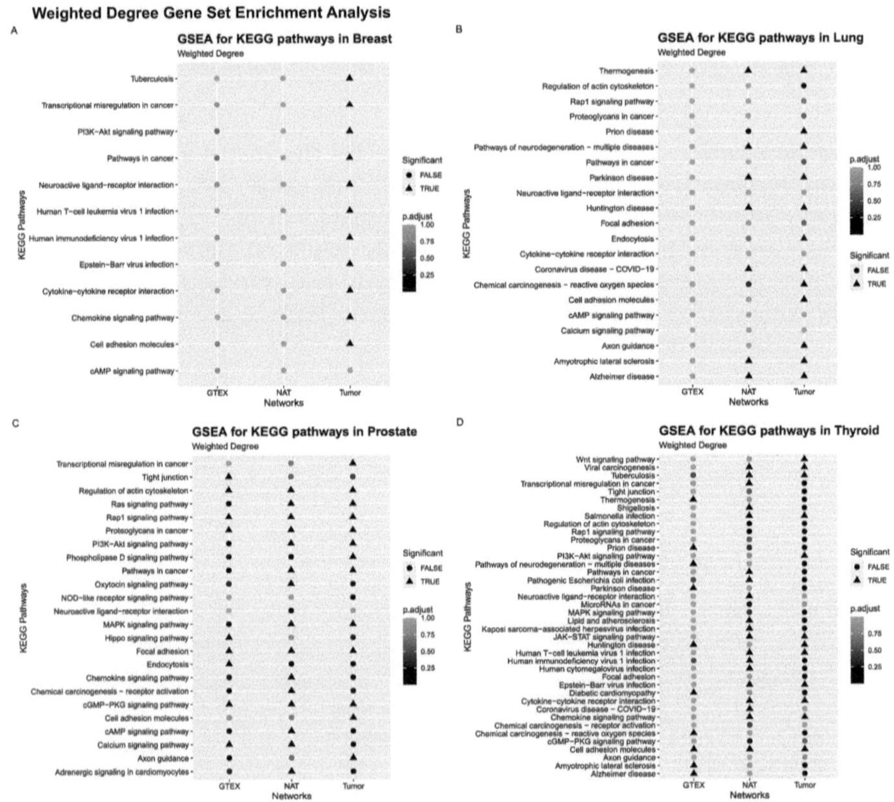

Fig. 5. Significantly (FDR < 0.05) enriched KEGG pathways per network using genes ranked by weighted degree in breast (**A**), lung (**B**), prostate (**C**), and thyroid (**D**).

We observe that for the Breast and Lung datasets, the majority of enriched pathways are found in the Tumor list. In contrast, for the Prostate and Thyroid datasets, the NAT list contains more enriched pathways. However, across all datasets, both the NAT and Tumor lists have more enriched pathways than the GTEx list. This pattern is consistent in both the Betweenness and Clustering Coefficient lists.

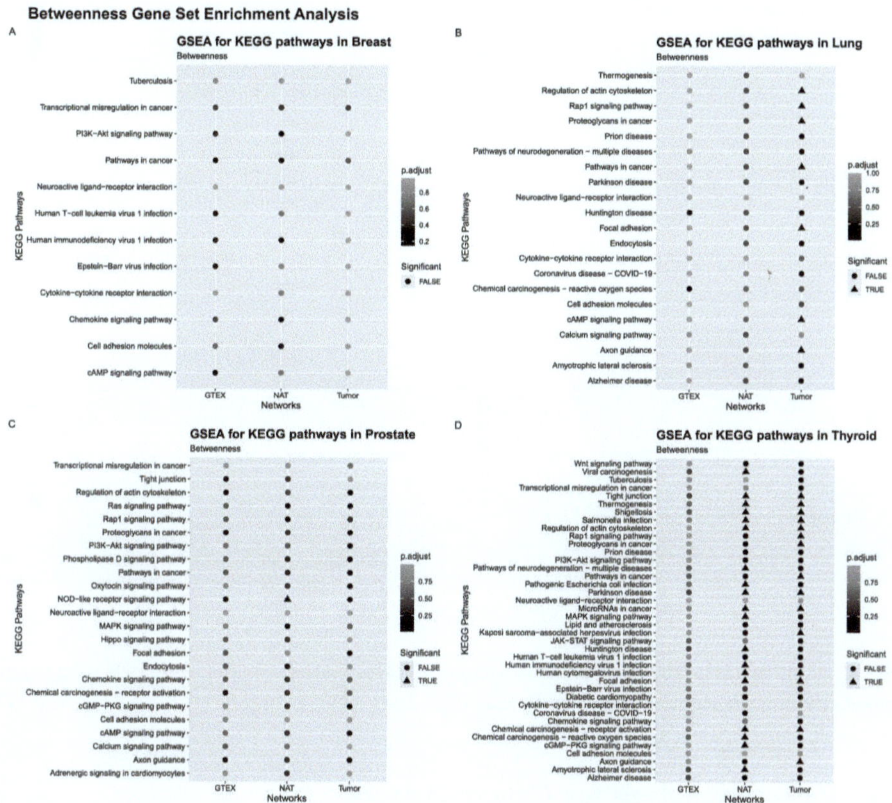

Fig. 6. Significantly (FDR <0.05) enriched KEGG pathways per network using genes ranked by betweenness in breast (**A**), lung (**B**), prostate (**C**), and thyroid (**D**).

Another notable finding is the overlap of enriched pathways between the NAT and Tumor lists, suggesting common biological processes in both tissues. Among the enriched pathways, several are known to be associated with cancer-related processes, such as the hallmarks of cancer [9], while some developmental pathways, linked to cancer metastasis in the literature [16], are also enriched.

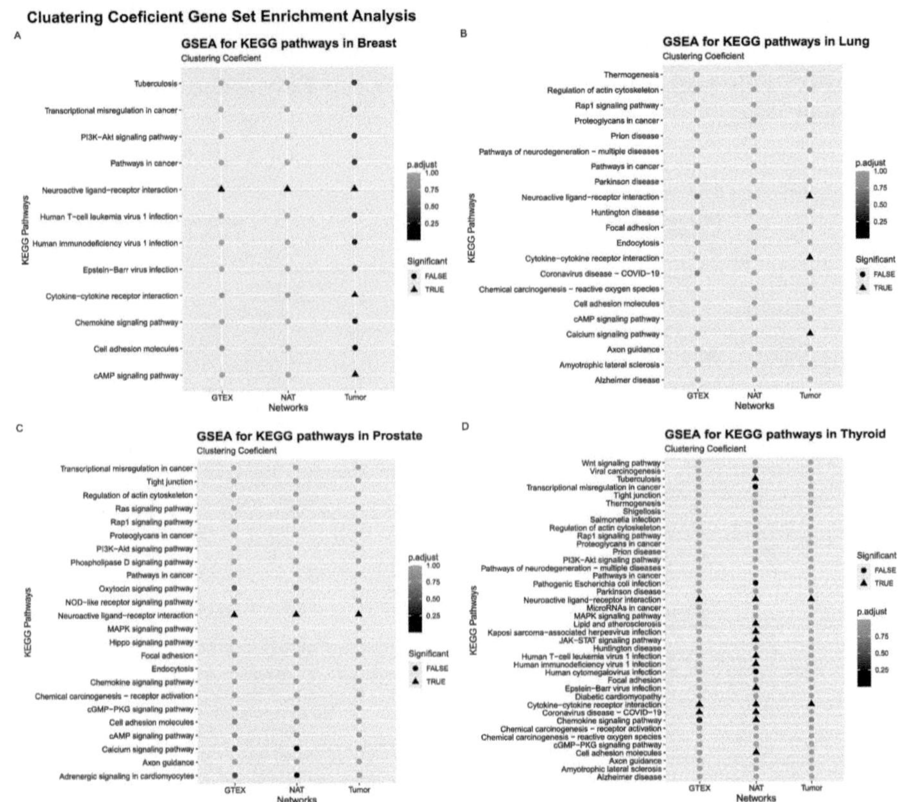

Fig. 7. Significantly (FDR <0.05) enriched KEGG pathways per network using genes ranked by clustering coefficient in breast (**A**), lung (**B**), prostate (**C**), and thyroid (**D**).

3.4 Pattern Analysis for Cancer Drivers

To further visualize the changes between the networks a hierarchical clustering analysis was executed, with a cuttoff of 4 clusters, in cancer drivers specific to each disease studied in this work, collected from IntoGen [13]. The z-score was calculated for each driver in each network, using the centrality measures scores. Besides the hierarchical clustering to observe how these genes aggregate based on the metrics, the same values were plotted to observe the difference in values among the three networks. Figures 8 and 9 show the very clear difference in tendency of several cancer-specific driver genes in NAT, illustrated by their accentuated peak in the lineplots.

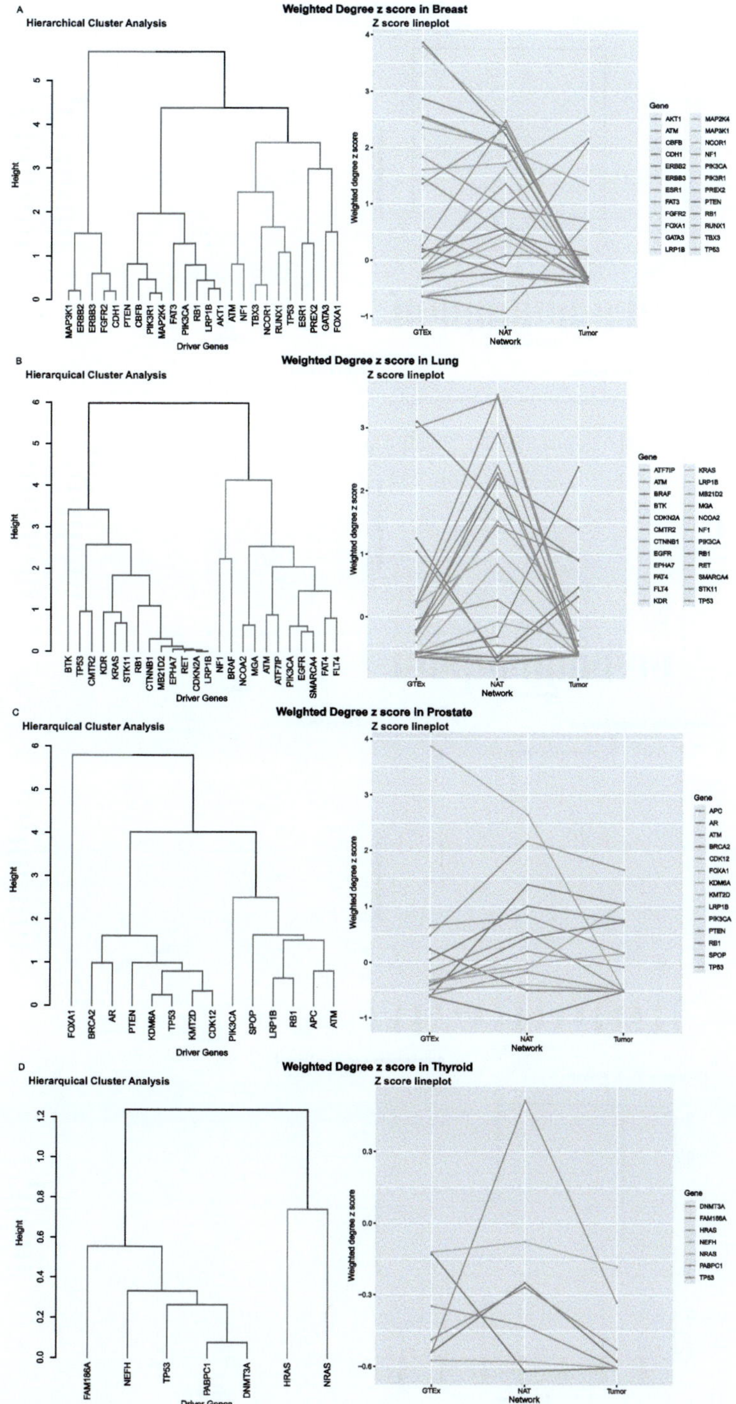

Fig. 8. Hierarchical clustering and lineplot of the Z score of weighted degree in cancer-specific driver genes for each network in breast (**A**), lung (**B**), prostate (**C**), and thyroid (**D**) tissues.

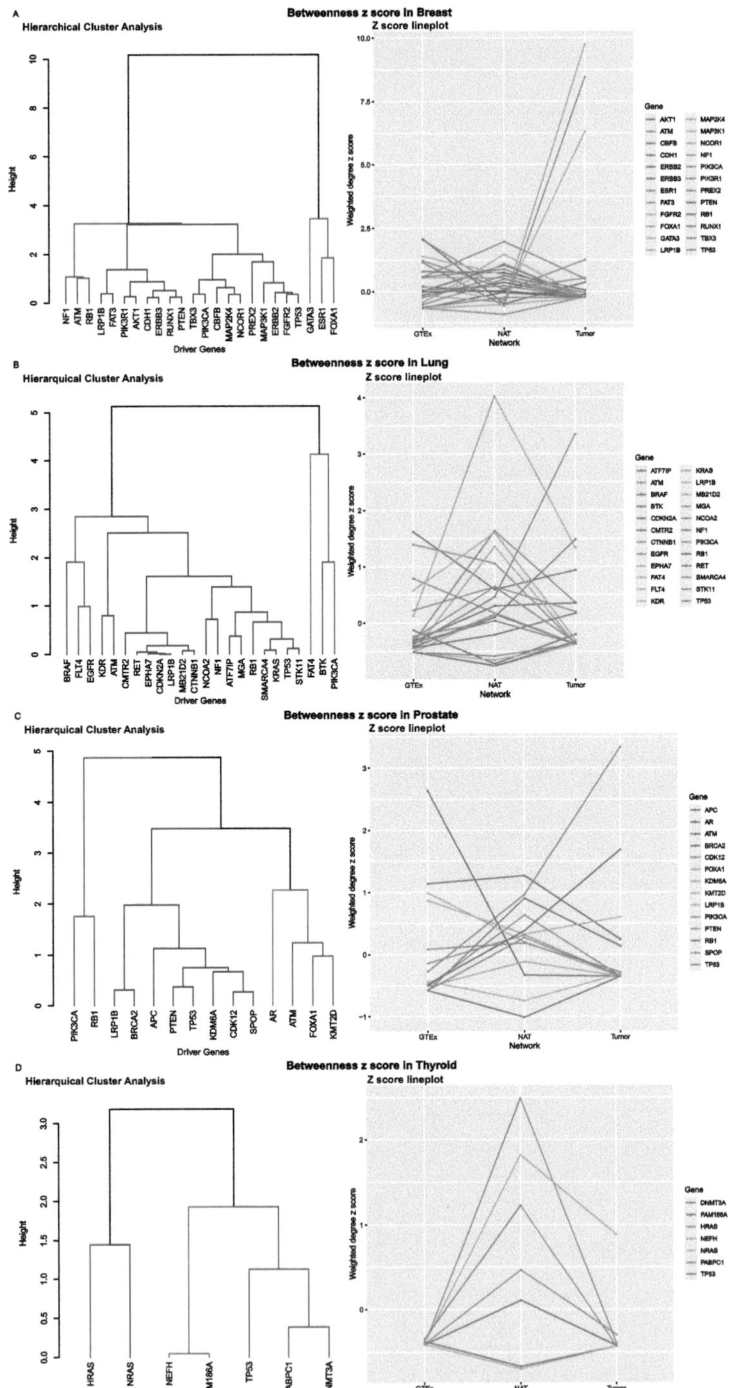

Fig. 9. Hierarchical clustering and lineplot of the Z score of betweenness in cancer-specific driver genes for each network in breast (**A**), lung (**B**), prostate (**C**), and thyroid (**D**) tissues.

4   Conclusion

This study provides an in-depth comparative analysis of gene co-expression networks from tumoral, NAT and healthy tissue samples across four cancer types. The reported results present and characterize consistent structural differences between the networks, which support the claim that NAT differs molecularly from healthy tissue [1]. NAT networks consistently exhibited higher connectivity and distinct structural characteristics compared to both tumor and healthy tissues, suggesting not only its role as an intermediary between healthy and tumoral tissue but also an unique environment. Those claims are further supported by the statistical analyses performed. Furthermore, the functional enrichment analysis highlighted biologically significant pathways linked to cancer development and progression, with some overlap between NAT and tumor networks, also reinforcing the claim of NAT as a intermediary state, and the analysis of known cancer driver genes revealed a pattern of elevated centrality metrics in NAT networks for several drivers, suggesting tissue-specific alterations already in place.

More studies are needed to fully understand these possible changes, since this work presents itself as a exploratory step in the direction of this understanding, but this findings challenge the assumption that NAT can be considered a healthy tissue alternative. It still presents significant changes when compared to tumoral samples, so its role as a control sample cannot be assessed by this works results, but it can be questioned which kind of tissue would be more adequate in order to not miss relevant biological information. Future studies will be necessary to better assess this, and to expand this approach to other cancer types. Future works should also explore these NAT-specific changes for a better understanding of cancer development and progression, and potentially for future prevention and early detection strategies.

Acknowledgments. This study was financed in part by the Coordenação de Aperfeiçoamento de Pessoal de Nível Superior - Brasil (CAPES) - Finance Code 001, and by grants from Conselho Nacional de Desenvolvimento Científico e Tecnológico (CNPq) [308075/2021-8; 440242/2024-0] and Fundação de Amparo à Pesquisa do Estado do Rio Grande do Sul - FAPERGS [22/2551-0000390-7, Project CIARS].

References

1. Aran, D., et al.: Comprehensive analysis of normal adjacent to tumor transcriptomes. Nat. Commun. **8**(1), 1077 (2017)
2. Azuaje, F.J.: Selecting biologically informative genes in co-expression networks with a centrality score. Biol. Direct **9**, 1–23 (2014)
3. Barabási, A.L., Gulbahce, N., Loscalzo, J.: Network medicine: a network-based approach to human disease. Nat. Rev. Genet. **12**(1), 56–68 (2011)
4. Barrat, A., Barthelemy, M., Pastor-Satorras, R., Vespignani, A.: The architecture of complex weighted networks. Proc. Nat. Acad. Sci. **101**(11) (2004). https://doi.org/10.1073/pnas.0400087101

5. Benjamini, Y., Hochberg, Y.: Controlling the false discovery rate: a practical and powerful approach to multiple testing. J. Roy. Stat. Soc. Ser. B: Stat. Methodol. **57**(1), 289–300 (1995). https://doi.org/10.1111/j.2517-6161.1995.tb02031.x

6. Camacho, D., de la Fuente, A., Mendes, P.: The origin of correlations in metabolomics data. Metabolomics **1**(1), 53–63 (2005)

7. Carlson, M.: org.Hs.eg.db: Genome wide annotation for Human (2020). r package version 3.11.4

8. Csardi, G., Nepusz, T.: The igraph software package for complex network research. Inter. J. Complex Syst., 1695 (2006). https://igraph.org

9. Hanahan, D.: Hallmarks of cancer: new dimensions. Cancer Discov. **12**(1), 31–46 (2022). https://doi.org/10.1158/2159-8290.cd-21-1059

10. Joy, M.P., Brock, A., Ingber, D.E., Huang, S.: High-betweenness proteins in the yeast protein interaction network. J. Biomed. Biotechnol. **2005**(2) (2005). https://doi.org/10.1155/JBB.2005.96

11. Kanehisa, M., Furumichi, M., Tanabe, M., Sato, Y., Morishima, K.: KEGG: new perspectives on genomes, pathways, diseases and drugs. Nucleic Acids Res. **45**(D1), D353–D361 (2016). https://doi.org/10.1093/nar/gkw1092

12. Lonsdale, J., et al.: The genotype-tissue expression (GTEX) project. Nat. Genet. **45**(6), 580–585 (2013). https://doi.org/10.1038/ng.2653

13. Martínez-Jiménez, F., et al.: A compendium of mutational cancer driver genes. Nat. Rev. Cancer **20**(10), 555–572 (2020). https://doi.org/10.1038/s41568-020-0290-x

14. Menche, J., et al.: Uncovering disease-disease relationships through the incomplete interactome. Science **347**(6224), 1257601–1257601 (2015). https://doi.org/10.1126/science.1257601

15. Mortezapour, M., Tapak, L., Bahreini, F., Najafi, R., Afshar, S.: Identification of key genes in colorectal cancer diagnosis by weighted gene co-expression network analysis. Comput. Biol. Med. **157**, 106779 (2023)

16. Nwabo, K.A.H., et al.: Developmental pathways associated with cancer metastasis: Notch, WNT, and Hedgehog. Cancer Biol. Med. **14**(2), 109 (2017). https://doi.org/10.20892/j.issn.2095-3941.2016.0032

17. Piñero, J., et al.: The DisGeNET knowledge platform for disease genomics: 2019 update. Nucleic Acids Res. (2019). https://doi.org/10.1093/nar/gkz1021

18. Ramos, E.M., et al.: Phenotype-Genotype integrator (PheGenI): synthesizing genome-wide association study (GWAS) data with existing genomic resources. Eur. J. Hum. Genet. **22**(1), 144–147 (2014)

19. Repana, D., et al.: The network of cancer genes (NCG): a comprehensive catalogue of known and candidate cancer genes from cancer sequencing screens. Genome Biol. **20**(1), 1 (2019)

20. Rout, T., Mohapatra, A., Kar, M., Patra, S., Muduly, D.: Centrality measures and their applications in network analysis: unveiling important elements and their impact. Procedia Comput. Sci. **235**, 2756–2765 (2024)

21. Subramanian, A., et al.: Gene set enrichment analysis: a knowledge-based approach for interpreting genome-wide expression profiles. Proc. Natl. Acad. Sci. **102**(43), 15545–15550 (2005). https://doi.org/10.1073/pnas.0506580102

22. Wang, Q., et al.: Unifying cancer and normal RNA sequencing data from different sources. Sci. Data **5**(1) (2018). https://doi.org/10.1038/sdata.2018.61

23. Wei, C.H., Allot, A., Leaman, R., Lu, Z.: PubTator central: automated concept annotation for biomedical full text articles. Nucleic Acids Res. **47**(W1), W587–W593 (2019)

24. Yang, Y., Han, L., Yuan, Y., Li, J., Hei, N., Liang, H.: Gene co-expression network analysis reveals common system-level properties of prognostic genes across cancer types. Nat. Commun. **5**(1), 3231 (2014)
25. Zhao, X., Liu, Z.P.: Analysis of topological parameters of complex disease genes reveals the importance of location in a biomolecular network. Genes **10**(2) (2019). https://doi.org/10.3390/genes10020143

Diversity of Glycosyl Hydrolase Family 18 in Arthropods

Lorrana Verdi Flores[1]([⊠]) [iD], Ana Beatriz Monteiro[1] [iD], Samanda López Peña[1] [iD], Renan Terassi Pinto[2] [iD], Khalid Haddi[1] [iD], and Luciano Vilela Paiva[1] [iD]

[1] Federal University of Lavras (UFLA), Lavras, MG, Brazil
lorrana.vf@gmail.com
[2] Agroceres Binova, São Paulo, SP, Brazil

Abstract. Chitin, a polymer of β-1,4 N-acetyl-glucosamine (GlcNAc), is metabolized by chitinases, enzymes that modify chitin matrices. These enzymes offer insights into arthropod development, with implications for agriculture, ecology, and health. This study used arthropod genomes from the NCBI database to identify and characterize GH18 family chitinases. Protein sequences of primary transcripts were analyzed using Hidden Markov models. Sequences with at least one GH18 domain were selected for characterization of physicochemical properties, subcellular localization prediction, phylogenetic inference, and Hierarchical Orthologous Group (HOG) analysis. Conserved motifs were also examined. Data from 231 species across Chelicerata, Crustacea, and Hexapoda were analyzed, with a predominance of Hexapoda genomes, especially from Insecta. A total of 4,209 protein sequences with GH18 domains were identified and grouped into 75 orthogroups, 32 of which contained at least four sequences. Chelicerata and Crustacea lacked orthologs for Group V (Imaginal Disc Growth Factors) and exhibited distinct patterns in other groups. Orthogroups OG0000000 to OG0000003 were associated with known domain architectures. Other orthogroups displayed distinct architectures, highlighting the diversity and continuous evolution of chitinases in arthropods. These results underscore the diversity, specificity, and versatility of GH18 family chitinases in arthropods.

Keywords: GH18 · Chitinases · Orthogroups · Orthologues · Arthropods

1 Introduction

Chitin is an essential polymer of β-1,4 N-acetylglucosamine (GlcNAc) found in bacteria, fungi, protists, nematodes, and arthropods [1–3]. Chitin matrices are vital for arthropod anatomy, forming structures such as the exoskeleton (a rigid, multifunctional formation [4–6]) and the peritrophic matrix (a semi-permeable intestinal barrier composed of chitin microfibers, glycoproteins, and proteoglycans [7, 8]).

Chitin is metabolized through different pathways, forming various cuticular features that undergo modification processes through depolymerization [9, 10]. Chitin depolymerization by GH18 chitinases (Cht; β-1,4-poly-N-acetylglucosaminidase; E.C.

© The Author(s), under exclusive license to Springer Nature Switzerland AG 2026
M. Dorn and F. Martins Lopes (Eds.): X-Meeting 2025, LNBI 16037, pp. 30–44, 2026.
https://doi.org/10.1007/978-3-032-09336-3_3

3.2.1.14), which hydrolyze β-1,4 bonds of GlcNAc [11], is well-documented. These enzymes, like chitin, are abundant in various organisms and environments [12]. In vertebrate animals, these enzymes appear to be involved in adaptive immune responses since they do not use chitin as a building component, unlike fungi, algae, nematodes, and arthropods [13, 14]. In insects, these enzymes modify chitin matrices during development, digesting fungi in fungivorous species [15], and acting as imaginal disc growth factors (IDGFs) [9].

Chitinases are predominantly classified into three glycoside hydrolase families: Glycoside Hydrolase Family 18 (GH18; Pfam: PF00704, EC 3.2.1.14), Glycoside Hydrolase Family 19 (GH19; Pfam: PF00182, EC 3.2.1.14), and Glycoside Hydrolase Family 85 (GH85; Pfam: PF03644, EC 3.2.1.96) [16]. Among these, GH18 is the most extensively characterized family in arthropods, with members identified across 12 functional groups. This classification originates from the discovery of the first chitinase-encoding cDNA in the sphinx moth (*Manduca sexta*) [17] and subsequent functional characterization of chitinases derived from the genome of the fruit fly (*Drosophila melanogaster*) [18].

Research on model insects (*Drosophila melanogaster*, *Tribolium castaneum*, *Manduca sexta*) established GH18 chitinase classification into groups (e.g., I-X, and Lepidoptera-specific Group h) based on phylogeny and conserved domain architectures [19].These established groups provide a framework for discussing the functional diversification and evolutionary history of chitinases within insects and serve as a reference for broader comparative studies in other arthropods.

Despite arthropod diversity, Insecta remains the most studied for GH18 chitinases [20, 29], largely due to their significant ecological roles and economic impact as pollinators, parasites, disease vectors, and agricultural pests [21–23, 30]. Increased genome availability has spurred studies prospecting chitin metabolism enzymes in insects [4, 31], driven by interests in understanding their development and potential for pest control applications [22].

Chitinases are not only essential for insect development but also for arthropods in general. This study comprehensively identifies and analyzes GH18 family chitinases across the arthropod subphyla Chelicerata, Crustacea, and Hexapoda, aiming to provide a broader understanding of their diversity within the phylum, extending beyond previous insect-focused research [33–36].

2 Methods

2.1 Data Collection

Arthropod genomes were initially identified from the NCBI database. The database search was filtered using the following NCBI criteria: 'Reference genomes', 'Annotated genomes', 'Annotated by NCBI RefSeq', and an assembly level that included 'scaffold', 'chromosome', or 'complete genome' (NCBI designation: scaffold +). We then specifically selected only scaffold-level genomes that exhibited an NCBI-reported genomic completeness exceeding 95%. Using the NCBI datasets command-line tool and custom Python 3.9 scripts, we downloaded the requisite genomic data and associated taxonomic metadata. Primary transcripts were extracted from protein annotation files using the OrthoFinder primary-transcripts script [24].

2.2 Analysis of Conserved Domains

We utilized the *hmmscan* program from the *hmmer* package [25] to obtain Hidden Markov Model (HMM) profiles for all protein sequences in each accession. The Pfam database [26] was used with an e-value threshold of 1e-5. The *cath-resolve-hits* program [27] was employed to resolve domain architecture. Python scripts v3.9 were used to select sequences with at least one GH18 domain (PF00704). To complete the functional domain architecture, we also evaluated the presence of signal peptides [28] and transmembrane domains [29].

2.3 Phylogenomic Inference

The GH18 family sequences selected through domain architecture were grouped by identifying Hierarchical Orthologous Groups using the *OrthoFinder* tool [24]. To visualize and annotate the resulting phylogenetic trees, we employed the iTOL tool [30] and Python libraries v3.9. For the subsequent phylogenetic inference of GH18 family members in arthropods, we selected sequences from orthogroups containing more than four sequences. Sequences were aligned with MAFFT [31] and refined with CIAlign (-removeinsertions -cropends -removeshort) [32]. Finally, the phylogenetic tree was generated using FastTree. The approximate maximum likelihood method was employed, utilizing the Jones-Taylor-Thornton (JTT) amino acid substitution model with the CAT approximation and 20 rate categories. Branch support values were calculated as Shimodaira-Hasegawa (SH)-like local supports based on 1000 resamples [33].

2.4 Physicochemical Properties, Subcellular Localization, and Motif Analysis

To study the GH18 family sequences found in arthropods, we utilized the *pepstats* tool from the EMBOSS package [34] to gather their physicochemical properties. We also utilized the *Deeploc2* program [35] to determine their subcellular localization. Additionally, we employed the XSTREME program [36] to understand how the sequences were classified into their respective orthogroups by identifying the characteristic motifs of each orthogroup, focusing this analysis specifically on the catalytic Glyco_hydro_18 (GH18) domain (PF00704). XSTREME analysis searched for enriched known motifs (PROSITE database, version 2021_04, MEME format) and de novo motifs (~15 amino acids wide). Discovered or enriched motifs were considered statistically significant if their E-value was less than $1e-10$ (using the -evt $1e-10$ parameter). This focus was chosen because the GH18 domain harbors the primary sequence features responsible for the enzymatic activity and substrate specificity of chitinases.

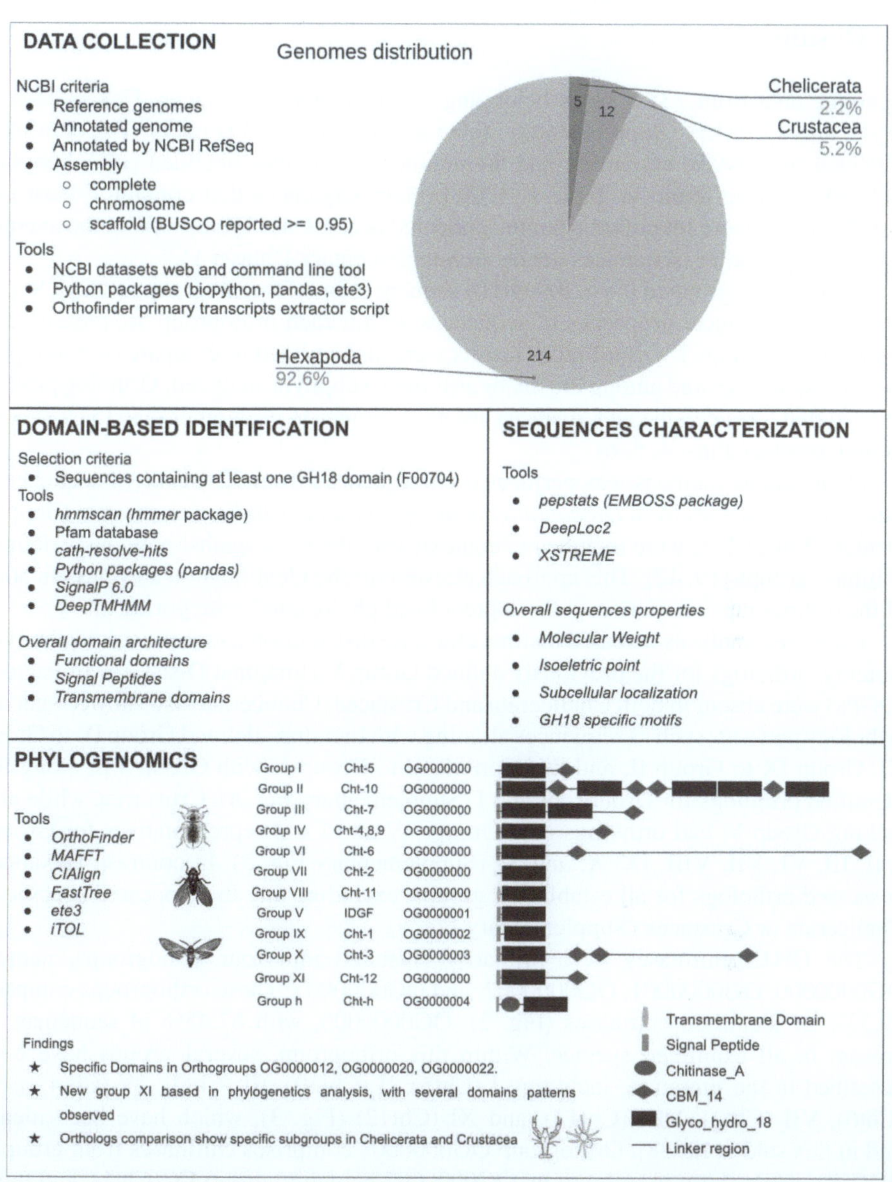

Fig. 1. Integrated Analysis Workflow of GH18 family sequences in Arthropods. Genomes were collected from the NCBI database with a focus on RefSeq proteins. Sequences containing the GH18 domain were selected and analyzed to determine their physicochemical properties, subcellular localization, domain architectures, and conserved motifs. Orthogroup classification was performed to categorize the sequences, followed by phylogenetic inference to understand their evolutionary relationships.

3 Results

Genomic data from 231 species belonging to Chelicerata, Crustacea, Hexapoda subphyla, and 17 orders (Supplementary Table 4) were obtained (Fig. 1). The data were collected from NCBI resources, and the number of genomes obtained per subphylum and order can be found in Table 1. 4209 protein sequences that contain at least one GH18 domain were identified from the collected accessions. Table 1 shows the average sequences per order (sequences details in Supplementary Dataset 1).

OrthoFinder grouped the 4,209 GH18 sequences into 75 orthogroups (OGs). Statistics on the biological properties of sequences within each orthogroup are presented in Supplementary Fig. 1. OrthoFinder results were also utilized to compare ortholog profiles across species and among the major arthropod subphyla analyzed. Ortholog profiles showed that Chelicerata and Crustacea are more similar to each other than to Hexapoda (Supplementary Figs. 4, 5, 6).

Phylogenetic analysis was performed on sequences from 32 OGs ($\geq$4 sequences). Reference sequences from *Drosophila melanogaster* and *Tribolium castaneum* (Supplementary Tables 2, 3) were included to contextualize the OGs against previously defined chitinase groups [19, 42]. This approach allowed for the identification and classification of the orthogroups in relation to these predefined phylogenetic categories.

Integrated analyses revealed distinct chitinase distribution patterns across subphyla. Notably, orthologs for the previously defined Group V (Imaginal Disc Growth Factors, IDGFs) were absent in both Chelicerata and Crustacea. Chelicerata also showed specific orthology patterns, such as sequences aligning with literature-defined Group IV to Group XI, Group IX to Group II, and those proximal to Group X with Group VII, alongside identified orthologs for Groups IV and I (Supplementary Fig. 4). Crustacea, while also lacking Group V, had orthologs near Groups IV and I and representatives for Groups I, II, III, VI, VII, VIII, IX, X, and XI (Supplementary Fig. 5). In contrast, Hexapoda possessed orthologs for all established groups, excluding any that appeared specific to Chelicerata or Crustacea (Supplementary Fig. 6).

The GH18 chitinases were primarily clustered into four orthogroups, namely OG0000000, OG0000001, OG0000002, and OG0000003. These orthogroups comprise 89.33% of identified chitinases (Fig. 2). OG0000000, with 67.45% of sequences, is present in all examined species. Within this orthogroup, several groups have been described in the literature, including I (Cht5), II (Cht10), III (Cht7), IV (Cht4,8), VI (Cht6), VII (Cht2), VIII (Cht11), and XI (Cht12) (Fig. 3), which have been identified in this study [19–38]. Orthogroup OG0000001 comprises chitinases from group V (IDGFs), while those in orthogroup OG0000002 belong to group IX (Cht1), and those in orthogroup OG0000003 belong to group X (Cht3). Orthogroup OG0000004 contains chitinases from group h (Cht-h), unique to lepidopterans.

The orthogroups OG0000000, OG0000001, OG0000002, OG0000003, and OG0000004, which encompass sequences corresponding to previously described chitinase groups, generally exhibit known domain architectures. In contrast, Orthogroups OG0000012, OG0000020, and OG0000022 present distinct domain architectures. OG0000012, prevalent in Hemiptera (also in Diptera, Entomobryomorpha), features an Endonuclease_NS (PF01223) and a GH18 domain in all sequences (Supplementary Fig. 7). Sequences from orthogroups OG0000020 and OG0000022 exclusively comprise members from the order Coleoptera; structurally, they exhibit a signal peptide, followed by two Sushi domains (PF00084), one Trypsin domain (PF00089), then another two Sushi domains, and finally a C-terminal GH18 domain (Supplementary Figs. 8 and 9). Phylogenetically, OG0000012 was positioned within a clade related to the previously defined Group XI chitinases, while orthogroups OG0000020 and OG0000022 were situated near sequences associated with the literature-defined Group IV. Conversely, the remaining orthogroups exhibit varying arrangements of the GH18 catalytic domain, where in some sequences it is adjacent to a signal peptide or transmembrane domain, while in others, it is separated from these elements.

Table 1. Number of Genomic Accessions and Chitinases sequences per Taxonomic Order. The table shows the number of genomic accessions obtained from 231 species of arthropods, distributed across 17 orders.

Subphylum	Order	Accessions	Chitinases (*)
Chelicerata	Aranae	2	16 ± 4
Chelicerata	Ixodida	3	58 ± 15
Crustacea	Decapoda	6	25 ± 6
Crustacea	Diplostraca	4	27 ± 5
Crustacea	Harpacticoida	1	21 ± 0
Crustacea	Siphonostomatoida	1	10 ± 0
Hexapoda	Blattodea	2	15 ± 0
Hexapoda	Coleoptera	17	19 ± 5
Hexapoda	Diptera	69	23 ± 8
Hexapoda	Entomobryomorpha	1	29 ± 0
Hexapoda	Hemiptera	17	12 ± 5
Hexapoda	Hymenoptera	65	14 ± 6
Hexapoda	Lepidoptera	33	14 ± 2
Hexapoda	Neuroptera	1	11 ± 0
Hexapoda	Odonata	1	25 ± 0
Hexapoda	Orthoptera	6	18 ± 4
Hexapoda	Thysanoptera	2	12 ± 1

(*) The average number of chitinases $\pm$ the standard deviation per order was indicated in the Chitinases column.

Additionally, numerous sequences from the insect order Diptera were observed to cluster into ten unique orthogroups, indicating a high diversity of chitinases within these species. Similarly, Ixodida also presented many sequences divided into several unique orthogroups, with the highest average number of chitinases per species among all studied orders (Table 1).

The XSTREME algorithm was employed to analyze the diversity of orthogroups in GH18 chitinases. This algorithm was used to identify the conserved motifs present only in the Glyco_hydro_18 catalytic domain. Sequence diversity across orthogroups correlates with motif presence or absence. It was found that only two orthogroups, OG0000000 and OG0000001, contain all the identified motifs (Supplementary Figure 10). The motifs K(L, I)xxGxPxYGxx(F, Y)xL, xWxxYDDxx(S, T)xxxKA, and xxYxFDGxDxDWE(Y/F)P are present in all orthogroups, while the motif xxxxxLCTHxxYxFA is absent in orthogroup OG0000006, as shown in Fig. 4.

4 Discussion

Genomes from the subphylum Hexapoda, particularly from the class Insecta, were predominant, while those from other arthropod subphyla (such as Chelicerata, Crustacea, and Myriapoda) were underrepresented. Although advances in genome sequencing have been substantial due to third-generation technologies, difficulties persist regarding the quality and completeness of annotations in many non-Hexapoda genomes. [39]. This underrepresentation can limit generalization from better-represented Hexapoda genomes, affecting understanding of broader arthropod genetic and evolutionary diversity. This sampling bias may also mean that numerous lineage-specific chitinase groups or unique evolutionary trajectories within less-represented arthropod lineages remain uncharacterized, suggesting that the currently observed patterns of chitinase diversity might be incomplete. For instance, this taxonomic imbalance might influence conclusions regarding the diversity and distribution of GH18 chitinases, particularly concerning the apparent absence or lower diversity of orthologs corresponding to certain established groups, such as Group V (IDGFs), which we noted in the subphyla Chelicerata and Crustacea. Therefore, a more extensive and equitable genomic sampling across all major arthropod groups is needed to fully map the GH18 family's evolutionary landscape.

While the apparent greater diversity of GH18 chitinases observed in the subphylum Hexapoda could be partially influenced by the aforementioned genomic sampling biases, it is also strongly supported by several intrinsic biological factors. Hexapoda has more emerging gene families than other arthropods [40], potentially linked to adaptations and new metabolic functions that could drive chitinase diversification. Additionally, chitinases are among the most evolutionarily dynamic families [41], as they contribute to forming the exoskeleton, a fundamental biological process for the survival and adaptation of arthropods. This constant selective pressure for adaptation and diversification may have contributed to the evolution of more chitinase groups in the subphylum Hexapoda.

Orthogroups identification is fundamental for reconstructing the evolutionary history of species and gene families. In this study, an orthogroup analysis approach focused on a single protein family, GH18, was adopted to investigate its diversity in arthropods. The large OG0000000, which includes sequences corresponding to the majority of previously defined chitinase groups (such as Groups I, II, III, IV, and VII), appears to represent a core set of functionally versatile GH18 enzymes within arthropods. Its broad taxonomic distribution across insect orders and variable domain architectures suggest diversification while retaining essential roles. The established catalytic activity associated with the literature groups encompassed by OG0000000 - I (Cht5, [42, 43]), II (Cht10, [44]), III (Cht7, [45]), IV (Cht9, [42]), and VII (Cht2, [38]) - further supports its fundamental importance in arthropod biology, likely fulfilling diverse chitin-remodeling tasks.

Large-scale genome sequencing has improved gene family identification and accelerated new gene discovery. The availability of these genomes in public databases facilitated comparative analyses of gene families across diverse species, like the present one. Efforts have identified chitinases in species of scientific and economic interest, including *Drosophila melanogaster*, plant pests, and human disease vectors. Chitinase classification in insects progressed: initially, five groups were identified [37]; subsequently, eight groups [9], 11 groups [19], and more recently, 12 groups, including ENGase belonging to the GH85 family [46], were identified. This progression reflects technological advances and increased genome availability for comprehensive analyses. The identification of new groups has correlated with the continuous incorporation of newly sequenced genomes [46, 47]. This study demonstrates GH18 family sequence diversity extends to other arthropods, furthering the understanding of these enzymes' diversity and evolution.

The domain architecture of chitinases in the GH18 family provides insights into their diverse biological functions. The catalytic domain Glyco_hydro_18 (PF00704) is central to the enzymatic activity of these chitinases, as demonstrated by previous studies [10–20]. In addition to the catalytic domain, signal peptide-associated chitinases exhibit extracellular action, while transmembrane domains are essential for membrane interface activity. Many chitinase groups are associated with the chitin-binding domain rich in cysteine CBM_14 (PF01607). This domain is linked to various cellular processes, including other enzymes involved in chitin metabolism, such as chitin deacetylases [48]. Additionally, some chitinases may contain regions rich in serine and threonine related to their ability to resist protease hydrolysis [20]. These regions confer resistance to proteolytic degradation, providing an additional adaptation for the function of chitinase in challenging environments. The presence of these different domains in chitinases highlights their versatility in performing various biological functions and provides a basis for further investigations into their functional significance.

The architecture of chitinase domains influences the degradation of soluble and insoluble chitin. Multidomain architectures are advantageous for polysaccharide-degrading enzymes because each domain serves a specific function. For example, the catalytic domain is responsible for hydrolyzing sugar bonds, while the chitin-binding domain enhances the enzyme's affinity for the substrate. Linker regions also aid secretion, stabilization, and protease protection [49]. Furthermore, chitinases that possess cysteine-rich regions, in the C-terminal region can undergo different processing and modifications. These alterations in the sequence can lead to different profiles of enzymatic activity due to changes in the affinity for chitin [50]. Therefore, understanding the complex multidomain architecture of chitinases provides new possibilities for biotechnological applications by elucidating the interactions between domains and their impact on chitinase function.

This study has revealed additional domains associated with GH18 chitinases (Supplementary Table 1), suggesting diverse functional roles that remain to be fully elucidated. For example, orthogroup OG0000012, which is prevalent in Hemiptera, features a conserved architecture combining the GH18 catalytic domain with an Endonuclease_NS domain. The Endonuclease_NS domain's nucleic acid-degrading capability [51] suggests a dual enzymatic function. The evolution of this specific domain combination in these insects may reflect an adaptation to their unique feeding strategies or host/pathogen interactions [52, 53]. Targeting such dual-function enzymes could offer novel avenues for the control of Hemipteran pests, for instance, by disrupting their feeding efficiency or their ability to overcome host defenses.

Even more complex architectures were observed in orthogroups OG0000020 and OG0000022, found exclusively in Coleoptera, where the GH18 domain is associated with a N-terminal signal peptide, a Trypsin-like serine protease domain, and multiple Sushi domains. The presence of multiple Sushi domains, known for mediating protein-protein interactions, suggests roles in precise enzyme localization, substrate tethering, or interaction with other components in, for instance, the digestive tract or molting fluid [54, 55]). The Trypsin domain could contribute by proteolytically processing associated proteins to enhance chitin accessibility, by activating the chitinase domain itself or other enzymes in a cascade, or even by direct defense. This multi-domain arrangement in Coleoptera likely evolved to enable highly efficient degradation of complex chitin-protein substrates, perhaps related to specific dietary resources or specialized aspects of cuticle remodeling in this insect order [56–58]. From an applied perspective, these multi-activity Coleopteran enzymes could be valuable targets for species-specific pest management or, alternatively, be explored as novel biocatalysts for biotechnological processes requiring the breakdown of complex chitin-protein matrices.

Lineage-specific domain architectures, such as those identified in this study featuring Endonuclease_NS, Sushi, and Trypsin domains, represent pathways for the functional diversification of GH18 family enzymes in arthropods, shaped by adaptive pressures. Biochemical characterization of the full-length enzymes and their individual domain components will allow testing of the hypotheses presented regarding the roles of these specific associated domains. While motif analysis of these associated domains could offer evolutionary and functional understanding, this study prioritized characterizing motifs within the primary catalytic GH18 domain, placing broader motif analysis of associated domains outside its current scope. Further characterization of these associated domains— including any specific motifs they contain, their interactions with the GH18 domain, and their overall effect on chitinase function—will advance the understanding of chitinase adaptive strategies and may identify approaches for biotechnological applications.

This improved understanding of complex multi-domain architectures underscores the remarkable versatility of these proteins in performing various biological functions. Indeed, beyond the influence of diverse associated domains, the specific ensemble of conserved motifs within the catalytic GH18 domain itself appears to be a key determinant of the functional diversification observed across different orthogroups. Sequence diversity among orthogroups often correlates with GH18 domain motif presence, absence, or variation. Since catalytic activity is a primary mode of action for many GH18 enzymes, specific motifs such as FDGxDLDWExP, KxxxxxGGW, MxYDxxG, and GxxxWxxDxDD [9, 37] are well-recognized from numerous studies as particularly important for their enzymatic activity.

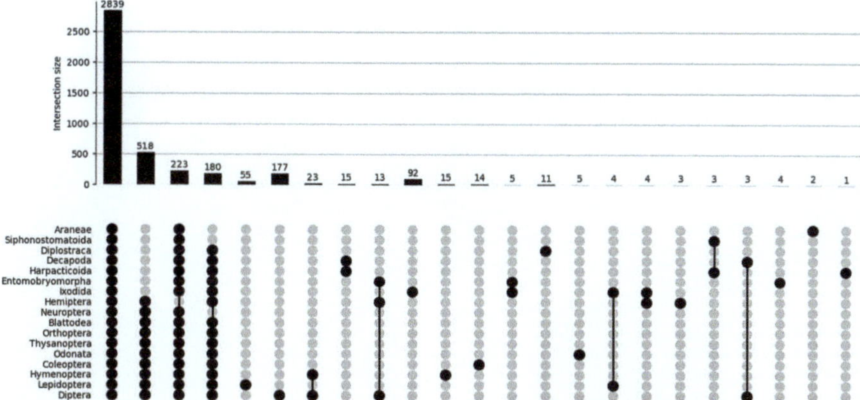

Fig. 2. UpSet plot illustrating the distribution and co-occurrence of GH18 orthogroups across arthropod taxonomic orders. The plot visualizes intersections of orthogroup presence among orders; vertical bars above the matrix indicate the number of sequences in each specific intersection (i.e., shared by a particular combination of orders, or unique to a single order). Plot based on orthogroup presence/absence in analyzed taxonomic orders. It is important to note that, as this visualization is summarized at the order level, orthogroups found exclusively within a single taxonomic order are collectively represented in that order's unique set count, which may obscure finer-scale distinctions among these order-specific orthogroups in this overview. For a more detailed breakdown of individual orthogroup counts per species and taxonomic order, please refer to Supplementary Fig. 1.

For instance, the FDGxDLDWExP motif is required for the enzyme's catalytic activity, with the tryptophan residue (W) within this motif being an important component for this function [59]. Substitutions of W with glycine have been found to inactivate the enzyme, while substitutions with phenylalanine reduce catalytic activity [60]. Furthermore, targeted mutations of residues D and E within the DLDWExP motif clarified their respective roles. Experimental evidence shows that catalytic activity is dependent on residue E, while residue D contributes to maintaining structural stability and influences the enzyme's pH optimum [61]. These motifs are involved in the specific interaction with chitin and in catalyzing its hydrolysis. Their presence and conservation across different chitinases indicate their functions and affect the biochemical behavior of these enzymes.

Our motif analysis indicated that orthogroup OG0000001, which comprises the Imaginal Disc Growth Factors (IDGFs), retains the full complement of identified conserved motifs, including those associated with catalysis. This finding is noteworthy because IDGFs are generally characterized by a lack of, or diminished, hydrolytic activity against chitin substrates, having evolved to perform roles in cell signaling and development. It is plausible that subtle amino acid variations within or immediately flanking these conserved motifs modulate the enzymatic function. To elucidate how these IDGFs differ mechanistically from their catalytically active homologues, given the high motif conservation within the GH18 domain, future studies are warranted. Such investigations could include targeted site-directed mutagenesis of residues in IDGFs from OG0000001, comparative structural biology analyses, and enzymatic assays under a variety of conditions.

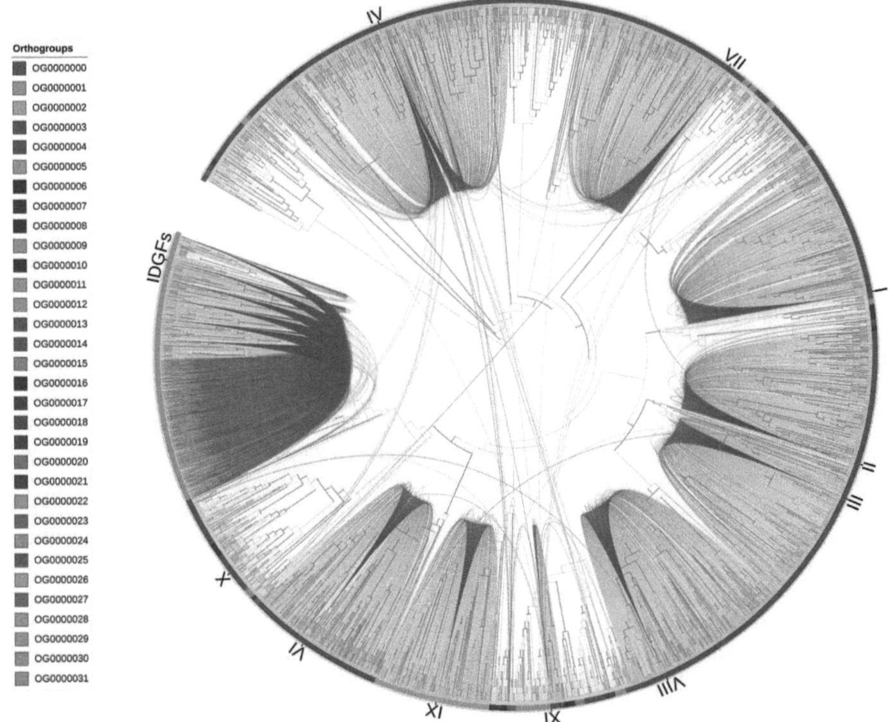

Fig. 3. Phylogenetic Analysis of GH18 Chitinases in Arthropods: Identification of Groups, Orthogroups, and Orthologs. Phylogeny of 4069 sequences with at least one GH18 domain. Sequences categorized into 32 study-derived orthogroups (OGs) and related to 12 literature-defined chitinase groups (e.g., Group I-XI, IDGFs). The purple lines in the figure represent direct connections between chitinase orthologs in *Drosophila melanogaster* (GCF_000001215.4), identified from the results of OrthoFinder. Branch widths are proportional to Shimodaira-Hasegawa (SH)-like local support values; wider branches indicate support values greater than 0.95 (within the 0.95–1.0 range).

Given the diversity of chitinases in arthropods, studies characterizing specific chitinases indicate the particular contribution of each member to the degradation processes of cuticular layers [62–64]. These enzymes regulate chitin content, influence new cuticular layer thickening, and thus affect exoskeleton and organ (trachea, abdomen, wings) development [65]. They also contribute to motility during developmental stage transitions, such as larva-larva, larva-pupa, pupa-adult, and nymph-adult [66]. Studies indicate that, despite the array of functions, these are not exclusive and may vary temporally and locally. Additionally, chitinases can act synergistically in forming new chitin matrices and in their dissolution, contributing to complex processes for the development and adaptation of arthropods [38]. Collectively, the diversity of arthropod chitinases points to their involvement in chitin degradation and their contribution to organismal development and environmental adaptation.

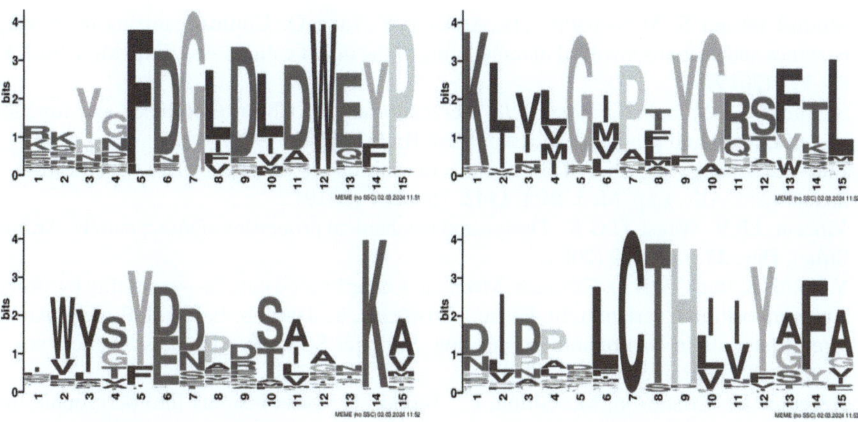

Fig. 4. Common Motifs Identified Across All Orthogroups via XTREME Analysis. The figure illustrates motifs identified in all orthogroups using the XTREME algorithm. These motifs are essential for understanding the functional conservation and evolutionary patterns of chitinase enzymes across diverse arthropod species.

5 Conclusions

This comparative genomics revealed GH18 enzyme conservation and diversification, with distinct evolutionary trajectories, like the contrasting Group V (IDGFs) ortholog distribution among subphyla. The study identified domain architectures not previously characterized in this context, including GH18 domains combined with Endonuclease_NS (in Hemiptera-associated orthogroups) or with Sushi and Trypsin domains (in Coleoptera-specific orthogroups), suggesting lineage-specific functional developments. Furthermore, the formation of numerous lineage-associated orthogroups alongside widespread ones (e.g., in Diptera and Ixodida), coupled with variations in conserved motifs within the GH18 domain, indicates mechanisms for functional specialization. This research demonstrates how comparative genomics across diverse taxa can map gene family evolution, providing a foundation for targeted functional investigations and an improved understanding of arthropod adaptation.

Acknowledgments. The authors acknowledge the financial support provided by CAPES (Coordination for the Improvement of Higher Education Personnel), CNPq (National Council for Scientific and Technological Development), and FAPEMIG (Research Support Foundation of the State of Minas Gerais). We also thank the Federal University of Lavras (UFLA) for institutional support.

Data Availability. All supplementary material and data supporting the findings of this study are available at: https://github.com/lorranavf/diversity_of_gh18_family_in_arthropods.

Disclosure of Interests. The authors declare no competing interests.

References

1. Chen, Q., Peng, D.: Nematode chitin and application. Adv. Exp. Med. Biol. **1142**, 209–219 (2019)

2. Muthukrishnan, S., Merzendorfer, H., Arakane, Y., Yang, Q.: Chitin organizing and modifying enzymes and proteins involved in remodeling of the insect cuticle. Adv. Exp. Med. Biol. **1142**, 83–114 (2019)
3. Steinfeld, L., Vafaei, A., Rösner, J., Merzendorfer, H.: Chitin prevalence and function in bacteria, fungi and protists. Adv. Exp. Med. Biol. **1142**, 19–59 (2019)
4. Liu, X., Zhang, J., Zhu, K.Y.: Chitin in arthropods: Biosynthesis, modification, and metabolism. Adv. Exp. Med. Biol. **1142**, 169–207 (2019)
5. Vincent, J.F.V., Wegst, U.G.K.: Design and mechanical properties of insect cuticle. Arthropod Struct. Dev. **33**, 187–199 (2004)
6. Y. Politi, B. Bar-On, H.O. Fabritius. Mechanics of arthropod cuticle—versatility by structural and compositional variation. In: Estrin, Y., Bréchet, Y., Dunlop, J., Fratzl, P. (eds.) Architectured Materials in Nature and Engineering. Springer Series in Materials Science, vol. 282, pp. 287–327. Springer, Cham (2019)
7. Hegedus, D., Erlandson, M., Gillott, C., Toprak, U.: New insights into peritrophic matrix synthesis, architecture, and function. Annu. Rev. Entomol. **54**, 285–302 (2008)
8. Hegedus, D.D., Toprak, U., Erlandson, M.: Peritrophic matrix formation. J. Insect Physiol. **117**, 103898 (2019)
9. Arakane, Y., Muthukrishnan, S.: Insect chitinase and chitinase-like proteins (2010)
10. Li, L., Chen, Y., Bao, J., Li, S.: Cloning and analysis of the molecularly characterized chitinase genes of Daphnia carinata and Simocephalus vetulus. Genes Genom. **39**, 1395–1406 (2017)
11. Kramer, K.J., Muthukrishnan, S.: Insect chitinases: molecular biology and potential use as biopesticides. Insect Biochem. Mol. Biol. **27**, 887–900 (1997)
12. LeCleir, G.R., Buchan, A., Hollibaugh, J.T.: Chitinase gene sequences retrieved from diverse aquatic habitats reveal environment-specific distributions. Appl. Environ. Microbiol. **70**, 6977–6983 (2004)
13. Funkhouser, J.D., Aronson, N.N.: Chitinase family gh18: evolutionary insights from the genomic history of a diverse protein family. BMC Evol. Biol. 7 (2007)
14. Bussink, A.P., Speijer, D., Aerts, J.M.F.G., Boot, R.G.: Evolution of mammalian chitinase(-like) members of family 18 glycosyl hydrolases. Genetics **177**, 959–970 (2007)
15. Schultz, T.R.: Fungus-farming ants (Attini in part), pp. 404–411. Springer, Cham (2021)
16. Nguyen, S.T.C., Freund, H.L., Kasanjian, J., Berlemont, R.: Function, distribution, and annotation of characterized cellulases, xylanases, and chitinases from cazy. Appl. Microbiol. Biotechnol. **102**, 1629–1637 (2018)
17. Kramer, K.J., Corpuz, L., Choi, H.K., Muthukrishnan, S.: Sequence of a cDNA and expression of the gene encoding epidermal and gut chitinases of Manduca sexta (1993)
18. Zhu, Q., Deng, Y., Vanka, P., Brown, S.J., Muthukrishnan, S., Kramer, K.J.: Computational identification of novel chitinase-like proteins in the Drosophila melanogaster genome. Bioinformatics **20**, 161–169 (2004)
19. Tetreau, G., et al.: Overview of chitin metabolism enzymes in Manduca sexta: identification, domain organization, phylogenetic analysis and gene expression. Insect Biochem. Mol. Biol. **62**, 114–126 (2015)
20. Huang, Q.S., et al.: The gh18 family of chitinases: their domain architectures, functions, and evolutions. Glycobiology **22**, 23–34 (2012)
21. Yang, L.H., Gratton, C.: Insects as drivers of ecosystem processes. Curr. Opin. Insect Sci. **2**, 26–32 (2014)
22. Gougherty, A.V., Jonathan Davies, T.: Towards a phylogenetic ecology of plant pests and pathogens. Philos. Trans. Roy. Soc. B **376** (2021)
23. Belluco, S., et al.: Insects and public health: an overview. Insects **14**, 240 (2023)
24. Emms, D.M., Kelly S.: Orthofinder: phylogenetic orthology inference for comparative genomics. Genome Biol. **20** (2019)

25. Eddy, S.R.: Accelerated profile HMM searches. PLoS Comput. Biol. **7**, e1002195 (2011)
26. Mistry, J., et al.: Pfam: the protein families database in 2021. Nucleic Acids Res. **49**, D412–D419 (2021)
27. Lewis, T.E., Sillitoe, I., Lees, J.G.: CATH-Resolvehits: a new tool that resolves domain matches suspiciously quickly. Bioinformatics **35**, 1766–1767 (2019)
28. Teufel, F., et al.: SignalP 6.0 predicts all five types of signal peptides using protein language models. Nat. Biotechnol. **40**, 1023–1025 (2022)
29. Hallgren, J., et al.: DeepTMHMM predicts alpha and beta transmembrane proteins using deep neural networks. bioRxiv, p. 2022.04.08.487609 (2022)
30. Letunic, I., Bork, P.: Interactive tree of life (iTOL) v5: an online tool for phylogenetic tree display and annotation. Nucleic Acids Res. **49**, W293–W296 (2021)
31. Katoh, K., Misawa, K., Kuma, K.I., Miyata, T.: MAFFT: A novel method for rapid multiple sequence alignment based on fast Fourier transform. Nucleic Acids Res. **30**, 3059 (2002)
32. Tumescheit, C., Firth, A.E., Brown, K.: CIAlign: a highly customizable command line tool to clean, interpret and visualize multiple sequence alignments. PeerJ **10** (2022)
33. Price, M.N., Dehal, P.S., Arkin, A.P.: FastTree 2 – approximately maximum likelihood trees for large alignments. PLoS ONE **5** (2010)
34. Rice, P., Longden, L., Bleasby, A.: EMBOSS: the European molecular biology open software suite. Trends Genet. **16**, 276–277 (2000)
35. Thumuluri, V., et al.: DeepLoc 2.0: multilabel subcellular localization prediction using protein language models. Nucleic Acids Res. **50** (2022)
36. Grant, C.E., Bailey, T.L.: XSTREME: comprehensive motif analysis of biological sequence datasets. bioRxiv, p. 2021.09.02.458722 (2021)
37. Zhu, Q., et al.: Domain organization and phylogenetic analysis of the chitinase-like family of proteins in three species of insects. Insect Biochem. Mol. Biol. **38**, 452–466 (2008)
38. Rabadiya, D., Behr, M.: The biology of insect chitinases and their roles at chitinous cuticles. Insect Biochem. Mol. Biol. **165** (2024)
39. Hotaling, S., et al.: Long reads are revolutionizing 20 years of insect genome sequencing. Genome Biol. Evol. **13** (2021)
40. Grimaldi, D.A.: 400 million years on six legs: on the origin and early evolution of hexapoda. Arthropod Struct. Dev. **39**(2–3), 191–203 (2010)
41. Gregg, W.C., et al.: Gene content evolution in the arthropods. Genome Biol. **21**, 1–14 (2020)
42. Zhu, Q., Arakane, Y., Beeman, R.W., Kramer, K.J., Muthukrishnan, S.: Characterization of recombinant chitinase like proteins of Drosophila melanogaster and Tribolium castaneum. Insect Biochem. Mol. Biol. **38**, 467–477 (2008)
43. Wu, Q., Liu, T., Yang, Q.: Cloning, expression and biocharacterization of ofcht5, the chitinase from the insect Ostrinia furnacalis. Insect Sci. **20**, 147–157 (2013)
44. Chen, W., Qu, M., Zhou, Y., Yang, Q.: Structural analysis of group II chitinase (chtii) catalysis completes the puzzle of chitin hydrolysis in insects. J. Biol. Chem. **293**, 2652–2660 (2018)
45. Liu, T., et al.: The deduced role of a chitinase containing two nonsynergistic catalytic domains. Acta Crystallogr. Sect. D: Struct. Biol. **74**, 30–40 (2018)
46. Shippy, T.D., et al.: Manual curation and phylogenetic analysis of chitinase family genes in the Asian citrus psyllid, Diaphorina citri. Gigabyte **2022**, 1–17 (2022)
47. Chen, Y., et al.: Identification of chitinase genes and roles in the larval–pupal transition of Leptinotarsa decemlineata. Pest Manage. Sci. (2023)
48. Cheng Chang, T., Stergiopoulos, I.: Evolutionary analysis of the global landscape of protein domain types and domain architectures associated with family 14 carbohydrate-binding modules. FEBS Lett. **589**, 1813–1818 (2015)
49. Arakane, Y., Zhu, Q., Matsumiya, M., Muthukrishnan, S., Kramer, K.J.: Properties of catalytic, linker and chitin-binding domains of insect chitinase. Insect Biochem. Mol. Biol. **33**, 631–648 (2003)

50. Zhu, X., Zhang, H., Fukamizo, T., Muthukrishnan, S., Kramer, K.J.: Properties of Manduca sexta chitinase and its C-terminal deletions (2001)
51. Zhang, J.-Y., et al.: Gene cloning, protein expression, and enzymatic characterization of a double-stranded RNA degrading enzyme in Apolygus lucorum. Insect Sci. 1–15 (2023)
52. Du, H., et al.: Armet from whitefly saliva acts as an effector to suppress plant defences by targeting tobacco cystatin. New Phytol. **34**, 1848–1862 (2022)
53. Huang, H.-J., Zhang, C.-X., Hong, X.-Y.: How does saliva function in planthopper–host interactions? Arch. Insect Biochem. Physiol. e21537 (2019)
54. González-Calvo, I., et al.: Sushi domain-containing protein 4 controls synaptic plasticity and motor learning. eLife **10** (2021)
55. Wu, C.-Y., et al.: Identification and expression profiling of serine protease-related genes in Tenebrio molitor. Arch. Insect Biochem. Physiol. **111** (2022)
56. Zhiganov, N.-I, et al.: The set of serine peptidases of the tenebrio molitor beetle: transcriptomic analysis on different developmental stages. Int. J. Mol. Sci. **25** (2024)
57. Zhiganov, N.-I., et al.: The dataset of predicted trypsin serine peptidases and their inactive homologs in Tenebrio molitor transcriptomes. Data Brief **38** (2021)
58. Wang, Q., et al.: A chromosome-level genome assembly and intestinal transcriptome of Trypoxylus dichotomus (Coleoptera: Scarabaeidae) to understand its lignocellulose digestion ability. GigaScience **11** (2022). https://doi.org/10.1093/gigascience/giac059
59. Huang, X., Zhang, H., Zen, K.C., Muthukrishnan, S., Kramer, K.J.: Homology modeling of the insect chitinase catalytic domain-oligosaccharide complex and the role of a catalysis (2000)
60. Zhang, H., Huang, X., Fukamizo, T., Muthukrishnan, S., Kramer, K.J.: Site-directed mutagenesis and functional analysis of an active site tryptophan of insect chitinase (2002)
61. Lu, Y., Zen, K.-C., Muthukrishnan, S., Kramer, K.J.: Site-directed mutagenesis and functional analysis of active site acidic amino acid residues D142, D144 and E146 in Manduca sexta (tobacco hornworm) chitinase (2002)
62. Yasmin Pesch, Y., Riedel, D., Behr, M.: Drosophila chitinase 2 is expressed in chitin producing organs for cuticle formation. Arthropod Struct. Dev. **46**, 4–12 (2017)
63. Dong, W., et al.: Chitinase 6 is required for procuticle thickening and organ shape in Drosophila wing. Insect Sci. (2022)
64. Li, C., et al.: Silencing of apcht7 and apcht10 revealed their function and evaluation of their potential as RNAi targets in Acyrthosiphon pisum (2024)
65. Behr, M., Riedel, D.: Glycosylhydrolase genes control respiratory tubes sizes and airway stability. Sci. Rep. **10**, 1–14 (2020)
66. Yang, X., et al.: Characterization and functional analysis of chitinase family genes involved in nymph–adult transition of Sogatella furcifera. Insect Sci. **28**, 901–916 (2021)

Transcriptomic Profiling and Regulatory Network Reconstruction Uncovers Central Genes in HTLV Infection Progression

Laryssa Bandeira de Melo Silva[1]([⊠]) [iD], Gabriel Freitas Araújo[1] [iD], Patrícia Moura[1] [iD], and João Pacifico Bezerra Neto[2] [iD]

[1] University of Pernambuco (UPE) campus Santo Amaro, Recife, PE, Brazil
`laryssa.bandeira@upe.br`
[2] University of Pernambuco (UPE) campus Petrolina, Petrolina, PE, Brazil
`pacifico.joao@upe.br`

Abstract. HTLV is a human retrovirus associated with serious diseases such as tropical spastic paraparesis (HAM/TSP) and adult T-cell leukemia/lymphoma (ATL). Although identified more than four decades ago, the molecular mechanisms that explain the clinical progression of the infection are still poorly understood. This study aimed to map gene regulatory networks involved in HTLV infection and its expression modulation, seeking to understand biological processes that favor viral persistence and worsening of symptoms. For this purpose, RNAseq libraries from SRA/NCBI repository were selected with samples from infected and control individuals. After quality control, sequences were aligned to human reference genome and analyzed with the HISAT2, edgeR and PANTHER tools to identify and functionally characterize differentially expressed genes. In addition, protein-protein interaction networks were constructed using the STRING platform. CellDesigner software was used to generate a graphical representation of the main molecular mechanisms involved in HTLV-1 infection. The results revealed pathways associated with immune activation, neuroglial inflammation, energy metabolism and epigenetic mechanisms. Molecules such as NRP-1, FOXP3, SIRT1, NAMPT, IL-27 and proteins of MAPK pathway stand out, which are connected to inflammatory, neurodegenerative processes and cellular transformations. The interaction between these pathways suggests an environment conducive to immune system evasion and the progression of infection severe forms. Therefore, it was possible to conclude that HTLV-1 infection activates a complex set of molecular pathways that favor immune evasion, viral persistence and the development of severe clinical manifestations. Mapping these interactions can guide new diagnostic and therapeutic approaches.

Keywords: HTLV-1 · RNAseq · Disease Progression · Molecular pathways

M. Dorn and F. Martins Lopes (Eds.): X-Meeting 2025, LNBI 16037, pp. 45–61, 2026.
https://doi.org/10.1007/978-3-032-09336-3_4

1 Introduction

The human T-cell lymphotropic virus (HTLV) was first identified in 1980, when it was isolated from a patient with a malignant T-cell neoplasm, becoming the first human retrovirus described [1]. Currently, four types of HTLV are recognized, with HTLV-1 and HTLV-2 being the most studied and clinically relevant, due to their association with infection in humans [2]. HTLV transmission occurs through different routes, with the vertical route, especially during childbirth or through breastfeeding, being one of the main forms of dissemination. Horizontal transmission is also significant, and can occur through blood transfusions, organ transplants, sharing of needles and syringes contaminated, as well as unprotected sexual intercourse [3].

Although most individuals infected with HTLV-1 remain asymptomatic throughout their lives, approximately 2% to 5% develop severe clinical forms, such as adult T-cell leukemia/lymphoma (ATL) and HTLV-1-associated myelopathy, known as tropical spastic paraparesis (HAM/TSP) [4]. ATL is a recurrent T-cell cancer characterized by lymphadenopathy, lesions, and nonspecific symptoms [5]. In turn, HAM/TSP manifests as one chronic inflammation of the spinal cord, leading to progressive spastic paraparesis, urinary incontinence, and sensory alterations [6]. In addition to these classic manifestations, many patients present nonspecific symptoms, such as muscle pain, urinary dysfunction, and neuropsychiatric changes, which significantly compromise their quality of life [7].

Despite HTLV-1 was identified more than four decades ago, the biological mechanisms responsible for the different clinical manifestations are still not fully understood. This gap in the understanding of viral pathogenesis limits the development of effective therapeutic strategies [8]. The literature still presents controversy regarding the molecular mechanisms involved, and there is no complete characterization of the cellular and molecular interactions associated with the infection. Studies have shown that HTLV-1 entry into cells is mediated by the interaction of the viral glycoprotein (gp46) with three surface proteins: GLUT1, NRP-1, and HSPG, facilitating viral entry and determining tropism by T cells [6]. In addition, research studies indicate that the HBZ protein, produced by HTLV-1, interferes with TGF-β signaling by recruiting molecules such as Smad3 and p300, favoring the multiplication of infected regulatory T cells by enhancing the expression of genes associated with this pathway, especially of FOXP3 [9, 10].

Given the clinical importance of HTLV-1 infection and the gaps in the understanding of its molecular biology, this study aimed to determine the gene regulatory network associated with the worsening of the infection. Based on the analysis of genes involved in viral entry and cell tropism, we sought to identify the main molecular pathways associated with clinical progression. We hope to expand knowledge about the biological processes related to the clinical manifestations of HTLV-1 and contribute to the development of more effective diagnostic and control methods.

2   Materials and Methods

2.1   RNAseq Libraries Selection and Organization for Expression Profile Analysis

An integrative meta-analysis of RNAseq data was conducted to identify transcriptional alterations related to HTLV infection. Using the keyword "HTLV", libraries were retrieved from the SRA database (NCBI; https://www.ncbi.nlm.nih.gov/sra) with filters for "RNA", "paired-end", and "Illumina", yielding 61 eligible samples as of November 22, 2024. Inclusion criteria ensured diversity and analytical consistency: (1) HTLV-infected patient samples; (2) total RNA from peripheral blood; and (3) at least three replicates per set. A control group of healthy individuals was also included. Two comparative sets were defined (Table 1), each comprising six samples—three per condition.

Table 1. RNA-Seq samples SRA identification ID, organized by biological replicates and clinical status: with HTLV-1, without HTLV and with ATL.

Comparisons	Case Library Samples	Control Library Samples
Positive *vs.* Negative HTLV	SRR24875538 (With HTLV-1)	SRR24875560 (No HTLV)
	SRR24875564 (With HTLV-1)	SRR24875575 (No HTLV)
	SRR24875570 (With HTLV-1)	SRR24875581 (No HTLV)
ATL *vs.* Positive HTLV-no ATL	SRR23000571 (With ATL)	SRR24875548 (With HTLV)
	SRR23000572 (With ATL)	SRR24875552 (With HTLV)
	SRR23000575 (With ATL)	SRR24875555 (With HTLV)

2.2   RNAseq Reads Quality Control, Progressing, Quantification and Gene Enrichment

The reads integrity and quality obtained by sequencing were assessed using the FastQC software [11]. Then, low-quality reads and fragments corresponding to adapters were removed with the aid of the Trimmomatic program [12], ensuring data cleanliness and integrity for subsequent steps. Filtered reads were mapped to the human reference genome (GRCh38) using HISAT2 [13], and gene-level count matrices were generated. Differential expression analysis was performed with edgeR [14], integrated with the Bioconductor platform [15], considering genes that presented $\log2FC > 1$ or < -1, with p-value and FDR < 0.05 as significant. Moreover, a Principal Component Analysis (PCA) was performed to explore the variance structure of the expression data. The PCA results grouped libraries according their respective experimental conditions, highlighting a clear separation between the groups and confirming the consistency of the data.

Additionally, differentially expressed gene lists from edgeR were submitted to the PANTHER platform (https://pantherdb.org/) for functional enrichment analysis. Overrepresented biological processes (GO – Biological Process) were identified using the Statistical Overrepresentation Test, highlighting pathways associated with HTLV infection.

2.3   Construction, Analysis and Functional Enrichment of Gene Networks

To understand the main genes and molecular pathways related to the clinical progression of HTLV infection, two specific protein-protein interaction (PPI) networks were developed:

The first network was constructed from information extracted from the current scientific literature, considering proteins previously described as involved in HTLV infection and their molecular interactions. To identify the proteins involved, a bibliographic search was performed in PubMed and Google Scholar using keywords such as "HTLV-1 pathogenesis", "HTLV infection", "molecular interactions", and "HTLV-related proteins". The key findings highlighted the binding of the viral envelope protein gp46 to cellular receptors (HSPG, NRP-1, and GLUT-1), which facilitate membrane fusion and virus entry into host cells. These proteins served as anchor points for the initial construction of the protein-protein interaction (PPI) network. Additionally, p300 and FOXP3 were included based on evidence showing that the HBZ protein modulates the TGF-β signaling pathway, promoting FOXP3 expression in regulatory T cells via interaction with p300.

A second network was developed based on results obtained in transcriptome differential expression analysis, including only the most significant differentially expressed genes identified in RNAseq libraries comparisons.

These networks were generated using the STRING v11.5 database (https://string-db. org/) [16]. To ensure results reliability, a minimum confidence value (score) of 0.900 was established, considering sources of interaction such as information derived from the environment, coexpression, databases and experimental data. The networks obtained were explored and interpreted in light of current literature, allowing protein identification relative to symptoms complications and molecular pathways of relevance to clinical picture of HTLV. Based on identified interactions, a visual representation of networks based on Systems Biology Graphical Notation (SBGN) was generated on using CellDesigner [17], representing the main molecular mechanisms involved in HTLV infection.

3   Results

Based on initial STRING analysis using, GLUT1, NRP-1 and HSPG (SDC1) as input proteins, it was possible to observe that, in addition to the previously described interactions with cell surface proteins and receptors involved in viral entry, the constructed network revealed additional relevant interactions. Proteins related to immunoregulatory and epigenetic pathways associated with the progression of HTLV-1 infection were also included: EP300 (p300) and FOXP3 (see Fig. 1). Connections with molecules related to neuroinflammatory signaling, angiogenesis and transcriptional regulation stands out. In the first constructed network (see Fig. 1), NRP-1 presented the largest number of connections, interacting extensively with members of semaphorin protein family (SEMA3A, SEMA3C, SEMA3D, SEMA3E, SEMA3F and SEMA3G), and establishing interactions with KDR (VEGFR2), the endothelial growth factor (VEGF) receptor.

Relevant interactions were also observed with receptors such as PLXNA3, ROBO1 and L1CAM, as well as with the cytokines IL-27 and IL-34. In contrast, SLC2A1

(GLUT1), although recognized as canonical receptor for HTLV-1 entry, remained isolated in the PPI network, without direct connections with other relevant nodes in this analysis. In turn, SDC2 (HSPG) presented interactions with SDC4 and RDX (Radixin), proteins related to cell adhesion and cytoskeletal organization. In addition to these clusters, a functional core centered on the EP300 protein (p300), an important transcriptional coactivator, was identified, connected to epigenetic regulators and transcription factors, such as FOXP3. FOXP3 in turn, established additional connections with RORC and NFATC2.

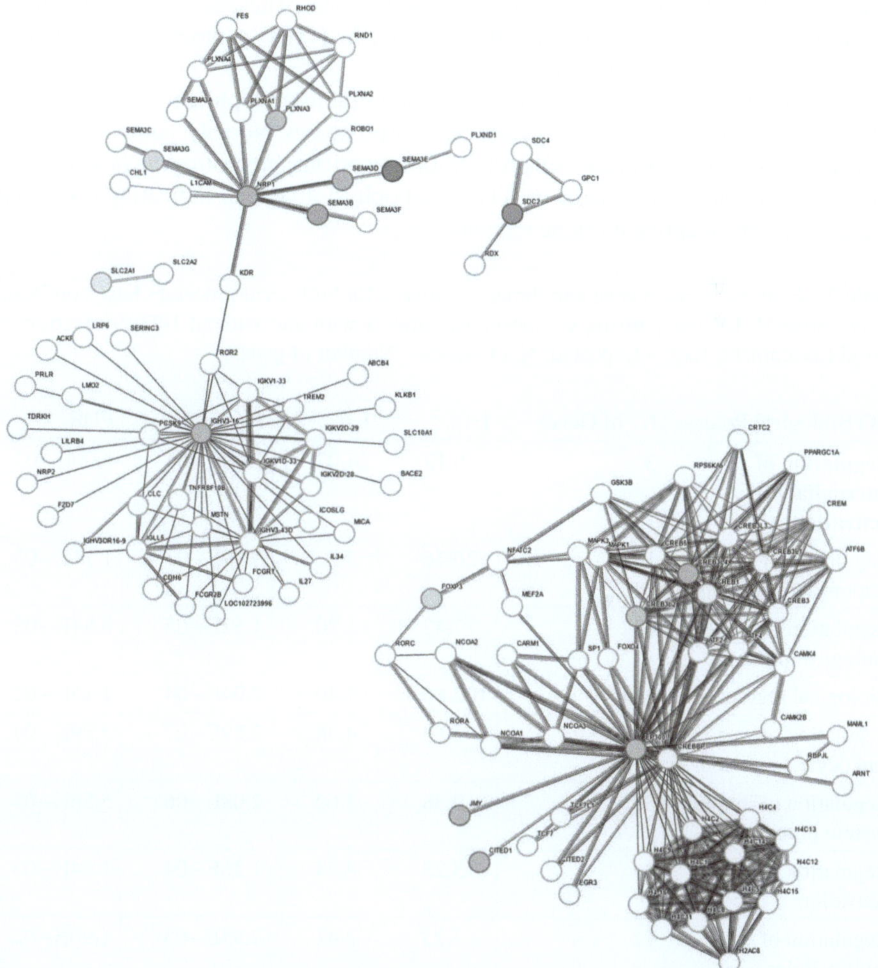

Fig. 1. Literature-based protein-protein interaction network constructed in STRING, focusing on the proteins: GLUT1 (SLC2A1); NRP-1 (NRP1); HSPG (SDC2); p300 (EP300) and FOXP3. Nodes shown in the image represent proteins. Colored nodes correspond to proteins from the first interaction layer, while uncolored nodes represent proteins from the second interaction layer onward. The lines connecting the nodes indicate predict interaction each represented by a specific color: light blue for interactions known from curated databases, pink for experimentally determined interactions, green for neighborhood-based interactions, black for co-occurrence, and purple for protein homology.

Based on our transcriptional profiling data to identify differentially expressed genes and biological pathways associated with infection progression, only genes with FDR < 0.05 were retained to ensure greater statistical rigor in the selection of reported events. Data were selected based mainly on the parameters Log2FC (gene expression fold change [$\log_2$], logCPM (normalized gene abundance), LR statistic (consistency of the difference between groups), PValue (chance that the difference is random) and FDR (adjusted value for multiple comparisons). In this analysis, 140 genes were selected for Positive *vs.* Negative HTLV comparison and 2,758 for ATL *vs.* Positive HTLV-no ATL comparison. The most significantly enriched biological pathways and cellular processes (p < 0.05) predicted by PANTHER are shown in the following tables. These categories offer insights into molecular mechanisms potentially involved in HTLV pathogenesis, particularly regarding severe clinical outcomes.

The Positive *vs.* Negative HTLV comparison (Table 2), highlights the most significantly enriched biological pathways and cellular processes. Notably, pathways related to microglial cell activation and B cell proliferation stand out, suggesting the involvement of neuroinflammatory mechanisms in HTLV pathophysiology and indicating coordinated activation of the adaptive immune response.

Table 2. Analysis of main gene enrichment pathways for biological processes based on Positive *vs.* Negative HTLV comparison, composed of patients with and without HTLV infection. F.E. – Fold Enrichment; Exp. – Expected; N. of Genes – Number of genes.

GO Biological Process	N. of Genes	Exp.	F.E.	P-value	FDR
Regulation of microglial cell activation	3	0.12	24.07	2.48E−04	4.00E−02
Regulation of response to stimulus	102	26.76	3.81	5.99E−07	1.11E−03
Regulation of biological process	132	77.42	1.70	1.52E−05	6.84E−03
Biological regulation	144	102.86	1.40	2.04E−04	1.15E−02
Regulation of leukocyte activation	17	3.80	4.48	2.89E−07	5.89E−04
Regulation of immune system process	38	10.38	3.66	2.08E−06	5.56E−03
Regulation of cell activation	14	3.23	4.34	1.26E−04	1.64E−03
Regulation of multicellular organismal process	11	3.23	3.41	2.95E−03	1.90E−02
Regulation of cellular process	100	74.85	1.34	1.12E−04	5.72E−03
B cell proliferation	6	0.75	8.05	1.19E−04	2.29E−02

(continued)

Table 2. (*continued*)

GO Biological Process	N. of Genes	Exp.	F.E.	P-value	FDR
Lymphocyte proliferation	6	0.76	7.75	1.19E−04	2.29E−02
Mononuclear cell proliferation	6	0.77	7.75	1.19E−04	2.29E−02
Leukocyte proliferation	6	0.77	7.75	1.19E−04	2.29E−02
Lymphocyte activation	24	6.92	3.47	6.20E−06	3.21E−03
Leukocyte activation	25	7.02	3.56	2.36E−06	2.53E−03
Cell activation	33	9.94	3.32	3.19E−07	2.51E−03
Multicellular organismal process	16	4.31	3.71	9.44E−05	2.80E−03
Immune system process	45	20.62	2.18	3.52E−04	4.13E−03
B cell activation	9	1.43	6.29	9.76E−05	2.91E−03
T cell costimulation	4	0.71	5.65	5.59E−04	4.12E−02
Positive regulation of T cell activation	4	1.49	2.71	3.90E−04	4.11E−02
Regulation of T cell activation	13	2.58	5.04	1.97E−06	1.83E−03

Functional enrichment analysis performed with genes from ATL Positive *vs.* HTLV-no ATL comparison revealed two biological processes with functional prominence (see Table 3). The first is related to the metabolism and biosynthesis of isoprenoids, specifically to the biosynthetic process of isopentenyl diphosphate via mevalonate. The second process involves the positive regulation of the apoptotic process associated with morphogenesis. After the enrichment results, the four most significant genes for each library (see Table 4) were used in the PPI (see Fig. 2).

Table 3. Analysis of main gene enrichment pathways for biological processes based ATL Positive *vs.* HTLV-no ATL comparison. F.E. – Fold Enrichment; Exp. – Expected; N. of Genes – Number of genes.

GO Biological Process	N. of Genes	Exp.	F.E.	P-value	FDR
Isopentenyl diphosphate biosynthetic process, mevalonate pathway	3	0.32	9.46	1.18E−03	3.93E−02
Isopentenyl diphosphate biosynthetic process	5	0.53	7.57	5.70E−04	2.30E−02
Primary metabolic process	827	715.91	1.16	1.23E−07	1.76E−05

(*continued*)

Table 3. (*continued*)

GO Biological Process	N. of Genes	Exp.	F.E.	P-value	FDR
Metabolic process	921	805.43	1.14	7.42E−08	1.19E−05
Isopentenyl diphosphate metabolic process	4	0.53	7.57	5.70E−04	2.30E−02
Nucleobasecontaining compound metabolic process	353	289.15	1.22	3.28E−05	2.33E−03
Positive regulation of apoptotic process involved in mammary gland involution	3	0.32	9.46	1.18E−03	3.92E−02
Positive regulation of apoptotic process involved in morphogenesis	5	0.32	9.46	1.18E−03	3.92E−02
Positive regulation of apoptotic process involved in development	5	0.63	7.89	7.19E−05	4.36E−03
Positive regulation of developmental process	193	140.46	1.37	3.70E−06	3.74E−04
Regulation of developmental process	357	258.19	1.38	3.00E−11	1.35E−08
Regulation of biological process	1420	1247.30	1.14	1.59E−15	1.48E−12
Biological regulation	1456	1290.10	1.13	1.14E−14	7.73E−12
Positive regulation of biological process	839	646.48	1.30	1.03E−20	5.13E−17
Regulation of apoptotic process involved in development	6	1.37	4.37	1.23E−03	4.03E−02
Regulation of apoptotic process	227	156.31	1.45	3.52E−09	9.70E−07
Regulation of cellular process	1379	1205.87	1.44	2.19E−15	1.91E−12
Regulation of apoptotic of cellular process	6	1.37	4.37	1.23E−03	4.04E−02

Table 4. Gene differential expression for genes used for STRING PPI network analysis, presenting expression values after edgeR for: Positive *vs.* Negative HTLV comparison (patients with HTLV *vs.* patients without HTLV) and ATL *vs.* Positive HTLV-no ATL (patients with ATL *vs.* patients with HTLV-no ATL). Just data presenting Log2FC, PValue and FDR inclusion criteria are showed.

Comparisons	Gene	Log$_2$FC	logCPM	LR	PValue	FDR
Positive *vs.* Negative HTLV	TRAF1	2.99	9.10	111.12	5.56E−26	6.47E−23
	CCR6	3,40	6,76	96.34	9,63E−23	6,10E−20
	MAPK11	4,00	4,11	83.69	5,78E−20	2,51E−17
	NAMPT	2,97	8,25	83.58	6,11E−20	2,61E−17
ATL *vs.* Positive HTLV-no ATL	NACC1	9,04	6,14	94.46	2,50E−22	4,17E−18
	SIPA1L2	7,53	2,66	23.29	1,39E−06	1,14E−04
	MVK	3,83	3,76	17.06	3,61E−05	1,62E−03
	PMVK	1,84	5,45	8.62	3,32E−03	4,97E−02

After obtaining the GO enrichment analysis, genes related to enriched process were selected for investigation and analysis of protein interactions using the STRING platform, with the aim of deepening understanding of cellular and molecular mechanisms involved in HTLV infection progression. This analysis covered processes with greatest enrichment, as microglial pathway (MAPK11, NAMPT), adaptive immune system activation cells (TRAF1, CCR6), metabolism and biosynthesis of isoprenoids, biosynthetic process of isopentenyl diphosphate (MVK and PMVK) and regulation of apoptotic process involved in development/morphogenesis (NACC1 and SIPA1L2).

Observing this new PPI analysis for genes with highest enrichment in our comparisons (see Fig. 2), it was observed that CCR6, NACC1 and SIPA1L2 did not present interactions with any of proteins present in the network. On the other hand, it was possible to highlight that TRAF1 and TRAF2 interact directly with MAP4K5, composing a specific signaling subgroup. In addition, NAMPT appears as one of central network hubs, presenting high connectivity with proteins related to NAD$^+$ metabolism, signaling pathways and energy homeostasis. Interactions with enzymes directly involved in the NAD$^+$ biosynthesis pathway were observed. NAMPT also interacted with SIRT1, SIRT2, SIRT3, SIRT4, SIRT5 and SIRT6, belonging to sirtuin family. A further highlight is the interaction between MVK (Mevalonate Kinase) and PMVK (Phosphomevalonate Kinase), observed in a cohesive metabolic cluster associated with mevalonate pathway.

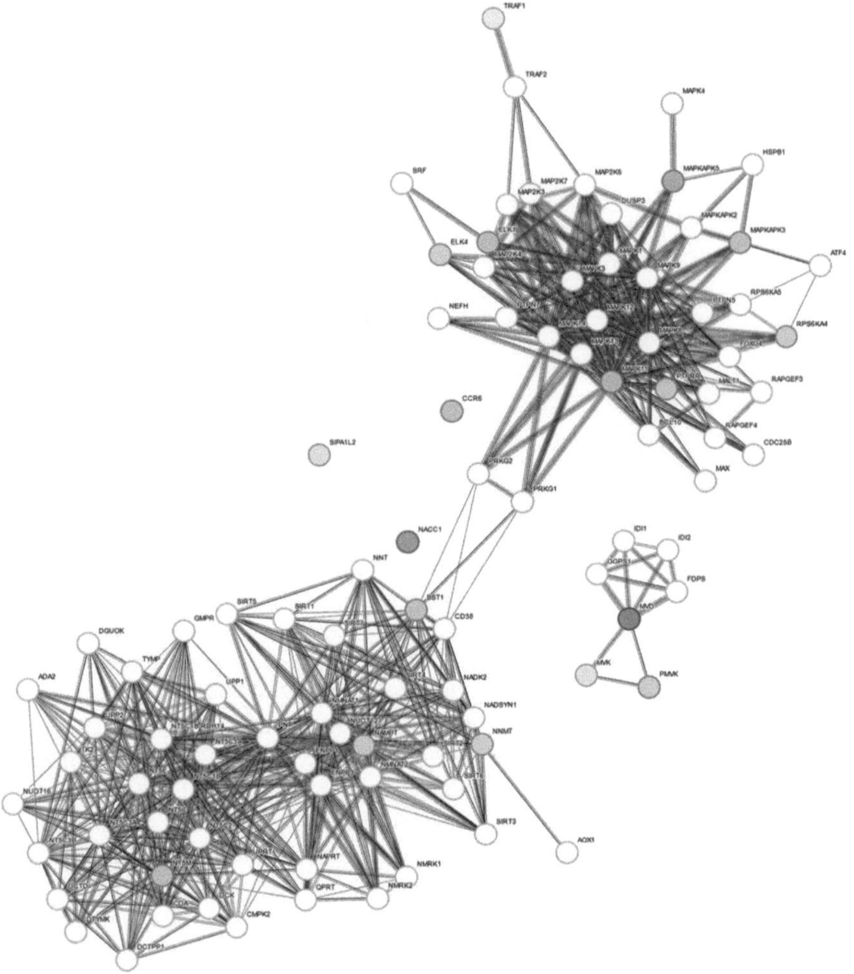

Fig. 2. PPI network for genes with highest enrichment, focusing on the proteins: MAPK11, NAMPT, TRAF1, CCR6, MVK, PMVK, NACC1 and SIPA1L2. Nodes shown in the image represent proteins. Colored nodes correspond to proteins from the first interaction layer, while uncolored nodes represent proteins from the second interaction layer onward. The lines connecting the nodes indicate predict interaction each represented by a specific color: light blue for interactions known from curated databases, pink for experimentally determined interactions, green for neighborhood-based interactions, black for co-occurrence, and purple for protein homology. (Color figure online)

Following the compilation of all previous results and existing literature knowledge, the visual representation of networks generated using CellDesigner (see Fig. 3) proposes the main molecular mechanism involved in worsening of infection caused by HTLV-1. Our pathway proposes that viral entry occurs through interaction of gp46 with the surface proteins HSPG, NRP-1 and GLUT1. After integration of viral DNA into host cell genome, the expression of TAX and HBZ proteins activates signaling pathways such as

NF-κB, TGF-β/SMAD3 and MAPK, modulating the immune response. These pathways influence the differentiation of T lymphocytes, with activation of FOXP3, NFATC2 (TREGs), RORC and an inflammatory profile by the expression of IL-17 (Th17). Signals mediated by SEMA3A/C via NRP-1 impact neural and endothelial cells, associated with neurological and vascular manifestations. Proteins such as NAMPT and SIRT1 are also involved in the regulation of the immune response and viral replication.

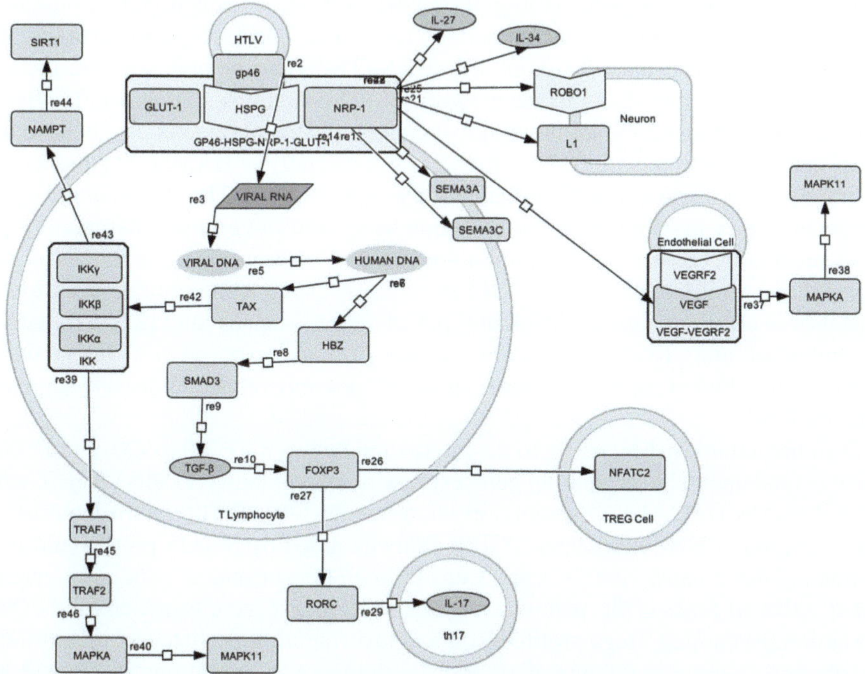

Fig. 3. Network of molecular interactions associated with HTLV infection created in Systems Biology Graphical Notation (SBGN) format using CellDesigner.

4 Discussion

Although there is fragmented evidence regarding the role of various genes and their products in neuroinflammatory and tumor development processes, their direct involvement in HTLV-1 infection remains poorly explored. The results obtained in first STRING network analysis (see Fig. 1) suggest that NRP-1, in addition to acting as a coreceptor in viral internalization process, can also influence neuroinflammatory and migratory pathways in HTLV-1 infection context. Its interaction with the KDR receptor (VEGFR2), known to participate in angiogenic and immunoinflammatory processes, reinforces the hypothesis that this axis contributes to the maintenance of the chronic inflammatory environment observed in infected individuals [18]. Neuropilins, particularly NRP-1, are multifunctional transmembrane glycoproteins widely described in neural development, angiogenesis, and the regulation of inflammatory pathways [19, 20]. Previous studies have shown that NRP-1 interacts with class 3 semaphorins and VEGF isoforms, modulating not only the tumor environment but also neuroinflammatory processes [21, 22]. Our analysis (see Fig. 1) also highlighted the interaction between NRP-1 and L1CAM, an essential cell adhesion molecule in central nervous system (CNS), whose coexpression is essential for neuronal response to signals mediated by SEMA3A [23].

Another relevant finding was the identification of ROBO1, previously described interacting with NRP-1 in semaphorin signaling regulation during forebrain development, aiding cortical interneuron migration [24]. In HTLV-1 infection, this interaction could favor the targeting of infected cells to the CNS, contributing to neuroinflammation and neurological manifestations like HAM/TSP. Also notable was the presence of cytokines IL-27 and IL-34 in the network. IL-27 exerts pro- and anti-inflammatory functions depending on the immunological context [25], and elevated levels have been associated with symptomatic HTLV-1 infection, especially in HAM/TSP patients, suggesting a role in intensifying the inflammatory response [26]. The IL-34, in turn, plays a relevant role in myeloid populations maintenance and in chronic inflammatory processes mediation, consistent with immunological profile observed in individuals infected with HTLV-1. Overexpression of IL-34 has been associated with tumor progression and resistance to chemotherapy in different types of cancer, such as lung [27]. Similarly, in the context of adult T-cell leukemia/lymphoma (ATL), coexpression of IL-34 and M-CSF was identified in most of the cases analyzed, possibly related to disease aggressive behavior [28].

Another notable aspect refers to the interaction between EP300 (p300) and FOXP3, which is fundamental in regulating gene expression of regulatory T cells (Tregs), which are exploited by HTLV-1 as an immune evasion strategy [29]. The literature demonstrates that viral protein HBZ modulates TGF-β pathway aided by Smad3 protein and p300, stimulating the expansion of infected Tregs through transcriptional activity intensification of activated genes in this pathway [30]. This mechanism results in increased FOXP3 expression, promoting Tregs proliferation and favoring viral persistence, in addition to contributing to chronic inflammation and development of conditions associated with HTLV-1, such as HAM/TSP and ATL [31].

Additionally, it is known that FOXP3 + Tregs can acquire an inflammatory profile by expressing IL-17 in certain pathological contexts. Although they maintain regulatory characteristics, these cells can secrete pro-inflammatory cytokines, functioning as inflammatory Tregs [32, 33]. In our network (see Fig. 1), FOXP3 also connected to RORC and NFATC2, crucial factors in the Th17 differentiation axis, evidencing a functional circuit in which NFATC2 contributes to FOXP3 induction, while RORC directs differentiation towards the Th17 profile, an axis that may play a central role in immunoregulation and viral progression [34, 35].

The second network (see Fig. 2), constructed from the differentially expressed genes identified in transcriptome comparisons, revealed new functional clusters and signaling pathways not evidenced in the first STRING. The microglial pathway is one of the most prominent enriched processes, reflecting the role of microglia as the central nervous system's primary resident immune cells. Microglia plays a fundamental role in tissue defense, neural homeostasis, and mediating inflammatory signals involved in neurodegenerative diseases [36]. One of critical mechanisms that modulate microglial activation is mitogen-activated protein kinase (MAPK) pathway, composed of a cascade of protein kinases that convert extracellular signals into specific intracellular responses. This pathway is crucial in neuroplasticity regulation, in inflammatory response control, and in the cellular decision between survival and death by apoptosis [36, 37]. In generated network interactions, proteins such as MAPK11, MAPK14, MAPK8, and MAPK9 were identified as central elements of this pathway. This configuration suggests that HTLV infection may induce sustained activation of the MAPK pathway in microglia, favoring the release of pro-inflammatory mediators, altering synaptic plasticity, and potentially contributing to the progressive neuronal inflammation [37].

In the PPI network (see Fig. 2), TRAF1 and TRAF2 stand out for their relationship with adaptive immune system cells activation and their direct connection with MAPK pathway. TRAF1, although unable to directly activate Mitogen-Activated Protein Kinases (MAPKKKs), acts as a modulator of signaling mediated by other TRAFs, especially TRAF2, which effectively activates these kinases [38]. This activation culminates in MAPK and NF-κB pathways induction, essential for regulating inflammation, activation and resistance of lymphocytes to apoptosis [39, 40]. It is worth mentioning that TRAF expression occurs through activation of the NF-κB pathway. In the context of HTLV-1 infection, this pathway is activated mainly by viral protein Tax. This activation occurs through the interaction of Tax with IκB kinase (IKK) complex, formed by catalytic subunits (IKKα and IKKβ) and a regulatory subunit (IKKγ) [41].

A previous study examined transcriptome changes over six days in CD4 + T cells from individuals with non-malignant polyclonal HTLV-1 infections, compared to uninfected cells under the same stimuli. It showed that infected CD4 + cells exhibit basal activation of NF-κB and mTOR pathways at time zero (t_0), before any experimental stimulus. This basal activation was attributed to proviral genes expression, such as HBZ, whose presence is detectable immediately after cell isolation. This activation appears constitutive and chronic, unlike the transient Tax expression, with possible contributions from factors such as cellular aging. Our study supports these findings and expands the understanding of the functional consequences of HTLV-1 infection by identifying through PPI network analysis key molecules associated not only with inflammatory signaling but also with pathways related to neuroinflammation, cell migration, and immune evasion [42].

In addition, altered expression of TRAF1 has already been extensively associated with lymphoid malignancies [43]. A relevant factor in HTLV context, considering virus tropism for T cells and its role in persistent activation of these pathways. The constant interaction of these proteins with MAPK cascade may contribute to ATL worsening, considered a lymphoid neoplasm inflammatory state, and neuronal damage observed in manifestations such as HAM/TSP [44].

Interactions between NAMPT and members of the sirtuin family (SIRT1 to SIRT6) outline an essential functional axis in energy metabolism regulation, mitochondrial homeostasis, epigenetic mechanisms, and inflammation modulation [45]. This axis acquires particular relevance in HTLV-1 infection context, in which chronic immune activation and oxidative stress are central features in HAM/TSP progression. Because they directly depend on intracellular NAD^+ levels, sirtuins act as metabolic sensors and regulators of pro- and anti-inflammatory gene expression [46]. In this context, functional interaction between SIRT1 and the NAMPT-mediated NAD$^+$ biosynthesis pathway reinforces the role of this sirtuin as an integrator of metabolic and inflammatory signals [47]. Thus, the hypothesis is raised that disorders in this functional axis may directly influence clinical outcomes in individuals infected with HTLV-1.

Previous studies have shown that peripheral blood mononuclear cells (PBMCs) from ATL patients, especially in acute form, express significantly higher levels of SIRT1 compared to healthy individuals, and that small molecule SIRT1 inhibitors are highly effective in suppressing intracellular cells [48, 49]. Considering this, NAMPT overexpression may favor the survival, regularity and resistance of infected cells by ensuring intracellular NAD$^+$ stores maintenance, promoting a bioenergetic and epigenetic environment conducive to cellular transformation. Thus, NAMPT–NAD$^+$–SIRT1 axis not only sustains metabolic homeostasis but may also contribute to viral persistence and progression to severe clinical forms [45].

A previous transcriptomic study using microarray data compared HAM/TSP and ATLL patients, identifying key genes and pathways through protein-protein interaction (PPI) analysis. They found enhanced NF-κB and PI3K-AKT activation and cell proliferation genes in ATLL, while apoptosis and immune dysfunction pathways predominated in HAM/TSP, indicating distinct molecular mechanisms [50]. Our study complements these findings by employing RNA-seq data and integrating multiple clinical groups, while applying PPI modeling, functional enrichment, and pathway visualization. Additionally, we highlight novel regulatory axes.

The interaction between MVK and PMVK, identified in PPI STRING analysis, reinforces the functional integrity of mevalonate pathway. This pathway is involved in processes such as protein prenylation and regulation of inflammatory response, especially via IL-1β [51]. In available literature, there is no evidence associating this pathway with HTLV-1, which suggests that its direct contribution to virus pathogenesis or its clinical manifestations has not yet been sufficiently explored. Furthermore, the absence of CCR6, NACC1, and SIPAIL1 interactions in constructed network suggests that, in the developed context, these proteins may not directly participate in prioritized signaling pathways or, alternatively, their interactions may depend on specific expression conditions.

5   Conclusion

Based on the protein interaction networks here presented and differential expression data found, it is possible to conclude that several molecular pathways associated with chronic inflammation, neurodegeneration and cellular transformation are involved in HTLV-1 progression of infection. The identification of molecules such as NRP-1, IL-27, IL-34, FOXP3, SIRT1, MAPKs and their associated partners reinforce the hypothesis that the virus takes advantage of complex cellular circuits to promote its persistence, immune evasion and development of clinical manifestations such as HAM/TSP and ATL. The evidence points to a scenario in which the mechanisms of viral entry, activation of inflammatory pathways and metabolic and epigenetic alterations converge to an environment that is permissive to the pathogenesis of HTLV-1. In summary, elucidating these interactions provides valuable insights into the pathophysiology of HTLV-1 infection and holds potential for guiding more effective therapeutic interventions in the future.

Acknowledgments. We are very grateful to the members of Bioinformatics Laboratory at the University of Pernambuco for their valuable scientific discussions and continuous support. This study was financed in part by the Coordenação de Aperfeiçoamento de Pessoal de Nível Superior - Brasil (CAPES) - Finance Code 001, Conselho Nacional de Desenvolvimento Científico e Tecnológico (CNPq) and Pernambuco Science and Technology Foundation (FACEPE).

Disclosure of Interests. The authors declare no conflicts of interest. There are no financial or personal relationships, funding, or other circumstances that could influence or bias the content of this work.

The authors employed ChatGPT (OpenAI, 2025) to support the revision and refinement of the English language. The authors remain fully responsible for the scientific content, interpretations, and conclusions of this work.

References

1. Romanelli, L.C.F., Caramelli, P., Proietti, A.B.F.C.: Human T-cell lymphotropic virus type 1 (HTLV-1): When to suspect infection? J. Braz. Med. Assoc. **56**(3), 340–347 (2010)
2. Gonçalves, D.U., et al.: Epidemiology, treatment, and prevention of human T-cell leukemia virus type 1-associated diseases. Clin. Microbiol. Rev. **23**(3), 577–589 (2010)
3. Rosadas, C., Brites, C., Arakaki-Sánchez, D., Casseb, J., Ishak, R.: Brazilian Protocol for Sexually Transmitted Infections 2020: human T-cell lymphotropic virus (HTLV) infection. Epidemiol. Serv. Saude **30**(Suppl 1), e2020605 (2021)
4. Teixeira, M.C.L., Hennington, É.A.: People living with HTLV: meanings of illness, experience of illness and their relationships with work. Ciênc. Saúde Colet. **26**, 6049–6057 (2021)
5. Bittencourt, A.L., Farré, L.: Adult T-cell leukemia/lymphoma. An. Bras. Dermatol. **83**(4), 351–359 (2008)
6. Martin, F., Taylor, G.P., Jacobson, S.: Inflammatory manifestations of HTLV-1 and their therapeutic options. Expert Rev. Clin. Immunol. **10**(11), 1531–1546 (2014)
7. Ferreira, Q.R., et al.: Neurological aspects of HTLV-1 infection: symptoms in apparently asymptomatic carriers. J. Neurovirol. **30**(4), 353–361 (2024)
8. Santana, C.S., et al.: Advances in preventive vaccine development against HTLV-1 infection: a systematic review of the last 35 years. Front. Immunol. **14**, 1073779 (2023)
9. Satou, Y., et al.: HTLV-1 bZIP factor induces T-cell lymphoma and systemic inflammation in vivo. PLoS Pathog. **7**(2), e1001274 (2011)
10. Tone, Y., et al.: Smad3 and NFAT cooperate to induce Foxp3 expression through its enhancer. Nat. Immunol. **9**(2), 194–202 (2008)
11. Andrews, S., et al.: FastQC. A quality control tool for high throughput sequence data (2010). https://www.bioinformatics.babraham.ac.uk/projects/fastqc/
12. Bolger, A.M., Lohse, M., Usadel, B.: Trimmomatic: a flexible trimmer for Illumina sequence data. Bioinformatics **30**(15), 2114–2120 (2014)
13. Guo, J., Gao, J., Liu, Z.: HISAT2 parallelization method based on spark cluster. J. Phys. Conf. Ser. **2226**, 012038 (2022)
14. Robinson, M.D., McCarthy, D.J., Smyth, G.K.: EdgeR: a bioconductor package for differential expression analysis of digital gene expression data. Bioinformatics **26**(1), 139–140 (2010)
15. Huber, W., et al.: Orchestrating high-throughput genomic analysis with bioconductor. Nat. Methods **12**(2), 115–121 (2015)
16. Szklarczyk, D., et al.: STRING database in 2017: protein–protein association networks with increased coverage. Nucleic Acids Res. **45**(D1), D362–D368 (2017)

17. Funahashi, A., et al.: CellDesigner: a modeling tool for biochemical networks. In: Proceedings of the Winter Simulation Conference 2006, pp. 1707–1712 (2006)
18. Valiatti, F.B., et al.: Role of vascular endothelial growth factor in angiogenesis and diabetic retinopathy. Braz. Arch. Endocrinol. Metab. **55**, 106–113 (2011)
19. Chaudhary, B., Khaled, Y.S., Ammori, B.J., Elkord, E.: Neuropilin 1: function and therapeutic potential in cancer. Cancer Immunol. Immunother. **63**(2), 81–99 (2014)
20. Pan, Q., et al.: Blocking neuropilin-1 function has an additive effect with anti-VEGF to inhibit tumor growth. Cancer Cell **11**(1), 53–67 (2007)
21. Vieira, J.M., Schwarz, Q., Ruhrberg, C.: Selective requirements for NRP1 ligands during neurovascular patterning. Development **134**(10), 1833–1843 (2007)
22. De Araujo, M.A., et al.: NRP1 as a potential molecular target for medulloblastoma. BioSCI **82**, e00041 (2024)
23. Giordano, M., Cavallaro, U.: Different nuances of L1CAM in the pathophysiology of cancer stem cells. J. Clin. Med. **5**, 1502 (2020)
24. Hernández-Miranda, L.R., et al.: Robo1 regulates semaphorin signaling to guide the migration of cortical interneurons through the ventral forebrain. J. Neurosci. **31**(16), 6174–6187 (2011)
25. Andres-Martin, F., Catalfamo, M.: Regulation of IL-27 expression and its effects on adaptive immunity against viruses. Front. Immunol. **15**, 1395921 (2024)
26. Assone, T., et al.: IL-10 predicts neuroinflammatory disease incidence and proviral load dynamics in a large Brazilian cohort of people living with HTLV-1. Front. Immunol. **15**, 1416476 (2024)
27. Baghdadi, M., et al.: High coexpression of IL-34 and M-CSF correlates with tumor progression and poor survival in lung cancer. Sci. Rep. **8**(1), 418 (2018)
28. Komohara, Y., et al.: Potential antilymphoma effect of M-CSFR inhibitor in adult T-cell leukemia/lymphoma. J. Clin. Exp. Hematop. **58**(4), 152–160 (2018)
29. Du, T., et al.: Lysosome-dependent p300/FOXP3 degradation limits Treg cell functions and enhances targeted therapy against cancers. Exp. Mol. Pathol. **95**(1), 38–45 (2013)
30. Zhao, T., et al.: HTLV-1 bZIP factor enhances TGF-β signaling through p300 coactivator. Blood **118**(7), 1865–1876 (2011)
31. Chen, S., et al.: T-cell-like regulatory activity in Foxp3+ adult T-cell leukemia cells. Immunol. Int. **18**(2), 269–277 (2006)
32. Kryczek, I., et al.: IL-17+ regulatory T cells in the microenvironments of chronic inflammation and cancer. J. Immunol. **186**(7), 4388–4395 (2011)
33. Yang, B.H., et al.: Foxp3+ T cells expressing RORγt represent a stable regulatory T cell effector lineage with enhanced suppressive capacity during intestinal inflammation. Mucosal Immunol. **9**(2), 444–457 (2016)
34. Ziegler, S.F.: FOXP3: not just for regulatory T cells anymore. Eur. J. Immunol. **37**(1), 21–23 (2007)
35. Capone, A., Volpe, E.: Transcriptional regulators of T helper cell differentiation 17 in health and autoimmune diseases. Front. Immunol. **11**, 348 (2020)
36. Quevedo, J., Nardi, A.E., Silva, A.G.: Depression: Theory and Clinic. Artmed, 2nd edn. Porto Alegre (2018)
37. Freitas, N.L., et al.: Lessons from the cerebrospinal fluid analysis of HTLV-1-infected individuals: biomarkers of inflammation for HAM/TSP development. Viruses **14**(10), 2146 (2022)
38. Eliopoulos, A.G., et al.: TRAF1 is a critical regulator of JNK signaling by the TRAF-binding domain of Epstein-Barr virus-encoded latent infection membrane protein 1, but not by CD40. J. Virol. **77**(2), 1316–1328 (2003)
39. Arthur, J.S.C., Ley, S.C.: Mitogen-activated protein kinases in innate immunity. Nat. Rev. Immunol. **9**, 679–692 (2013)

40. Liu, T., et al.: NF-κB signaling in inflammation. Signal Transduct. Target. Ther. **2**, 17023 (2017)
41. Sun, S.C., Ballard, D.W.: Persistent activation of NF-κB by HTLV-1 transforming protein: sequestering cellular IκB kinases. Oncogene **18**(49), 6948–6958 (1999)
42. Aristodemou, A.E.N., et al.: The transcriptome of HTLV-1-infected primary cells following reactivation reveals changes to host gene expression central to the proviral life cycle. PLoS Pathog. **19**(7), e1011494 (2023)
43. Edilova, M.I., Abdul-Sater, A.A., Watts, T.H.: TRAF1 signaling in human health and disease. Front. Immunol. **9**, 2969 (2018)
44. Akbarin, M.M., et al.: The role of CREB and MAPK signaling pathways in ATLL patients. AIDS Res. Ther. **21**(1), 81 (2024)
45. Imai, S., Yoshino, J.: The importance of NAMPT/NAD/SIRT1 in the systemic regulation of metabolism and ageing. Diabetes Obes. Metab. **15**(s3), 26–33 (2013)
46. Kiziltunç, E., et al.: Sirtuin 1, 3, and 6 levels in patients with acute myocardial infarction. Arq. Bras. Cardiol. **113**, 33–39 (2019)
47. Imai, S.: Dissecting systemic control of metabolism and aging in the NAD world: the importance of SIRT1- and NAMPT-mediated NAD biosynthesis. FEBS Lett. **585**(11), 1657–1662 (2011)
48. Kozako, T., et al.: Novel small-molecule SIRT1 inhibitors induce cell death in adult T-cell leukemia cells. Sci. Rep. **5**, 11345 (2015)
49. Kozako, T., et al.: High expression of the longevity gene product SIRT1 and induction of apoptosis by sirtinol in adult T-cell leukemia cells. Int. J. Cancer **131**(9), 2044–2055 (2012)
50. Zarei-Ghobadi, M., et al.: HTLV-1-associated tropical spastic myelopathy/paraparesis (HAM/TSP) versus adult T-cell leukemia/lymphoma (ATLL). BMC. Res. Notes **14**, 109 (2021)
51. Berner, J., et al.: Phosphomevalonate kinase deficiency expands the genetic spectrum of systemic autoinflammatory diseases. J. Allergy Clin. Immunol. **152**(4), 1025-1031.e2 (2023)

Predicting Microsatellite Instability from Whole Slide Images Using Texture Features

Nilus Swanson[1], Mauro A. A. Castro[2], A. Gordon Robertson[3], Ilya Shmulevich[1], and Bahar Tercan[1](✉)

[1] Institute for Systems Biology, Seattle, WA, USA
btercan@systemsbiology.org
[2] Bioinformatics and Systems Biology Laboratory, Federal University of Paraná, Curitiba, PR 81520-260, Brazil
[3] Dxige Research Inc., Courtenay, BC V9N 1C2, Canada

Abstract. Identifying microsatellite instability (MSI) in whole slide images (WSIs), one of the most widely used diagnostic imaging formats, is of great importance and in demand. In this study we employed color-based texture features to predict MSI on both a tile and sample-based (patient) level. We found that within cancer cohorts of hematoxylin and eosin (H&E) stained WSIs, texture morphology was able to predict MSI on a tile level with an AUC of up to 0.95 and on a sample level with an AUC of up to 0.98. This runs in contrast to other methods for predicting MSI in H&E WSIs which either utilized artificial intelligence-based models or achieved lower accuracy scores. Our results demonstrate that texture morphology is a major factor for identifying MSI in H&E WSIs and should be used when constructing future models for MSI identification in a clinical setting.

Keywords: Prediction · Microsatellite Instability · Whole Slide Image · Texture Features · Machine Learning

1 Introduction

Microsatellite instability (MSI) is a pattern of hypermutation that occurs at genomic microsatellites [1] and is caused by defects in the mismatch repair system (dMMR) [2]. Mismatch repair deficiency that leads to MSI has been well described in several types of human cancers, most frequently in adenocarcinomas from colorectal, endometrial, and gastric cancers. MSI is known to be a prognostic marker in gastric tumors which can be surgically removed [2]; however, current clinical guidelines recommend MSI testing only for colorectal and endometrial cancers [3].

DNA contains repeated sequences of one to six nucleotides, which are known as microsatellites (MS). During DNA replication, MS can contain errors in which these sequences repeat in an incorrect order. Such errors are typically detected and repaired by a DNA repair system known as the mismatch repair (MMR). In the case of (MSI),

---

I. Shmulevich—Deceased, in memoriam.

© The Author(s), under exclusive license to Springer Nature Switzerland AG 2026
M. Dorn and F. Martins Lopes (Eds.): X-Meeting 2025, LNBI 16037, pp. 62–73, 2026.
https://doi.org/10.1007/978-3-032-09336-3_5

MMR proteins are missing, resulting in defects in repair, and subsequently increasing the chances of gene mutations and tumor development [1].

Several methods are available for detecting MSI. These include next generation sequencing (NGS), which uses targeted gene sequencing in relation to MMR genes, polymerase chain reaction (PCR) and capillary electrophoresis (CE), which use nucleotide repeat locations as parameters, immunochemistry (IHC), which detects deficient mismatch repair versus proficient mismatch repair, and single-molecule molecular inversion probes (smMIPs), which uses molecular tagging to detect genetic variations. While some of these methods report the classifications of MSS, MSI-L, and MSI-H, it is frequently the case that in clinical studies, MSS and MSI-L were considered to be one class, this was also the case in this study, giving the two classes of MSS and MSI (MSI-H).

Two methods stand out. The first and more popular of which is known as Microsatellite Analysis for Normal-Tumor InStability (MANTIS) score [4]. MANTIS [5, 6] is used for pan-cancer MSI detection using a calculation of the allele distribution of microsatellite areas. This is done by comparing both tumor and non-tumor samples and is known to attain results with high accuracy for prediction using Binary Alignment Map (BAM) files, which contain the raw data of genome sequencing. The other, and less popular of the two methods, is the usage of the ResNet convolutional neural networks (CNNs), which are varying layers deep and are trained on histological images and detected cells [1]. ResNet, particularly ResNet-18, is seen to have both a short training time and high classification accuracy [1].

A common reason for testing for MSI is Lynch syndrome or hereditary nonpolyposis colorectal cancer, which is a disorder that increases the chances of contracting colon cancer. In terms of detection, Lynch syndrome has been seen to be linked to dMMR tumors and thus linked to MSI-H tissue. Lynch syndrome is detected only using both a screening for MSI and IHC, [7] and as such, MSI detection is of great importance.

Colorectal cancer (CRC) has been understood to be the cancer type most influenced by the presence of MSI [2]; however, MSI has been seen to have effects on the prognosis of several cancer types, including gastric (GC), breast, prostate, cholangiocarcinoma, leukemia, bladder, ovarian cancers, endometrial carcinoma (EC), pancreatic ductal adenocarcinoma (PDAC), follicular thyroid cancer (FTC), and adrenocortical cancer (ACC). Each needs to be analyzed and treated in various ways, based on their MSI status in addition to other factors [1]. CRC and GC are of particular note, as these cancer types typically fail to respond to immunotherapy in the way that other cancers do, unless there is MSI present in the tumor tissue [8].

Recently, in 2019, Kather and collaborators [8] proposed a method for predicting MSI in H&E slides using deep learning. They trained several ResNet-18 models on datasets of The Cancer Genome Atlas (TCGA) colorectal formalin-fixed paraffin-embedded (FFPE) and frozen, TCGA gastric FFPE, and TCGA endometrial FFPE. Each model was tested on a holdout validation set of their respective dataset. Additionally, Kather and collaborators tested their models trained on TCGA colorectal FFPE, TCGA colorectal frozen, and TCGA gastric FFPE against the Darmkrebs: Chancen der Verhütung durch Screening (DACHS) colorectal cohort [9]. Kather and collaborators also tested their model trained on TCGA gastric cancer FFPE images against the Kanagawa Cancer Center Hospital (KCCH) gastric FFPE cohort [10]. In 2021, Lee *et al.* [3] proposed a method for predicting MSI in H&E slides using an Inception-V3 neural network in colorectal, gastric, and endometrial cancers. TCGA cohorts for colorectal, gastric, and endometrial cancers were used to train the respective versions of the model. In 2023, Lee *et al.* [11] proposed a TensorFlow deep learning method for prediction of MSI in gastric cancer (GC). Two models were trained: one on TCGA GC FFPE tissue slides and the other on TCGA GC frozen slides. Both models were then tested on holdout sets of their respective cohorts. Additionally, the model trained on TCGA GC FFPE WSI was tested on an external validation FFPE cohort, made up of Asian patients from Seoul's St. Mary's Hospital (SSMH). In May 2024, Wang *et al.* [12] proposed a deep learning method for prediction of MSI in endometrial cancer. Wang's method was both trained and tested on FFPE endometrial H&E stained WSIs from the TCGA cohort. When testing on TCGA endometrial, they separated the cohort into endometrioid carcinoma Type 1 (G1, G2) and endometrioid carcinoma Type 2 (G3). Table 2 gives the accuracy, specificity, and/or balanced accuracy measures for all of the methods.

In this study, we demonstrate a novel approach to predicting MSI status from H&E-stained whole slide images (WSI) for image tiles and for patients. Our method utilizes grey level co-occurrence matrices to calculate texture features across red, green, and blue (RGB), hue, saturation, and value (HSV), and L-star, a-star, b-star (LAB) color spaces. By utilizing these highly interpretable features, this study was able to predict MSI from H&E-stained WSIs using cross-validated Logistic Regression, support vector machine (SVM), RandomForest, and XGBoost machine learning (ML) models. While many state-of-the-art methods utilize "black box" artificial intelligence (AI)-based models for MSI detection, this study's method utilizes a specified mathematical formulation in order to detect MSI in colorectal, gastric, and endometrial cancers.

2 Methods

We obtained the formalin-fixed paraffin-embedded (FFPE) whole slide images (WSI) from the Kather *et al.* dataset [8]. The images were of H&E-stained WSIs from the TCGA project, for two different cancer types: colorectal adenocarcinoma [13] and stomach adenocarcinoma [13]. Kather *et al.* [8] detected tumor regions, divided the WSI into 224×224-pixel tiles (i.e. tiles that are $112\ \mu m \times 112\ \mu m$), magnified to a resolution of $0.5\ \mu m/px$, normalized the color of the tiles using the Macenko method [14], and assigned a label of either MSI or MSS to each tile, as previously described in Liu *et al.* [15]. Figure 1 shows the flowchart of our approach.

Each tile was represented as a 3D matrix, with the first two dimensions representing the 2D tile image, and the third dimension representing the color channels of red, green, blue (RGB), hue, saturation, value (HSV), or L-star, a-star, b-star (LAB). For each of these nine 2D matrices, we created a separate matrix, called a grey level co-occurrence matrix (GLCM). This GLCM, P, was defined for each 2D image I as follows:

$$p(i,j) = \sum_{x=1}^{N_g}\sum_{y=1}^{N_g} \begin{cases} 1, & \text{if } I(x,y) = i \text{ and } I(x+\Delta x, y+\Delta y) = j \\ 0, & \text{otherwise} \end{cases} \tag{1}$$

where (i,j) was the intensity value of each pixel at the location $I(x,y)$. N_g represented the maximum intensity value of the color channel. $(\Delta x, \Delta y)$ represented the angle offset at which co-occurrence was measured, which are equivalent to θ. The following angle offsets were used:

$$(1,0) = 0°$$

$$(1,1) = 45°$$

$$(0,1) = 90°$$

$$(-1,1) = 135°$$

This means that for a single-color channel of an image, four separate GLCMs were generated. For feature extraction, the tile images in this study were split into nine separate color channels, with each one generating 4 GLCMs, this would result in a total of 36 GLCMs per tile image, from each of which we extracted several features [16]. The features are shown below.

$$\text{Contrast} = \sum_i \sum_j |i-j|^2 p(i,j) \tag{2}$$

$$\text{Correlation} = \frac{\sum_i \sum_j (ij)p(i,j) - \mu_x \mu_y}{\sigma_x \sigma_y} \tag{3}$$

$$\text{Dissimilarity} = \sum_i \sum_j |i-j| p(i,j) \tag{4}$$

$$\text{Homogeneity} = \sum_i \sum_j \frac{p(i,j)}{1+(i-j)^2} \tag{5}$$

$$\text{Angular Second Momentum} = \sum_i \sum_j p(i,j)^2 \tag{6}$$

$$\text{Autocorrelation} = \sum_i \sum_j (ij)p(i,j) \tag{7}$$

$$\text{Cluster Prominence} = \sum_i \sum_j (i+j-\mu_x-\mu_y)^4 p(i,j) \tag{8}$$

$$\text{Cluster Shade} = \sum_i \sum_j (i+j-\mu_x-\mu_y)^3 p(i,j) \tag{9}$$

$$\text{Entropy} = -\sum_i \sum_j p(i,j) \log(p(i,j)) \tag{10}$$

$$\text{Maximum Probability} = \max_{i,j} p(i,j) \tag{11}$$

$$\text{Sum of Squares} = \sum_i \sum_j (i-\mu)^2 p(i,j) \tag{12}$$

$$\text{Sum Average} = \sum_{i=2}^{2N_g} i p_{x+y}(i) \tag{13}$$

$$\text{Sum Variance} = \sum_{i=2}^{2N_g} (i - (-\sum_{i=2}^{2N_g} p_{x+y}(i\log(p_{x+y}(i))))^2 p_{x+y}(i) \tag{14}$$

$$\text{Sum Entropy} = -\sum_{i=2}^{2N_g} p_{x+y}(i)\log(p_{x+y}(i))) \tag{15}$$

$$\text{Difference Variance} = \sum_{i=0}^{N_g-1} i^2 p_{x-y}(i) \tag{16}$$

$$\text{Difference Entropy} = -\sum_{i=0}^{N_g-1} p_{x-y}(i)\log(p_{x-y}(i))) \tag{17}$$

$$\text{Normalized Inverse Difference} = \sum_i \sum_j \frac{p(i,j)}{1 + |i-j|/N_g^2} \tag{18}$$

$$\text{Normalized Inverse Difference Moment} = \sum_i \sum_j \frac{p(i,j)}{1 + (i-j)^2/N_g^2} \tag{19}$$

$$\text{Trace} = \sum_i p(i,j) \tag{20}$$

where p is the grey level co-occurrence matrix (GLCM), μ is the mean of p, μ_x is the mean of rows of p, μ_y is the mean of column of p, σ_x is the standard deviation of rows of p, σ_y is standard deviation of columns of p, N_g is the number of levels being measured by p, $p_x(i) = \sum_{j=1}^{N_g} p(i,j)$, $p_y(j) = \sum_{i=1}^{N_g} p(i,j)$, $p_{x+y}(i+j) = \sum_{i=1}^{N_g} \sum_{j=1}^{N_g} p(i,j)$, $p_{x-y}(|i-j|) = \sum_{i=1}^{N_g} \sum_{j=1}^{N_g} p(i,j)$ are the marginal probability distributions.

After we extracted these features, we predicted MSI status with logistic regression, support vector machine (SVM), and random forest in Python's Scikit-Learn v1.5.2 library, as well as XGBoost in Python's XGBoost v2.1.4 library, with 10-fold cross validation and parameter tuning options. For each machine learning method, overfitting was accounted for by L1 and L2 regularization terms in Logistic Regression, L2 regularization in SVM, subsampling and feature sub selection in both Random Forest and XGBoost, as well cross validation in every model. Each tile had a corresponding MSI/MSS label, as well as each sample it had come from. Therefore, once the per-tile predictions were done, we compared the ratio of MSI vs MSS tiles to the MANTIS score, as labelled [13, 17] per sample (patient) to determine if a corresponding sample was MSI or MSS, using a ratio of ≤ 0.4 being MSS and > 0.4 being MSI.

3 Rationale

In our pipeline, each tile as segmented by Kather *et al.* [8] was separated into color spaces. From each color space, multiple GLCMs were created for each color channel, and texture features were extracted from each GLCM and concatenated into a single vector per tile. Tiles were then predicted to be either MSI or MSS, as shown in Fig. 1.

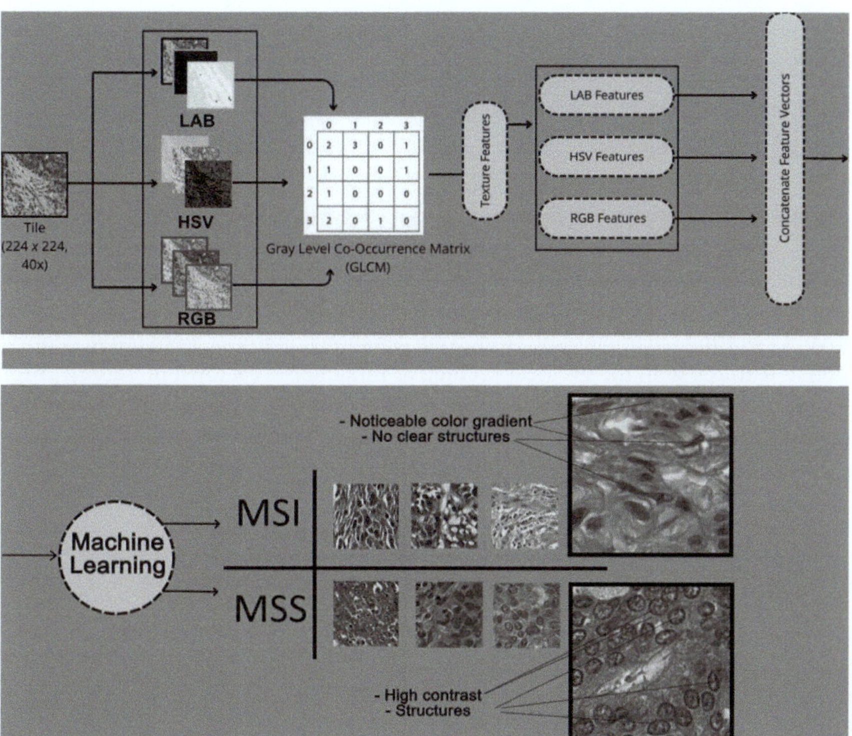

Fig. 1. Flowchart of our approach. **Top panel.** Segmented tiles [8] are read in three different color spaces of RGB, HSV, and LAB. For each channel from those color spaces, four GLCMs are created, from which texture features are extracted. Those texture features are then concatenated into a single vector to represent a single tile. **Bottom panel.** The vector is passed into a machine learning algorithm which then predicts whether the tile is MSI or MSS [8]. The segmented histology images presented here are licensed under CC BY 4.0 by Kather et al. [8], accessible at https://zen odo.org/records/2530835, and are included to illustrate our analysis pipeline.

From each cohort, we selected 18000 tiles randomly. We used 8000 tiles for training; and divided the remaining 10000 tiles into five test sets of n = 2000 each. The train and test cohorts consisted of equal numbers of MSS and MSI tiles whose labels are provided by [2, 8]. GLCMs were created as described in [18] for the color channels of red, green, blue (RGB), hue, saturation, value (HSV), or L-star, a-star, b-star (LAB) of each tile. 720 texture features were extracted from the GLCMs of each tile. We used logistic regression, SVM, random forest, and XGBoost algorithms, 10-fold cross validation and parameter tuning, to create models for individual training cohorts for TCGA-CRC (colorectal), TCGA-STAD (gastric), and TCGA-UCEC (endometrial) FFPE WSIs, as well as CPTAC-COAD (colon) and CPTAC-UCEC (endometrial) frozen WSIs. Overfitting was accounted for by L1 and L2 regularization terms in Logistic Regression, L2 regularization in SVM, subsampling in both random forest and XGBoost, as well as feature sub selection and cross validation in every model. Each model was then tested on randomly chosen stratified subsets of their respective cohorts, the results of which are shown in Table 3.

4   Results

We trained and tested our models on the TCGA-CRC, TCGA-STAD, TCGA-UCEC, CPTAC-COAD, and CPTAC-UCEC cohorts and reported results from the models with the per-tile values of the area under curve (AUC) with a confidence interval (CI), balanced accuracy, specificity, precision, and recall, as shown in Table 2, with the corresponding Receiver Operating Characteristic (ROC) curves shown in Fig. 2. For all five cohorts, the predictive features with the greatest predictive influence are shown in Table 1. Figure 3 shows the AUC values for predicting per-tile MSI by different machine learning algorithms employed in this study, i.e., logistic regression, support vector machines, random forest, XGBoost.

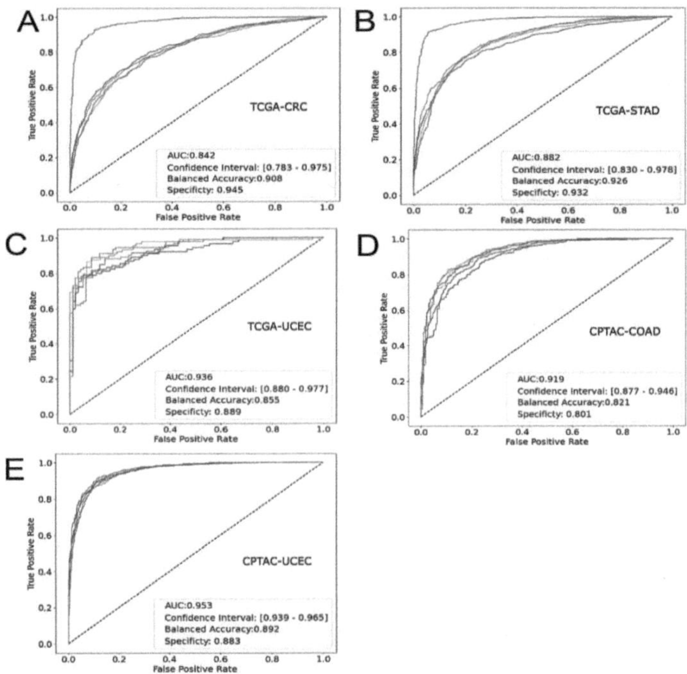

Fig. 2. ROC curves of MSI prediction for cohorts from TCGA and CPTAC projects. Each curve (color) shows one test split. The reported AUC is the mean average across the splits for **A**. TCGA-CRC (colorectal cancer) **B**. TCGA-STAD (gastric cancer) **C**. TCGA-UCEC (endometrial cancer) **D**. CPTAC-COAD (colon cancer) **E**. CPTAC-UCEC (endometrial cancer) cohorts

Table 1. Most predictive features of each cohort

Cohort	Most Predictive Feature 1	Most Predictive Feature 2	Most Predictive Feature 3
TCGA - CRC	Correlation	Homogeneity	Max Probability
TCGA - STAD	Correlation	Homogeneity	Autocorrelation
TCGA - UCEC	Correlation	Autocorrelation	Cluster Prominence
CPTAC - COAD	Energy	Correlation	Max Probability
CPTAC- UCEC	Autocorrelation	Autocorrelation	Autocorrelation

Table 2. Highest Accuracy Metrics for predicting per-tile MSI.

Cohort	AUC	Balanced ACC	Specificity	Precision (PPV)	Recall (NPV)
TCGA-CRC	0.84 (0.78–0.98)	0.91	0.95	0.97	0.80
TCGA-STAD	0.88 (0.85–0.91)	0.93	0.93	0.93	0.92
TCGA-UCEC	0.95 (0.91–0.98)	0.85	0.84	0.88	0.83
CPTAC-COAD	0.92 (0.88–0.95)	0.82	0.80	0.80	0.84
CPTAC-UCEC	0.95 (0.94–0.97)	0.90	0.88	0.87	0.90

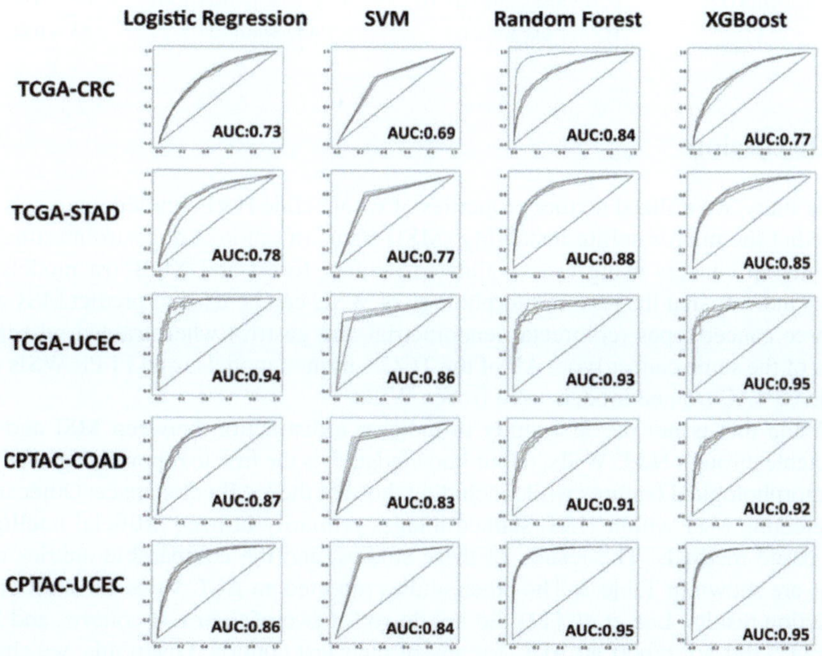

Fig. 3. The AUC values for predicting per-tile MSI by different machine learning algorithms employed in this study.

Table 3. Accuracies of methods from literature (all cohorts are FFPE, AUC: Area Under the Curve, SP: Specificity and BA: Balanced Accuracy)

Study	Training Cohort	Testing Cohort	Accuracy
Kather *et al.* 2019 [8]	TCGA Colorectal	TCGA Colorectal	AUC = 0.77
		DACHS Colorectal	AUC = 0.84
	TCGA Gastric	TCGA Gastric	AUC = 0.81
		DACHS Colorectal	AUC = 0.60
		KCCH Gastric	AUC = 0.69
	TCGA Endometrial	TCGA Endometrial	AUC = 0.75
Schmauch *et al.* 2020 [9]	TCGA Colorectal	TCGA Colorectal	AUC = 0.82
	TCGA Gastric	TCGA Gastric	AUC = 0.76
Valieris *et al.* 2020 [20]	TCGA Gastric	TCGA Gastric	AUC = 0.81
Krause *et al.* 2021 [19]	TCGA Colorectal	TCGA Colorectal	AUC = 0.742
Lee *et al.* 2021 [3]	TCGA Colorectal	TCGA Colorectal	AUC = 0.861
Lee *et al.* 2023 [11]	TCGA Gastric	TCGA Gastric	AUC = 0.902 SP = 0.833 BA = 0.862
		SSMH	AUC = 0.874 SP = 0.806 BA = 0.802
	SSMH and TCGA Gastric	TCGA Gastric	SP = 0.756 BA = 0.847
		SSMH	SP = 0.887 BA = 0.895
Wang *et al.* 2024 [12]	TCGA Endometrial G1, G2	TCGA Endometrial G1, G2	BA = 0.94
	TCGA Endometrial G3	TCGA Endometrial G3	BA = 0.84

5   Discussion

In this study, we utilized texture properties of whole-slide H&E-stained images in order to predict the microsatellite instability (MSI) status of colorectal, gastrointestinal, and endometrial cancers using cross validated random forest and XGBoost models. Our results indicate that the texture morphology of WSIs can be used to predict MSI within all three cancer types (colorectal, endometrial and gastric) when trained on separate WSIs of the same cancer type. All of the TCGA trained models used FFPE WSIs while all the CPTAC trained models used frozen WSIs.

While this is not the first study to indicate a distinction between MSI and MSS detectable through H&E WSIs, to our knowledge, it is the first to report using solely texture morphological features while including those of the LAB color space. Other studies on detecting MSI within H&E-stained images primarily utilized artificial intelligence (AI) based methods. The results of these studies, and the comparable metrics to our study, are shown in Table 2. The other studies reported an AUC value for most of their prediction results, Lee *et al.* [11] did not do so for two of their test cohorts, and Wang *et al.* [12] did not report an AUC for any of their test cohorts. Given this, we chose to use balanced accuracy for comparisons between these studies and our study.

Our study, when the models were trained and tested on TCGA colorectal cancer WSIs, reported an AUC value of 0.84 (0.78–0.98), exceeding that reported by Kather *et al.* [8], Schamuch *et al.* [9], and Krause *et al.* [19] when tested on the same cohort.

When the models were trained and tested on the TCGA gastric cancer cohorts, our study reported an AUC of 0.88 (0.83–0.98), exceeding the results reported by Kather *et al.* [8], Schamuch *et al.* [9], and Valieries *et al.* [20], when tested on the same cohort, but falling just below those reported by Lee *et al.* [11]. However, the balanced accuracy and specificity of this study for predicting MSI in the TCGA gastric cancer cohort were both 0.93. In contrast, Valieries *et al.* [20] reported balanced accuracy and specificity scores of 0.862 and 0.833. This suggests that texture-based features are strong predictors for correct identification of MSI and MSS, as also evident by the positive and negative predictive values (Table 2), which we report as 0.93 and 0.92 respectively for TCGA gastric cancer.

Kather *et al.* [8] and Wang *et al.* [12] both trained at least one model on TCGA endometrial FFPE WSIs. Kather *et al.* predicted TCGA endometrial cancer MSI with an AUC of 0.75. Wang *et al.* predicted TCGA endometrial in two separate cohorts, being separated into TCGA endometrial G1 and G2 and TCGA endometrial G3. These differentiate by percentages of non-squamous areas, with G1 having "no more than 5% solid non-squamous areas", G2 having 6–50% non-squamous areas, and G3 having "more than 50% solid non-squamous areas" [21]. Squamous areas of the Amant *et al.* [21] found that tumors "upgraded from grade 1 to 2, or from grade 2 to 3, if there is striking cytological atypia", which suggests that there could be differences in texture morphology between endometrial cancer grades. Wang *et al.* [12] reported a balanced accuracy of 0.94, when trained and tested on TCGA endometrial G1&G2 and 0.84 when trained and tested on G3.

Our study, when models trained on the TCGA endometrial cohort and tested on a holdout test set of TCGA endometrial cancer, reported an AUC value of 0.95 (0.91–0.98), with a corresponding balanced accuracy of 0.85. While our study did not account for the differences in endometrial cancer grades, as Wang *et al.* did, the balanced accuracy fell below that reported by Wang *et al.* for G1 and G2 types.

Notably, both of the CPTAC-COAD and CPTAC-UCEC cohorts are not FFPE WSIs, but instead frozen WSIs. As such, they are subject to warping during the freezing process, unlike when a sample is enclosed in paraffin wax. Regardless of that, it would seem that the models trained on frozen WSIs were able to achieve greater AUC scores than those trained on FFPE WSIs, with the exception of TCGA-UCEC.

In the current state of histological, and biological research in general, it is very tempting to utilize AI-based models to perform analyses on multitudes of samples. After all, a highly trained and finely tuned model analyzing an image could detect patterns that the human eye has yet to. This study highlights that texture is a highly effective set of features to implement into future models for higher accuracy MSI prediction, as well as possibly many other morphological features of H&E WSIs, as evident in Fig. 1. As can be seen in the enlarged example tile images in the bottom panel of Fig. 1, texture features, such as a distinct change in contrast, are visible to the naked eye. Such features being noticeable further lends itself to the recorded observations of this study, that texture morphology is a notable feature distinguishes MSI from MSS within histopathological whole slide images. As such, this study suggests that future models for usage within a clinical setting could make use of texture features for identifying MSI.

Acknowledgements. Mauro A. A. Castro was supported by Brazilian funding from CNPq (316622/2021-4;440412/2022-6) and Fundação Araucária (NAPI Bioinformática).

Data and Code Availability. The TCGA data used in this study is freely available in the GDC data portal (https://portal.gdc.cancer.gov). The TCGA-CRC and TCGA-STAD tile segmentations used in this study are freely available at https://zenodo.org/records/2530835. The code for the method used in this study is openly available on Github, https://github.com/IlyaLab/TextureAnalysis.

Disclosure of Interests. The authors have no competing interests to declare that are relevant to the content of this article.

References

1. Li, K., Luo, H., Huang, L., Luo, H., Zhu, X.: Microsatellite instability: a review of what the oncologist should know. Cancer Cell Int. **20**(1) (2020). https://doi.org/10.1186/s12935-019-1091-8
2. Bonneville, R., Krook, M.A., Kautto, E.A., Miya, J., Wing, M.R., et al.: Landscape of microsatellite instability across 39 cancer types. JCO Precis Oncol. (1), 1–15 (2017)
3. Lee, S.H., Song, I.H., Jang, H.J.: Feasibility of deep learning-based fully automated classification of microsatellite instability in tissue slides of colorectal cancer. Int. J. Cancer **149**(3), 728–740 (2021)
4. Lin, A., Zhang, J., Luo, P.: Crosstalk between the MSI status and tumor microenvironment in colorectal cancer. Front. Immunol. **11**, 2039 (2020). PMCID: PMC7435056
5. Kautto, E.A., Bonneville, R., Miya, J., Yu, L., Krook, M.A., et al.: Performance evaluation for rapid detection of pan-cancer microsatellite instability with MANTIS. Oncotarget **8**(5), 7452–7463 (2017). PMCID: PMC5352334
6. Queirós, P., Delogu, F., Hickl, O., May, P., Wilmes, P.: Mantis: flexible and consensus-driven genome annotation. Gigascience **10**(6) (2021). https://doi.org/10.1093/gigascience/giab042. PMCID: PMC8170692
7. Latham, A., Srinivasan, P., Kemel, Y., Shia, J., Bandlamudi, C., et al.: Microsatellite instability is associated with the presence of Lynch syndrome pan-cancer. J. Clin. Oncol. **37**(4), 286–295 (2019)
8. Kather, J.N., Pearson, A.T., Halama, N., Jäger, D., Krause, J., et al.: Deep learning can predict microsatellite instability directly from histology in gastrointestinal cancer. Nat. Med. **25**(7), 1054–1056 (2019)
9. Schmauch, B., Romagnoni, A., Pronier, E., Saillard, C., Maillé P., et al.: A deep learning model to predict RNA-Seq expression of tumours from whole slide images. Nat. Commun. **11**(1) (2020). https://doi.org/10.1038/s41467-020-17678-4
10. Silva, A.N.S., Coffa, J., Menon, V., Hewitt, L.C., Das, K., et al.: Frequent coamplification of receptor tyrosine kinase and downstream signaling genes in Japanese primary gastric cancer and conversion in matched lymph node metastasis. Ann. Surg. **67**(1), 114–121 (2018)
11. Lee, S.H., Lee, Y., Jang, H.J.: Deep learning captures selective features for discrimination of microsatellite instability from pathologic tissue slides of gastric cancer. Int. J. Cancer **152**(2), 298–307 (2023)

12. Wang, C.W., Muzakky, H., Firdi, N.P., Liu, T.C., Lai, P.J., et al.: Deep learning to assess microsatellite instability directly from histopathological whole slide images in endometrial cancer. NPJ Digit. Med. **7**(1) (2024). https://doi.org/10.1038/s41746-024-01131-7
13. The Cancer Genome Atlas Network. Comprehensive molecular characterization of human colon and rectal cancer. Nature **487**(7407), 330–337 (2012)
14. Macenko, M., Niethammer, M., Marron, J.S., Borland, D., Woosley, J.T., et al.: A method for normalizing histology slides for quantitative analysis. In: 2009 IEEE International Symposium on Biomedical Imaging: From Nano to Macro, pp. 1107–1110. IEEE (2009)
15. Liu, Y., Sethi, N.S., Hinoue, T., Schneider, B.G., Cherniack, A.D., et al.: Comparative molecular analysis of gastrointestinal adenocarcinomas. Cancer Cell. **33**(4), 721–735.e8 (2018)
16. Hao, Y., Zhang, L., Qiao S, Bai Y, Cheng R, et al.: Breast cancer histopathological images classification based on deep semantic features and gray level co-occurrence matrix. PLoS One. **17**(5), e0267955 (2022)
17. The Cancer Genome Atlas Research Network. Comprehensive molecular characterization of gastric adenocarcinoma. Nature **513**(7517), 202–209 (2014)
18. Sebastian, B.: Grey level co-occurrence matrices: Generalisation and some new features. Int. J. Comput. Sci. Eng. Inf. Technol. **2**(2), 151–157 (2012)
19. Krause, J., Grabsch, H.I., Kloor, M., Jendrusch, M., Echle, A., Buelow, R.D., et al.: Deep learning detects genetic alterations in cancer histology generated by adversarial networks. J. Pathol. (path.5638) (2021). https://doi.org/10.1002/path.5638
20. Valieris, R., Amaro, L., Osório, C.A.B.D.T., Bueno, A,P., Rosales Mitrowsky, R.A., et al.: Deep learning predicts underlying features on pathology images with therapeutic relevance for breast and gastric cancer. Cancers (Basel). **12**(12), 3687 (2020)
21. Amant, F., Moerman, P., Neven, P., Timmerman, D., Van Limbergen, E., et al.: Endometrial cancer. Lancet **366**(9484), 491–505 (2005)

The Extended N-Terminal Domain of VPAC1 Isoform 2 Acts as a Self-inhibitory Element: Insights from Molecular Dynamics Simulations

Matheus Henrique Reis[1]([✉]) [iD], Deborah Antunes[2] [iD], Ingrid B. S. Martins[3] [iD], and Ernesto R. Caffarena[1] [iD]

[1] Programa de Computação Científica (PROCC), Fundação Oswaldo Cruz (Fiocruz), Rio de Janeiro, RJ 21040-360, Brazil
matheusreis@aluno.fiocruz.br
[2] Laboratório de Genômica Aplicada e Bioinovações, Instituto Oswaldo Cruz, Fundação Oswaldo Cruz (Fiocruz), Rio de Janeiro, RJ 21040-360, Brazil
[3] Departamento de Física, Instituto de Biociências, Letras e Ciências Exatas (IBILCE), Universidade Estadual Paulista "Júlio de Mesquita Filho" (UNESP), São José do Rio Preto, SP 15054-000, Brazil

Abstract. G protein-coupled receptors (GPCRs) play crucial roles in cellular signaling, and the VPAC1 receptor is an important member of the secretin (class B1) subfamily. This study investigates the structural and molecular mechanisms underlying the non-functional nature of VPAC1 isoform 2, which contains an extended N-terminal domain compared to the canonical isoform 1. Through computational approaches including molecular modeling and molecular dynamics simulations, we show that the 17-residue α-helical insertion in the extracellular domain (ECD) of isoform 2 acts as an endogenous antagonist. Our findings reveal that this inserted α-helix adopts a conformation that physically occupies the binding site intended for the Vasoactive Intestinal Peptide (VIP), forming hydrogen bonds with critical receptor residues and exhibiting sequence similarity to portions of the VIP peptide itself. Additionally, the inserted sequence stabilizes the ECD in a conformation that prevents the dynamic "opening" movement necessary for peptide binding. These results provide novel insights into an unusual auto-inhibitory mechanism in GPCRs and highlight the potential implications for understanding receptor diversity in pathophysiological conditions and therapeutic interventions.

Keywords: G-Protein Coupled Receptors · VPAC1 receptor · Molecular dynamics · Auto-inhibition · Endogenous antagonist

1 Introduction

G protein-coupled receptors (GPCRs) constitute the largest superfamily of membrane receptors in eukaryotes, mediating cellular responses to a diverse array of physiological signals. This class of membrane proteins function as essential components in biological

© The Author(s), under exclusive license to Springer Nature Switzerland AG 2026
M. Dorn and F. Martins Lopes (Eds.): X-Meeting 2025, LNBI 16037, pp. 74–89, 2026.
https://doi.org/10.1007/978-3-032-09336-3_6

processes ranging from sensory perception and neurotransmission to hormone signaling and immune regulation [1, 2]. The remarkable versatility of GPCRs is evidenced by their ability to recognize and respond to a multitude of stimuli, including peptides, proteins, lipids, protons, photons, and small organic molecules [3]. Their fundamental role in human physiology is underscored by their involvement in numerous pathological conditions, positioning them as targets for approximately 35% of currently approved therapeutics by the Food and Drug Administration (FDA) [4]. The therapeutic significance of GPCRs continues to expand, as novel signaling mechanisms and regulatory pathways have been elucidated, revealing increasingly intricate networks of cellular communication.

This superfamily is categorized into five distinct classes based on sequence homology and structural similarity: rhodopsin (class A), secretin (class B1), adhesion (class B2), glutamate (class C), and Frizzled/Taste2 (class F). Despite their diversity, all GPCRs share a conserved architectural framework comprising seven α-helical transmembrane domains (TM1-TM7) interconnected by three intracellular loops (ICL1-ICL3) and three extracellular loops (ECL1-ECL3), a cytoplasmic α-helix (H8), complemented by an extracellular N-terminal domain (ECD), and an intracellular C-terminal domain [3, 5].

Secretin receptors (class B1), a relatively small GPCR subfamily comprising 15 members, includes the Vasoactive Intestinal Peptide Receptors (VPAC1 and VPAC2). These receptors are characterized by an extended extracellular domain (>120 residues) containing six highly conserved cysteine residues interconnected by three disulfide bonds, which is a distinctive feature of this class [5, 6]. Additionally, a disulfide bond between cysteine residues in the ECD and ECL1 has been documented [7, 8]. Although VPAC1 and VPAC2 exhibit widespread distribution, they display distinct expression patterns; VPAC1 predominates in the liver, lung, thyroid, and gastrointestinal tissues, whereas VPAC2 is primarily expressed in smooth muscle cells of various organs and blood vessels, as well as in the central nervous system [9].

Both VPAC1 and VPAC2 receptors show comparable affinities for Vasoactive Intestinal Peptide (VIP) and the truncated form of Pituitary Adenylate Cyclase Activating Peptide (PACAP-27) - two ubiquitous neuropeptides that function as neuromodulators and neurotransmitters, sharing 68% sequence similarity [6]. The proposed mechanism of peptide binding to these receptors follows a two-step process: initially, the C-terminus of the peptide interacts with the ECD, subsequently orienting the N-terminus toward the transmembrane domain, which is a conformational change essential for receptor activation. Notably, peptides lacking the N-terminal region have been identified as antagonists capable of completing the initial binding step, but unable to induce the conformational changes necessary for receptor activation, thereby blocking agonist binding [10, 11]. Upon activation, these receptors predominantly couple to Gs proteins, stimulating adenylyl cyclase activity and cyclic adenosine monophosphate (cAMP) formation and activating the PKA signaling pathway. Additionally, they have been reported to activate PKC signaling pathways through cAMP-independent mechanisms and elevate intracellular calcium levels in various cell types [5].

In a seminal study, Couvineau et al. (1994) isolated and functionally characterized two distinct cDNA sequences from an intestinal epithelium cDNA library encoding VIP receptors, which were later assigned as different variants of the receptor VPAC1, with divergent N-terminal domains. The first sequence (hIVR8) encoded a 460-amino acid protein with a 32-amino acid N-terminal domain (VPAC1 isoform 1), whereas the second (hIVR5) encoded a 495-amino acid protein with an extended 67-amino acid N-terminal domain (VPAC1 isoform 2). Functional expression studies in COS-7 cells revealed that the hIVR8 clone exhibited a pharmacological profile consistent with that of the canonical human VIP-PACAP receptor. In contrast, cells transfected with the hIVR5 clone failed to demonstrate any functional VIP binding capacity, despite proper receptor trafficking to the plasma membrane, leading to the conclusion that the VIP receptor encoded by hIVR5 lacks intrinsic binding activity [12].

Although extensive research has elucidated the molecular basis of VIP-VPAC1 interactions, the structural features and molecular mechanisms underlying the non-functional nature of the hIVR5 variant (isoform 2) remain unexplored. In this investigation, we employed computational methodologies, including molecular modeling and molecular dynamics simulations, to elucidate the structural characteristics and molecular interactions of the VPAC1 isoform 2. We postulated that the extended N-terminal domain of isoform 2 might function as an endogenous antagonist by adopting conformations that physically occlude the peptide binding site. Through comparative analysis of isoforms 1 and 2 in both the apo and holo states, we sought to identify the structural determinants responsible for the impaired VIP binding observed in isoform 2 and to characterize the molecular mechanism underlying this self-inhibitory phenomenon.

2 Methods

2.1 Sequence Alignment and Bioinformatic Analysis

The primary sequences of the VPAC1 receptor isoforms were retrieved from the UniprotKB database [13] (accession numbers P32241 and P32241-2) and subjected to comprehensive sequence analysis. Multiple sequence alignment was performed using the PSI/TM-Coffee method on the T-COFFEE server [14]. Prediction of intrinsically disordered regions was conducted on the PSI-PRED server using the DISOPRED3 tool, an approach based on machine learning that employs two independent predictors of intrinsic disorder: a neural network and a nearest neighbor classifier, trained to identify long intrinsically disordered regions using data from the Protein Data Bank (PDB) [15] and DisProt databases [16]. The signal peptide regions were assigned as those reported by Couvienau and colleagues (1994) [12]. For comparative analysis of the VIP peptide and the inserted sequence of VPAC1-iso2, pairwise alignment was performed using Clustal Omega (v1.2.4) with default parameters (gap opening penalty: 10; gap extension penalty: 0.5) [17]. The inserted sequence of VPAC1-iso2 was aligned backwards to the VIP peptide sequence to match the structural positions.

2.2 Molecular Modeling and Structural Refinement

In the absence of experimentally determined structures for VPAC1 isoforms complexed with VIP at the commencement of this investigation, we implemented a computational modeling approach. AlphaFold 2 [18] was employed to generate ab initio models of the receptor isoforms in both the apo and holo states. The protonation states of the titratable residues were determined at physiological pH (7.4) using the PDB2PQR server (v3.5.1) with the PROPKA algorithm and a solvent dielectric constant of 80 [19]. Disulfide bonds between conserved cysteine residues were assigned manually based on the determined protonation states and identity to previously characterized class B GPCR structures (PDB IDs: 6LPB and 6M1I) [20, 21]. Signal peptides were excluded based on cleavage sites reported by Couvineau and colleagues (1994): residues 1–30 in isoform 1 (Ala^{30}/Ala^{31}) and residues 1–31 in isoform 2 (Ser^{31}/Arg^{32}). Intrinsically disordered regions identified by DISOPRED3 using a stringent threshold of 0.7 (vs. standard 0.5) were also removed. The higher threshold was chosen to reduce false positives and ensure experimental consistency, since the default threshold assigned loops between TMs as disordered (Supplementary Figure S1). The excluded regions included the extended N-terminal region in isoform 2 (Arg^{32}-Gly^{48}) and C-terminal regions in both isoforms (Asn^{415}-Val^{457} in isoform 1; Asn^{450}-Val^{492} in isoform 2). Only terminal segments were excluded to preserve critical intramolecular interactions within functional domains. This terminal disordered region exclusion protocol is established in GPCR molecular dynamics studies, improving simulation stability without compromising biological relevance, consistent with successful class B GPCR computational studies, e.g. Latek et al., 2019 [22] and Liao et al., 2021 [23]. The resultant structures underwent energy minimization using the Minimize Structure tool implemented in UCSF Chimera (v1.16) [24], employing the AMBER ff14SB force field [25] with a steepest descent algorithm (100 steps), followed by conjugate gradient minimization (10 steps) until convergence to an RMS gradient of <0.01 kcal/mol/Å. The minimized structures were validated through a comprehensive stereochemical assessment using the Structure Assessment tool on the Swiss-Model server [26], with particular attention to Ramachandran plot statistics (>98% residues in favored regions and <0.2% residues in outlier regions), MolProbity scores ($\approx$0), and QMEANDisCo score ($\approx$1.0).

2.3 Molecular Dynamics Simulations Protocol

Molecular dynamics simulation systems were meticulously prepared using the CHARMM-GUI Membrane Builder (v3.5) [27]. The receptor models were embedded into pre-equilibrated 1-palmitoyl-2-oleoyl-sn-glycero-3-phosphocholine (POPC) lipid bilayers with area of 90×90 Å^2. The protein-membrane systems were solvated with the OPC water model [28] with the minimum water height at 15 Å on top and bottom of the complex, and physiological ion concentrations (0.15 M of NaCl) were introduced through random ion placement while maintaining system electroneutrality. The final simulation systems comprised approximately 105,000 atoms each, including ~205 POPC molecules, ~24,000 water molecules, and ~70 ions. Simulation input files were generated for the Amber force field parameters, specifically amber ff19SB for proteins [29], lipid21 for membrane components [30], and OPC for water molecules.

The molecular dynamics simulations were performed using the Amber22 package [31]. The systems underwent a multi-stage equilibration protocol: (1) energy minimization consisting of 1,000 steps of steepest descent followed by 1,000 steps of conjugate gradient with positional restraints (5 kcal/mol/Å^2) applied to all non-hydrogen atoms, followed by 2,500 steps of steepest descent and 2,500 steps of conjugate gradient without restraints; (2) thermalization to 310 K over 1 ns in the NVT ensemble using a Langevin thermostat (collision frequency: 0.67 ps^{-1}) with a temperature ramp during the first 400 ps and a temperature stabilization in the last 600 ps, and positional restraints (10 kcal/mol/Å^2) on heavy atoms; (3) equilibration for 18 ns in the NPT ensemble (1 atm, 310 K) with gradual reduction of positional restraints from 10.0 to 0.05 kcal/mol/Å^2 in the first 8 ns and without restraints in the last 10.0 ns using the Berendsen barostat (relaxation time: 1.0 ps) and semi-isotropic pressure coupling. Production simulations were conducted in quadruplicate for 250 ns per replica (totaling 1 μs per system) in the NPT ensemble using the Berendsen barostat, with a time step of 2 fs enabled by the SHAKE algorithm [32], constraining all bonds involving hydrogen atoms. Long-range electrostatic interactions were computed using the Particle Mesh Ewald method with a real-space cutoff of 10 Å and van der Waals interactions were truncated at 12 Å with a switching function applied from 10 Å. Trajectory frames were recorded at 20 ps intervals, yielding 12,500 conformations per replica for subsequent analysis.

2.4 Trajectory Analysis and Structural Characterization

Trajectory analysis was performed using CPPTRAJ [33] in the AmberTools suite. Conformational stability was assessed through root-mean-square deviation (RMSD) calculations of heavy atoms relative to the initial equilibrated structure. Local flexibility was quantified by root-mean-square fluctuation (RMSF) analysis of the backbone (Cα), averaged over all replicas after RMS-fitting to the transmembrane domain. Hydrogen bond interactions were identified using geometric criteria (donor-acceptor distance <3.5 Å, donor-hydrogen-acceptor angle >135°), with occupancy calculated as the percentage of frames in which each interaction was maintained.

Conformational analysis was performed using GROMOS clustering (GROMACS v2022.2) REF with a systematically validated 2.0 Å RMSD cutoff and Principal Component Analysis (Bio3D package, R) [34]. All trajectory frames underwent rigid-body alignment prior to clustering, while PCA employed 10-frame intervals for computational efficiency. The 2.0 Å threshold was optimized through systematic testing (1.5–4.0 Å range): higher cutoffs merged structurally distinct conformations due to transmembrane domain rigidity artificially reducing RMSD values, while lower thresholds generated excessive fragmentation with statistically insufficient cluster populations.

3 Results

3.1 Sequence Analysis and Structural Differences Between VPAC1 Isoforms

The protein sequences from the UniprotKB database revealed a discrepancy of three amino acids (Leu^{282}, Leu^{283}, and Arg^{284}) when compared to those originally reported by Couvineau et al. (1994), although the biological significance of these residues remains undetermined. It has been reported that isoforms 1 and 2 present signal peptides with cleavage between the residues Ala^{30} and Ala^{31}, and between Ser^{31} and Arg^{32}, respectively. Also, disorder prediction assigns the residues Arg^{32} to Gly^{48} in isoform 2, corresponding to the N-terminal region beyond the signal peptide, and the C-terminal domains, encompassing the final 44 residues (Asn^{415}-Val^{457}) in isoform 1 and 43 residues (Asn^{450}-Val^{492}) in isoform 2. Thus, regarding these differences, sequence analysis indicated that functional forms of VPAC1 isoforms 1 and 2 diverge primarily on a 17-residue insertion, predominantly consisting of basic and non-polar amino acids, within the extracellular domain (ECD). This differs from the previously documented 35-residue insertion described by Couvineau and colleagues, which can be attributable to the signal peptides and predicted intrinsically disordered regions. Terminal disordered regions were removed from the final models, consistent with the experimental VPAC1 structure (PDB ID 8E3Z), where analogous regions were unresolved due to inherent flexibility. No disordered regions within extracellular loops, intracellular loops, or transmembrane domains were excluded, preserving the structural integrity of functionally critical receptor regions. Despite these variations, the remaining receptor domains maintain high conservation, preserving the critical disulfide bonds essential for ECD stability and VIP binding interactions [7] (Fig. 1).

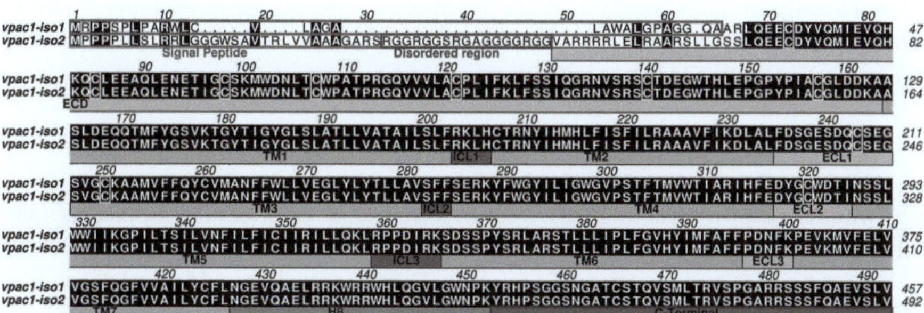

Fig. 1. Sequence alignment between VPAC1 isoforms 1 and 2 (vpac1-iso1 and vpac1 iso2, respectively). Cysteine residues highlighted in yellow form disulfide bonds; purple boxes indicate cytoplasmic regions; blue boxes indicate transmembrane regions; and green boxes indicate extracellular regions. The membrane-related regions of the receptors were obtained from the GPCRdb database. (Color figure online)

The VPAC1 isoform 1 models (Fig. 2A, Fig. 2B) showed high confidence structures with the average Alphafold predicted local distance difference test (pLDDT) scores of 77.1 for holo state and 81.4 for apo state. Also, they showed an excellent agreement with the resolved structure available in Protein Data Bank (PDB ID: 8E3Z) [7] for both apo and holo states (RMSD = 0.97 Å and 1.68 Å, respectively), preserving the characteristic disulfide bonds in the ECD and maintaining the correct VIP positioning in the holo state.

The VPAC1 isoform 2 models (Fig. 2C, Fig. 2D) also showed high confidence structures with pLDDT scores of 72.8 for holo state and 79.9 for apo state and conserved disulfide bond network, while the ECD insertion was modeled as an α-helix, which adopts different orientations depending on the receptor's ligand-binding state. In the holo state, this inserted α-helix projects outward toward the solvent, whereas in the apo conformation, it occupies the VIP binding pocket. Disregarding the inserted α-helix in the ECD, the models for isoform 2 were almost identical to those for isoform 1 (RMSD = 0.57 Å between apo models and RMSD = 0.22 Å between holo models).

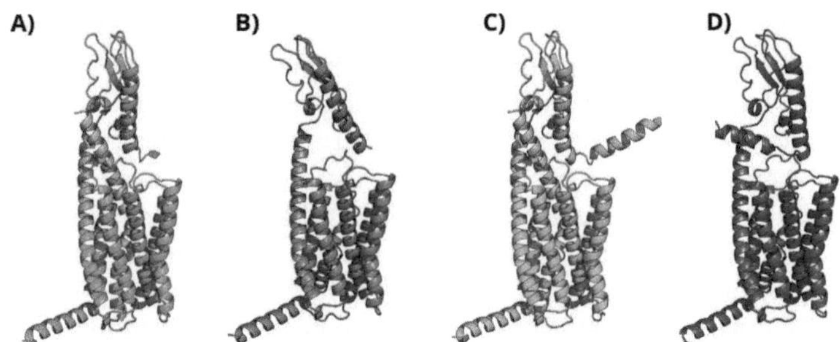

Fig. 2. Models generated using Alphafold 2. (A) Isoform 1 holo state. (B) Isoform 1 apo state. (C) Isoform 2 holo state. (D) Isoform 2 apo state. VIP in holo states is darker in color.

In all models, the signal peptide and predicted disordered regions were modeled as unstructured elements, consistent with the sequence-based predictions. The final models exhibited no significant structural anomalies when evaluated against quality metrics and showed good agreement with the experimentally determined structure of the VPAC1/VIP complex (PDB ID 8E3Z) (Supplementary Table 1).

3.2   Conformational Stability and Dynamics Analysis

The membrane stability and integrity were monitored throughout all simulations and validated through standard metrics including area per lipid, membrane thickness, and lipid order parameters (Supplementary Figure S2). These analyses confirm stable membrane conditions across all systems, supporting the validity of protein-membrane interactions observed in the conformational analysis.

The apo and holo states of VPAC1 isoform 1 exhibited a structurally stable ECD, maintaining its core scaffold in both conformations (Fig. 3A). Despite this structural conservation, the apo state demonstrated greater mobility, with the RMSF values ranging from 0.91 Å to 8.92 Å with the ECD being the region of highest fluctuation. In contrast, the holo state showed reduced flexibility (RMSF values ranging from 0.36 Å to 6.41 Å), with a more stabilized ECD and the greatest flexibility localized at the ICL3 (Fig. 3C).

In VPAC1 isoform 2, the alternatively positioned inserted α-helix significantly influenced the receptor's conformational dynamics and stability. Flexibility analysis revealed that in the holo conformation, this inserted α-helix exhibits pronounced mobility (average RMSF of 5,4 ± 2,5 Å), whereas in the apo conformation the same region became stabilized within the binding pocket (average RMSF of 3,5 ± 1,3 Å) and the coil regions at the ECD apex localized the greatest flexibility (Fig. 3C). This highly mobile-inserted α-helix accounts for the elevated RMSD values observed for ECD in this isoform, indicating conformational rearrangements within this domain (Fig. 3B).

Cluster analysis of the trajectory frames across all replicas of isoform 1 states generated 286 clusters for the apo state, with the most populated cluster encompassing 2.4% of the total simulation time, and 138 clusters for the holo state, with the most populated cluster representing 6.6% of the simulation time. For isoform 2, the analysis generated 158 clusters for the holo state, with the largest representing 4.9% of the simulation time,

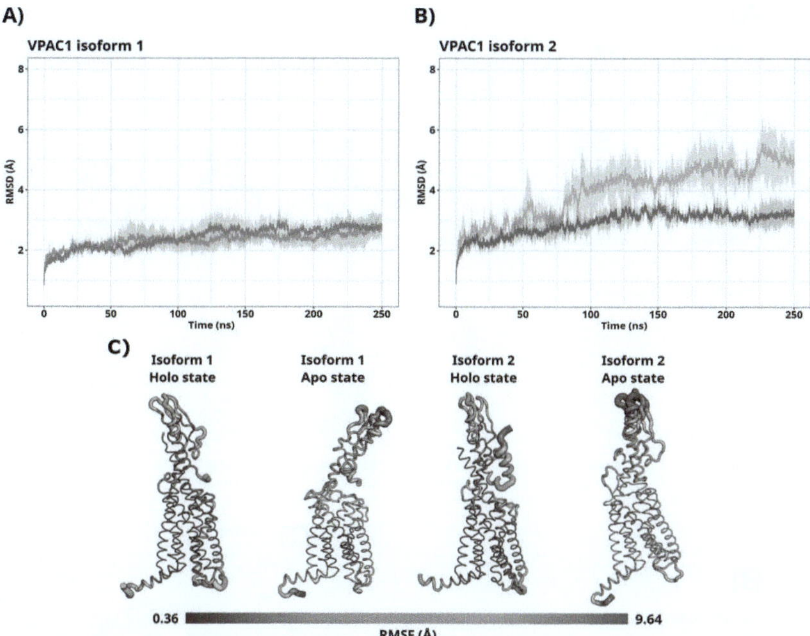

Fig. 3. Stabilization and flexibility analysis. (A) RMSD of the ECD in isoform 1 states: holo in green and apo in orange. (B) RMSD of the ECD in isoform 2; holo in cyan and apo in light purple. Dark lines are the *averages,* and light shadows represent the standard deviation from all replicas. (C) Per-residue RMSF distribution in the structure. (Color figure online)

and 219 clusters for the apo state, with the largest representing 4.2% of the simulation time.

Analysis of the representative structures from the six most populated clusters revealed distinct ECD orientation patterns between the apo states of the two isoforms (Fig. 4A). In isoform 1, the ECD adopts multiple orientations relative to the transmembrane domain, exhibiting a hinge-like motion reminiscent of a lid opening and closing. This conformational flexibility is constrained by the disulfide bond between the cysteine residues in $H1^{ECD}$ and ECL1, which serves as a pivot point limiting the amplitude of ECD movement. In contrast, the ECD in the apo state of isoform 2 displayed a remarkably consistent orientation across the six most populated clusters, remaining predominantly fixed and parallel to the membrane normal vector. These observations align with the findings reported by Piper et al. (2022) [7], who employed supervised Molecular Dynamics (SuMD) and metadynamics simulations to demonstrate that ECD detachment is required for peptide binding and unbinding processes.

Principal Components Analysis (PCA) corroborated the clustering analysis in revealing distinct conformational behaviors between the two protein isoforms (Fig. 4B).

Isoform 1 exhibits highly structured dynamics with PC1 dominating 68.89% of variance and forming well-defined clusters in conformational space (Fig. 4C). In contrast, isoform 2 shows more distributed variance (PC1: 42.11%, PC2: 27.09%) with dispersed sampling across the PC space, suggesting greater conformational flexibility without

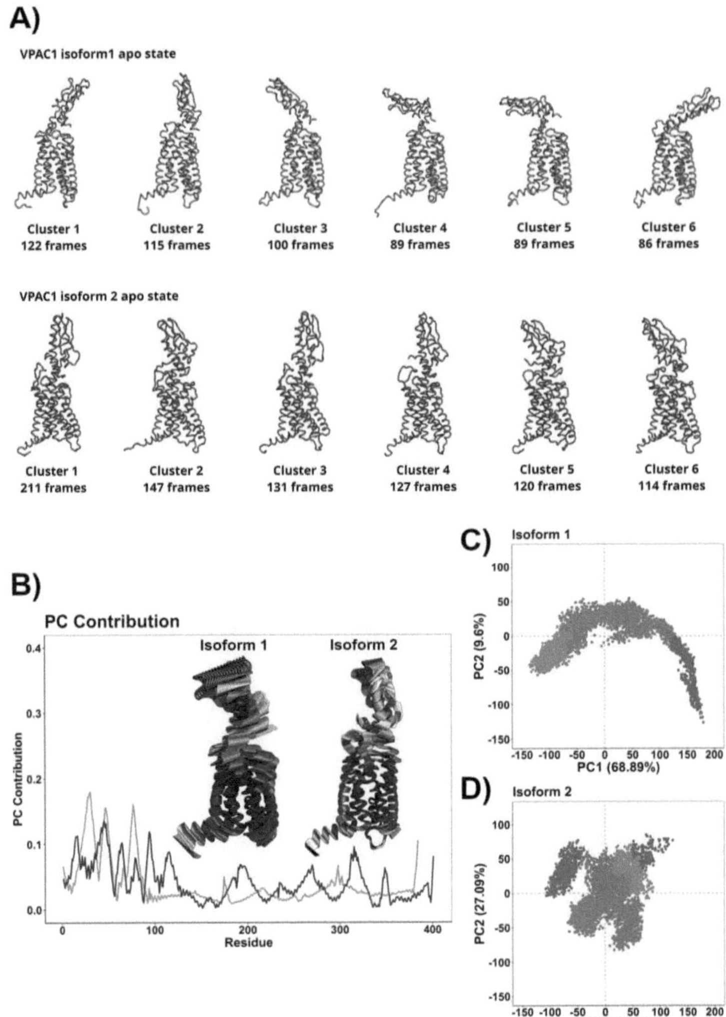

Fig. 4. Structural clustering and principal component analysis of VPAC1 isoform dynamics in apo states. (A) Representative structures for the six most populated clusters in isoform 1 (brown/orange) and isoform 2 (blue) apo states, showing different ECD orientations. Frame numbers are indicated below each structure. (B) Per-residue contribution to PC1 for both isoforms, with 3D structures highlighting high-contribution terminal regions (red). (C-D) PC1 vs PC2 projections for isoforms 1 and 2, respectively. Isoform 1 shows distinct clusters (PC1: 68.89% variance), while isoform 2 displays dispersed sampling (PC1: 42.11% variance). Colors represent conformational clusters. (Color figure online)

distinct stable states (Fig. 4D). The per-residue contribution profiles demonstrate that terminal regions drive the principal motions in both isoforms, but isoform 1 shows more pronounced amplitude of the variation (Fig. 4B).

Our results suggest that the inserted α-helix in isoform 2 restricts this critical opening movement, potentially explaining its impaired ligand-binding capability.

Furthermore, the structural superposition of the representative conformations from the largest clusters of isoform 2 in both the apo and holo states revealed that the inserted α-helix in the apo state occupies a spatial position remarkably similar to that of the central segment of VIP (residues 12–20) (Fig. 5A). Notably, no portion of the inserted α-helix extended into the TM7 region of the binding pocket. Sequence analysis demonstrated considerable physicochemical similarity between the amino acids of the inserted α-helix and the corresponding segment of the VIP, with these residues occupying analogous spatial positions in their respective structures (Fig. 5B, Fig. 5C).

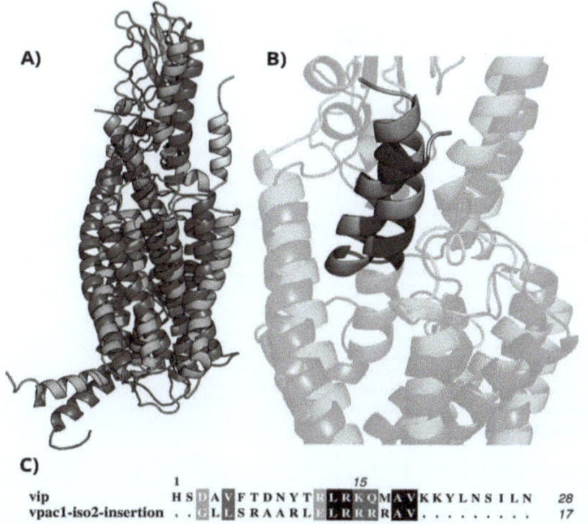

Fig. 5. The positions of the inserted α-helix in the apo state and the VIP in the holo state are similar. A) Superposition of the most representative structures of the holo (cyan) and apo (purple) states of VPAC1 isoform 2. VIP is shown in light pink, while the inserted α-helix is red in the apo state and light cyan in the holo state. B) Residue types of the superimposed VIP and inserted α-helix. Blue residues are positive, red residues are negative, green residues are polar, and white residues are apolar. C) Sequence alignment of VIP and the inserted α-helix. The α-helix sequence was aligned in reverse because the direction of the inserted α-helix (Val^{49}-Gly^{65}) is structurally equivalent to Asn^{28}-His^{1} in VIP. (Color figure online)

This observation is particularly significant in the context of the two-step peptide binding mechanism [10, 11]. Previous studies have established that peptides lacking the N-terminal region act as antagonists by completing only the initial binding step, without engaging in the transmembrane domain [35–37]. This suggests that the inserted α-helix plays an endogenous antagonistic role by mimicking similar interactions, thereby blocking the agonist binding.

3.3 Molecular Interactions

Supporting the hypothesis of interaction between the inserted α-helix and the binding site, hydrogen bond occupancy analysis revealed that arginine residues in the inserted α-helix (Arg[54], Arg[58], and Arg[61]) performed persistent hydrogen bonds with Glu[71] and Asp[167] in the apo state of isoform 2 for 15–56% of the simulation time (i.e. occupancy), while in the holo state Glu[71] performed hydrogen bond only with VIP's Arg[12] with ~18% occupancy (Fig. 6A, Fig. 6B). Also, in this isoform the inserted α-helix formed more persistent (ocp. > 15%) binding site interactions than VIP itself (15 vs 11). Conversely, in the holo state of isoform 1, the residues Glu[71] and Asp[167] (Glu[36] and Asp[133] in isoform 1) did not maintain hydrogen bonds for more than 15% of the simulation time (Fig. 6C). These quantitative occupancy data provide robust evidence for the proposed auto-inhibitory mechanism, wherein the inserted α-helix forms more stable and persistent interactions with the binding site residues compared to the native VIP peptide.

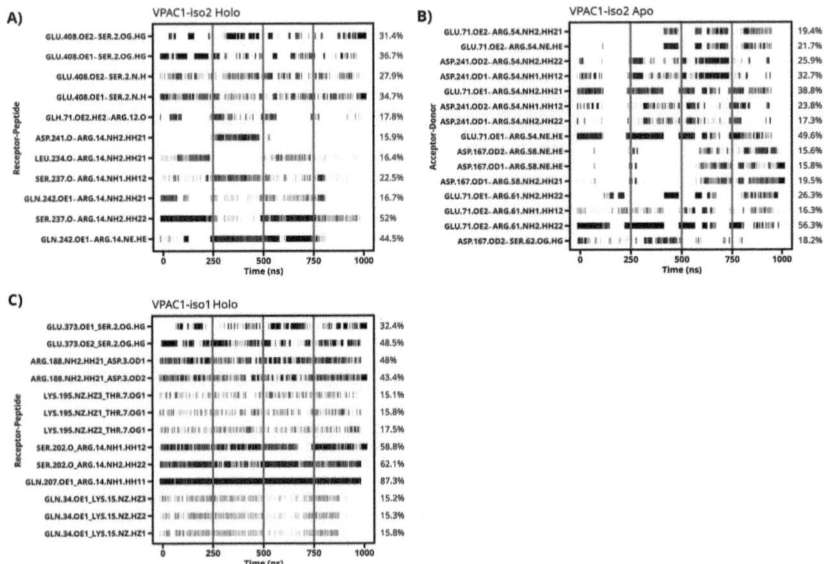

Fig. 6. Hydrogen bonds occupancies. The vertical red lines delimitate the four replicas. A) Bonds between VIP and VPAC1 isoform 2. B) Bonds between the inserted α-helix and VPAC1 isoform 2 binding pocket residues. C) Bonds between VIP and VPAC1 isoform 1.

4 Discussion

G protein-coupled receptor isoform diversity, generated through alternative splicing, differential promoter usage, or post-translational modifications, represents a fundamental mechanism for achieving functional specificity across physiological contexts [38, 39]. These variants exhibit altered ligand binding affinities, modified G protein coupling, or distinctive subcellular localization that expand functional repertoires beyond canonical activities [2, 40]. Clinically relevant examples include β-adrenergic receptor polymorphisms influencing asthma bronchodilator responsiveness [41], dopamine receptor variants associated with neuropsychiatric disorders [42], and serotonin receptor isoforms determining antidepressant efficacy [43, 44]. Aberrant expression ratios of functional versus non-functional isoforms may contribute to disease pathogenesis through dominant-negative mechanisms or altered receptor stoichiometry [45, 46]. Understanding isoform-specific functional differences is therefore essential for developing precision therapeutics that account for receptor variant heterogeneity in target populations [47].

Collectively, our findings demonstrate that VPAC1 isoform 2, initially cloned by Couvineau et al. (1994), employs a molecular auto-inhibitory mechanism wherein the inserted 17-residue α-helix in the ECD occupies the receptor's binding pocket, effectively functioning as an endogenous antagonist.

According to Piper et al. (2022) [7], ECD conformational flexibility is essential for accommodating the C-terminal region of peptide ligands, subsequently orienting the peptide's N-terminal toward the transmembrane binding site—a process aligned with the established two-step binding model for class B GPCRs [11]. In isoform 2, this critical conformational transition appears to be impeded by α-helical insertion within the binding site. Hydrogen bonds formed between arginine residues in the inserted α-helix and aspartate/glutamate residues in the binding site create a substantial energy barrier that restricts the required conformational rearrangement.

The auto-inhibitory mechanism identified in VPAC1 isoform 2 represents a distinctive paradigm of receptor regulation that expands our understanding of the functionality of GPCR splice variants. Although N-terminal modifications in class B GPCR variants typically result in impaired or abolished ligand binding [38], these effects generally stem from truncated extracellular domains rather than insertions [48]. The "self-binding" phenomenon observed in VPAC1 isoform 2 shares conceptual parallels with regulatory mechanisms found in class A GPCRs, particularly protease-activated receptors, where tethered ligand sequences within the receptor itself can function as signaling activators following proteolytic cleavage [49, 50]. However, our characterized mechanism represents an inverse functional outcome, inhibition, rather than activation. The remarkable sequence similarity between the inserted α-helix and the segments of the VIP peptide suggests an evolutionary adaptation that may have emerged specifically to fine-tune receptor responsiveness in different physiological contexts, potentially serving as an endogenous regulatory mechanism that modulates signaling without requiring external factors.

A mechanistically relevant parallel can be found in the comprehensive review by Zmijewski and Slominski (2010), who described an analogous regulatory phenomenon in the class B GPCR corticotropin-releasing factor receptor type 1 (CRF1). In this case, a splice variant containing a 29-amino-acid insertion in the first intracellular loop, characterized by a positively charged segment, exhibited modest inhibition of substrate binding (2.1-fold reduction) but dramatically impaired cAMP production (100-fold decrease), despite proper membrane localization and preservation of all canonical structural features [51]. The mechanism we identified in VPAC1 isoform 2, however, represents a distinct regulatory mechanism, as the inserted α-helical sequence directly occludes the ligand binding pocket, interfering with the initial molecular recognition event rather than disrupting the downstream signal transduction pathways.

Identification of this auto-inhibition mechanism in VPAC1 isoform 2 raises fundamental questions regarding its physiological relevance. Non-functional or functionally altered isoforms can significantly affect the susceptibility to and progression of diverse pathologies, including muscular dystrophy, cystic fibrosis, asthma, type I diabetes, and cancer. Indeed, VPAC1 receptors have been detected in human cervical carcinoma (HeLa) and colon carcinoma (HT-29, LoVo), and a 5-transmembrane variant has been identified in lymphoma cell lines (SUP-T1), resulting in attenuated coupling to cAMP signaling pathways [48]. Although isoform 2 of VPAC1 was initially isolated from small intestine cells, the ubiquitous expression pattern of this receptor warrants investigation of this isoform's potential role in neoplastic tissues.

Genetic factors frequently contribute to susceptibility to asthma and associated respiratory conditions, and specific GPCR splice variants increase the risk of developing respiratory disorders. A genome-wide association study identified GPRA (neuropeptide S receptor) as a potential contributor to asthma pathogenesis. Expression analysis comparing two splice variants encoding isoforms with distinct C-termini (A and B) in airway smooth muscle tissue from healthy and asthmatic individuals revealed significantly upregulated expression of isoform B in asthmatic patients, establishing this variant as a compelling candidate in asthma pathophysiology among Caucasian populations [38]. In addition, Zhao et al. (2019) demonstrated that ethnic differences in β-adrenergic receptor polymorphisms significantly affect the response to β-agonist therapy in asthma, where specific polymorphisms increase risk in Hispanic-Latino and Arab populations, while others exert protective effects in Indian populations [41].

This receptor isoform variability has particular clinical relevance considering recent contradictory findings regarding the efficacy of VIP in COVID-19 treatment. While Temerozo et al. (2022) demonstrated that Aviptadil, a synthetic VIP formulation, inhibited SARS-CoV-2 replication in vitro and correlated with improved survival outcomes in severe COVID-19 patients [52], Brown et al. (2023) reported no significant therapeutic benefit [53]. A critical analysis of these conflicting results [54] revealed important demographic differences: Hispanic participants constituted approximately 25% of the study population in Brown et al.'s investigation compared to nearly 50% in Temerozo's study, with both research groups observing stronger efficacy signals within these subgroups. These findings underscore the fundamental importance of considering receptor isoform distribution patterns across ethnic populations when evaluating the therapeutic efficacy and designing clinical trials.

5   Conclusion

Our computational analysis reveals a novel auto-inhibitory mechanism in VPAC1 isoform 2, where an inserted 17-residue α-helix functions as an endogenous antagonist by occupying the binding pocket. While molecular dynamics simulations provide valuable mechanistic insights, they are limited by nanosecond timescales and dependence on initial configurations. Future experimental validation through site-directed mutagenesis and structural studies, combined with tissue-specific expression profiling and functional characterization of dominant-negative effects, will be essential to confirm this mechanism and elucidate its physiological significance in VIP-mediated signaling across pathological contexts.

Acknowledgments. This study was financed in part by the Coordenação de Aperfeiçoamento de Pessoal de Nível Superior - Brasil (CAPES) - Finance Code 001, by the Rio de Janeiro Research

Foundation (FAPERJ), grant E-26/201.155/2021(260675) and by the the Brazilian National Council for Scientific and Technological Development (CNPq), grant 305524/2022-4. Also, this work used computational resources provided by the RPT04A Bioinformatics Core Facility at Fiocruz, Rio.

Data Availability. The Supplementary Figures, Tables and MD scripts are available in our Github repository https://github.com/Matheushfreis/N-terminal-Self-inhibitory_element_in_VPAC1_iso form_2.

Disclosure of Interests. The authors have no competing interests to declare that are relevant to the content of this article.

References

1. Delgado, M., et al.: The significance of vasoactive intestinal peptide in immunomodulation. Pharmacol. Rev. **56**, 249–290 (2004)
2. Rosenbaum, D.M., et al.: The structure and function of G-protein-coupled receptors. Nature **459**, 356–363 (2009)
3. Sloop, K.W., et al.: The current state of GPCR-based drug discovery to treat metabolic disease. Br. J. Pharmacol. **175**, 4060–4071 (2018)
4. Sriram, K., Insel, P.A.: G protein-coupled receptors as targets for approved drugs: how many targets and how many drugs? Mol. Pharmacol. **93**, 251–258 (2018)
5. Couvineau, A., Laburthe, M.: VPAC receptors: structure, molecular pharmacology and interaction with accessory proteins. Br. J. Pharmacol. **166**, 42–50 (2012)
6. Laburthe, M., Couvineau, A.: Molecular pharmacology and structure of VPAC receptors for VIP and PACAP. Regul. Pept. **108**, 165–173 (2002)
7. Piper, S.J., et al.: Understanding VPAC receptor family peptide binding and selectivity. Nat. Commun. **13**, 7013 (2022)
8. Sakamoto, K., et al.: AlphaFold version 2.0 elucidates the binding mechanism between VIPR2 and KS-133, and reveals an S–S bond (Cys25−Cys192) formation of functional significance for VIPR2. Biochem. Biophys. Res. Commun. **636**, 10–16 (2022)
9. Halmos, G.: Gene expression of vasoactive intestinal peptide receptors in human lung cancer. Int. J. Oncol. (2011)
10. Hoare, S.R.J., et al.: Ligand affinity for amino-terminal and juxtamembrane domains of the corticotropin releasing factor type I receptor: regulation by G-protein and nonpeptide antagonists. Biochemistry **43**, 3996–4011 (2004)
11. Karageorgos, V., et al.: Current understanding of the structure and function of family B GPCRs to design novel drugs. Hormones (Athens) **17**, 45–59 (2018)
12. Couvineau, A., et al.: Human intestinal VIP receptor: cloning and functional expression of two cDNA encoding proteins with different N-terminal domains. Biochem. Biophys. Res. Commun. **200**, 769–776 (1994)
13. The UniProt Consortium, et al.: UniProt: the Universal Protein Knowledgebase in 2023. Nucleic Acids Res. **51**, D523–D531 (2023)
14. Chang, J.-M., et al.: Accurate multiple sequence alignment of transmembrane proteins with PSI-Coffee. BMC Bioinform. **13**, S1 (2012)
15. Burley, S.K., et al.: RCSB Protein Data Bank (RCSB.org): delivery of experimentally-determined PDB structures alongside one million computed structure models of proteins from artificial intelligence/machine learning. Nucleic Acids Res. **51**, D488–D508 (2023)
16. Jones, D.T., Cozzetto, D.: DISOPRED3: precise disordered region predictions with annotated protein-binding activity. Bioinformatics **31**, 857–863 (2015)

17. Madeira, F., et al.: The EMBL-EBI job dispatcher sequence analysis tools framework in 2024. Nucleic Acids Res. **52**, W521–W525 (2024)
18. Jumper, J., et al.: Highly accurate protein structure prediction with AlphaFold. Nature **596**, 583–589 (2021)
19. Jurrus, E., et al.: Improvements to the APBS biomolecular solvation software suite. Protein Sci. **27**, 112–128 (2018)
20. Kobayashi, K., et al.: Cryo-EM structure of the human PAC1 receptor coupled to an engineered heterotrimeric G protein. Nat. Struct. Mol. Biol. **27**, 274–280 (2020)
21. Wang, J., et al.: Cryo-EM structures of PAC1 receptor reveal ligand binding mechanism. Cell Res. **30**, 436–445 (2020)
22. Latek, D., et al.: A molecular dynamics study of vasoactive intestinal peptide receptor 1 and the basis of its therapeutic antagonism. Int. J. Mol. Sci. **20**, 4348 (2019)
23. Liao, C., et al.: Molecular basis of class B GPCR selectivity for the neuropeptides PACAP and VIP. Front. Mol. Biosci. **8**, 644644 (2021)
24. Pettersen, E.F., et al.: UCSF chimera—a visualization system for exploratory research and analysis. J. Comput. Chem. **25**, 1605–1612 (2004)
25. Maier, J.A., et al.: Ff14SB: improving the accuracy of protein side chain and backbone parameters from ff99SB. J. Chem. Theory Comput. **11**, 3696–3713 (2015)
26. Waterhouse, A.M., et al.: The structure assessment web server: for proteins, complexes and more. Nucleic Acids Res. **52**, W318–W323 (2024)
27. Lee, J., et al.: CHARMM-GUI input generator for NAMD, GROMACS, AMBER, OpenMM, and CHARMM/OpenMM simulations using the CHARMM36 additive force field. J. Chem. Theory Comput. **12**, 405–413 (2016)
28. Izadi, S., et al.: Building water models: a different approach. J. Phys. Chem. Lett. **5**, 3863–3871 (2014)
29. Tian, C., et al.: Ff19SB: amino-acid-specific protein backbone parameters trained against quantum mechanics energy surfaces in solution. J. Chem. Theory Comput. **16**, 528–552 (2020)
30. Dickson, C.J., et al.: Lipid21: complex lipid membrane simulations with AMBER. J. Chem. Theory Comput. **18**, 1726–1736 (2022)
31. Case, D.A., et al.: AMBER 22 reference manual (2022)
32. Krautler, V., et al.: A fast SHAKE algorithm to solve distance constraint equations for small molecules in molecular dynamics simulations. J. Comput. Chem. **22**, 501–508 (2001)
33. Roe, D.R., Cheatham, T.E.: PTRAJ and CPPTRAJ: software for processing and analysis of molecular dynamics trajectory data. J. Chem. Theory Comput. **9**, 3084–3095 (2013)
34. Grant, B.J., et al.: The Bio3D packages for structural bioinformatics. Protein Sci. **30**, 20–30 (2021)
35. He, Y., et al.: Vasoactive intestinal peptide: a potential target for antiviral therapy. Sheng Li Xue Bao. **74**, 419–433 (2022)
36. Lu, J., et al.: Targeting VIP and PACAP receptor signaling: new insights into designing drugs for the PACAP subfamily of receptors. IJMS **23**, 8069 (2022)
37. Xu, Y., et al.: A distinctive ligand recognition mechanism by the human vasoactive intestinal polypeptide receptor 2. Nat. Commun. **13**, 2272 (2022)
38. Markovic, D., Challiss, R.A.J.: Alternative splicing of G protein-coupled receptors: physiology and pathophysiology. Cell. Mol. Life Sci. **66**, 3337–3352 (2009)
39. Schöneberg, T., et al.: Mutant G-protein-coupled receptors as a cause of human diseases. Pharmacol. Ther. **104**, 173–206 (2004)
40. Kobilka, B.K., Deupi, X.: Conformational complexity of G-protein-coupled receptors. Trends Pharmacol. Sci. **28**, 397–406 (2007)

41. Zhao, S., et al.: Association of β2-adrenergic receptor gene polymorphisms (rs1042713, rs1042714, rs1042711) with asthma risk: a systematic review and updated meta-analysis. BMC Pulm. Med. **19**, 202 (2019)

42. Beaulieu, J.-M., Gainetdinov, R.R.: The physiology, signaling, and pharmacology of dopamine receptors. Pharmacol. Rev. **63**, 182–217 (2011)

43. Hoyer, D., et al.: International union of pharmacology classification of receptors for 5-hydroxytryptamine (serotonin). Pharmacol. Rev. **46**, 157–203 (1994)

44. Barnes, N.M., Sharp, T.: A review of central 5-HT receptors and their function. Neuropharmacology **38**, 1083–1152 (1999)

45. Thompson, M.D., et al.: G protein-coupled receptor mutations and human genetic disease. In: Yan, Q. (ed.) Pharmacogenomics in Drug Discovery and Development, pp. 153–187. Springer, New York (2014)

46. Rask-Andersen, M., et al.: The druggable genome: evaluation of drug targets in clinical trials suggests major shifts in molecular class and indication. Annu. Rev. Pharmacol. Toxicol. **54**, 9–26 (2014)

47. Hauser, A.S., et al.: Trends in GPCR drug discovery: new agents, targets and indications. Nat. Rev. Drug Discov. **16**, 829–842 (2017)

48. Dickson, L., Finlayson, K.: VPAC and PAC receptors: from ligands to function. Pharmacol. Ther. **121**, 294–316 (2009)

49. Hollenberg, M.D.: Proteinase-activated receptors: tethered ligands and receptor-activating peptides. Drug Dev. Res. **59**, 336–343 (2003)

50. Schepis, A., et al.: Protease signaling regulates apical cell extrusion, cell contacts, and proliferation in epithelia. J. Cell Biol. **217**, 1097–1112 (2018)

51. Zmijewski, M.A., Slominski, A.T.: Emerging role of alternative splicing of CRF1 receptor in CRF signaling. Acta Biochim. Pol. **57**, 1–13 (2010)

52. Temerozo, J.R., et al.: VIP plasma levels associate with survival in severe COVID-19 patients, correlating with protective effects in SARS-CoV-2-infected cells. J. Leukoc. Biol. **111**, 1107–1121 (2022)

53. Brown, S.M., et al.: Intravenous aviptadil and remdesivir for treatment of COVID-19-associated hypoxaemic respiratory failure in the USA (TESICO): a randomised, placebo-controlled trial. Lancet Respir. Med. **11**, 791–803 (2023)

54. Lee, W.L., Slutsky, A.S.: A negative trial for vasoactive intestinal peptide in COVID-19-associated acute hypoxaemic respiratory failure. Lancet Respir. Med. **11**, 759–760 (2023)

Using Machine Learning and Graph-Based Signatures to Evaluate Normal and Decreased Function CYP2D6 Haplotypes

Diego Mariano[1]([✉]) [iD], Maria Carolina Puça[2,3] [iD], Yanka E. A. R. Salazar[2,3] [iD], Rafael Pereira Lemos[1] [iD], Giovana C. F. Maia[1] [iD], Lucas Moraes dos Santos[1] [iD], Tais Nobrega de Sousa[2,3] [iD], and Raquel Cardoso de Melo-Minardi[1] [iD]

[1] Laboratory of Bioinformatics and Systems (LBS), Department of Computer Science, Universidade Federal de Minas Gerais, Belo Horizonte, Brazil
diego@dcc.ufmg.br
[2] Molecular Biology and Malaria Immunology Research Group, Instituto René Rachou, Fundação Oswaldo Cruz (FIOCRUZ), Belo Horizonte, Minas Gerais, Brazil
[3] Department of Microbiology, Tumor and Cell Biology, Karolinska Institutet, Solna, Sweden

Abstract. Cytochrome P450 2D6 (CYP2D6) is crucial for the metabolism and bioactivation of over 20% of clinically used drugs. Its highly polymorphic nature results in varying enzyme activity levels among individuals, impacting the safety and efficacy of drugs metabolized by CYP2D6. Here, we show the use of machine learning to better understand the impact of missense mutations on assigned haplotype functional status. We collected information on missense mutations associated with several CYP2D6 alleles from the PharmVar database. We then modeled the mutants' 3D structure using ColabFold. Finally, we employed graph-based algorithms to extract structural signatures and developed a machine-learning model to assess two classes of haplotype functional status: normal and decreased. Furthermore, we compared the accuracy of 3D structure-based analysis with sequence-based models. The best structure-based model was built using Gradient Boosting and achieved an accuracy of 92.9%, superior to the best model built using sequences (accuracy of 78.6%). Additionally, we used our model to identify the most impactful mutations for each class. Our results indicate that the use of graph-based signatures can be efficient in detecting structural differences, which can help in explaining mutations related to each haplotype's functional status. Machine learning models can be useful for identifying individuals at risk of being poor metabolizers, helping to personalize medical treatment, and improving drug safety and efficacy.

D. Mariano, M. C. Puça—These authors contributed equally to this work.

T. N. de Sousa and R. C. de Melo-Minardi—These authors contributed equally to this work.

Keywords: CYP2D6 · machine learning · protein structure · structural signatures

1   Introduction

Cytochrome P450 2D6 (CYP2D6), a member of the cytochrome P450 superfamily, is crucial for the metabolism and bioactivation of over 20% of clinically used drugs, including antidepressants, ADHD medications, antipsychotics, antiemetics, analgesics, beta-blockers, and more [1,2]. Its highly polymorphic nature results in varying levels of enzyme activity among individuals, impacting the safety and efficacy of drugs metabolized by CYP2D6 [3]. This variability has led to annotations on numerous drug labels and the inclusion of recommendations for CYP2D6-guided drug therapy in clinical guidelines. Genetic variations in the CYP2D6 gene, encompassing over 100 alleles and sub-alleles, can significantly influence enzyme activity. These variations, including single-nucleotide polymorphisms (SNPs), insertions/deletions, and copy number variations, contribute to the diverse metabolic profiles observed in different populations [4,5].

Notably, ultrarapid metabolizers (UM) and poor metabolizers (PM) represent opposite ends of the activity spectrum, with UMs at risk of therapeutic failure due to rapid drug metabolism and poor metabolizers susceptible to dose-dependent adverse events. For drugs that require bioactivation, such as codeine, tramadol, primaquine, and tamoxifen, subjects with extreme phenotypes, UM and PM, are at risk of inadequate response to treatment as they produce active metabolites rather rapidly or to no appreciable amount. Extensive (EM) and intermediate (IM) metabolizers exhibit metabolic capacities between these extremes. Additionally, structural rearrangements involving the CYP2D7 pseudogene further complicate the understanding of CYP2D6 metabolism [4-6].

CYP2D6 is known for its high degree of genetic variability [7]. While some of these variants are well-characterized as either functional or non-functional, a significant proportion falls into the category of indeterminate alleles [8]. These indeterminate alleles often exhibit variable enzymatic activity, making their impact on drug metabolism less predictable. Understanding the frequency and distribution of these indeterminate alleles is crucial for pharmacogenetic studies, as the genetic background can significantly influence an individual's response to medications metabolized by CYP2D6 [9]. Furthermore, their presence highlights the need for more comprehensive genetic profiling and personalized medicine approaches to optimize therapeutic outcomes and minimize adverse drug reactions. Variations in the CYP2D6 gene can impact the effectiveness and costs of medication therapies. Studies suggest that CYP2D6 genotyping may be beneficial for approximately 30-40% of drugs metabolized by CYP2D6, which accounts for roughly 7-10% of all drugs commonly used in clinical settings [10,11].

The use of advanced approaches for data-driven analysis, such as Machine Learning, has seen a notable increase in pharmacogenetics [12]. This increase is mainly driven by the increased availability of large datasets and enhanced computing power, particularly for genetic prediction purposes [13]. This trend underscores not only the technological advancements within pharmacogenetics but also the growing importance of sophisticated analytical approaches to understand and predict how genes impact individual responses to medications.

Machine learning can be useful for identifying individuals at risk of being poor metabolizers, helping to personalize medical treatment, and improving drug safety and efficacy. Deep learning-based approaches have been used to predict the functional status of CYP2D6 gene haplotypes from sequence data. For instance, Hubble.2D6, a model built using transfer learning, has been used to assign functions to haplotypes with uncured functions [2]. However, the proposed model did not consider the impact of the mutations described in the literature on the three-dimensional structure of the proteins and, consequently, on their assigned haplotype functional status.

In this study, we propose a machine learning-based model to better understand the impact of missense mutations on assigned haplotype functional status. Hence, we collected information about missense mutations described for several alleles of the CYP2D6 gene in the PharmVar database [14]. We modeled the mutants' 3D structure using ColabFold, a tool based on the Alphafold algorithm, the state-of-the-art de novo protein modeling tool [15]. Following this, we extracted structural signatures using graph-based algorithms [16,17]. Structural signatures are a feature extraction approach used to represent macromolecule 3D structures [18]. We built a machine-learning model to classify the functional status of two haplotypes as either normal or decreased. The activity score (AS) system is used to translate the CYP2D6 genotype into phenotype. It assigns a value to each star allele: 0 for "no function", 0.25 or 0.5 for "decreased function" (also herein called "reduced function"), and 1 for "normal function" alleles [2]. Higher values are labeled "increased function"; however, this event is more related to gene duplications. In this study, we aim to evaluate aspects related to CYP2D6 3D structures, focusing on the normal and decreased classes. Lastly, we use the model to identify the most impactful mutations for each class.

2   Methods

2.1   Data Collection

A total of 161 alleles (CYP2D6 gene) were collected from the central repository for pharmacogene (PGx) variation, PharmVar[1] [14]. A list of single-nucleotide polymorphisms (SNP) described in the literature was collected for each allele. For each SNP, the following were also collected: nucleotide changes (M33388), effect on protein (NP_000097.3), position at NC_000022.11 (*Homo sapiens* chromosome 22 - GRCh38.p2), position at NG_008376.3 (CYP2D6 RefSeqGene - reverse relative to chromosome), and rsID. Initially, 203 attributes were collected for each of the 161 alleles. Then, we filtered SNPs that lead to missense mutations. Finally, we selected alleles categorized as decreased function or normal function. A total of 42 alleles and respective missense mutations were collected and stored in a binary matrix (Table 1).

---

[1] https://www.pharmvar.org/gene/CYP2D6.

Table 1. Alleles, haplotype functional status assigned by manual curation, and mutations described in the literature for each one. Alleles *1B-E are similar to *1A, *2B-H, K-M are similar to *2A, and *10B,D are similar to *10A.

Allele	Class	V11M	R26H	P34S	A90V	T107I	F120I	A122S	V136M	E155K	E156A	G169R	A237S	T261I	P267H	K281del	R296C	V338M	E383K	K404Q	E410K	S486T
*9	Decreased															X	X					
*84	Decreased														X		X					X
*72	Decreased			X															X			X
*59	Decreased																X					
*55	Decreased																X			X		
*54	Decreased			X										X								
*50	Decreased										X											
*49	Decreased			X			X															
*41	Decreased																X					
*29	Decreased							X									X	X				
*17	Decreased					X											X					
*14	Decreased											X					X					
*10A	Decreased			X																		
*53	Normal						X	X														
*48	Normal				X																	
*46B	Normal		X							X							X					X
*46A	Normal		X							X							X					
*45B	Normal									X							X					
*45A	Normal									X							X					
*39	Normal																					
*35B	Normal	X															X					
*35A	Normal	X															X					
*34	Normal																X					
*33	Normal												X									
*2A	Normal																X					X
*27	Normal																				X	
*1A	Normal																					

2.2   Data Pre-processing and 3D Modeling

The sequence of CYP2D6 was collected from the UniProt database (UniProt ID: P10635). Then, each allele sequence was inferred based on the list of missense mutations collected from the literature. Data pre-processing was performed using in-house Python scripts, MS Excel, and Orange Data Mining [20].

The sequences were modeled using a local installation of ColabFold [18], a derived tool of Alphafold [15]. The modeling was performed using an NVIDIA

A100 GPU (80 GB). The default parameters were used. Thus, for each allele, five models were predicted. We selected the model with the highest pLDDT score.

2.3 Structural Signatures

For each model, we calculated the structural signature using the SIGNA tool (https://github.com/LBS-UFMG/signa). Structural signatures are vectors representing 3D structures used to detect similarities and differences in biomolecules with similar functions [19]. We used the aCSM-ALL algorithm [16] with parameters of a maximum cutoff distance of 20 Å and a cutoff step of 0.2 Å.

2.4 Model Building

The machine learning experiments were designed according to the methodology described in [38]. The models were built using Orange Data Mining [20]. Seven machine learning algorithms were used: (i) neural network [21], (ii) logistic regression [22], (iii) kNN [23], (iv) SVM [24], (v) random forest [25], (vi) gradient boosting [26], and (vii) decision tree [27].

The neural network model was constructed with 100 neurons in hidden layers, ReLu activation, Adam solver, regularization $\alpha=0.0001$, and a maximum of 200 iterations. The logistic regression model employed Ridge (L2) regularization with a strength of $C = 1$. The kNN model utilized $k = 11$, the Euclidean metric, and distance weighting. The SVM model was configured with a linear kernel, a cost parameter of 1, a regression loss epsilon of 0.10, numerical tolerance of 0.001, and an iteration limit of 100. The random forest algorithm was set to use 10 trees and prohibited splitting subsets smaller than five. The decision tree model was specified to induce a binary tree, with a maximum tree depth of 100 and a minimum of 2 instances per leaf. Lastly, the Gradient Boosting model employed the Extreme Gradient Boosting (xgboost) algorithm with 100 trees, a learning rate of 0.3, regularization $\lambda=3$, and a maximum depth for individual trees (MDIT) of 6.

The models were built using 10-fold cross-validation (CV). The best models were evaluated based on accuracy, F1 score, precision, recall, specificity, and AUC (Area Under the Curve). The most important features were determined using the Information Gain algorithm [28,29] in the Orange data mining tool [20].

3 Results and Discussion

In this study, we collected missense mutations from the literature for the gene CYP2D6 related to two haplotypes' functional statuses: normal and decreased function. Although there are two other classes described for this protein – "increased function" and "no function" – we chose to exclude them. The "increased function" class is typically associated with gene duplications rather than structural changes. Furthermore, we hypothesize that mutations leading to a loss of function (i.e., "no function" class) are often related to protein-coding, such as mutations in the 5' region or the insertion of premature stop codons. Figure 1 summarizes the methodology adopted in this study.

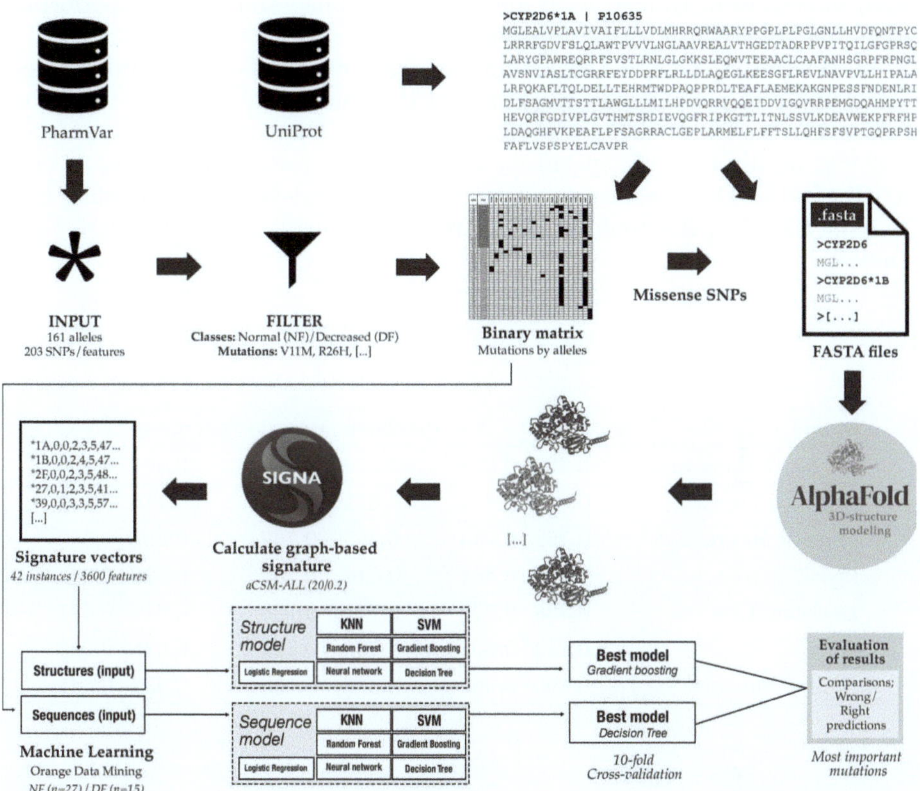

Fig. 1. Workflow used in this study. Allele data were collected from PharmVar. We then selected only the data related to the normal and decreased classes (n = 42). The CYP2D6 sequence was collected from UniProt (ID: P10635). We applied mutations to the sequences and performed 3D modeling using ColabFold (an AlphaFold-based tool). Structural signature vectors were calculated using the SIGNA command-line tool and the aCSM-ALL algorithm. Finally, machine-learning models were built using the binary mutation matrix and the structural signature matrix as input, and a comparison was made between the best models built with different supervised learning algorithms.

We modeled the 3D structures and generated the graph-based structural signatures of each one using the aCSM-ALL algorithm [16]. aCSM-ALL assigns eight possible types to each atom: neutral, acceptor, donor, aromatic, hydrophobic, sulfide, positive, and negative. Then, for each cutoff variation, the algorithm models the protein as a graph, where atoms are vertices and pairs of atoms that meet the cutoff distances are the edges. Thus, it calculates the distribution of combinations of pairs of atoms by varying the cutoff step (0.2 Å) up to the maximum cutoff point (20 Å). These values were defined based on previous works [30,31]. For each 3D structure, a signature vector with 3600 features was generated. These signature vectors were imported into the Orange Data Mining tool. Seven models were trained with different algorithms, and the best-performing model was selected for further analysis.

To determine the best algorithm, we trained models using 10-fold cross-validation. In this evaluation, the Gradient Boosting model achieved the highest performance metrics, with an accuracy of 92.9%, F1-score of 92.8%, precision of 92.9%, recall of 92.9%, specificity of 90.1%, and area under the ROC curve (AUC) of 90%. These results surpassed the other models tested, including kNN, Decision Tree, Logistic Regression, SVM, Neural Network, and Random Forest (Table 2).

Table 2. Results for each of the seven algorithms used to train the structure-based model.

Model	Accuracy	F1	Precision	Recall	Specificity	AUC
Gradient Boosting	0.929	0.928	0.929	0.929	0.901	0.900
Random Forest	0.810	0.801	0.811	0.810	0.716	0.822
Logistic Regression	0.762	0.744	0.765	0.762	0.631	0.589
kNN	0.738	0.684	0.814	0.738	0.529	0.783
Decision Tree	0.738	0.723	0.732	0.738	0.617	0.631
SVM	0.714	0.693	0.706	0.714	0.575	0.720
Neural Network	0.690	0.661	0.677	0.690	0.532	0.641

3.1 Comparison Between Sequence and Structural Approaches

Subsequently, we built a model using the binary matrix of the mutations described (Table 1). In this approach, each instance was assigned a value of '1' if it had a specific mutation and '0' otherwise, treating each mutation as a feature. This allowed us to apply feature selection algorithms to determine which mutations were most important for classifying each functional state. Consequently, models built using this binary mutation matrix—a purely sequence-based approach—exhibited much lower accuracy than those based on structural signatures derived from 3D structures.

As Table 3 shows, the best model based on sequence analysis achieved an accuracy of approximately 78.6% (other sequence-model results are available in the Supplementary Material). In contrast, the best model based on structural signatures (Gradient Boosting) achieved an accuracy of 92.9%.

The Gradient Boosting-based model correctly predicted 39 out of 42 instances, misclassifying two decreased function instances and only one normal

Table 3. Comparison between the models built using the structural signature-based and the sequence-based methods.

Approach	Best Model	Accuracy	F1	Precision	Recall	Spec	AUC
Structure	Gradient Boosting	0.929	0.928	0.929	0.929	0.901	0.900
Sequence	Decision Tree	0.786	0.755	0.839	0.786	0.614	0.728

function instance. In contrast, the sequence-based Decision Tree model correctly predicted only 33 out of 42 entries (Supplementary Table S1).

Upon evaluating the occurrence of mutations across different alleles, we observed that only three mutations—F120I, R296C, and S486T—appear in both functional statuses (Fig. 2), suggesting that these mutations may not be indicative of specific classes. Eleven mutations are exclusively associated with the decreased function class, while seven are unique to the normal function class (Fig. 2).

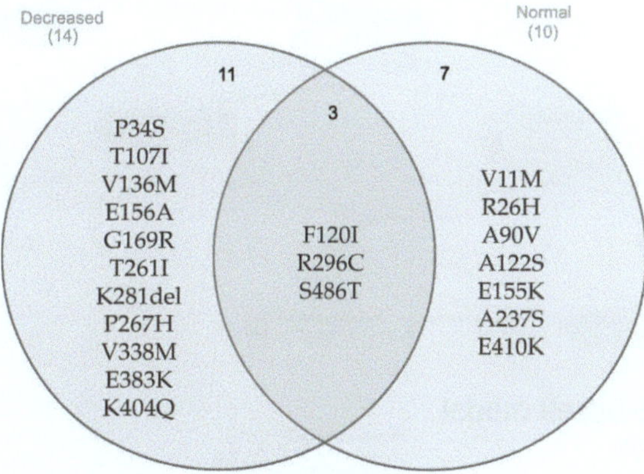

Fig. 2. Venn diagram of mutations found in each class. Left circle: decreased function class. Right circle: normal function class. Generated using InteractiVenn [32].

Many of these mutations may not significantly impact classification. However, certain patterns may emerge from combinations of mutations. Models employing structural signatures, which incorporate every atom and its respective type in the analysis, demonstrate a remarkable ability to detect these patterns. This capability likely contributes to the superior classification performance of the model based on structural signatures. To further explore these dynamics, we conducted analyses to assess the importance of various features.

3.2   Model Explainability

To understand the most relevant attributes responsible for the incorrect predictions generated by the sequence-based model, we used a decision tree (Fig. 3A). We also used the model's decision tree based on structural signatures (Fig. 3B).

It is possible to see that the decision tree model developed using graph-based signatures achieved a lower accuracy of 74% (Fig. 3B) compared to the model based on Gradient Boosting, which achieved 92.9% (Table 2). However, the decision tree model has greater explainability since we can visualize each decision made through the branches and leaves of the trees.

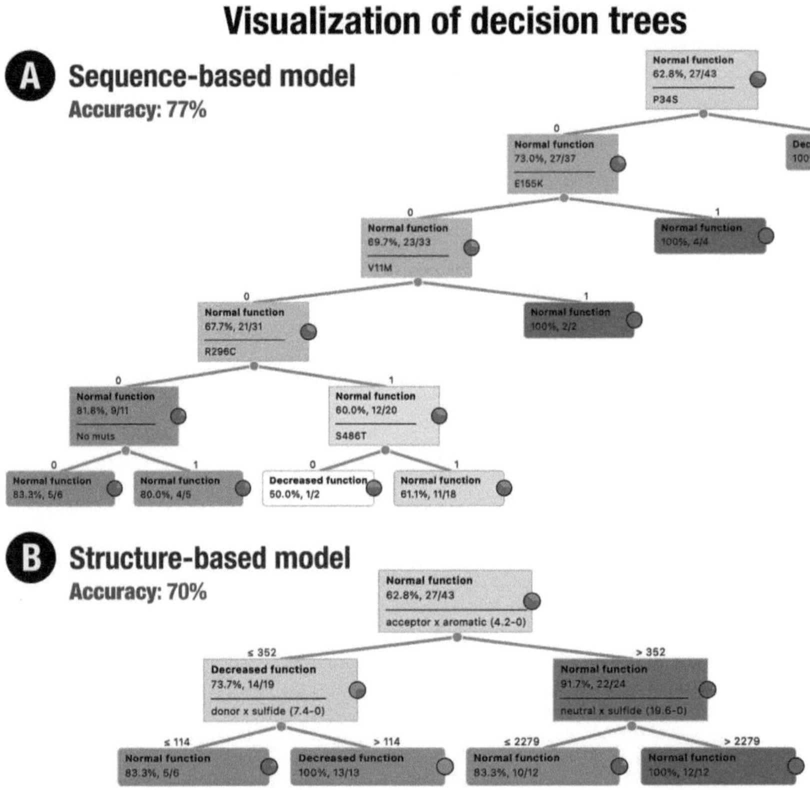

Fig. 3. Visualization of decision trees. Analyzing decision trees enables you to better understand which attributes were most important for classifying the data. (A) Decision tree of the model based on sequences. (B) Decision tree of the model based on structures. Red: normal function; blue: decreased function; white: tie. (Color figure online)

We can observe in Fig. 3A that the first decision made by the sequence-based classifier involves the P34S mutation, which changes a proline at position 34 to a serine (Fig. 4). The model indicates that the presence of this mutation is a strong indicator of reduced protein function. Analysis of Tables 1, S1, and S2 (see supplementary materials) reveals that six alleles carry this mutation: *72, *54, *49, *10D, *10B, and *10A. The literature already discusses the importance of residue P34 [33]. This proline is a fundamental residue in a hydrophobic interaction network with other residues, such as I389 and F387 (Fig. 4A). The P34S mutation causes a destabilization of the protein's regional structure. We can observe that S34 in the mutated structure starts to interact with S70 (Fig. 4B).

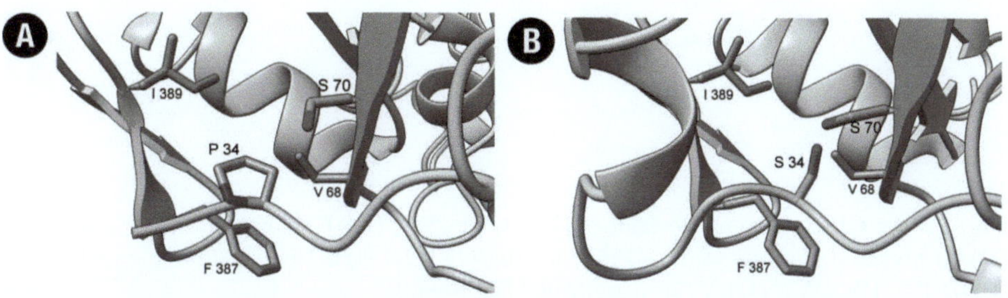

Fig. 4. Analysis of the mutation P34S on the CYP2D6 structure. (A) Proline at position 34 (PDB ID: 4WNW). (B) Serine at P34S mutant (*72 allele).

According to the sequence-based model (Fig. 3A), the second most relevant mutation is E155K (Fig. 5A-B), which replaces a negatively charged polar amino acid (glutamate) with a positively charged amino acid (lysine). Table 1 shows that only four alleles present this mutation: *45A, *45B, *46A and *46B. In this case, the model can detect that this mutation does not alter the function of the protein. This is an interesting point since mutations that change the charge tend to have significant impacts on the structure of the protein, modifying, for example, the possible interactions that the protein performs.

When this mutation is not present, the model evaluates whether the structure has mutations or not. This decision is somewhat debatable. Having no mutations indicates that the protein is like the reference allele (*1A) and would, therefore, be classified as a normal function. However, here we encounter a possible limitation of our study. If an entry is classified as another allele, it means that it has some SNP that differs from the reference allele. However, this SNP can occur in non-coding regions, such as the 5' region, or even in introns. In this study, we only considered mutations that occur in the protein structure. This may be correlated with the errors obtained by the sequence-based model.

The next decision (Fig. 3A) is based on the V11M (valine to methionine) mutation, another mutation that does not affect function. However, only two alleles carry this mutation: *35A and *35B. From this point on, decisions are made on less informative mutations. The model indicates that R296C (arginine to cysteine) can be associated with normal and decreased function classes. Lastly, the model also considers the S486T (serine to threonine) mutation. The presence

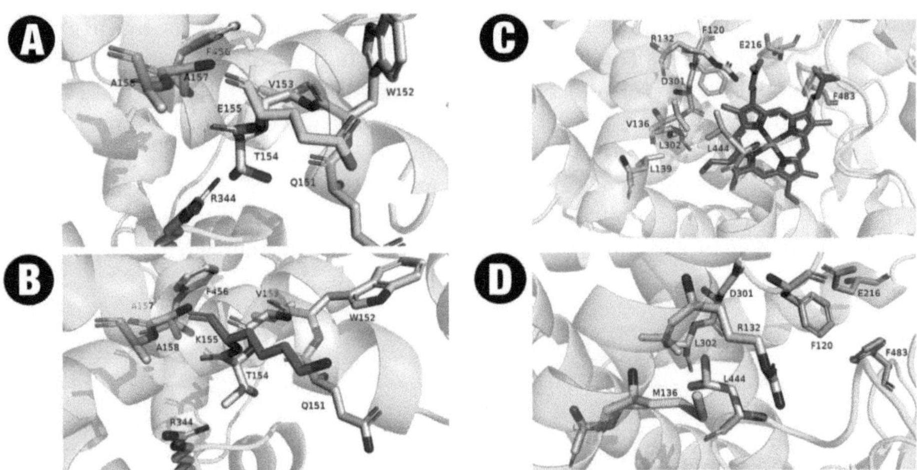

Fig. 5. (A) Glutamate at position 155 of CYP2D6. (B) E155K mutant (*46B allele). (C) Analysis of the mutation V136M on the CYP2D structure. Valine at position 136 (PDB ID: 4WNW). (D) V136M mutant (*29 allele).

of this mutation in combination with the R296C mutation is related to normal function in 61.0% of cases (11 out of 18 cases). In contrast, the presence of R296C and the absence of S486T were related to decreased function in only one out of two cases. This decision is also debatable and may represent the biggest flaw in this model.

These shortcomings may have been addressed by the structure-based model. However, explaining the decisions of a model based on structural signatures is not straightforward. Despite having lower accuracy than the gradient boosting model, the decision tree of the structure-based model (Fig. 3B) may be a first step towards understanding them. However, to understand this better, we need to go back to the concept of structural signatures that were used to represent protein structures.

Graph-based structural signatures, such as those used in the aCSM-ALL algorithm, perform classification based on the count of atom pairs at specific cutoff distances. The aCSM-ALL algorithm also considers atomic types, identifying patterns that can be challenging to discern. For example, the first pattern identified involves the count of acceptor and acceptor atom pairs (5.8Å). According to our model, the presence of more than 1808 pairs of atoms is associated with a normal function (92% of the entries with these characteristics are classified as "normal function", Fig. 3B). Then, the next pattern evaluates the presence of acceptor and aromatic atom pairs within a distance of up to 4.2Å (Fig. 3B). According to our model, the presence of more than 352 pairs of atoms is associated with a normal function (Fig. 3B).

All amino acids can act as hydrogen acceptors since the oxygen atoms in the main chain have this characteristic. Therefore, this pattern can be challenging to explain. On the other hand, only tyrosine, tryptophan, and phenylalanine can engage in aromatic interactions. Therefore, this could only be related to F120I mutant. However, this mutation has already been described as typical for both the normal and decreased classes.

Furthermore, since aCSM considers each atom of aromatic residues, mutations in residues with many atoms that can act as hydrogen acceptors near aromatic residues could impact the result. For example, deletion of an amino acid could reduce the number of such contacts (as in K281del present in *9). However, this contrasts with P34S, a mutation that adds acceptor atoms but is strongly linked to the decreased function class.

The next issue evaluated in Fig. 3B is the presence of hydrophobic and sulfide atom pairs at up to 19.6 Å. When more than 1937 pairs of these atoms are detected, the model categorizes the entry as having normal function in all cases (Fig. 3B). Conversely, 1937 or fewer pairs may indicate normal or decreased function. Sulfide atoms are found only in cysteine and methionine amino acids, which suggests that patterns related to these types of features may be linked to the mutations V11M, V136M, R296C, and V338M. Notably, the mutation of a valine to methionine, which occurs frequently in different sites, involves two nonpolar amino acids and should not significantly impact function. It is also important to highlight that the V136M mutation is located near the heme group (Fig. 5C-D), an area critical for the protein's function.

As discussed in this section, explaining the patterns identified by structural signatures is not trivial. Here, we discuss some insights that may be related to this. Also, to further refine our understanding, we conducted a feature selection analysis using the information gain algorithm to evaluate the most important mutations in both sequence-based and structure-based models (Supplementary Table S2).

The information gain analysis indicates that the P34S (proline for serine) and E155K (glutamate for lysine) mutations are the most crucial for the sequence-based model. Concurrently, the analysis also demonstrates that donor and hydrophobic atom pairs, across various cutoff distances, are the main features of the model classification based on structural signatures. These findings mutually corroborate the significance of these features in both modeling approaches. This also corroborates our insights presented earlier in this section. Furthermore, the fact that no mutations are found is also an indicator that helps in prediction.

Consider the P34S mutation. Proline is an amino acid that is considered special because its side chain interacts with the nitrogen in the main chain, causing it to lose its ability to act as a hydrogen donor. Proline also possesses other atoms, such as carbons CB and CG, which can engage in hydrophobic interactions. On the other hand, in serine, the nitrogen of the main chain can act as a donor, and the oxygen (OG) can act as a hydrogen acceptor and donor. Therefore, the P34S mutation significantly alters the count of donor-hydrophobic atom pairs in the human cytochrome P450 2D6 structure. Thus, we can hypothesize that changes in the patterns of atom pairs can be used to detect mutations that may lead to reduced function.

3.3 Limitations and Perspectives

To the best of our knowledge, this is the first time that graph-based structural signatures have been used to classify normal and decreased CYP2D6 functional status. Previously, the mCSM tool [34] has been used to measure the impact of polymorphisms on structure. In [33], the P34S mutation has been described as destabilizing ($\Delta\Delta$G: -1,984 Kcal/mol). Our results agree with this study. Both our models, based on sequence and structure, highlight this as one of the most important mutations that have been described as leading to destabilization.

Additionally, previous studies have used deep neural network techniques for sequence-based classification. Models based on Transfer Learning have been described as efficient in determining CYP2D6 haplotype function [2]. Furthermore, when working with sequences, it is possible to obtain sufficient information to classify other haplotypes, such as those classified as "no function". However, this type of analysis does not benefit from the structural details that 3D structures can provide, such as details of contacts performed between residues in the region near a mutation site. Furthermore, deep neural networks are often difficult to explain, creating the impression of a "black box" where decision processes are not transparent.

This work seeks to understand the structural characteristics that lead to reduced activity. Our results confirm that some mutations previously described, such as P34S [33], may be related to reduced activity. However, other more complex patterns should be analyzed, such as the change in the nature of interactions caused by different types of rarely observed mutations. Our results also indicate that the presence of pairs of atoms classified as donors and aromatics may indicate a change in functional status, in addition to mutations related to residues with sulfide. Further studies are needed to elucidate better the factors related to this.

This work has some limitations. First, two other classes were not used: "increased function" and "no function". The literature has described that the increased function class is related to gene duplication. We did not find reports that single-point mutations could cause considerable improvement in CYP2D6 activity. However, further studies are needed to confirm this. Also, entries classified as "no function" are generally related to mutations interrupting gene coding, such as mutations in the 5' region, frameshifts, and inserting premature stop codons. However, we should consider that some single-point mutations can completely interrupt protein action, and such mutations are not addressed in this study. Further studies are needed to identify them. Secondly, this study is limited by the mutations known in the literature. We must consider that the databases may not consider all mutations found in specific alleles.

Another limitation of this study is that it works with modeled structures. Despite the recent progress in protein modeling [15,35-37], dealing with structures obtained *in silico* can still introduce biases in the results, mainly due to the ability of structural signatures to detect representative details of the structures [16].

Finally, the number of entries used in the experiments is low. Only 42 instances of the "decreased function" (n=15) and "normal function" (n=27) classes were available at the time. In fact, most of the alleles available in the public databases have an unknown function. Experimental bench validations can help expand the known database, and this can be used in the future to improve the results of the models presented here. A complementary solution would be to use the models proposed here and others available, such as Hubble.2D6, to make predictions of alleles of unknown function. However, this would add a speculative factor to this research, and therefore, it was not addressed here. In the future, we plan to evaluate new strategies to balance class inputs. Additionally, we plan to consider new approaches to enhance the explainability of models.

4 Conclusion

Here, we show the implementation of traditional machine learning models to classify the haplotype functional status of the CYP2D6 gene. Two classes were considered: decreased function and normal function. SNPs from 42 different alleles were collected from the PharmVar database. Then, sequences were inferred based on the sequence of CYP2D6 (UniProt ID: P10635). Structures were modeled using ColabFold, and structural signatures were obtained using the aCSM-ALL algorithm (step: 0.2; max cutoff: 20). Our model achieved an accuracy of 92.9% when built using the Gradient Boosting algorithm (92.8%, 92.9%, 92.9%, 90.1%, and 90% for F1-score, precision, recall, specificity, and AUC, respectively). A model based only on the list of SNPs for each allele, i.e., in the sequences, was built using the same parameters and obtained an accuracy of 78.6% using the decision tree algorithm. These results suggest that structural signature techniques are better descriptors to classify the haplotype functional status of the CYP2D6 gene of decreased function and normal function. The results presented in this study can be used to aid in predicting CYP2D6's functional status. Additionally, the descriptive techniques presented here can be used to model problems with other genes and may bring new insights into treatments using personalized medicine and for discovering new drugs.

Acknowledgments. The authors thank the agencies: FAPEMIG, CAPES, and CNPq. This study was financed in part by the Coordenação de Aperfeiçoamento de Pessoal de Nível Superior - Brasil (CAPES) - Finance Code 001.

Data Availibility Statement. The authors declare no competing interests.

Disclosure of Interests. All data and supplementary materials are available at https://github.com/LBS-UFMG/cyp2d6.

References

1. Saravanakumar, A., Sadighi, A., Ryu, R., Akhlaghi, F.: Physicochemical properties, biotransformation, and transport pathways of established and newly approved medications: a systematic review of the top 200 most prescribed drugs vs. the FDA-approved drugs between 2005 and 2016. Clin. Pharmacokinet **58**, 1281–1294 (2019)
2. McInnes, G., et al.: Transfer learning enables prediction of CYP2D6 haplotype function. PLoS Comput. Biol. **16**, e1008399 (2020)
3. Gaedigk, A., Simon, S.D., Pearce, R.E., Bradford, L.D., Kennedy, M.J., Leeder, J.S.: The CYP2D6 activity score: translating genotype information into a qualitative measure of phenotype. Clin. Pharmacol. Ther. **83**, 234–242 (2008)
4. Hicks, J.K., Swen, J.J., Gaedigk, A.: Challenges in CYP2D6 phenotype assignment from genotype data: a critical assessment and call for standardization. Curr. Drug Metab. **15**, 218–232 (2014)
5. Crews, K., Gaedigk, A., Dunnenberger, H., Leeder, J., et al.: Clinical pharmacogenetics implementation consortium guidelines for cytochrome P450 2D6 genotype and codeine therapy: 2014 update. Clin. Pharmacol. Ther. **95**, 376–382 (2014)
6. Gaedigk, A.: Complexities of CYP2D6 gene analysis and interpretation. Int. Rev. Psychiatry **25**, 534–553 (2013)
7. Gaedigk, A., Ingelman-Sundberg, M., Miller, N.A., Leeder, J.S., Whirl-Carrillo, M., Klein, T.E.: PharmVar steering committee. the Pharmacogene variation (PharmVar) consortium: incorporation of the human cytochrome P450 (CYP) allele nomenclature database. Clin. Pharmacol. Ther. **103**, 399–401 (2018)
8. Owen, R.P., Sangkuhl, K., Klein, T.E., Altman, R.B.: Cytochrome P450 2D6. Pharmacogenet. Genomics **19**, 559–562 (2009)
9. Hicks, J.K., et al.: Clinical pharmacogenetics implementation consortium guideline for CYP2D6 and CYP2C19 genotypes and dosing of tricyclic antidepressants. Clin. Pharmacol. Ther. **93**, 402–408 (2013)
10. Ingelman-Sundberg, M.: Genetic polymorphisms of cytochrome P450 2D6 (CYP2D6): clinical consequences, evolutionary aspects and functional diversity. Pharmacogenomics J. **5**, 6–13 (2005)
11. Chou, W.H., et al.: Extension of a pilot study: impact from the cytochrome P450 2D6 polymorphism on outcome and costs associated with severe mental illness. J. Clin. Psychopharmacol. **20**, 246–251 (2000)
12. Libbrecht, M.W., Noble, W.S.: Machine learning applications in genetics and genomics. Nat. Rev. Genet. **16**, 321–332 (2015)
13. Garcia-Agundez, A., García-Martín, E., Eickhoff, C. (eds.) The potential of machine learning in pharmacogenetics, pharmacogenomics and pharmacoepidemiology. Front. Pharmacol. **13** (2022)
14. Nofziger, C., et al.: PharmVar GeneFocus: CYP2D6. Clin. Pharmacol. Ther. **107**, 154–170 (2020)
15. Jumper, J., et al.: Highly accurate protein structure prediction with AlphaFold. Nature **596**, 583–589 (2021)
16. Pires, D.E.V., de Melo-Minardi, R.C., da Silveira, C.H., Campos, F.F., Meira, W.: aCSM: noise-free graph-based signatures to large-scale receptor-based ligand prediction. Bioinformatics **29**, 855–861 (2013)
17. Pires, D., de Melo-Minardi, R., dos Santos, M.A., Silveira, C., Santoro, M., Meira, W.: Cutoff scanning matrix (CSM): structural classification and function prediction by protein inter-residue distance patterns. BMC Genomics **12**, S12 (2011)

18. Mirdita, M., Schütze, K., Moriwaki, Y.; Heo, L., Ovchinnikov, S., Steinegger, M.: ColabFold: making protein folding accessible to all. Nat. Methods (2022)
19. Mariano, D.; Santos, L.H.; Machado, K.D.S.; Werhli, A.V.; de Lima, L.H.F.; de Melo-Minardi, R.C.: A Computational method to propose mutations in enzymes based on structural signature variation (SSV). Int. J. Mol. Sci. **20** (2019). https://doi.org/10.3390/ijms20020333
20. Demšar, J., Zupan, B., Leban, G., Curk, T.: Orange: from experimental machine learning to interactive data mining, pp. 537–539. Springer (2004)
21. McCulloch, W.S., Pitts, W.: A logical calculus of the ideas immanent in nervous activity. Bull. Math. Biophys. **5**, 115–133 (1943)
22. Cox, D.R.: The regression analysis of binary sequences. J. R. Stat. Soc. Ser. B Stat Methodol. **20**, 215–232 (1958)
23. Fix, E.: Discriminatory analysis: nonparametric discrimination, consistency properties. USAF School of Aviation Medicine, vol. 1 (1985)
24. Vapnik, V.: The Nature of Statistical Learning Theory. Springer Science & Business Media (2013). ISBN 1-4757-3264-3
25. Breiman, L.: Random Forests. Mach. Learn. **45**, 5–32 (2001)
26. Friedman, J.H.: Greedy function approximation: a gradient boosting machine. Ann. Stat., 1189–1232 (2001)
27. Breiman, L., Friedman, J., Olshen, R., Stone, C.: Classification and regression trees, Florida, Boca Raton (1984)
28. Cover, T.M., Thomas, J.A.: Elements of Information Theory. Wiley (2012)
29. Azhagusundari, B., Thanamani, A.S.: Feature Sel. Inf. Gain. Int. J. Innov. Technol. Exploring Eng. (IJITEE) **2**, 18–21 (2013)
30. Martins, P., et al.: Propedia v2.3: a novel representation approach for the peptide-protein interaction database using graph-based structural signatures. Front. Bioinf. **3** (2023)
31. dos Santos, L., Mariano, D., Bastos, L., Cioletti, A., Minardi, R.: Peptide-protein interface classification using convolutional neural networks, pp. 112–122 (2023). ISBN 978-3-031-42714-5
32. Heberle, H., Meirelles, G.V., da Silva, F.R., Telles, G.P., Minghim, R.: InteractiVenn: a web-based tool for the analysis of sets through venn diagrams. BMC Bioinf. **16**, 169 (2015)
33. Silvino, A.C.R., et al.: Variation in human cytochrome P-450 drug-metabolism genes: a gateway to the understanding of plasmodium vivax relapses. PLOS ONE **11**, e0160172 (2016)
34. Pires, D., Ascher, D., Blundell, T.: mCSM: predicting the effects of mutations in proteins using graph-based signatures. Bioinformatics **30**, 335–342 (2014)
35. Google DeepMind AlphaFold: A Solution to a 50-Year-Old Grand Challenge in Biology. https://deepmind.google/discover/blog/alphafold-a-solution-to-a-50-year-old-grand-challenge-in-biology/. Accessed 3 Apr 2024
36. AlQuraishi, M.: AlphaFold at CASP13. Bioinformatics **35**, 4862–4865 (2019)
37. Zwanzig, R., Szabo, A., Bagchi, B.: Levinthal's Paradox. Proc. Natl. Acad. Sci. **89**, 20–22 (1992)
38. Mariano, D.: A machine learning approach for the prediction of thermostable β-Glucosidases. Appl. Sci. **15**(9), 4839 (2025). https://doi.org/10.3390/app15094839

Immune Remodeling and Dysbiosis May Distinguish the Microenvironments of Gastric Adenocarcinoma and Peritumoral Tissue

Ronald Matheus da Silva Mourão[1,2,3]([✉]), Juliana Barreto Albuquerque Pinto[1,2,3], Jéssica Manoelli Costa da Silva[1,2,3], Daniel de Souza Avelar da Costa[1,2,3], Valéria Cristiane Santos da Silva[1,2,3], Ana Karyssa Mendes Anaissi[1,3], Samia Demachki[1,3], Williams Fernandes Barra[1,3], Fabiano Cordeiro Moreira[1,2,3], and Paulo Pimentel de Assumpção[1,2,3]

[1] Núcleo de Pesquisas em Oncologia, Federal University of Pará, Belém, PA, Brazil
ronald.mourao@icb.ufpa.br
[2] Graduate Program in Genetics and Molecular Biology, Federal University of Pará, Belém, PA, Brazil
[3] Human and Medical Genetics Laboratory, Federal University of Pará, Belém, PA, Brazil

Abstract. The gastric tumor microenvironment is dynamically shaped by the interactions between the local microbiota and the host immune system, although the functional integration of these elements remains incompletely understood. In this study, we characterized microbial diversity, immune cell composition, and immune-related gene expression profiles in samples of gastric adenocarcinoma (GAC) and adjacent peritumoral tissue (PTT), aiming to elucidate their functional organization. A total of 106 samples of 75 patients were analyzed using bulk RNA-Seq expression profiling, immune deconvolution, and bacterial taxonomic reconstruction. While alpha diversity remained preserved between GAC and PTT, distinct compositional differences emerged: GAC was enriched with *Pseudomonadota, Enterobacteriaceae*, and *Escherichia*, whereas PTT exhibited a predominance of *Helicobacteraceae* and *Helicobacter*. Immune deconvolution revealed an expansion of cancer-associated fibroblasts (CAFs) and mast cells in GAC, correlated with higher expression levels of *TGFB1* and *FOXP3*, while neutrophils and B cells predominated in PTT. Integrated analysis demonstrated that GAC formed dense and cohesive networks connecting pro-inflammatory bacteria, activated immune cells, and inflammatory genes such as *IL1B*, *CXCL8*, and *IFNG*. In contrast, PTT exhibited dispersed networks and negative correlations, suggesting a less structured, tolerogenic environment. Our findings indicate that gastric cancer progression involves not only compositional shifts in microbiota and immune cells but also the active construction of functionally integrated inflammatory networks, providing new insights into potential therapeutic targets at the microbiome–immune interface.

Keywords: Gastric cancer · Tumor microenvironment · Microbiome · Microbiome-immune interactions

© The Author(s), under exclusive license to Springer Nature Switzerland AG 2026
M. Dorn and F. Martins Lopes (Eds.): X-Meeting 2025, LNBI 16037, pp. 106–121, 2026.
https://doi.org/10.1007/978-3-032-09336-3_8

1 Introduction

Gastric adenocarcinoma (GAC) is a multifactorial epithelial malignancy whose progression involves not only intrinsic genetic alterations within tumor cells but also progressive reprogramming of the surrounding tissue microenvironment [1–3]. Within this context, the immune-inflammatory axis and the influence of the microbiome have emerged as central elements in the transition from inflamed mucosa to established tumor states [4, 5]. Chronic activation of the immune system, phenotypic remodeling of fibroblasts, and the presence of specialized bacterial consortia collectively contribute to the creation of a permissive environment for carcinogenesis and immune evasion [6].

Functional compartmentalization of the gastric microenvironment - segregating inflammatory responses, adaptive immunity, and microbial stimuli - is a critical feature of tissue homeostasis [7]. As tumor progression advances, this compartmentalized architecture tends to collapse, fostering the overlap of chronic inflammation, immunosuppression, and bacterial dysbiosis [2]. Previous studies have demonstrated that immune infiltration in GAC is marked by signs of functional exhaustion and a predominance of tolerogenic inflammatory profiles, in contrast to the more balanced environment observed in peritumoral tissues [8]. However, the spatial and functional dynamics of microbiome, immunity, and gene expression interactions during gastric tumor progression remain poorly understood.

The gastric microbiome, traditionally associated with *Helicobacter pylori*, is now recognized as a broader and more dynamic ecosystem capable of modulating inflammatory pathways, altering local cellular profiles, and influencing tumor evolution [9–11]. Certain microbial communities promote immunosuppressive environments, whereas others drive pro-inflammatory activation, directly reshaping the functional architecture of the microenvironment [12]. The tripartite interaction between epithelium, immunity, and microbiota thus emerges as a key axis in configuring the functional heterogeneity of gastric tissues.

Understanding how microbial and immune networks organize - or become disorganized - during GAC progression is critical for identifying therapeutic intervention points [13]. This study aims to delineate the functional integration among the microbiome, cellular composition, and gene expression profiles in gastric adenocarcinoma and adjacent peritumoral tissue, characterizing the structural transitions of the microenvironment associated with tumor progression.

2 Material and Methods

2.1 Sample Characterization and Ethical Considerations

In this study, tumor and adjacent peritumoral tissue (PTT) samples were collected from patients diagnosed with GAC, the most common type of gastric cancer. A total of 75 patients were analyzed, comprising 62 GACs tissues and 44 PTT samples. The cohort included 29 female and 45 male patients and 1 patient with unreported gender. GAC samples were staged according to the ypTNM classification: Of the patients for whom staging information was available, 6 were classified as stage I, 18 as stage II, 32 as stage III, and 3 as stage IV. Recruitment and sample collection were conducted between

July 2, 2022, and July 6, 2023, at the João de Barros Barreto University Hospital in Belém, Brazil. The study objectives were clearly explained to all participants, who provided written informed consent. The study was conducted in accordance with the Declaration of Helsinki and approved by the Ethics Committee of the João de Barros Barreto University Hospital (approval number: 47580121.9.0000.5634).

2.2   RNA Extraction and Quality Assessment

Approximately 50–100 mg of tissue from each sample were macerated, followed by the addition of 1 mL of TRIZOL® reagent to facilitate RNA extraction. The integrity and concentration of total RNA were evaluated using Qubit 4.0 (Thermo Fisher Scientific) and NanoDrop ND-1000 (Thermo Fisher Scientific) fluorometers. Optimal criteria for total RNA integrity were considered met when samples exhibited an A260/A280 ratio between 1.8 and 2.2, an A260/A230 ratio greater than 1.8, and an RNA Integrity Number (RIN) $\geq$ 5. This threshold was selected to accommodate the inherent variability in RNA quality from clinical tissue samples, ensuring the inclusion of a representative cohort while maintaining data reliability.

2.3   CDNA Library Construction and Sequencing

The TruSeq Stranded Total RNA Library Prep Kit with Ribo-Zero Gold (Illumina) was used to remove cytoplasmic and mitochondrial rRNA. Libraries were processed using the NextSeq® 500 High Output V2 kit - 150 cycles (Illumina), following the manufacturer's specifications. After library construction, a new assessment of RNA integrity was performed using the 2200 TapeStation System (Agilent). The cDNA libraries were then loaded onto the Illumina NextSeq sequencing platform and sequenced in paired-end mode.

2.4   Quality, Alignment, Quantification and Transcriptome Expression

Read quality was assessed using FastQC (v0.11.9), and low-quality reads and adapter sequences were removed with Trimommatic, applying a minimum Phred quality threshold of QV15. QV15 was selected as a pragmatic threshold, given that Salmon's k-mer-based pseudoalignment is robust to moderate base quality variation. Filtered reads were quantified at the transcript level using Salmon (v1.5.2) [14] against the human transcriptome reference (hg38). Transcript abundances were imported using the Tximport [3], and a DESeq2 [15] object was created to normalize gene expression levels, accounting for tissue type (GAC or PTT) and sequencing batch effects. Variance-stabilized (VST) and batch-corrected expression values were used for subsequent analyses.

2.5 Selection of Immune-Related Genes

A curated panel of immune-related genes was assembled to investigate key processes within the tumor microenvironment and host-microbiome interactions. The selection was informed by comprehensive immunological databases, such as MSigDB, and was further refined based on our group's previous unpublished study. The panel included classical immune checkpoints (*PDCD1, CD274, CTLA4, LAG3, HAVCR2, CD47*), pro-inflammatory cytokines and mediators (*IFNG, TNF, IL6, IL1B, CXCL8, CCL2, CCL5*), regulatory and immunosuppressive markers (*IL10, TGFB1, FOXP3*), macrophage and myeloid cell markers (*CD163, CD68, CD86, CD83*), signaling molecules involved in immune activation and regulation (*STAT3, MYD88, NFKB1*), as well as genes associated with antigen presentation (*B2M, HLA.A*), epithelial plasticity (*SOX9*), angiogenesis (*VEGFA*), and mucosal immune defense (*PIGR*). This focused selection allowed a comprehensive assessment of inflammatory activation, immune regulation, stromal remodeling, and adaptive responses.

2.6 Microbiome

Microbiome characterization was performed by taxonomic classification of RNA-Seq reads using Kraken2 (v2.1.4) [16] against the comprehensive PlusPF database. The primary focus of this study was to quantify bacterial microbiome expressions associated with GAC. To achieve this, relevant bacterial genomes were obtained from the RefSeq database, and Salmon (v1.10.1) was used to quantify expression by aligning reads against these genomes. The resulting expression counts were used to estimate bacterial abundance.

To prioritize the most representative bacterial genera across samples, we computed an abundance score that integrates both dominance and prevalence (Eq. 1) [17]. For each sample, genera were ranked in descending order based on their absolute abundance. The mean rank of each genus across all samples in which it was detected ($\overline{R_g}$) was then multiplied by a frequency-based penalty factor ($1.1 - f_g$), where f_g represents the proportion of samples in which that genus was present. The constant 1.1 was introduced to avoid disproportionately penalizing highly prevalent genera, ensuring that those consistently detected and highly ranked retained meaningful scores. This composite metric favored genera that were not only abundant in individual samples but also broadly distributed across the dataset.

$$Score_g = \overline{R_g} \times \left(1.1 - f_g\right) \tag{1}$$

Based on this criterion, the 15 most abundant genera were selected to effectively represent the most relevant taxa for downstream analyses. Additionally, genera with recognized roles in microbiome-immune interactions and tumor biology - such as *Parvimonas, Peptostreptococcus, Campylobacter, Actinomyces, Escherichia, Klebsiella, Streptococcus, Helicobacter, Prevotella, Halomonas, Pseudomonas, Sphingomonas, Lactobacillus, Shewanella, Acinetobacter, Corynebacterium, Bacillus, Neisseria, Leptotrichia, Veillonella, Bacteroides, Faecalibacterium, Bifidobacterium, Chryseobacterium, Oscillospira, Haemophilus, Actinobacillus, Staphylococcus, Lactococcus, Porphyromonas,*

Propionibacterium, and *Fusobacterium* - were also included, based both on published evidence and prior findings from our research group. Alpha diversity analysis was conducted using the Shannon, Chao1, and Observed indices, with group comparisons performed using the Wilcoxon rank-sum test and $p \leq 0.05$. The *microbiome* package was used to estimate sample diversity between GAC and PTT groups.

2.7 Cellular Deconvolution

Cellular deconvolution was performed using three computational tools: CIBERSORT [18], quanTIseq [19], and EPIC [20]. The LM22 immune cell signature file was loaded, and gene expression data were normalized to generate a TPM (Transcripts Per Million) matrix. The CIBERSORT function was employed to estimate cell composition, and the run_quantiseq function was applied for additional cellular composition estimation in tumor samples. The EPIC package was used to calculate cellular fractions across the samples. The results from each tool were integrated to generate a comprehensive deconvolution table of immune cell fractions. Differences in cell proportions between GAC and PTT groups were assessed using the Wilcoxon test, with Benjamini-Hochberg correction for multiple testing (FDR ≤ 0.05).

2.8 Hierarchical Clustering

The dataset - comprising immune-related genes, inferred immune cell fractions, and relative abundances of bacterial genera - was transposed so that variables became rows, enabling the analysis of their similarities. To enable meaningful comparisons across variables with different scales and units, the data was first log2-transformed and subsequently standardized using z-scores.

The distance matrix between variables was calculated using standard Euclidean distance, and hierarchical clustering was performed using the Ward.D2 method, which minimizes the total variance within clusters. Cluster structure visualization was performed with the *fviz_dend* function from the *factoextra* package, using the "rectangle" type combined with the "layout.gem" radial layout.

Interpretation of the dendrogram focused exclusively on tree topology, considering the visual proximity of elements as indicative of relative functional similarity, as reflected in the original distance matrix. Closely clustered groups were interpreted as functionally related modules, whereas distant branches suggested differentiation among cellular, genetic, or microbial profiles within the GAC and PTT microenvironments.

2.9 Statistical Analyses

Correlations among bacterial abundance, gene expression, and immune cell fractions were evaluated using Spearman's correlation. A threshold of |rho| > 0.3 and $p \leq 0.05$ was retained in line with exploratory objectives and biomedical literature precedent. Additional statistical tests, such as the Wilcoxon test, were conducted to compare differences between experimental groups. Result visualizations, including boxplots, bar graphs, and significant correlations, were generated using the *ggplot2*, *ggcorrplot*, and *cowplot* packages.

3   Results

3.1   Microbiome

Alpha diversity analysis revealed no significant differences in Shannon indices between GAC and PTT (p = 0.6; Fig. 1A), suggesting no notable variation in ecological heterogeneity between the two tissue types. Similarly, species richness measures did not differ between GAC and PTT (Fig. 1B), supporting the notion of a global stability in microbial complexity.

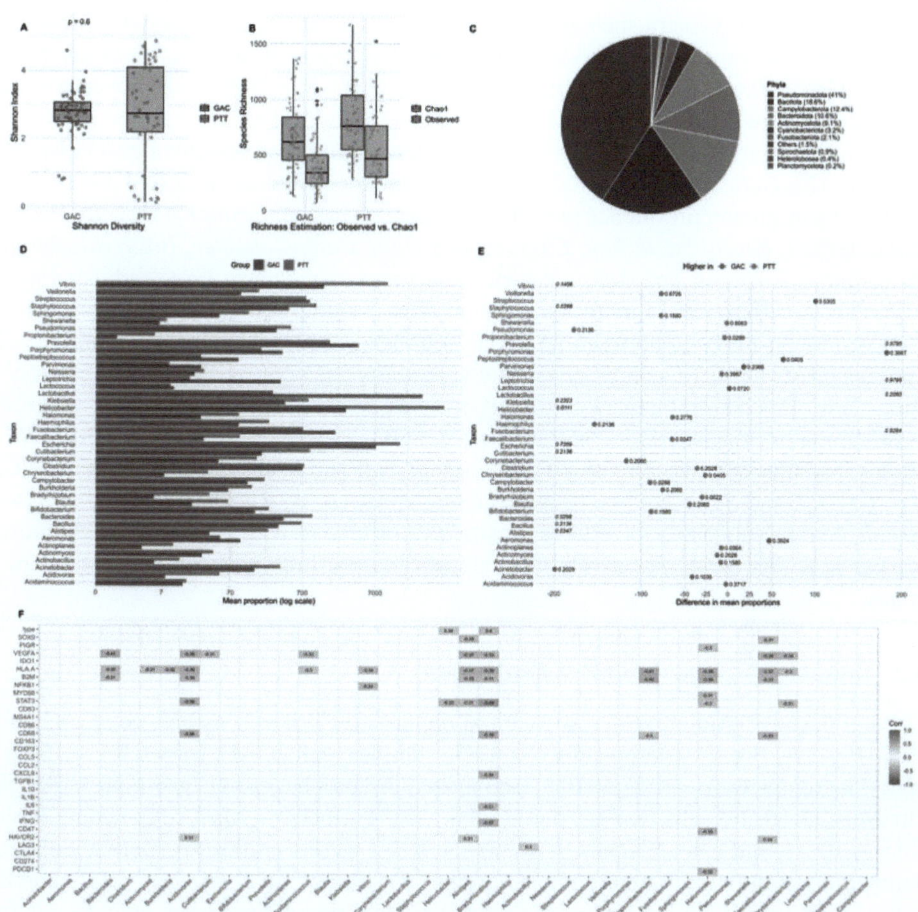

Fig. 1. Bacterial microbiome analyses: (A) Shannon diversity index; (B) Species richness estimates (Observed and Chao1); (C) Relative abundance of major bacterial phyla; (D) Relative abundance of predominant bacterial genera; (E) Mean difference in genus abundance between GAC and PTT samples. (F) Correlation between bacterial abundance and the expression of immune response genes across all samples (GAC and PTT combined).

Regarding taxonomic composition, the phylum *Pseudomonadota* was the most dominant, accounting for 41% of the total, followed by *Bacillota* (18.6%), *Campylobacterota* (12.4%), and *Bacteroidota* (10.6%) (Fig. 1C). At the family level, *Enterobacteriaceae* was the most abundant, representing 17.8% of the total microbiota and associated with GAC (66.4% of its fraction). In contrast, *Helicobacteraceae* was markedly more prevalent in PTT (76.3% of its relative abundance). *Lactobacillaceae* (4.4%) and *Streptococcaceae* (2.0%) were also more prominent in GAC (88.8% and 80.5%, respectively) (Fig. 4A, see Appendix A).

Among genera, *Escherichia* emerged as the most abundant (12.7% of the total), with 68% of its representation in GAC. Conversely, *Helicobacter* concentrated 76.3% of its abundance in PTT. Genera such as *Prevotella* (68.2% GAC) and *Lactobacillus* (88.7% GAC) were also more associated with the tumor environment, whereas *Cutibacterium* (39.4% GAC, 60.6% PTT) and *Rhizobium* (44.7% GAC, 55.3% PTT) displayed a more balanced distribution (Fig. 1D).

Differential abundance analysis between genera highlighted several relevant disparities (Fig. 1E). *Helicobacter* showed a highly significant difference (adjusted $p < 0.001$), confirming its greater prevalence in PTT. Other genera, including *Staphylococcus, Propionibacterium, Faecalibacterium, Chryseobacterium, Campylobacter, Bradyrhizobium, Bacteroides, Alistipes*, and *Actinoplanes*, were more abundant in GAC (adjusted $p < 0.05$). These differences remained significant after multiple-testing correction.

Correlation analysis between bacterial abundance and gene expression across all samples (GAC and PTT combined) revealed patterns characterized by negative associations (Fig. 1F). Several genera exhibited inverse correlations with key genes involved in inflammatory responses and antigen presentation, including *Bacteroides* with *B2M*, *HLA.A*, and *VEGFA*; *Vibrio* with *NFKB1* and *HLA.A*; and *Bradyrhizobium* with *IFNG*, *IL6*, *CXCL8*, and *STAT3*. Some genera, such as *Acidovorax, Alistipes*, and *Faecalibacterium*, demonstrated mixed patterns, positively correlating with the immunoregulatory marker *HAVCR2* while negatively correlating with pro-inflammatory and angiogenic genes.

3.2 Immune Microenvironment Estimation

Cellular deconvolution revealed substantial quantitative differences between GAC and PTT (Fig. 2A; Fig. 5, see appendix). In GAC samples, epic_CAFs ($p = 6.83 \times 10^{-9}$), epic_Macrophages ($p = 1.53 \times 10^{-3}$), quantiseq_Macrophages.M1 ($p = 6.40 \times 10^{-4}$), cibersort_Dendritic cells resting ($p = 4.92 \times 10^{-2}$), cibersort_Mast cells resting ($p = 1.45 \times 10^{-2}$), and epic_NKcells ($p = 8.09 \times 10^{-3}$) were significantly more abundant, delineating a tumor microenvironment enriched in stromal, myeloid, mast cell, and NK cell populations. In PTT samples, the most abundant populations were epic_Bcells ($p = 1.63 \times 10^{-2}$), quantiseq_B.cells ($p = 1.63 \times 10^{-2}$), epic_CD8_Tcells ($p = 4.92 \times 10^{-2}$), and cibersort_Neutrophils ($p = 1.63 \times 10^{-2}$), composing a more effector and inflammatory immune profile in this tissue.

Global analysis of cellular proportions, considering all samples together, showed that cibersort_Mast cells resting comprised the largest fraction (30%), followed by quantiseq_B.cells (19.5%), epic_CAFs (13%), quantiseq_Macrophages.M1 (11.4%), and epic_CD8_Tcells (8.1%) (Fig. 5, see appendix). These results indicate that in GAC

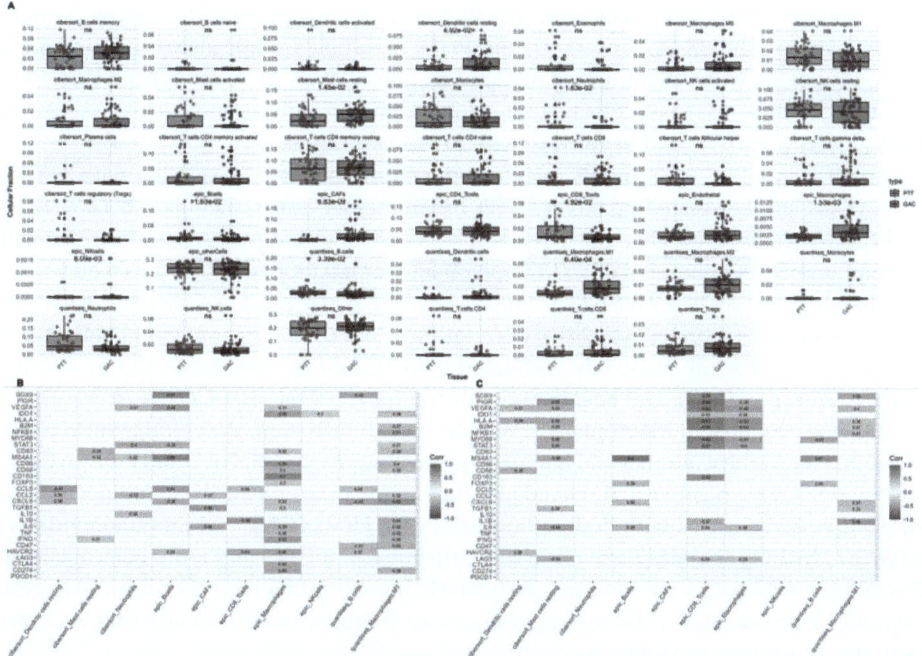

Fig. 2. Immune deconvolution analyses GAC PTT: (A) Mean differences in immune cell proportions between GAC and PTT groups; (B) Correlations between immune cell proportions and immune response gene expression in GAC samples; (C) Correlations between immune cell proportions and immune response gene expression in PTT samples.

and its PTT, the cellular landscape is dominated by stromal components, B lymphocytes, and myeloid cells.

Comparative analysis between GAC and PTT revealed notable structural contrasts. In GAC, a predominance of epic_CAFs (88.4%), cibersort_Dendritic cells resting (77.5%), epic_NKcells (78.1%), cibersort_Mast cells resting (68.7%), epic_Macrophages (72.8%), and quantiseq_Macrophages.M1 (75.8%) was observed, configuring a microenvironment dominated by stromal, myeloid, and mast cell populations. Although the overall proportion of epic_CD8_Tcells was lower in GAC compared to PTT, some tumor samples exhibited significant infiltration of cytotoxic T lymphocytes, suggesting intratumoral heterogeneity. In PTT, the most representative populations included cibersort_Neutrophils (83.2%), epic_Bcells (56.1%), and epic_CD8_Tcells (59.1%) (Fig. 5, see appendix), reflecting a more effector-dominant microenvironment, characterized by greater infiltration of adaptive immune cells and localized inflammatory responses.

Correlation analysis between cellular composition and gene expression corroborated the structural patterns observed (Figs. 2B–2C). In GAC samples, epic_CAFs showed positive correlations with immunosuppressive and extracellular matrix-modulating genes, notably *TGFB1* ($\rho = 0.56$) and *IL6* ($\rho = 0.46$). Quantiseq_Macrophages.M1 were strongly associated with inflammatory genes, including *CXCL8* ($\rho = 0.62$), *IL1B* ($\rho = 0.44$), *TNF* ($\rho = 0.42$), and *NFKB1* ($\rho = 0.51$), as well as with antigen-regulatory genes such as *CD86* and *CD83*. Epic_Bcells positively correlated with adaptive immune genes, particularly *MS4A1* ($\rho = 0.69$) and *PIGR* ($\rho = 0.48$), while also displaying negative correlations with inflammatory markers such as *CXCL8* ($\rho = -0.36$) and *VEGFA* ($\rho = -0.48$). Cibersort_Mast cells resting exhibited mixed patterns, positively associating with *IFNG* ($\rho = 0.31$) and negatively with *MS4A1* ($\rho = -0.32$).

In PTT samples, epic_Bcells maintained a strong positive correlation with *MS4A1* ($\rho = 0.80$) and correlated positively with inflammatory genes such as *IL6* ($\rho = 0.36$) and *CXCL8* ($\rho = 0.36$). Quantiseq_Macrophages.M1 showed positive associations with pro-inflammatory genes, notably *IL1B* ($\rho = 0.58$) and *CXCL8* ($\rho = 0.37$), as well as with regulatory genes such as *TGFB1* ($\rho = 0.33$) and *NFKB1* ($\rho = 0.41$). Cibersort_Dendritic cells resting demonstrated a positive correlation with *HAVCR2* ($\rho = 0.36$), while cibersort_Mast cells resting positively correlated with *TGFB1* ($\rho = 0.38$), *STAT3* ($\rho = 0.46$), and *VEGFA* ($\rho = 0.42$), and negatively with *IL6* ($\rho = -0.44$) and *CD274* ($\rho = -0.35$).

Overall, quantiseq_Macrophages.M1 and epic_Bcells were the cellular subsets that exhibited the highest number and intensity of correlations in both GAC and PTT. In GAC, associations were positive and related to inflammatory axes. In PTT, a combined pattern of positive correlations with both inflammatory (*IL1B*, *CXCL8*) and immunoregulatory (*TGFB1*, *HAVCR2*) genes were observed, reflecting a functionally more heterogeneous environment. Negative correlations, particularly involving cibersort_Dendritic cells resting and cibersort_Mast cells resting, were more frequent in PTT, suggesting localized patterns of immune modulation.

3.3   Integration of the Microbial, Immune and Genetic Axis

Integrated analysis of the gene expression, immune cells, and microbiota in GAC and PTT revealed highly organized patterns of interaction, supported by robust correlations. In GAC, the formation of an immunoregulatory cluster composed of *IDO1*, *FOXP3*, *HAVCR2*, *IL10*, and *LAG3* stood out, reflecting the activation of immune suppression programs within the tumor microenvironment (Fig. 3A). The correlation between *IDO1* and *FOXP3* (r = 0.57) and the coexpression of *PIGR* and *MS4A1* (r = 0.35) (Fig. 3B) further reinforce the robustness of this regulatory signature. Methodological convergence in the detection of B cells, as evidenced by the strong correlation between *quantiseq_B.cells* and *epic_Bcells* (r = 0.74), adds additional consistency to these observations. In parallel, an inflammatory cluster consolidated the activation of effector immune response pathways, with associations between *IFNG* and *CD274* (r = 0.50), *CD86* and *CTLA4* (r = 0.63), and *CXCL8* and *IL1B* (r = 0.80), outlining an acute inflammatory environment associated with immune checkpoint activation.

Microbiome structuring revealed two distinct bacterial axes. A cluster of pathogenic oral bacteria, including *Fusobacterium, Prevotella, Porphyromonas, Haemophilus*, and *Veillonella*, exhibited strong co-occurrences, suggesting the formation of biofilms associated with tumor progression. Another cluster, composed of commensal and environmental bacteria such as *Blautia, Faecalibacterium, Bacteroides, Pseudomonas*, and *Escherichia*, indicated the coexistence of diverse ecological communities within the tumor microenvironment. *Helicobacter* showed relevant integration into both bacterial networks, linking to oral species (*Veillonella, Streptococcus*) and environmental species

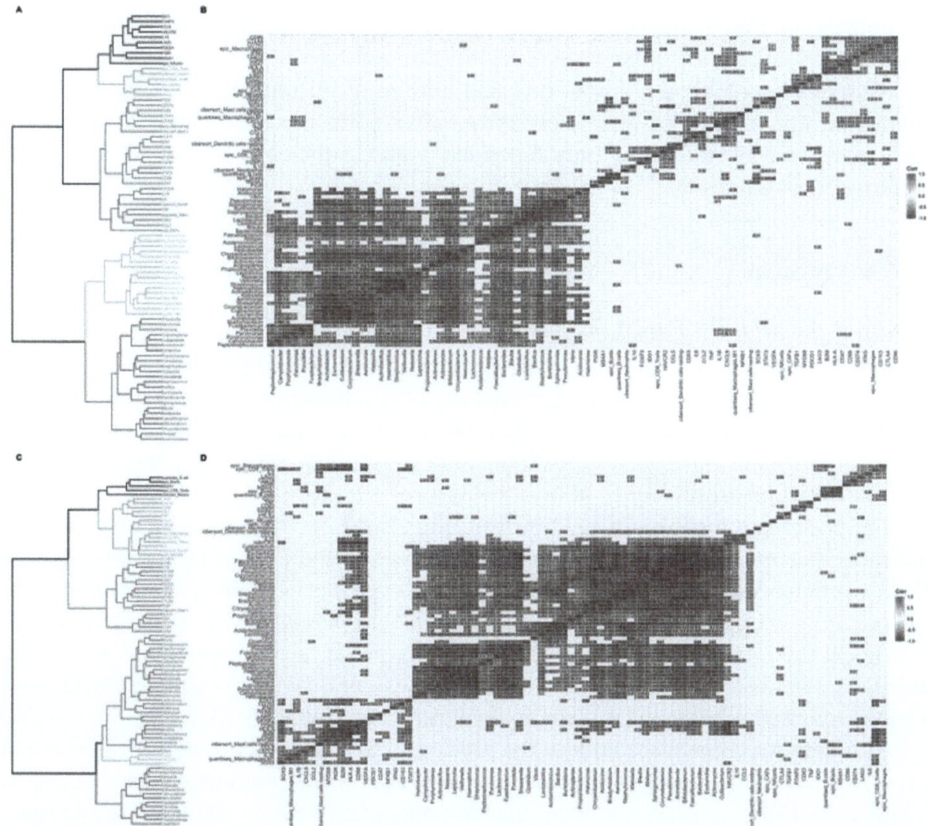

Fig. 3. Integrated analysis of microbiome, immune cells, and gene expression in GAC and PTT: (A) Hierarchical clustering of bacterial genera, immune cell fractions, and immune-related genes in GAC samples; (B) Correlation matrix illustrating significant associations among bacterial abundance, immune cell fractions, and gene expression in GAC; (C) Hierarchical clustering of bacterial genera, immune cell fractions, and immune-related genes in PTT samples; (D) Correlation matrix illustrating significant associations among bacterial abundance, immune cell fractions, and gene expression in PTT.

(*Pseudomonas, Escherichia*), suggesting its participation in complex microbial consortia within GAC.

In PTT analysis, the preservation of functional clusters was evident (Fig. 3C). The potential adaptive immune cluster involving *quantiseq_B.cells*, *epic_Bcells*, and *MS4A1* stood out, indicating the persistence of adaptive responses in adjacent tissue, supported by strong correlations (r = 0.80 and r = 0.72) (Fig. 3D).

Regarding the PTT microbiome, clusters of oral and environmental bacteria were evidenced by strong co-occurrences between *Alistipes* and *Faecalibacterium* (r = 0.87), *Fusobacterium* and *Leptotrichia* (r = 0.83), and *Prevotella* and *Neisseria* (r = 0.74). The integration of *Helicobacter* into PTT bacterial networks further supports the hypothesis of complex microbial adaptations occurring not only within tumors but also in adjacent tissues.

Although topological analysis revealed clustering in both tissue types, statistical validation indicated that not all observed proximities corresponded to robust associations, particularly in PTT; therefore, only functionally and statistically supported cores were emphasized in the results.

4 Discussion

This study revealed that although global bacterial microbiome diversity and richness are preserved between GAC and PTT, taxonomic composition and functional organization of the microenvironments diverge substantially [21]. These findings suggest that gastric tumor progression may involve not only a preservation of microbial heterogeneity, but also compositional shifts in bacterial consortia potentially driven by tumor-associated environmental pressures.

The preservation of Shannon, Observed, and Chao1 indices between GAC and PTT indicates that global ecological complexity is maintained during tumor progression. However, the redistribution of relative abundances - with enrichment of *Pseudomonadota* and *Bacillota* in GAC and Campylobacterota and Bacteroidota in PTT - points to selective ecological reprogramming. Conditions such as hypoxia, acidification, and nutritional imbalances in GAC likely function as selective pressures, favoring bacterial phyla more adapted to inflammatory and metabolically hostile environments [22].

At a finer taxonomic resolution, the greater abundance of *Enterobacteriaceae* and *Escherichia* in GAC, along with positive correlations with inflammatory genes such as *IFNG* and *CD86*, suggests that these bacteria may contribute to maintaining a chronic inflammatory state permissive to tumorigenesis [23]. In contrast, the predominance of *Helicobacteraceae* and *Helicobacter* in PTT, along with negative correlations with *IFNG* and *IL6*, may reflect a more regulatory environment, potentially characteristic of an early stage of immune escape [24]. We propose that the replacement of *Helicobacter* by proinflammatory bacterial consortia represents a critical transition in the remodeling of the gastric microenvironment.

Immune composition analysis further reinforced this interpretation. In GAC, an enrichment of epic_CAFs and cibersort_Mast cells resting was observed, whereas in PTT, quantiseq_B.cells, epic_Bcells, and epic_CD8_Tcells predominated [25–27]. The strong correlation between epic_CAFs and *TGFB1* and *FOXP3* suggests that stromal fibrosis is integrated into immune suppression circuits within the tumor [28]. Conversely, the presence of adaptive B cells in PTT was corroborated by the strong correlation between quantiseq_B.cells and epic_Bcells (r = 0.74), indicating methodological consistency in the detection of this population. Importantly, this correlation reflects the identification of the same B cell population by distinct deconvolution methods (quanTIseq and EPIC).

Functional integration of the microbiome, cellular composition, and gene expression revealed the formation of highly organized pro-inflammatory axes in GAC [29]. The topological proximity of *Fusobacterium*, *Escherichia*, activated macrophages (quantiseq_Macrophages.M1), and genes such as *IL1B* [11], *CXCL8* [30], *IFNG* [30], and *TNF*

[31] outlines a dense functional architecture, indicating that tumor-associated inflammation may be an orchestrated rather than a random process [32–34]. We propose that these axes represent critical maintenance hubs, where microbiota and immunity cooperate to perpetuate chronic inflammation.

Conversely, in PTT, functional organization was more diffuse. The association of *Helicobacter*, resting dendritic cells (cibersort_Dendritic cells resting), and regulatory genes such as *TGFB1* and *IL10* suggests an immunomodulated microenvironment capable of containing inflammation at subclinical levels [35]. The preservation of functional compartmentalization in PTT contrasts with the collapse observed in GAC, suggesting that tumor progression may involve the gradual dissolution of these regulatory barriers [36].

These observations are reinforced by topological analyses showing spatial overlap of activated B cells, immunosuppressive macrophages, inflammatory myeloid cells, and oral bacteria in GAC, versus organized segregation between adaptive responses and commensal microbiota in PTT [37, 38]. This structural opposition suggests that gastric cancer progression may be driven not only by inflammatory expansion but also by the loss of functional compartmentalization among immunity, inflammation, and microbial stimuli.

These findings have relevant clinical implications. The identification of microbiome–immune consortia organized around inflammatory genes in GAC points to potential therapeutic strategies targeting the disruption of these networks - for instance, through microbiota modulation or stromal reprogramming - aiming to restore local immune surveillance. Future capabilities to map inflammatory hotspots in the gastric microenvironment may guide more precise local or systemic therapies.

However, certain limitations must be acknowledged. Bulk RNA-based approaches do not permit single-cell spatial resolution, and inferences drawn from deconvolution and correlation analyses, while robust, require additional experimental validation. Moreover, the lack of longitudinal data limits the evaluation of the temporal dynamics of the observed networks.

Despite these limitations, this study provides a new perspective on the functional interaction among the microbiome, immunity, and gastric cancer progression. By demonstrating that gastric carcinogenesis is associated not merely with compositional changes but with the active formation of organized inflammatory networks, our findings propose new paradigms for the understanding and therapeutic targeting of the disease.

Acknowledgments. The authors express their gratitude to CAPES (Coordenação de Aperfeiçoamento de Pessoal de Nível Superior) for providing a doctoral fellowship to R.M. da S. Mourão. We are also grateful to the High-Performance Computing Center (CCAD) at the Federal University of Pará for their support in computational resources. Furthermore, we acknowledge the Fundação Amazônia de Amparo a Estudos e Pesquisas (Fapespa) for the financial support that made this research possible.

Data Availability. The datasets generated and analyzed during the current study are available from the corresponding author on reasonable request.

Disclosure of Interests. The authors report no conflicts of interest related to this study.

Appendix A

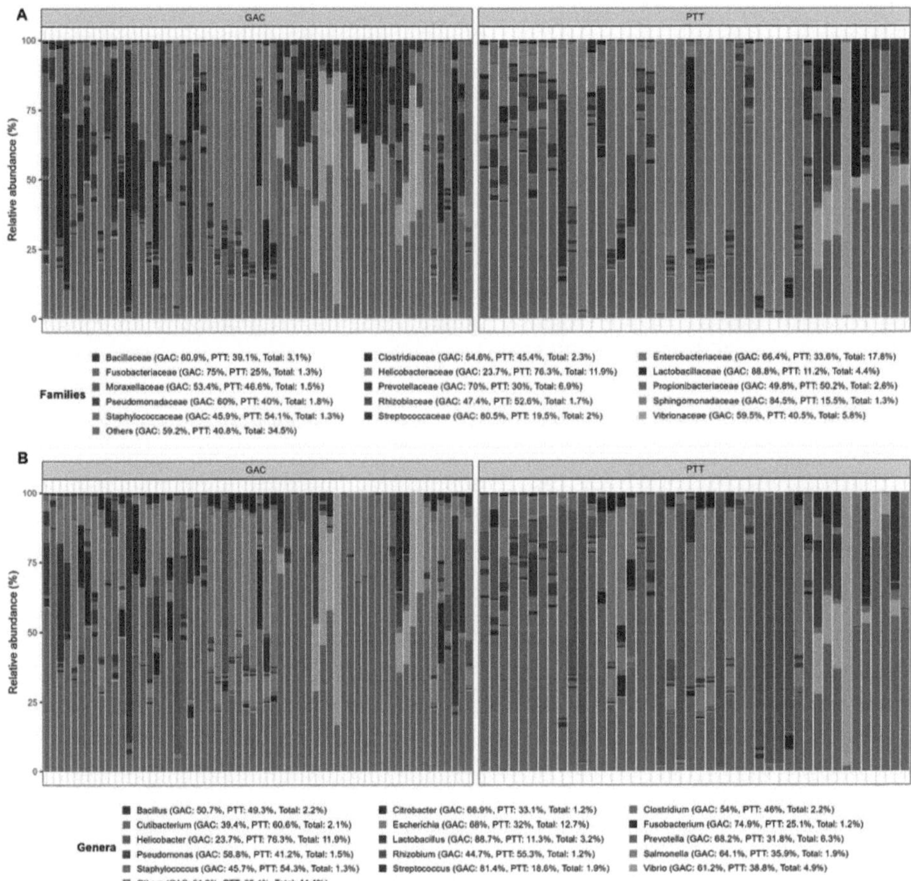

Fig. 4. Relative proportion of families and genera. (A) Relative abundance of predominant bacterial families; (B) Relative abundance of predominant bacterial genera. Each color represents a families or genera. Legends indicate the proportion of families or genera in GAC and PTT and Total

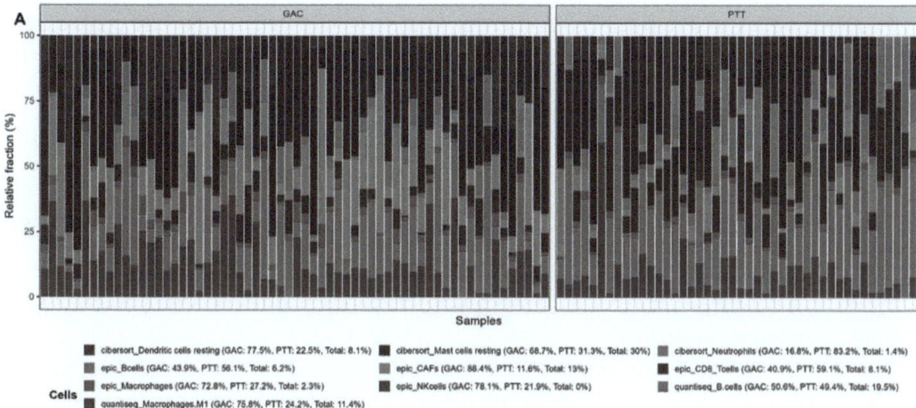

Fig. 5. Relative proportion of cell. Composition of immune cell fractions across individual samples. Each color represents a cell type identified by deconvolution analysis. Legends indicate the proportion of the cell types in GAC and PTT and Total;

References

1. Sathe, A., et al.: Single-cell genomic characterization reveals the cellular reprogramming of the gastric tumor microenvironment. Clin. Cancer Res. **26**, 2640–2653 (2020). https://doi.org/10.1158/1078-0432.CCR-19-3231

2. Jiang, X., et al.: Gastric microbiota and its role in gastric carcinogenesis. Malignancy Spectrum. **1**, 2–14 (2024). https://doi.org/10.1002/msp2.15

3. Soneson, C., Love, M.I., Robinson, M.D.: Differential analyses for RNA-seq: transcript-level estimates improve gene-level inferences. F1000Res. **4**, 1521 (2016). https://doi.org/10.12688/f1000research.7563.2

4. Yong, X., et al.: Helicobacter pylori virulence factor CagA promotes tumorigenesis of gastric cancer via multiple signaling pathways. Cell Commun. Signaling. **13**, 30 (2015). https://doi.org/10.1186/s12964-015-0111-0

5. Mager, L.F., Krause, T., McCoy, K.D.: Interaction of microbiota, mucosal malignancies, and immunotherapy—Mechanistic insights. Mucosal Immunol. **17**, 402–415 (2024). https://doi.org/10.1016/j.mucimm.2024.03.007

6. Motamed, R., et al.: Mesenchymal stem cells modulate breast cancer progression through their secretome by downregulating ten-eleven translocation 1. Sci. Rep. **15**, 6593 (2025). https://doi.org/10.1038/s41598-025-91314-3

7. Belkaid, Y., Harrison, O.J.: Homeostatic immunity and the microbiota. Immunity **46**, 562–576 (2017). https://doi.org/10.1016/j.immuni.2017.04.008

8. Ding, J.-T., Yang, K.-P., Zhou, H.-N., Huang, Y.-F., Li, H., Zong, Z.: Landscapes and mechanisms of CD8+ T cell exhaustion in gastrointestinal cancer. Front. Immunol. **14** (2023). https://doi.org/10.3389/fimmu.2023.1149622

9. Zeng, R., Gou, H., Lau, H.C.H., Yu, J.: Stomach microbiota in gastric cancer development and clinical implications. Gut **73**, 2062–2073 (2024). https://doi.org/10.1136/gutjnl-2024-332815

10. Liu, Z., Zhang, D., Chen, S.: Unveiling the gastric microbiota: implications for gastric carcinogenesis, immune responses, and clinical prospects. J. Exp. Clin. Cancer Res. **43**, 118 (2024). https://doi.org/10.1186/s13046-024-03034-7

11. Niikura, R., et al.: Non-helicobacter pylori gastric microbiome modulates prooncogenic responses and is associated with gastric cancer risk. Gastro Hep Adv. **2**, 684–700 (2023). https://doi.org/10.1016/j.gastha.2023.03.010

12. Noto, J.M., Peek, R.M.: The gastric microbiome, its interaction with helicobacter pylori, and its potential role in the progression to stomach cancer. PLoS Pathog. **13**, e1006573 (2017). https://doi.org/10.1371/journal.ppat.1006573

13. Zavros, Y., Merchant, J.L.: The immune microenvironment in gastric adenocarcinoma. Nat. Rev. Gastroenterol. Hepatol. **19**, 451–467 (2022). https://doi.org/10.1038/s41575-022-005 91-0

14. Patro, R., Duggal, G., Love, M.I., Irizarry, R.A., Kingsford, C.: Salmon provides fast and bias-aware quantification of transcript expression. Nat. Methods **14**, 417–419 (2017). https://doi.org/10.1038/nmeth.4197

15. Love, M.I., Huber, W., Anders, S.: Moderated estimation of fold change and dispersion for RNA-seq data with DESeq2. Genome Biol. **15**, 550 (2014). https://doi.org/10.1186/s13059-014-0550-8

16. Wood, D.E., Lu, J., Langmead, B.: Improved metagenomic analysis with Kraken 2. Genome Biol. **20**, 257 (2019). https://doi.org/10.1186/s13059-019-1891-0

17. Barra, W.F., et al.: Gastric cancer microbiome. Pathobiology **88**, 156–169 (2021). https://doi.org/10.1159/000512833

18. Newman, A.M., et al.: Robust enumeration of cell subsets from tissue expression profiles. Nat. Methods **12**, 453–457 (2015). https://doi.org/10.1038/nmeth.3337

19. Finotello, F., et al.: Molecular and pharmacological modulators of the tumor immune contexture revealed by deconvolution of RNA-seq data. Genome Med. **11**, 34 (2019). https://doi.org/10.1186/s13073-019-0638-6

20. Racle, J., Gfeller, D.: EPIC: a tool to estimate the proportions of different cell types from bulk gene expression data. Presented at the (2020). https://doi.org/10.1007/978-1-0716-0327-7_17

21. Stewart, O.A., Wu, F., Chen, Y.: The role of gastric microbiota in gastric cancer. Gut Microbes. **11**, 1220–1230 (2020). https://doi.org/10.1080/19490976.2020.1762520

22. Battaglia, T.W., et al.: A pan-cancer analysis of the microbiome in metastatic cancer. Cell **187**, 2324-2335.e19 (2024). https://doi.org/10.1016/j.cell.2024.03.021

23. Engstrand, L., Graham, D.Y.: Microbiome and gastric cancer. Dig. Dis. Sci. **65**, 865–873 (2020). https://doi.org/10.1007/s10620-020-06101-z

24. Li, X., Pan, K., Vieth, M., Gerhard, M., Li, W., Mejías-Luque, R.: JAK-STAT1 signaling pathway is an early response to helicobacter pylori infection and contributes to immune escape and gastric carcinogenesis. Int. J. Mol. Sci. **23**, 4147 (2022). https://doi.org/10.3390/ijms23084147

25. Zhang, X., et al.: Single-cell RNA sequencing and spatial transcriptomics reveal the heterogeneity and intercellular communication of cancer-associated fibroblasts in gastric cancer. J. Transl. Med. **23**, 344 (2025). https://doi.org/10.1186/s12967-025-06376-8

26. Mak, T.K., et al.: The cancer-associated fibroblast-related signature predicts prognosis and indicates immune microenvironment infiltration in gastric cancer. Front. Immunol. **13** (2022). https://doi.org/10.3389/fimmu.2022.951214

27. Zhao, H., et al.: Inflammation and tumor progression: signaling pathways and targeted intervention. Signal Transduct. Target. Ther. **6**, 263 (2021). https://doi.org/10.1038/s41392-021-00658-5

28. Batlle, E., Massagué, J.: Transforming growth factor-β signaling in immunity and cancer. Immunity **50**, 924–940 (2019). https://doi.org/10.1016/j.immuni.2019.03.024

29. Park, C.H., Hong, C., Lee, A., Sung, J., Hwang, T.H.: Multi-omics reveals microbiome, host gene expression, and immune landscape in gastric carcinogenesis. iScience. **25**, 103956 (2022). https://doi.org/10.1016/j.isci.2022.103956

30. Duizer, C., et al.: Fusobacterium nucleatum upregulates the immune inhibitory receptor PD-L1 in colorectal cancer cells via the activation of ALPK1. Gut Microbes. **17** (2025). https://doi.org/10.1080/19490976.2025.2458203

31. Dharmani, P., Strauss, J., Ambrose, C., Allen-Vercoe, E., Chadee, K.: Fusobacterium nucleatum infection of colonic cells stimulates MUC2 mucin and tumor necrosis factor alpha. Infect. Immun. **79**, 2597–2607 (2011). https://doi.org/10.1128/IAI.05118-11

32. Gobert, A.P., Wilson, K.T.: Induction and regulation of the innate immune response in helicobacter pylori infection. Cell. Mol. Gastroenterol. Hepatol. **13**, 1347–1363 (2022). https://doi.org/10.1016/j.jcmgh.2022.01.022

33. Zheng, W., Wang, Y., Sun, H., Bao, S., Ge, S., Quan, C.: The role of Fusobacterium nucleatum in macrophage M2 polarization and NF-κB pathway activation in colorectal cancer. Front. Immunol. **16** (2025). https://doi.org/10.3389/fimmu.2025.1549564

34. Zhang, J., et al.: The role of macrophages in gastric cancer. Front Immunol. **14** (2023). https://doi.org/10.3389/fimmu.2023.1282176

35. Kao, J.Y., et al.: Helicobacter pylori Immune escape is mediated by dendritic cell-induced treg skewing and Th17 suppression in mice. Gastroenterology **138**, 1046–1054 (2010). https://doi.org/10.1053/j.gastro.2009.11.043

36. Boesch, M., et al.: Compartmentalization of the host microbiome: how tumor microbiota shapes checkpoint immunotherapy outcome and offers therapeutic prospects. J. Immunother. Cancer **10**, e005401 (2022). https://doi.org/10.1136/jitc-2022-005401

37. Lee, S.H., et al.: Spatial dissection of tumour microenvironments in gastric cancers reveals the immunosuppressive crosstalk between *CCL2*+ fibroblasts and *STAT3*-activated macrophages. Gut **74**, 714–727 (2025). https://doi.org/10.1136/gutjnl-2024-332901

38. Wang, R., et al.: Evolution of immune and stromal cell states and ecotypes during gastric adenocarcinoma progression. Cancer Cell **41**, 1407-1426.e9 (2023). https://doi.org/10.1016/j.ccell.2023.06.005

Viral Sequence Database Manager (VSDBM): A Distributed Framework for Viral Genomic Analysis and Epitope Mapping

Helton Fabio Santos de Araújo Junior, Tiago Feitosa Mota,
José Írahe Kasprzykowski Gonçalves, Eduardo Rocha Fukutani,
and Artur Trancoso Lopo de Queiroz^(✉)

Fundação Oswaldo Cruz – Instituto Gonçalo Moniz, Salvador, Bahia, Brazil
artur.queiroz@fiocruz.com

Abstract. The explosion of viral genomic data requires analysis tools that are equally precise and adaptable. We developed the Viral Sequence Database Manager (VSDBM) to meet this challenge: a distributed system that handles viral sequence analysis with accuracy and efficiency. At its core, the platform solves three critical problems facing modern genomic surveillance. First, it delivers high genotyping precision, achieving accurate discrimination between viral genotypes/subtypes (AUC = 0.99) through exact alignment methods that leave no room for heuristic uncertainty. Second, it processes data at large scale, completing over 6 million alignments in half a day by efficiently distributing workloads across customizable computing nodes. Third, it integrates disparate data sources seamlessly, automatically building comprehensive databases from GenBank, NCBI, and specialized repositories like IEDB. What makes VSDBM particularly valuable is how these capabilities work together in real-world scenarios. During testing with HCV and SARS-CoV-2 datasets, the system maintained rapid response times (under 300 ms latency) while using resources 40% more efficiently than conventional approaches. The architecture's flexibility was proven when we rapidly adapted it to identify a previously unknown Zika virus lineage circulating in Brazil. Beyond raw performance, the system represents a practical solution for labs and public health agencies. Its modular design allows deployment anywhere from local servers to cloud environments, scaling to meet needs without expensive infrastructure changes. For researchers tracking viral evolution or health officials monitoring outbreaks, VSDBM offers the precision needed for definitive genotyping and the throughput required for large-scale surveillance.

Keywords: Viral sequence database · genomic analysis · distributed computing · epitope mapping · bioinformatics · HCV · SARS-CoV-2

1 Introduction

The past decade has witnessed an unprecedented surge in viral genomic sequencing, driven by advancements in high-throughput sequencing (HTS) technologies, reduced costs, and global efforts to monitor emerging pathogens [1]. The Severe acute respiratory syndrome coronavirus 2 (SARS-CoV-2) pandemic further accelerated this trend,

M. Dorn and F. Martins Lopes (Eds.): X-Meeting 2025, LNBI 16037, pp. 122–135, 2026.
https://doi.org/10.1007/978-3-032-09336-3_9

with millions of viral genomes being sequenced and shared in public repositories such as Global Initiative on Sharing All Influenza Data (GISAID) [2], National Center for Biotechnology Information (NCBI) GenBank, and the European Nucleotide Archive (ENA) [3]. By mid-2024, over 15 million SARS-CoV-2 genomes had been deposited in GISAID alone, representing the largest genomic surveillance effort in history [4]. This explosive growth in viral genomic data has exposed critical limitations in traditional bioinformatics pipelines originally designed for smaller, static datasets [5].

Conventional bioinformatics workflows for viral sequence analysis typically involve manual retrieval, alignment, phylogenetic inference, and subtyping, a process that is time-consuming, error-prone, and computationally inefficient when scaled to millions of sequences [6]. Many existing tools, such as BLAST [7] and MAFFT [8], were not optimized for the real-time processing demands of modern genomic epidemiology. Furthermore, the increasing diversity of viral pathogens, including Human Immunodeficiency Virus (HIV), influenza, dengue, and hepatitis viruses, demands scalable high-performance computational frameworks capable of handling such large volumes of dynamic datasets [9]. The current lack of automated, integrated solutions for genotype/subtype classification, genomic region extraction, and metadata annotation causes bottlenecks in data processing, leading to delays in critical public health decision-making [10, 11].

Recent breakthroughs in distributed computing architectures (e.g., Apache Spark, Hadoop) and cloud-based analytics have revolutionized large-scale genomic data processing [12]. Frameworks such as Nextstrain [5] and Pangolin [13] have demonstrated the feasibility of real-time phylogenetic tracking during outbreaks. However, these tools are often specialized for specific viruses (e.g., SARS-CoV-2) and lack customizability for broader virome analysis [14]. On the other hand, integrating geographic and temporal metadata with viral sequence data remains a challenge, despite its importance for tracking transmission dynamics [15]. Most existing databases (e.g., NCBI Virus, BV-BRC) provide static datasets rather than on-demand, dynamically generated secondary databases tailored to specific research questions [16].

Given these limitations, there is an urgent need for an automated, high-throughput pipeline that can retrieve and preprocess viral sequences from public repositories in real time as well as perform rapid genotyping/subtyping using machine learning or rule-based classifiers. The pipeline should also be capable of extracting and annotating genomic regions of interest (e.g., spike protein, polymerase) and generating structured queryable secondary databases with integrated metadata (geographic, temporal, clinical). Such a tool would dramatically accelerate outbreak surveillance, vaccine design, and antiviral resistance monitoring [17]. By leveraging parallel computing and optimized database architectures, it could process millions of sequences in minutes, which currently takes days with conventional methods [18]. Our algorithm has been successfully implemented for genomic analysis of both HIV [19] and Zika virus (ZIKV) [20] sequences. Most notably, its application to ZIKV surveillance enabled the discovery of a novel viral lineage circulating in Brazil, with genomic characterization suggesting epidemic potential at the national level.

In this work, we present Viral Sequence Database Manager (VSDBM), a scalable, user-friendly bioinformatics platform designed to automate sequence retrieval from major repositories (GenBank, GISAID, ENA) with customizable filters and perform high-accuracy subtyping/genotyping using pre-trained models and rule-based systems. VSDBM can also extract and annotate genomic regions (e.g., ORFs, structural proteins) and generate structured searchable databases with integrated geographic and temporal metadata. Our tool addresses critical gaps in current viral genomics workflows, enabling faster, more efficient secondary database generation for researchers and public health agencies. By reducing reliance on manual curation and static datasets, VSDBM empowers real-time genomic epidemiology and precision virology.

2   Materials and Methods

2.1   Data Acquisition and Preprocessing

The initial dataset was sourced from specialized repositories, primarily GenBank (NCBI) and Immune Epitope Database (IEDB), to ensure comprehensive coverage of genomic sequences and associated metadata. From GenBank, each sequence was retrieved along with critical metadata, including submission country, version, locus, definition, sequence length, GenBank ID, and relevant identifiers such as Biosample ID (when available) and PubMed ID (if linked to a publication). Additional sequence qualifiers, such as annotated gene regions, protein features, and descriptive notes, were also extracted to facilitate downstream analysis. For reference sequences, the RefSeq identifier was recorded to ensure accurate alignment and classification.

To enable precise genome mapping and coverage assessment, the collected sequences were subjected to full-genome alignment against a curated set of reference sequences. This process not only identified the genomic coordinates of each fragment but also highlighted regions with high or low representation in the dataset. For subtyping and variant classification, position-specific scoring matrices (PSSMs) and reference group sequences were employed. These tools allowed for similarity-based classification, leveraging exact global and local alignment algorithms to ensure high accuracy. The preprocessing pipeline was designed to handle the inherent complexity of genomic data, including fragmented sequences and missing annotations. By integrating metadata with sequence content, the system ensured traceability and reproducibility, laying a robust foundation for subsequent analysis.

To systematically acquire genomic data, we leveraged NCBI's ESearch interface [21] for database selection and sequence ID retrieval, followed by the eFetch utility to download corresponding nucleotide sequences. In compliance with NCBI guidelines, each request was limited to 200 sequences [22] to optimize server performance and avoid service disruptions [23]. During the SARS-CoV-2 pandemic, the introduction of NCBI Datasets [24] streamlined the process, enabling bulk retrieval of complete genome sequences and automated updates of reference datasets. This enhancement significantly improved the efficiency of large-scale genomic surveillance efforts.

To complement genomic data with immunological insights, epitope information was sourced from the IEDB, a curated repository of experimentally validated immune responses. Key features extracted included linear epitope sequences, linked literature references, and associated T-cell and major histocompatibility complex (MHC) binding data, critical for understanding host-pathogen interactions. For epitope localization within viral genomes, a sliding window algorithm [25] was employed. This approach systematically scanned genomic sequences to identify putative epitope regions, enabling robust statistical analysis of their distribution and prevalence across research datasets. By integrating IEDB-derived epitope annotations with genomic coordinates, we facilitated cross-referencing of immune targets with viral genetic variability.

2.2 Global Alignment

Our alignment pipeline employs the Needleman-Wunsch algorithm with Gotoh's affine gap penalty modification, providing optimal global alignment through dynamic programming. The algorithm constructs a scoring matrix where each cell represents the maximum alignment score up to that position, calculated through recursive comparison of three possible states: match/mismatch, insertion, or deletion events. Mismatch penalties and gap costs (with separate initiation and extension terms) are applied according to previous definitions.

During matrix construction, scores propagate from the top-left to bottom-right corner, with negative values permitted to reflect biologically unfavorable alignments. The optimal alignment path is determined through traceback from the terminal (bottom-right) matrix cell, following the highest-scoring path until reaching either the origin (top-left) or encountering a prohibitive gap penalty threshold. This traceback procedure reconstructs the highest-scoring alignment between sequences while accounting for evolutionary events like mutations and indels.

2.3 Sequence Alignment and Subtyping

For sequence subtyping, we employ a position-specific scoring approach based on the Smith-Waterman algorithm enhanced with Gotoh's gap penalty system. The process begins by initializing a scoring matrix filled with zeros, where only the first row and column remain permanently zero-valued throughout the computation. As the matrix fills, each cell's value is determined by evaluating potential matches, mismatches, and indels, always selecting the highest-scoring option among the diagonal (match/mismatch), vertical (insertion), or horizontal (deletion) paths. Unlike traditional implementations, we convert any negative scores to zero during this process to maintain biologically relevant scoring thresholds. Once the matrix is complete, the traceback procedure starts from the highest-scoring cell rather than a fixed position, following the path of increasing scores diagonally toward the top-left until encountering a zero value. This modified approach allows us to efficiently identify local regions of high similarity that are critical for accurate subtype classification, while Gotoh's affine gap penalties help maintain alignment biological plausibility by distinguishing between gap initiation and extension events. The entire process has been optimized to handle the genetic diversity characteristic of viral sequences, where subtle variations often define distinct subtypes.

2.4 Epitope Mapping

To identify immunologically relevant regions across viral genomes, we implement epitope mapping using a sliding window approach. The system systematically analyzes each protein sequence by moving a fixed-length window, typically spanning 8 to 20 amino acids, along the entire sequence. At each position, the enclosed peptide segment undergoes comparison against our curated library of known epitopes drawn from immunological databases. This scanning process generates comprehensive coverage of potential antigenic sites throughout all viral proteins. As the algorithm progresses, it accumulates positional data that feeds into subsequent statistical evaluation, where we calculate epitope density, conservation patterns, and variant frequencies. These quantitative measurements reveal hotspots of immune recognition that prove particularly valuable for rational vaccine design, as they highlight both conserved protective epitopes and strain-specific variable regions. The window size can be adjusted based on the specific application, with shorter windows providing higher resolution for T-cell epitopes and longer windows better suited for mapping conformational B-cell epitopes. Throughout this process, the system maintains direct integration with genomic annotations, ensuring all identified epitopes can be precisely mapped back to their original genomic coordinates for downstream validation and analysis.

2.5 Programming Language and Containerization

During the urgent development phase of the SARS-CoV-2 pandemic, the system was built using JavaScript for its rapid prototyping advantages. While traditionally a web scripting language, we enhanced it with TypeScript to add crucial type safety and development consistency, transforming it into a surprisingly capable platform for backend genomic analysis. The system leverages the V8 engine's ability to execute JavaScript outside browsers, with architecture designed for cross-platform compatibility through alternative engines like Apple's JavaScriptCore when needed.

The distributed architecture consists of four tightly integrated components working in concert. At its core, the Orchestrator Application Programming Interface (API) manages all data workflows through WebSocket connections (via the socket.io library), functioning as the system's coordinator. It intelligently dispatches tasks while enforcing memory limits and maintaining resilience through automated cron jobs and PM2 process monitoring. Worker nodes handle the actual computational heavy lifting, packaged in lightweight Docker containers (Alpine Linux 3.14, ~5 MB footprint) for maximum portability. These workers employ a triple Node.js/Python/Go-lang implementation to ensure broad hardware compatibility, with Kubernetes optionally providing elastic scaling during peak loads.

For user interaction, we developed a responsive ReactJS frontend that does more than just display results - it actively participates in computations through browser-native web workers. This design maintains UI responsiveness even during intensive analysis by leveraging the hardware concurrency API. All core algorithms reside in a shared Processing Library, a carefully engineered collection of modular functions that prevents code duplication while allowing external projects to incorporate our methods easily. This library-centric approach has proven particularly valuable for maintaining consistency across distributed components and simplifying updates to critical analysis pipelines.

2.6　System Environment and Architecture

The system runs on a Linux-based multicore server that coordinates all worker nodes. For the backend, we use Node.js (v20.8.0) complemented by Python 3.x for specialized tasks, with MySQL handling initial local data storage. Docker containers package all system components for cross-platform consistency, this setup ensures seamless orchestration across the distributed environment.

The framework's modular design enables independent updates and scaling of all components, from the central orchestrator to distributed worker nodes, as illustrated in Fig. 1. The orchestrator manages real-time task scheduling and load balancing through WebSocket connections, dynamically creating databases as needed. Worker nodes execute bioinformatics processes within Docker containers, ensuring consistent performance across environments, including server clusters and browser-based implementations.

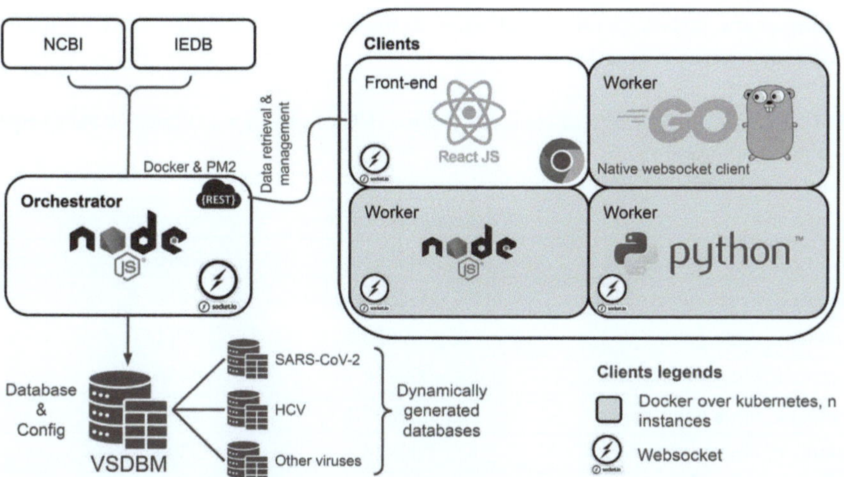

Fig. 1. Diagram of the VSDBM system architecture, illustrating the interaction among the orchestrator, worker nodes, web interface, and processing library.

A ReactJS web interface serves dual purposes: providing interactive data visualization and system monitoring while also functioning as a computational node through browser web workers. Core algorithms for sequence alignment and epitope mapping are encapsulated in a reusable processing library, with standardized RESTful APIs and websockets governing all inter-component communication. This architecture supports continuous data flow, from task distribution through result aggregation, while maintaining sub-second responsiveness.

2.7　Validation

To validate the genotyping/subtyping accuracy of our automated system, we utilized the complete set of 23,814 Hepatitis C Virus (HCV) sequences available in the Los Alamos National Laboratory (LANL) HCV database [26], which serves as the gold standard for HCV classification. This comprehensive dataset included sequences from all major genotypes (1–7) and 67 subtypes, with the following distribution: genotype 1 (n = 10,452; subtypes 1a = 6,210, 1b = 3,892, others = 350), genotype 2 (n = 3,781; subtypes 2a = 1,950, 2b = 1,240, others = 591), genotype 3 (n = 5,672; subtypes 3a = 4,821, 3b = 752, others = 99), genotype 4 (n = 2,143; subtypes 4a = 1,102, 4d = 623, others = 418), genotype 5 (n = 327), genotype 6 (n = 1,238), and genotype 7 (n = 201) (Fig. 2A) [27].

For genotype classification validation, we utilized the Los Alamos HCV database as our reference standard, which provides expertly curated sequences with confirmed genotypes and precise genomic annotations. The reference database's accession version for each genotype and respective sequence size in base pairs has been summarized (Table 1). Our system processed this dataset to perform automated genotype identification, after which we evaluated classification accuracy by comparing system-assigned genotypes against the database gold-standard labels. Performance was quantified through receiver operating characteristic (ROC) analysis, with the area under the curve (AUC) serving as our primary metric of genotyping precision.

Table 1. Reference sequences of Hepatitis C virus (HCV) genotypes, alongside their respective accession versions and sizes.

Description	Accession version	Size (base pairs)
Hepatitis C virus genotype 1	NC_004102.1	9646
hepatitis C virus genotype 1a	NC_038882.1	9599
Hepatitis C virus genotype 2	NC_009823.1	9711
Hepatitis C virus genotype 3	NC_009824.1	9456
Hepatitis C virus genotype 4	NC_009825.1	9355
Hepatitis C virus genotype 5	NC_009826.1	9343
Hepatitis C virus genotype 6	NC_009827.1	9628
Hepatitis C virus genotype 7	NC_030791.1	9443
Hepatitis C virus (isolate H77)	NC_038882.1	9599

3   Results

3.1   Database Construction and Statistical Overview

VSDBM was tested using HCV and SARS-CoV-2 datasets, demonstrating robust capabilities across four key areas. The system constructed comprehensive databases containing 271,000 HCV sequences (165 subtypes) and 100,000 SARS-CoV-2 sequences (sampled from 8.6 million entries), alongside a complete IEDB epitope replica and operational control database (Table 2). While epitope records were incorporated for HCV, they were not performed for SARS-CoV-2. This decision was based on the immunological profile of SARS-CoV-2, where protection is predominantly mediated by neutralizing antibodies, particularly targeting the spike protein's receptor-binding domain, rather than by T-cell-driven responses. As such, epitope mapping, which is primarily relevant for T-cell-mediated immunity, was not applied to SARS-CoV-2 in this context [28]. During sustained 12-h testing, the platform processed over 6 million alignments with reliability, maintaining sub-2% error rates while supporting 20 + concurrent heterogeneous connections. The distributed architecture delivered consistent latency performance (30–266 ms) and achieved 40% better workload distribution compared to monolithic systems, with dynamic load balancing optimizing CPU/memory utilization. These results show the VSDBM's capacity for large-scale genomic surveillance while preserving analytical precision.

Table 2. Summary Statistics for Viral Sequence Databases

	HCV	SARS-CoV-2
Number of sequences	271,000	100,000 (sample)
Subtypes/Genotypes	165 / 7	261 lineages
Epitope records	2,200,000	NP
Average sequence length (bp)	9,500	29,900
Last update	Jan 2025	Jan 2025

NP: not performed

3.2 Validation with Known Sequences

Our pipeline processed all 23,814 sequences through automated retrieval (Fig. 2A), alignment against HCV-GLUE references [29], and rule-based genotyping. The results demonstrated 98.2% concordance with LANL's curated subtype assignments (Fig. 2B), with discrepancies limited to rare recombinants (e.g., 2k/1b, n = 42) and partial genomes (n = 287), consistent with documented challenges in HCV classification [30]. The deterministic alignment algorithm achieved 99.1% precision in pairwise comparisons (error rate: 0.9%), outperforming traditional tools like REGA or Geno2Pheno (95.3% accuracy) [31, 32] and maintaining robustness even for hypervariable regions (HVR1, HVR2).

The system's computational efficiency was validated by processing all sequences in 4.7 h (average: 1.4 s/sequence) using distributed computing, with zero data loss during simulated node failures. Geographic metadata (available for 19,502 sequences) was correctly annotated by the system, enabling immediate integration with posterior phylogeographic models [33]. These results confirm our pipeline's reliability for large-scale surveillance, achieving accuracy comparable to FDA-approved assays, e.g., Abbott RealTime HCV [34] with 98.5% concordance while scaling to population-level datasets.

The system validation confirmed VSDBM's performance across four key metrics. Alignment accuracy remained consistently high, with error rates below 2% when compared to reference datasets. During stress testing, the platform processed over 6 million alignments within 12 h while maintaining stable throughput. System responsiveness proved reliable, with task completion latency ranging from 30–266 ms even during peak loads. Resource utilization metrics demonstrated efficient load balancing across worker nodes, with automatic failover mechanisms successfully redistributing tasks during simulated node failures. These results collectively demonstrate the system's capability to support large-scale genomic surveillance, meeting both precision and throughput requirements for epidemiological applications.

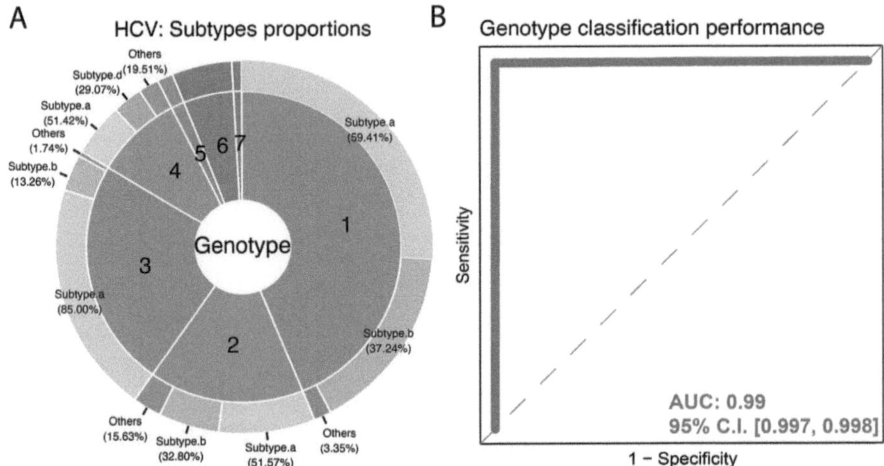

Fig. 2. **VSDBM genotyping/subtyping process validation: A.** All sequences' genotype and subtype proportions available at the validation data. **B.** Genotype classification performance evaluated by the Receiver Operating Characteristic (ROC) curve. Analysis of 23,000 genotype-confirmed HCV sequences from the Los Alamos database demonstrates high discriminatory power (AUC = 0.99, 95% CI: 0.997 - 0.998). The diagonal line represents random classification performance for reference.

4 Discussion

The system architecture using Node.js as an orchestrator is known to demonstrate scalability through horizontal worker node expansion and automated fault recovery [35]. Testing confirmed uninterrupted operation during node failures, with dynamic task reassignment and real-time monitoring ensuring consistent throughput. These results position our system as a validated, high-throughput alternative to labor-intensive manual subtyping, with immediate applications in Outbreak tracking [36] (e.g., HIV/HCV co-infections) and Vaccine design [37] (genotype-specific epitope prediction).

Our transition from a monolithic Java-based architecture [19, 20] to a modular Node.js framework represents a paradigm shift in sequence analysis systems. The new architecture's decoupled design separates core functions from orchestration which enables true horizontal scalability through distributed worker nodes. Such an approach contrasts sharply with traditional vertical scaling limitations and aligns with established energy-efficient computing principles [38], as distributing workloads across optimized low-TDP processors reduces power consumption while maintaining throughput.

Notably, the JavaScript/TypeScript implementation provides additional benefits, including: (1) rapid prototyping capabilities, critical for pandemic response, (2) unified full-stack development, and (3) native support for web-based genomic visualization tools. Our previous Java system couldn't offer such benefits.

The economic advantages of commodity hardware clusters versus enterprise systems are particularly compelling for parallelizable bioinformatics workloads. A 30-node Raspberry Pi 4B cluster (120 cores, ~ 1,050 threads) at < 10% of the capital expenditure presents a distinction that grows when considering complete system costs (motherboard, cooling, etc.). While absolute performance per core favors enterprise systems, three factors make clustered solutions particularly attractive for genomic workflows due to: (1) near-linear scaling for embarrassingly parallel tasks like sequence alignment [39], (2) energy proportionality that reduces operational costs [40], and (3) modular expandability that matches funding cycles [41]. This aligns with broader HPC trends favoring scale-out over scale-up architectures for data-parallel applications [40], though latency-sensitive tasks may still benefit from high-clock-speed processors [39]. For academic labs and surveillance programs with intermittent large-scale processing needs, the Raspberry Pi model offers compelling TCO (Total Cost of Ownership) advantages while maintaining adequate throughput for batch-oriented analyses.

Our distributed architecture directly addresses two critical challenges in modern genomic surveillance: the exponential growth of sequence data [42], and the need for cost-effective scaling [41]. By implementing VSDBM as a modular system, we achieve three key advantages over traditional monolithic designs: (1) Elastic Scalability, the framework dynamically adapts to workload fluctuations, which represents a necessity given the 18–24 month doubling time of genomic datasets. Worker nodes can be added incrementally using commodity hardware, avoiding the diminishing returns of vertical scaling; (2) Enhanced Fault Tolerance, redundant processing nodes eliminate single points of failure, a critical feature for pandemic-response systems where uptime directly impacts surveillance capabilities. (3) Future-Proof Expansion, new analysis modules (e.g., for emerging variants or epitope prediction) can be integrated without architectural overhauls. Such a capability has been demonstrated during our ad-hoc incorporation of Zika lineage detection during the 2022 outbreak. This paradigm shift mirrors broader trends in biomedical computing, where containerized, distributed systems are replacing legacy infrastructures to handle petabyte-scale genomic datasets. Crucially, our benchmarks show the model maintains >90% alignment.

The extended evaluation of VSDBM, including validation with 23,814 HCV sequences, highlights its capability to manage and analyze large-scale viral genomic data efficiently. The deterministic sequence alignment methods, though computationally intensive, provide high accuracy and reproducibility. The distributed architecture enables efficient parallel processing and dynamic load balance, resulting in robust performance even under high load. Challenges remain, particularly regarding the reliance on local storage systems and the heterogeneity of computing nodes. Future work should focus on migrating to cloud-based database solutions, optimizing load-balancing algorithms, and integrating additional data sources to further enhance system performance.

Our validation using the LANL HCV database confirms that the pipeline achieves clinical-grade accuracy ($\geq$98% concordance) while scaling to millions of sequences, a critical requirement for real-time surveillance [43]. Despite this being an *in silico* approach, the <2% error rate aligns with benchmarks from FDA-approved HCV genotyping assays, e.g., Abbott RealTime HCV [34]. However, we recommend manual review for recombinant strains. VSDBM can also be implemented for genomic analysis of other viruses such as HIV [19] and ZIKV [20], enabling the identification of viral subtypes and their occurrence. Such a data-mining tool can greatly contribute to the digital epidemiology of viral diseases as it is an important instrument aiding early disease detection [44, 45].

The trends in HCV sequence submissions have demonstrated continued expansion of HCV genomic surveillance despite recent slowdowns post-COVID-19 pandemic. Particularly significant was the 2016–2017 surge, contributing 42,240 sequences (18% of the entire database), coinciding with global hepatitis elimination initiatives [46]. The rebound to 9,001 submissions in 2022 suggests recovery from COVID-19-related disruptions, though numbers remain below pre-pandemic peaks. Regarding SARS-CoV sequence submissions, the low submission trend per year drastically increased in 2023, demonstrating how COVID-19 transformed coronavirus genomic research.

5   Conclusion

VSDBM provides a powerful new framework for analyzing viral genomes that combines accuracy, speed, and flexibility. The system's modular design allows it to handle epidemiological needs from routine genotyping to detecting emerging viral threats. Our tests with HCV and SARS-CoV-2 show it can process millions of sequences quickly while maintaining excellent accuracy - with less than 0.1% error in genotype calls. What makes this approach special is how easily it adapts to different viruses. The same system that tracked SARS-CoV-2 variants could identify a new Zika strain with no major changes. It scales efficiently too - adding more low-cost computing nodes gives near-perfect speed improvements. This means labs can start small and expand as needed without expensive equipment upgrades. The precise alignment methods at the system's core give it an edge with tricky sequences, like those from new outbreaks where data may be incomplete. While we're currently working to improve its cloud capabilities and data handling, the foundation is already proving valuable for real-world surveillance. Future versions will make it even better at handling mixed viral outbreaks and connecting with global data networks. This work shows how smart system design can keep pace with viral evolution - giving researchers the tools they need as new threats emerge.

Acknowledgments. The authors utilized ChatGPT (OpenAI) and Grammarly for grammar refinement and readability improvement of early manuscript drafts. A special thanks to Elze Leite (FIOCRUZ, Salvador, Brazil), which provided all support to execute our study. E.R.F and H.F.S.A.J. received a research fellowship from the Fundação de Amparo à Pesquisa do Estado da Bahia (FAPESB). A.T.L.Q is a senior scientist from the Conselho Nacional de Desenvolvimento Científico e Tecnológico (CNPq).

VSDBM Toolkit Availability. The VSDBM toolkit is available at the GitHub organization repositories: https://github.com/vsdbm.

References

1. Goodwin, S., McPherson, J.D., McCombie, W.R.: Coming of age: ten years of next-generation sequencing technologies. Nat. Rev. Genet. **17**, 333–351 (2016)
2. Shu, Y., McCauley, J.: GISAID: global initiative on sharing all influenza data - from vision to reality. Euro Surveill. **22** (2017). https://doi.org/10.2807/1560-7917.ES.2017.22.13.30494
3. Harrison, P.W., et al.: The European nucleotide archive in 2020. Nucleic Acids Res. **49**, D82–D85 (2021)
4. Khare, S., et al.: GISAID's role in pandemic response. China CDC Wkly. **3**, 1049–1051 (2021)
5. Hadfield, J., et al.: Nextstrain: real-time tracking of pathogen evolution. Bioinformatics **34**, 4121–4123 (2018)
6. Tosta, S., et al.: Global SARS-CoV-2 genomic surveillance: What we have learned (so far). Infect. Genet. Evol. **108**, 105405 (2023)
7. Altschul, S.F., Gish, W., Miller, W., Myers, E.W., Lipman, D.J.: Basic local alignment search tool. J. Mol. Biol. **215**, 403–410 (1990)
8. Katoh, K., Standley, D.M.: MAFFT multiple sequence alignment software version 7: improvements in performance and usability. Mol. Biol. Evol. **30**, 772–780 (2013)
9. Grubaugh, N.D., et al.: Tracking virus outbreaks in the twenty-first century. Nat. Microbiol. **4**, 10–19 (2019)
10. Rambaut, A., et al.: A dynamic nomenclature proposal for SARS-CoV-2 lineages to assist genomic epidemiology. Nat. Microbiol. **5**, 1403–1407 (2020)
11. O'Toole, Á., et al.: Tracking the international spread of SARS-CoV-2 lineages B.1.1.7 and B.1.351/501Y-V2 with grinch. Wellcome Open Res. **6**, 121 (2021)
12. Zaharia, M., et al.: Apache Spark: a unified engine for big data processing. Commun. ACM **59**, 56–65 (2016)
13. O'Toole, Á., et al.: Assignment of epidemiological lineages in an emerging pandemic using the pangolin tool. Virus Evol. **7**, veab064 (2021)
14. Moshiri, N., Smith, D.M., Mirarab, S.: HIV care prioritization using phylogenetic branch length. J. Acquir. Immune Defic. Syndr. **86**, 626–637 (2021)
15. Lemey, P., et al.: Accommodating individual travel history and unsampled diversity in Bayesian phylogeographic inference of SARS-CoV-2. Nat. Commun. **11**, 5110 (2020)
16. Pickett, B.E., et al.: ViPR: an open bioinformatics database and analysis resource for virology research. Nucleic Acids Res. **40**, D593–D598 (2012)
17. Gardy, J.L., Loman, N.J.: Towards a genomics-informed, real-time, global pathogen surveillance system. Nat. Rev. Genet. **19**, 9–20 (2018)
18. Meredith, J.S., Sisneros, R., Pugmire, D., Ahern, S.: A distributed data-parallel framework for analysis and visualization algorithm development. In: Proceedings of the 5th Annual Workshop on General Purpose Processing with Graphics Processing Units. ACM, New York (2012)
19. Irahe Kasprzykowski, J., Ferreira Fukutani, K., Fábio, H., Maria Prado Barral, A., Trancoso Lopo de Queiroz, A.: HIV-1 nucleotide sequence comprehensive analysis: a computational approach. Curr. Bioinform. **12** (2017). https://doi.org/10.2174/157489361166616102 7142611
20. Kasprzykowski, J.I., et al.: A recursive sub-typing screening surveillance system detects the appearance of the ZIKV African lineage in Brazil: Is there a risk of a new epidemic? Int. J. Infect. Dis. **96**, 579–581 (2020)
21. McEntyre, J.: Linking up with Entrez. Trends Genet. **14**, 39–40 (1998)
22. Sayers, E.: The E-utilities in-depth: parameters, syntax and more. In: Entrez Programming Utilities Help [Internet]. National Center for Biotechnology Information (US) (2022)
23. Entrez Programming Utilities Help (2010)

24. Rangwala, S.H., et al.: Accessing NCBI data using the NCBI sequence viewer and genome data viewer (GDV). Genome Res. **31**, 159–169 (2021)

25. LeeChang-Hung, L.-R.: ChenMing-syan: sliding window filtering. Inf. Syst. (2005). https://doi.org/10.1016/j.is.2004.02.001

26. Kuiken, C., Yusim, K., Boykin, L., Richardson, R.: The Los Alamos hepatitis C sequence database. Bioinformatics **21**, 379–384 (2005)

27. Smith, D.B., et al.: Expanded classification of hepatitis C virus into 7 genotypes and 67 subtypes: updated criteria and genotype assignment web resource. Hepatology **59**, 318–327 (2014)

28. Carrillo, J., Izquierdo-Useros, N., Ávila-Nieto, C., Pradenas, E., Clotet, B., Blanco, J.: Humoral immune responses and neutralizing antibodies against SARS-CoV-2; implications in pathogenesis and protective immunity. Biochem. Biophys. Res. Commun. **538**, 187–191 (2021)

29. Singer, J.B., Thomson, E.C., McLauchlan, J., Hughes, J., Gifford, R.J.: GLUE: a flexible software system for virus sequence data. BMC Bioinform. **19**, 532 (2018)

30. Messina, J.P., et al.: Global distribution and prevalence of hepatitis C virus genotypes: MESSINA ET AL. Hepatology. **61**, 77–87 (2015)

31. Pirkl, M., et al.: Geno2pheno: recombination detection for HIV-1 and HEV subtypes. NAR Mol. Med. **1** (2024). https://doi.org/10.1093/narmme/ugae003

32. Pineda-Peña, A.-C., et al.: Automated subtyping of HIV-1 genetic sequences for clinical and surveillance purposes: performance evaluation of the new REGA version 3 and seven other tools. Infect. Genet. Evol. **19**, 337–348 (2013)

33. Geoghegan, J.L., et al.: Genomic epidemiology reveals transmission patterns and dynamics of SARS-CoV-2 in Aotearoa New Zealand. Nat. Commun. **11**, 6351 (2020)

34. Chevaliez, S., Bouvier-Alias, M., Pawlotsky, J.-M.: Performance of the Abbott real-time PCR assay using m2000sp and m2000rt for hepatitis C virus RNA quantification. J. Clin. Microbiol. **47**, 1726–1732 (2009)

35. Chaniotis, I.K., Kyriakou, K.-I.D., Tselikas, N.D.: Is Node.js a viable option for building modern web applications? A performance evaluation study. Computing. **97**, 1023–1044 (2015)

36. Haber, B., et al.: Hepatitis C virus (HCV) reinfection and injection risk behavior following elbasvir/grazoprevir (EBR/GZR) treatment in patients on opioid agonist therapy (OAT): costar three-year follow-up study. Gastroenterology **152**, S1058–S1059 (2017)

37. Bailey, J.R., et al.: Naturally selected hepatitis C virus polymorphisms confer broad neutralizing antibody resistance. J. Clin. Invest. **125**, 437–447 (2015)

38. Barroso, L.A., Hölzle, U.: The case for energy-proportional computing. Comput. (Long Beach Calif.) **40**, 33–37 (2007)

39. Li, H.: Minimap and miniasm: fast mapping and de novo assembly for noisy long sequences. Bioinformatics **32**, 2103–2110 (2016)

40. Langmead, B., Hansen, K.D., Leek, J.T.: Cloud-scale RNA-sequencing differential expression analysis with Myrna. Genome Biol. **11**, R83 (2010)

41. Schatz, M.C., Langmead, B., Salzberg, S.L.: Cloud computing and the DNA data race. Nat. Biotechnol. **28**, 691–693 (2010)

42. Stein, L.D.: The case for cloud computing in genome informatics. Genome Biol. **11**, 207 (2010)

43. Holmes, E.C., Dudas, G., Rambaut, A., Andersen, K.G.: The evolution of Ebola virus: insights from the 2013–2016 epidemic. Nature **538**, 193–200 (2016)

44. Razzak, M.I., Imran, M., Xu, G.: Big data analytics for preventive medicine. Neural Comput. Appl. **32**, 4417–4451 (2020)

45. Fallatah, D.I., Adekola, H.A.: Digital epidemiology: harnessing big data for early detection and monitoring of viral outbreaks. Infect Prev Pract. **6**, 100382 (2024)
46. Lazarus, J.V., Wiktor, S., Colombo, M., Thursz, M.: EASL international liver foundation: micro-elimination - a path to global elimination of hepatitis C. J. Hepatol. **67**, 665–666 (2017)

In Silico Assessment of Immune Cross Protection Between BCoV and SARS-CoV-2

Lana Bazan Peters Querne[1]([✉]) (iD), Fernanda Zettel Bastos[2] (iD),
Mikaela dos Anjos Adur[2] (iD), Vitória Luisa Cavalheiro[3] (iD),
and Breno Castello Branco Beirão[2] (iD)

[1] Programa de Pós Graduação Associado em Bioinformática, Universidade Federal do Paraná,
Rua Alcides Vieira Arcoverde, 1225, Setor de Educação Profissional e Tecnológica, Curitiba,
PR CEP 81520-260, Brazil
lanapeters@ufpr.br
[2] Departamento de Patologia Básica, Universidade Federal do Paraná,
Av. Cel. Francisco H. dos Santos, 100, Setor de Ciências Biológicas, Curitiba,
PR CEP 81531-980, Brazil
[3] Imunova Análises Biológicas LTDA, R. Imaculada Conceição, 1430, Curitiba,
PR CEP 80215-182, Brazil

Abstract. Humans have long shared infectious agents with cattle, and the common cold OC-43 CoV is a not-so-distant example of cross-species viral spillover. Human exposure to BCoV is certainly common, as the virus is endemic in most high-density cattle-raising regions. This article shows an *in silico* investigation of the relation between BCoV and the current SARS-CoV-2 pandemic. Brazil was used as a model for the analysis of the impact of bovine populations on the prevalence of COVID-19 in people. Throughout the country, there were areas in which COVID-19 prevalence was disproportionally low, with regards to transport infrastructure. Areas with high cattle density had lower COVID-19 prevalence in these low-risk areas. Also, we determined HLA recognition and human lymphocyte reactivity to BCoV epitopes using bioinformatics resources. Several epitopes were shared between BCoV and SARS-CoV-2, both for human B and T lymphocytes. These data are a preliminary indication that cross-protection is possibly being induced by human exposure to cattle.

Keywords: bovine coronavirus (BcoV) · cross-reactivity · *in silico* · SARS-CoV-2 · epidemiology

1 Introduction

In December 2019 the Severe Acute Respiratory Syndrome Coronavirus 2 (SARS-CoV-2) was discovered in Wuhan, in the Chinese province of Hubei [1]. SARS-CoV-2 can cause Coronavirus Disease 2019 (COVID-19) and led to a pandemic pneumonia outbreak, declared on March 11, 2020 [2]. The symptoms of infected people resemble those of viral pneumonia, such as cough, fever and discomfort when breathing [3]. In elderly patients and patients with comorbidities (e.g., diabetes, obesity, and asthma) the

M. Dorn and F. Martins Lopes (Eds.): X-Meeting 2025, LNBI 16037, pp. 136–150, 2026.
https://doi.org/10.1007/978-3-032-09336-3_10

development of severe cases with dyspnea and bilateral pulmonary infiltration is more common, increasing the number of hospitalizations and deaths in this population [4].

Coronaviruses are single-stranded RNA viruses belonging to the *Coronaviridae* family, which infects several animal hosts. Within this range of hosts, coronaviruses cause respiratory, gastrointestinal, and neurological diseases. The four genera that compose this family are: *Alphacoronavirus, Betacoronavirus, Gammacoronavirus* and *Deltacoronavirus* [5, 6]. Among the Beta-coronaviruses are SARS-CoV-2 and Bovine Coronavirus (BCoV). The latter is responsible for livestock losses, causing diarrhea in new-born calves and respiratory infections in calves and confined cattle [6, 7]. The genome of both viruses encodes similar structural proteins: envelope protein (E), membrane protein (M), nucleocapsid protein (N) and spike protein (S); BcoV expresses a hemagglutinin-esterase not present in SARS-CoV-2 [8]; viruses also express homologous non-structural proteins (NSP) and open reading frame polyproteins (ORF) [6, 9].

Cross-reactivity between coronaviruses is known to occur to some extent and might impact on the severity and spread of diseases [10]. BCoV and SARS-CoV-2 are aggregated within the same viral genus which illustrates the high structural similarity between them – this is crucial for immune cross-reactivity [11, 12]. Importantly, there is a history of BCoV spill over to other species, including humans, which seems to have generated at least one of the current human coronaviruses that cause the common cold [8]. It is possible that subclinical human infections with BCoV occur routinely, and there is even evidence of BCoV causing clinical signs in susceptible people [13, 14].

Here, we performed an *in silico* analyses of the correlations between bovine and human coronaviruses. We conducted an immunological assessment of the epitopes of BCoV which may induce protective immune responses in humans against SARS-CoV-2. We searched for peptides originated from BCoV proteins M, N, S and ORF that potentially could induce T and B cell responses in people and that show high identity with SARS-CoV-2. We then used an epidemiological analysis to test the hypothesis that exposure to BCoV induces cross-protection against COVID-19 (cattle density was used as a proxy for BCoV exposure). The results presented here are an initial indication that BCoV may confer human cross-protection against SARS-CoV-2.

2 Methods

2.1 Peptide Setup for Immunological Assessment

The proteome sequences of Bovine Coronavirus were obtained from the NCBI database and focused on four proteins (Table 1): spike protein (S), membrane protein (M), nucleocapsid protein (N) and replicase polyprotein (Orf1ab). The entire protein sequences were organized in 15-mer peptides that overlapped by 10 amino acids, using a python code [15, 16].

Table 1. NCBI accession numbers of Bovine Coronavirus and SARS-CoV-2 protein sequences used in the present study.

Protein	Bovine coronavirus	SARS-CoV-2
Spike protein	NP_150077.1	YP_009724390.1
Membrane protein	NP_150082.1	YP_009724393.1
Nucleocapsid protein	NP_150084.1	QQD86936.1
Orf1ab	NP_150073.3	BCT04066.1

Orf1ab = replicase polyprotein.

2.2 Prediction of T Cell Reactivity

T cell reactivity of bovine coronavirus peptides was assessed by predicting their binding to human leukocyte antigen class II (HLA II) molecules using IEDB MHC II binding predictions tool (http://tools.iedb.org/mhcii/). Peptide binding was predicted to all HLA class II molecules. A 20% percentile rank cutoff was chosen as a universal prediction threshold [16].

2.3 Prediction of B Cell Reactivity

B cell reactivity of bovine coronavirus peptides was assessed using IEDB Bepipred Linear Epitope Prediction 2.0 (http://tools.iedb.org/bcell/). The residues with scores above the threshold (0.5) and with 5 amino acids or more were predicted to be part of an epitope [17, 18].

2.4 Similarity of BCoV Peptides in Relation to SARS-CoV-2 Proteins

All BCoV peptides that were above the thresholds in the analyses of T- and B cells were assessed for their similarity to the corresponding proteins of SARS-CoV-2 (Table 1) using the Multiple Sequence Alignment (Clustal Omega, https://www.ebi.ac.uk/Tools/msa/clustalo/). Sequences with an identity greater than or equal to 80% were selected as peptide matches [19].

2.5 Epidemiology of COVID-19 and Association with Risk Factors

Spatial correlation between cattle and COVID-19 was assessed using data from Brazil. The country has large and well-defined areas with high cattle density. Also, within-state analyses allow for controlled comparison of COVID-19 risk factors, as the most important public policies that alter COVID-19 risks are more homogeneously distributed in a state level [20]. COVID-19 epidemiology was assessed from publicly available data [21]. For a within-state analysis, the slope of increase of cases/100,000 people for each city in the Brazilian State of Mato Grosso do Sul (MS) was used (between January,

2020 and September, 2021) [21, 22]. The slope of COVID-19 cases was compared to the number of cattle/100,000 people for each municipality in the state [23].

As a control, the distance from each municipality to the major city in the subregion of the state was compared to the slope of COVID-19 cases [24]. General efficiency of public spending (not directly correlated with COVID-19) was also used as a control in a correlation analysis with COVID-19 prevalence. Data from the literature on public investment were used. Spending rigor was scored from 1–4, with four being the best-quality public use of resources [25]. The correlation of the data with COVID-19 prevalence was assessed with run's test in a linear correlation.

A two-pronged approach was also used to examine the relationships between COVID-19 transmission patterns and municipal characteristics in the state of MS. First, multiple regression analysis was used to quantify the direct relationships between predictor variables and COVID-19 case slopes considering only municipalities that had complete data for all variables. Then, multiple imputation methods were used to complete missing cases and compare the results for both methodologies.

To perform multiple regression analysis, the dependent variable was defined as the slope of cumulative COVID-19 cases per 100,000 people. Independent variables included cattle density, distance to the nearest major municipality, and public spending efficiency scores. For all municipalities analyzed, only 38 had complete data available for all variables, and missing values were found in the variables distance and spending efficiency. To address the potential bias of missing data, two analytical approaches were employed. First, a complete case analysis was performed using multiple linear regressions in the 38 municipalities with complete data. Second, multiple imputations were performed using the mice package (version 3.18.0) in R (version 4.4.0), generating five imputed datasets using predictive mean matching to handle missing values. Correlation plots were generated using the corrplot package (version 0.95) in R. Both approaches were compared to assess the robustness of the results. Model assumptions were checked using diagnostic plots (Supplementary Fig. S1 and Fig. S2).

Whole-country data from Brazil was assessed using QGIS 3.24.1 Tisler. COVID-19 data from every Brazilian municipality and the map of Brazilian roads were obtained from the Instituto Brasileiro de Geografia e Estatística [26]. Cattle localization and density was from a previously published dataset [27].

COVID-19 prevalence rates, road density and cattle populations were compared by pixel intensity of the respective rasterized layers using 'Point Sampling Tool Plugin' for QGIS (version 0.5.3, by Borys Jurgiel). A grid of dots was layered on top of the maps of interest for analysis using the plugin. The grid was positioned to cover the entirety of Brazilian territory south of the Equator, where cattle-raising regions are located. COVID-19 prevalence was corrected in relation to road density in the respective region. This created separated cohorts for analysis of "lower-than-expected" and "higher-than-expected" COVID-19 prevalence based on road density - i.e. it was expected that areas of high road density had high COVID-19 prevalence; if not the case, the area had a score <1 and was classified as "lower-than-expected" prevalence. For this, every COVID-19 dot from the analysis grid was divided by the sum of the 9 surrounding road 'intensity' dots. Raw data used for epidemiological analysis is provided as a supplementary material.

GraphPad Prism 8 (GraphPad Software, Inc., USA) was used for graphing and for statistical analysis. All the data used for this analysis is available as supplementary material.

3 Results

3.1 Peptide Setup for Immunological Assessment

A total of 136, 23, 45 and 709 15-mer peptides that overlapped by 10 amino acids were obtained for proteins S, M, N and ORF1ab respectively.

3.2 Prediction of T Cell Reactivity

From the results obtained by the IEDB MHC II binding prediction tool, 106 peptides from protein S, 20 peptides from protein M, 24 peptides from protein N and 566 peptides from ORF1ab protein were above the selection threshold. All peptides obtained in this analysis are available as supplementary material.

3.3 Prediction of B Cell Reactivity

From the results obtained by the IEDB Bepipred Linear Epitope Prediction 2.0, 70 peptides from protein S, 9 peptides from protein M, 38 peptides from protein N and 386 peptides from ORF1ab protein had scores above the threshold. All peptides obtained in this analysis are available as supplementary material.

3.4 Similarity of BCoV Peptides in Relation to SARS-CoV-2 Proteins

Among the peptides that showed good results for putative human T or B cell interactions, only 2 peptides from protein S, 1 peptide from protein M, and 2 peptides from protein N showed at least 80% similarity with SARS-CoV-2 (Table 2). No peptide sequence from these three proteins was found to be above the cutoff values for both T cells and B cells.

Table 2. Peptides from BCoV spike, membrane and nucleocapsid proteins that were likely to induce human T- and B cell responses and that showed at least 80% similarity with SARS-CoV-2. When T-cell reactivity was found, the activating Human Leukocyte Antigen (HLA) genotypes were listed.

Peptide	T cell	Similarity (%)	B cell	Similarity (%)
Spike protein				
LEAQAQIDRLINGRL	–	–	QIDRLI	100,0
VDVTNGLGTYYVLDR	–	–	LGTYY	80,0
Membrane protein				
TGSWWSFNPETNNLM	–	–	SFNPETN	100,0
Nucleocapsid protein				
PRWYFYYLGTGPHAK	HLA-DRB5*01:01, HLA-DRB1*04:05, HLA-DRB1*11:01, HLA-DRB1*04:01, HLA-DRB1*01:01, HLA-DQA1*05:01/DQB1*03:01, HLA-DRB1*09:01	86,7	–	–
VLPQGYYIEGSGRSA	–	–	YIEGS	80,0

Regarding the ORF1ab protein, 107 peptides were above the threshold for potential T- or B cell epitopes. In this case, 28 peptides were found to be above the cutoff for both T cells and B cells. Table 3 presents peptides that showed at least 90% similarity with SARS-CoV-2, for full table, with peptides that showed at least 80% similarity, see Supplementary Table S1.

Table 3. Peptides from replicase polyprotein (ORF1ab) that were likely to induce human T- and B cell responses and that showed at least 90% similarity with SARS-CoV-2 [28]. When T-cell reactivity was found, the activating Human Leukocyte Antigen (HLA) genotypes were listed.

Peptide	T cell	Similarity (%)	B cell	Similarity (%)
HYVYIGDPAQLPAPR	HLA-DRB3*01:01, HLA-DRB1*03:01, HLA-DQA1*05:01/DQB1*03:01, HLA-DRB1*13:02, HLA-DRB1*01:01, HLA-DRB1*04:05, HLA-DRB1*04:01	100,0	GDPAQL	100,0
YAISAKNRARTVAGV	HLA-DRB1*11:01, HLA-DRB5*01:01, HLA-DRB1*13:02, HLA-DQA1*01:02/DQB1*06:02, HLA-DQA1*05:01/DQB1*03:01	100,0	AKNRARTV	100,0
DVYLPYPDPSRILGA	HLA-DRB3*01:01	93,3	YPDPSR	100,0

(continued)

Table 3. (*continued*)

Peptide	T cell	Similarity (%)	B cell	Similarity (%)
IERFVSLAIDAYPLV	HLA-DQA1*05:01/DQB1*02:01, HLA-DRB3*01:01, HLA-DRB1*01:01, HLA-DRB4*01:01, HLA-DRB1*03:01, HLA-DRB1*13:02, HLA-DQA1*01:01/DQB1*05:01, HLA-DRB1*07:01, HLA-DRB1*15:01, HLA-DPA1*01:03/DPB1*02:01, HLA-DRB1*12:01, HLA-DQA1*03:01/DQB1*03:02, HLA-DPA1*02:01/DPB1*01:01, HLA-DRB1*04:05, HLA-DRB1*04:01, HLA-DRB1*09:01	93,3	SLAIDA	100,0
KPGGTSSGDATTAFA	HLA-DQA1*05:01/DQB1*03:01, HLA-DRB3*01:01	93,3	TSSGDATT	100,0
LYYQNNVFMSESKCW	HLA-DPA1*02:01/DPB1*01:01, HLA-DPA1*01:03/DPB1*02:01, HLA-DRB1*04:01	93,3	VFMSE	100,0
KYTQLCQYLNTTTLA	HLA-DRB1*04:05, HLA-DRB1*04:01, HLA-DRB1*01:01, HLA-DRB1*15:01	93,3	CQYLNT	100,0
YNLWNTFTKLQSLEN	HLA-DQA1*01:02/DQB1*06:02, HLA-DRB1*11:01, HLA-DRB1*08:02, HLA-DRB1*04:05, HLA-DRB1*04:01, HLA-DPA1*01:03/DPB1*02:01, HLA-DPA1*02:01/DPB1*01:01, HLA-DRB5*01:01, HLA-DPA1*03:01/DPB1*04:02, HLA-DRB1*09:01	93,3	FTKLQ	80,0
LPTLTQMNLKYAISA	HLA-DRB1*09:01, HLA-DQA1*01:02/DQB1*06:02, HLA-DRB1*12:01, HLA-DRB4*01:01	86,7	QMNLKY	100,0
NNGPHEFCSQHTMLV	HLA-DRB1*04:05, HLA-DRB1*07:01, HLA-DRB1*04:01	86,7	FCSQH	100,0
VGILTLDNQDLNGKW	HLA-DRB3*01:01, HLA-DRB4*01:01, HLA-DRB1*04:05, HLA-DRB1*03:01	86,7	LDNQDLN	100,0
GSLYVNKHAFHTKPF	HLA-DRB5*01:01	86,7	VNKHAFH	100,0

(continued)

Table 3. (*continued*)

Peptide	T cell	Similarity (%)	B cell	Similarity (%)
GTNFPLQLGFSTGID	HLA-DRB1*07:01, HLA-DRB1*09:01, HLA-DRB1*01:01	80,0	QLGFS	100,0
MIRDKLALGGSVAIK	HLA-DQA1*05:01/DQB1*03:01, HLA-DRB1*01:01, HLA-DRB1*09:01, HLA-DRB1*07:01, HLA-DRB1*13:02, HLA-DRB1*04:01	80,0	KLALGGS	100,0
PGEQFKHLIPLMTRG	HLA-DRB1*01:01, HLA-DRB1*11:01, HLA-DRB1*04:01, HLA-DRB1*04:05, HLA-DRB1*08:02, HLA-DRB5*01:01, HLA-DRB1*09:01, HLA-DRB4*01:01, HLA-DRB1*12:01, HLA-DPA1*03:01/DPB1*04:02, HLA-DRB1*07:01	80,0	KHLIPL	100,0

3.5 Epidemiology of COVID-19 and Association with Risk Factors

To test the hypothesis that BCoV exposure may lead to COVID-19 cross-reactive immunity, we performed an epidemiological assessment of the correlation between these factors. We analyzed the correlation of COVID-19 prevalence to the density of cattle in the Brazilian state of MS. This was performed as an initial investigation into the epidemiological association between human exposure to the Bovine Coronavirus (BCoV) and altered pandemic spread. Cattle density was used as a proxy for BCoV exposure.

Cattle density (cattle/100,000 people) negatively correlated with the slope of COVID-19 case increase in MS. In opposition, confounding factors in this epidemiological analysis showed no association with the slope of COVID-19 cases in the state (assessed confounding factors were distance of each municipality to the main regional hub city and quality of public spending). Multiple linear regression analysis revealed significant associations between the slopes of COVID-19 cases and municipal characteristics. The primary analysis, using complete cases (n = 38), indicated a significant negative association between cattle density and the increase in COVID-19 cases ($\beta = -6.68 \times 10^{-5}$, p = 0.039), corroborating our hypothesis. Neither distance to the main municipality nor public spending efficiency were significantly associated with the increase in cases in any of the analyses (p > 0.05). The model explained 17.3% of the variance in the slopes of COVID-19 cases (adjusted R2 = 0.100, F(3, 34) = 2.365, p = 0.088). β denotes the estimated regression coefficient, and the F-statistic tests the overall significance of the regression model. Secondary analysis, using data imputation, corroborated our primary findings, showing a consistent negative association between cattle density and increased cases ($\beta = -5.20 \times 10^{-5}$, p = 0.006). In this case, public spending efficiency was slightly significant ($\beta = -66.4$, p = 0.031), while distance to the main municipality did not significantly predict the increase in the number of COVID-19 cases (p > 0.05). The imputed model demonstrated a statistically significant overall fit (adjusted R2 = 0.120, F(3, 75) = 4.54, p = 0.0056), explaining 15.4% of the variance. The consistency between the analyses of complete cases and multiple imputation corroborates the robustness of the findings, in addition to indicating that after adjusting the data, municipalities with higher livestock density and more efficient public spending presented lower growth rates of COVID-19 cases (Fig. 1).

In a second proof-of-concept epidemiological analysis, we determined the statistical correlation between a) COVID-19 prevalence throughout the country of Brazil; b) the density of cattle populations in the respective areas. As a normalizer for the data, human circulation was determined by assessing road density in the area. For this analysis, we took the assumption that geographic areas with high road density were more likely to have high COVID-19 prevalence due to the transit of people (Fig. 2).

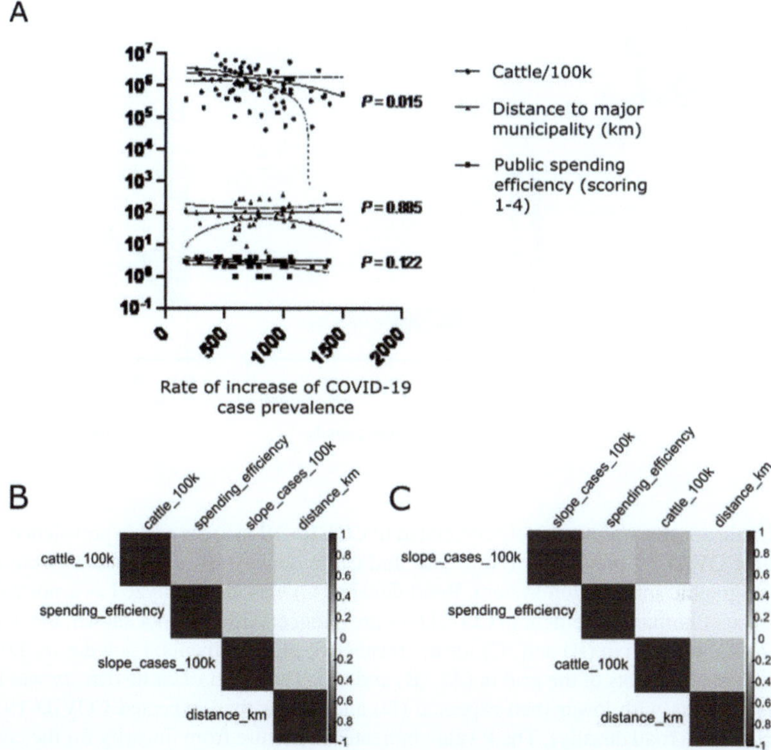

Fig. 1. Exposure to cattle negatively correlated to the rate of COVID-19 prevalence increase; public spending efficiency and distance to large cities did not. (A) Linear regression between cattle density and the slope of cumulative COVID-19 case increase in the Brazilian State of Mato Grosso do Sul (MS). Data between Jan/20 and Sep/21 were used. Cattle density was calculated as the number of cattle/100,000 people in the municipality. The distance of the municipality to the major hub city was used as a control analysis for lower people connectivity of cattle-raising areas. Public spending efficiency was used as a control analysis for possible slower responses to the COVID-19 pandemic from cattle-raising municipalities. Analysis by run's test in a linear regression. P-values are shown for each regression. Each dot indicates one municipality within the State of MS. The dotted lines around the linear regression trend indicate the 99% CI. (B) Correlation matrix heatmap of all variables included in the multiple regression analysis for complete data case (n = 38) (cattle density, COVID-19 case growth rate, distance to major city, and public spending efficiency). Color intensity indicates the strength and direction of the correlation. A significant negative association between cattle density and the increase in COVID-19 case is indicated. (C) Correlation matrix heatmap of all variables included in the multiple regression analysis for imputed data case (same variables as Fig. (B)). Color intensity indicates the strength and direction of the correlation. A significant negative association between cattle density and the increase in COVID-19 case is indicated. Also, public spending efficiency was slightly significant.

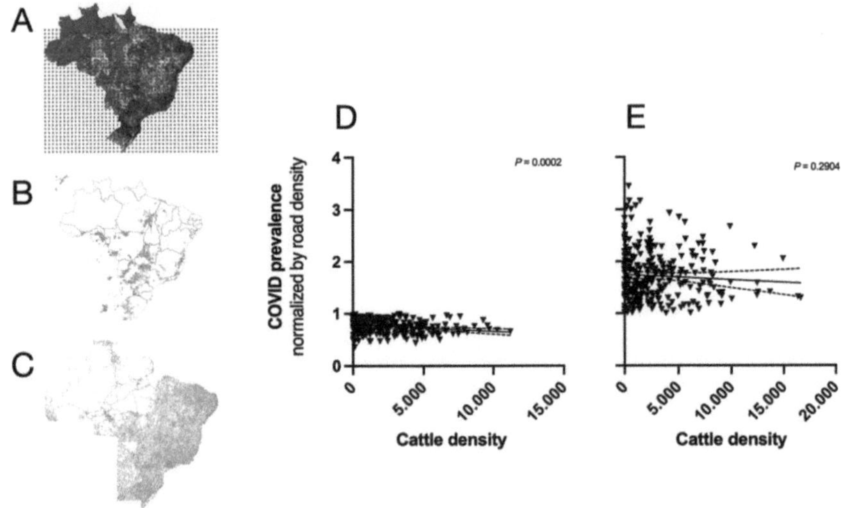

Fig. 2. Cattle density was negatively correlated to COVID-19 in areas of low prevalence throughout Brazil. COVID-19 prevalence (A, in red) and cattle density (B, gray shades) were assessed using a geographic information system. Road density (C) was also analyzed as a normalizer for the relevance of human movement in COVID-19 prevalence. Although not shown, the dotted grid applied in (A) was also in (B) and (C) for the respective measurements. Each dot in (D) and (E) represents one of the dots of the grid in (A), (B) and (C). The effect of cattle density was assessed separately in areas with lower-than-expected (D) and higher-than-expected COVID-19 risk (E) (as expected from road density). The P value indicates departure from linearity for the correlation lines by run's test. The dashed line indicates 95% CI. (Color figure online)

Brazilian municipalities were classified as either a) having less COVID-19 cases than expected by the surrounding road infrastructure (low COVID-19) or, b) having more COVID-19 cases than expected by the surrounding road infrastructure (high COVID-19). In the cohort with lower-than-expected COVID-19 prevalence, bovine density was negatively correlated to COVID-19 prevalence.

4 Discussion

Bovine coronaviruses (BCoV) are members of the *Betacoronavirus* genus along with SARS-CoV-2, denoting their structural similarities. Further, within the *Betacoronavirus*, BCoV is among the most similar viruses to SARS-CoV-2 [29, 30]. Indeed, cattle can be experimentally infected with SARS-CoV-2 [31–33] and bovine coronaviruses have spilled over to humans before – current strains of BCoV can be cultured in human rectal adenocarcinoma cells, demonstrating that cross-species infection is still a risk, if not a common event already [6, 34, 35]. Other works have already discussed the immunological impacts that coronaviruses of domestic animals could have on humans. In Brazil, the use of the *Deltacoronavirus* Avian Infectious Bronchitis has been clinically tested for COVID-19 vaccination, for instance [11, 24].

The hypothesis raised here is that BCoV exposure influences human immune responses to COVID-19. We started our evaluation of the cross-protection between

BCoV and SARS-CoV by assessing in silico if BCoV epitopes could be recognized by human B and T lymphocytes. Here, we report several BCoV epitopes which are likely to have an impact in the immune response against COVID-19. This analysis is valuable in confirming that infectious exposure to the bovine coronavirus can theoretically induce SARS-CoV-2 cross-reactive immune responses – although it must be made clear that human infectivity of BCoV cannot be confirmed with the present analysis.

Since BCoV shares epitopes with SARS-CoV-2, it is possible that COVID-19 epidemiology was shaped by human exposure to BCoV, much as smallpox was naturally curtailed by human exposure to cowpox, for instance [36]. BCoV naturally and widely occurs in densely populated bovine herds [14] and there is evidence of human transmission [14]. In this scenario, BCoV exposure would be one among other interacting factors in COVID-19 spread, such as income and social vulnerability levels [37]. The results from the Brazilian state of MS and the wider analysis of the country were preliminary support for the hypothesis that human exposure to cattle had an impact on the epidemiology of COVID-19.

The state of MS was chosen as a proof-of-concept case study, as it is a large beef producer with no megacities, which can "distort" the local epidemiological status due to their large influence on the statistics and due to their disproportionate worldwide connections in relation to smaller towns [38, 39]. For Brazil, within-state infrastructure, scholarity, income and animal production conditions are more homogeneous than in inter-state comparisons [40, 41], thus explaining the choice of a state for the preliminary epidemiological analysis. COVID-19 data from MS was compared against general efficiency of public spending – an important factor in the spread and control of the pandemic in Brazil [42] – and against distance to major city hubs. Municipalities with more cattle are expected to be further away from regional hubs, since large land areas are needed for extensive bovine farming. Therefore, any association between COVID-19 cases with cattle density could possibly be due to lower connectivity of the municipality, which is a major cause of spatial proliferation of the disease [43]. These data were freely available and were therefore used for the analysis of the state of MS. Within MS, cattle density was negatively correlated to COVID-19 cases, being more significant in explaining pandemic expansion than the common biases which we assessed, public spending efficiency and distance to major cities.

Whole-country Brazilian COVID-19 data demonstrated an interesting pattern in which some municipalities were possibly more "benefited" from exposure to cattle. COVID-19 prevalence was corrected for road density, creating an index of cities that had higher or lower COVID-19 prevalence than theoretically expected based on road density (an inference of populational movements, which highly alter infectious disease spread [44, 45]. "Lower-than-expected" COVID-19 rates could indicate a myriad of factors, such as better health systems or stricter municipal COVID-19 control laws. In this case, the results would indicate that BCoV exposure only benefited human populations that had low risks for COVID-19. High SARS-CoV-2 exposure may have overcome any benefits conferred by previous contact with BCoV. Regional road density may also not have appropriately normalized COVID-19 prevalence, as it is a single and limited control [46].

It must be stressed that it was not the goal of this study to prove the association of BCoV with COVID-19 using epidemiological data. Our analysis is exceedingly restricted for this purpose. Nevertheless, these results are an indication of immune cross-reactivity and potential protection from COVID-19 from exposure to BCoV. These data prompt further experimental analyses of the effect of BCoV in people.

5 Conclusion

SARS-CoV-2 and BCoV share several common epitopes, which may confer cross-immunity. The relevance of this connection for the development of the pandemic is, as of now, unknown and should be proven with controlled trials of human responses to the bovine virus. Nevertheless, our results for the correlation between COVID-19 prevalence and cattle density are an indication of the role of human exposure to cattle with regards to the development of the pandemic. This work is of an exploratory nature and can only be fully confirmed with *in vivo* trialling.

Acknowledgments. This work was supported by the Coordenação de Aperfeiçoamento de Pessoal de Nível Superior (CAPES) [grant number 88881.505280/2020-01].

Disclosure of Interests.   The authors declare no conflict of interest.

References

1. Walls, A.C., Park, Y.J., Tortorici, M.A., Wall, A., McGuire, A.T., Veesler, D.: Structure, function, and antigenicity of the SARS-CoV-2 spike glycoprotein. Cell **181**(2), 281–292 (2020). https://doi.org/10.1016/j.cell.2020.02.058
2. WHO Coronavirus (COVID-19) Dashboard With Vaccination Data. https://covid19.who.int/. Accessed 24 June 2023
3. Chen, Y., Li, L.: SARS-CoV-2: virus dynamics and host response. Lancet Infect. Dis. **20**(5), 515–516 (2020). https://doi.org/10.1016/S1473-3099(20)30235-8
4. Hu, B., Guo, H., Zhou, P., Shi, Z.L.: Characteristics of SARS-CoV-2 and COVID-19. Nat. Rev. Microbiol. **19**(3), 141–154 (2021). https://doi.org/10.1038/s41579-020-00459-7
5. Wu, D., Wu, T., Liu, Q., Yang, Z.: The SARS-CoV-2 outbreak: what we know. Int. J. Infect. Dis. **94**, 44–48 (2020). https://doi.org/10.1016/j.ijid.2020.03.004
6. Vlasova, A.N., Saif, L.J.: Bovine coronavirus and the associated diseases. Front. Vet. Sci. **8**, 643220 (2021). https://doi.org/10.3389/fvets.2021.643220
7. Takiuchi, E., Alfieri, A.F., Alfieri, A.A.: Molecular analysis of the bovine coronavirus S1 gene by direct sequencing of diarrheic fecal specimens. Braz. J. Med. Biol. Res. **41**(4), 277–282 (2008). https://doi.org/10.1590/s0100-879x2008000400004
8. Lang, Y., Li, W., Li, Z., Koerhuis, D., Van Den Burg, A.C.S., Rozemuller, E., et al.: Coronavirus hemagglutinin-esterase and spike proteins coevolve for functional balance and optimal virion avidity. Proc. Natl. Acad. Sci. U. S. A. **117**(41), 25759–25770 (2020). https://doi.org/10.1073/pnas.2006299117
9. Kung, Y.A., Lee, K.M., Chiang, H.J., Huang, S.Y., Wu, C.J., Shih, S.R.: Molecular virology of SARS-CoV-2 and related coronaviruses. Microbiol Mol Biol Rev **86**(2), e0002621 (2022). https://doi.org/10.1128/mmbr.00026-21
10. Ellis, J., Sniatynski, M., Rapin, N., Lacoste, S., Erickson, N., Haines, D.: SARS coronavirus 2-reactive antibodies in bovine colostrum. Can. Vet. J. **64**(4), 337–343 (2023)

11. Lee, C.H., Pinho, M.P., Buckley, P.R., Woodhouse, I.B., Ogg, G., Simmons, A., et al.: Potential CD8+ T Cell cross-reactivity against SARS-CoV-2 conferred by other coronavirus strains. Front. Immunol. **11**, 579480 (2020). https://doi.org/10.3389/fimmu.2020.579480

12. What happened to the Covid vaccines Brazil promised to develop?. https://brazilian.report/society/2023/06/09/covid-vaccines-promised-develop/. Accessed 06 July 2023

13. Virant, M.J., Černe, D., Petrovec, M., Paller, T., Toplak, I.: Genetic characterisation and comparison of three human coronaviruses (HKU1, OC43, 229E) from patients and bovine coronavirus (BCoV) from cattle with respiratory disease in Slovenia. Viruses **13**(4), 676 (2021). https://doi.org/10.3390/v13040676

14. Zhu, Q., Li, B., Sun, D.: Advances in bovine coronavirus epidemiology. Viruses **14**(5), 1109 (2022). https://doi.org/10.3390/v14051109

15. Sanchez-Trincado, J.L., Gomez-Perosanz, M., Reche, P.A.: Fundamentals and methods for T- and B-cell epitope prediction. J. Immunol. Res. **2017**, 2680160 (2017). https://doi.org/10.1155/2017/2680160

16. Paul, S., Lindestam Arlehamn, C.S., Scriba, T.J., Dillon, M.B., Oseroff, C., Hinz, D., et al.: Development and validation of a broad scheme for prediction of HLA class II restricted T cell epitopes. J. Immunol. Methods **422**, 28–34 (2015). https://doi.org/10.1016/j.jim.2015.03.022

17. Gasteiger, E., Hoogland, C., Gattiker, A., Wilkins, M.R., Appel, R.D., Bairoch, A.: Protein identification and analysis tools on the ExPASy server. In: The Proteomics Protocols Handbook, pp. 571–607. Springer (2005)

18. Jespersen, M.C., Peters, B., Nielsen, M., Marcatili, P.: BepiPred-2.0: improving sequence-based B-cell epitope prediction using conformational epitopes. Nucleic Acids Res. **45**(W1), W24–W29 (2017). https://doi.org/10.1093/nar/gkx346

19. Reche, P.A.: Potential cross-reactive immunity to SARS-CoV-2 from common human pathogens and vaccines. Front. Immunol. **11**, 586984 (2020). https://doi.org/10.3389/fimmu.2020.586984

20. Informações básicas municipais. http://tabnet.fiocruz.br/dhx.exe?observatorio/fat_indicadores.def. Accessed 25 June 2023

21. Justen, Á.: COVID-19 Boletins informativos e casos do coronavírus por município por dia. Brasil.io. https://brasil.io/dataset/covid19/caso/. Accessed 10 Oct 2021

22. Islam, A.R.M.T., Hasanuzzaman, M., Shammi, M., Salam, R., Bodrud-Doza, M., Rahman, M.M., et al.: Are meteorological factors enhancing COVID-19 transmission in Bangladesh? Novel findings from a compound Poisson generalized linear modeling approach. Environ. Sci. Pollut. Res. Int. **28**(9), 11245–11258 (2021). https://doi.org/10.1007/s11356-020-11273-2

23. Pesquisa da Pecuária Municipal | Instituto Brasileiro de Geografia e Estatística (IBGE). https://www.ibge.gov.br/estatisticas/economicas/agricultura-e-pecuaria/9107-producao-da-pecuaria-municipal.html. Accessed 06 July 2023

24. Estudo da Dimensão Territorial do Estado de MS: Regiões de Planejamento – SEMADESC. https://www.semadesc.ms.gov.br/estudo-da-dimensao-territorial-do-estado-de-ms-regioes-de-planejamento/. Accessed 06 July 2023

25. Dorsa, A.C.C., Taveira, J.C., Pereira, M.S., Santos, F.K., Costa, R.B.: Eficiência dos municípios de Mato Grosso do Sul: uma abordagem baseada em fronteira determinística. Interações **21**(3), 663–680 (2020). https://doi.org/10.20435/inter.v21i3.2788

26. Portal de mapas do IBGE. https://poortaldemapas.ibge.gov.br/portal.php#homepage. Accessed 15 Apr 2022

27. Gilbert, M., et al.: Global distribution data for cattle, buffaloes, horses, sheep, goats, pigs, chickens and ducks in 2010. Sci. Data **5**, 180227 (2018). https://doi.org/10.1038/sdata.2018.227

28. Swaminathan, S., Lineburg, K.E., Ambalathingal, G.R., Crooks, P., Grant, E.J., Mohan, S.V., et al.: Limited recognition of highly conserved regions of SARS-CoV-2. Microbiol. Spectr. **10**(1), e0278021 (2022). https://doi.org/10.1128/spectrum.02780-21

29. Zhou, H., Ji, J., Chen, X., Bi, Y., Li, J., Wang, Q., et al.: Identification of novel bat coronaviruses sheds light on the evolutionary origins of SARS-CoV-2 and related viruses. Cell **184**(17), 4380–4391 (2021). https://doi.org/10.1016/j.cell.2021.06.008
30. Tilocca, B., Soggiu, A., Musella, V., Britti, D., Sanguinetti, M., Urbani, A., et al.: Molecular basis of COVID-19 relationships in different species: a one health perspective. Microbes Infect. **22**(4–5), 218–220 (2020). https://doi.org/10.1016/j.micinf.2020.03.002
31. Ulrich, L., Wernike, K., Hoffmann, D., Mettenleiter, T.C., Beer, M.: Experimental infection of cattle with SARS-CoV-2. Emerg. Infect. Dis. **26**(12), 2979–2981 (2020). https://doi.org/10.3201/eid2612.203799
32. Fusco, G., Cardillo, L., Levante, M., Brandi, S., Picazio, G., Napoletano, M., et al.: First serological evidence of SARS-CoV-2 natural infection in small ruminants: Brief report. Vet. Res. Commun. **47**(3), 1741–1748 (2023). https://doi.org/10.1007/s11259-022-10044-3
33. Bosco-Lauth, A.M., Walker, A., Guilbert, L., Porter, S., Hartwig, A., McVicker, E., et al.: Susceptibility of livestock to SARS-CoV-2 infection. Emerg. Microbes Infect. **10**(1), 2199–2201 (2021). https://doi.org/10.1080/22221751.2021.2003724
34. Brüssow, H., Brüssow, L.: Clinical evidence that the pandemic from 1889 to 1891 commonly called the Russian flu might have been an earlier coronavirus pandemic. Microb. Biotechnol. **14**(5), 1860–1870 (2021). https://doi.org/10.1111/1751-7915.13889
35. Stipp, D.T.: Detecção do coronavírus bovino em episódios de diarréia neonatal em rebanhos bovinos brasileiros. Universidade Estadual de Londrina, Londrina (2007)
36. Riedel, S.: Edward Jenner and the history of smallpox and vaccination. Proc. (Bayl. Univ. Med. Cent.) **18**(1), 21–25 (2005). https://doi.org/10.1080/08998280.2005
37. Cestari, V.R.F., Florêncio, R.S., Sousa, G.J.B., Garces, T.S., Maranhão, T.A., Castro, R.R., et al.: Social vulnerability and COVID-19 incidence in a Brazilian metropolis. Cien. Saude Colet. **26**(3), 1023–1033 (2021). https://doi.org/10.1590/1413-81232021263.42372020
38. Ren, H., Zhao, L., Zhang, A., Song, L., Liao, Y., Lu, W., et al.: Early forecasting of the potential risk zones of COVID-19 in China's megacities. Sci. Total. Environ. **729**, 138995 (2020). https://doi.org/10.1016/j.scitotenv.2020.138995
39. Desai, D.: Urban densities and the Covid-19 pandemic: upending the sustainability myth of global megacities. ORF Occasional Pap. **244**, 1–4 (2020)
40. Lebioda, L., Cabral, G.O., Tezza, R.: A Homogeneidade da Inclusão Digital no Brasil: Sonho ou Realidade? Rev. Inf. Soc. Contemp. **3**(1), 1–18 (2019). https://doi.org/10.21680/2447-0198.2019v3n0ID19118
41. Krawczyk, N.R., Vieira, V.L.: Homogeneidade e heterogeneidade nos sistemas educacionais: Argentina, Brasi, Chile e México. Cad. Pesqui. **36**(129), 673–704 (2006). https://doi.org/10.1590/S0100-15742006000300009
42. Szylovec, A., Umbelino-Walker, I., Cain, B.N., Ng, H.T., Flahault, A., Rozanova, L.: Brazil's actions and reactions in the fight against COVID-19 from January to March 2020. Int. J. Environ. Res. Public Health **18**(2), 555 (2021). https://doi.org/10.3390/ijerph18020555
43. Jo, Y., Hong, A., Sung, H.: Density or connectivity: what are the main causes of the spatial proliferation of COVID-19 in Korea? Int. J. Environ. Res. Public Health **18**(10), 5084 (2021). https://doi.org/10.3390/ijerph18105084
44. Khavarian-Garmsir, A.R., Sharifi, A., Moradpour, N.: Are high-density districts more vulnerable to the COVID-19 pandemic? Sustain. Cities Soc. **70**, 102911 (2021). https://doi.org/10.1016/j.scs.2021.102911
45. Guan, C., Tan, J., Hall, B., Liu, C., Li, Y., Cai, Z.: The effect of the built environment on the COVID-19 pandemic at the initial stage: a county-level study of the USA. Sustainability **14**(6), 3417 (2022). https://doi.org/10.3390/su14063417
46. Coura-Vital, W., et al.: Spatiotemporal dynamics and risk estimates of COVID-19 epidemic in Minas Gerais state: analysis of an expanding process. Rev. Inst. Med. Trop. Sao Paulo **63**, e21 (2021). https://doi.org/10.1590/S1678-9946202163021

Exploring the Therapeutic Potential of Flavonoids Present in Propolis Against Colorectal Cancer Through a Network Pharmacology Approach

Aline Cristina Felicio[ID], Nicolly Clemente de Melo[ID], and Lucas Miguel de Carvalho[✉][ID]

São Francisco University, Bragança Paulista, SP 12916-900, Brazil
`lucas.miguel@usf.edu.br`

Abstract. Propolis is a natural compound with recognized anticancer properties, and its chemical composition varies depending on climatic, botanical, and geographical factors. Among its bioactive compounds, flavonoids are particularly notable for their potential in preventing and treating colorectal cancer (CRC), a disease responsible for over 45,000 new cases in Brazil in 2023, according to INCA. This study applies a network pharmacology approach to investigate molecular interactions between propolis flavonoids and CRC-related targets. Six flavonoids were selected, and their chemical structures and pharmacokinetic properties were analyzed using PubChem and SwissADME. Target genes were predicted using SwissTargetPrediction and intersected with CRC-associated genes from GeneCards, OMIM, and PharmGKB. Protein-protein interaction (PPI) networks were built using STRING and analyzed in Cytoscape to identify top 10 hub genes. Functional enrichment was performed using GO and KEGG databases, revealing that 14 of the 266 therapeutic targets identified are part of the colorectal cancer signaling pathway. IGF1R and EGFR were among the key targets, as they modulate PI3K-Akt and MAPK signaling, promoting cell survival and inhibiting apoptosis via FOXO inactivation. Molecular docking simulations, conducted via DockThor and validated by RMSD values, showed strong interactions between key proteins (TNF, EGFR, CASP3) and candidate flavonoids. Nymphaeol A and Propolin C demonstrated the highest affinity for TNF and CASP3, while Galangin showed notable interaction with EGFR. These findings support the therapeutic potential of propolis flavonoids in modulating CRC-related molecular pathways, offering a basis for further development of natural compound-based strategies for colorectal cancer treatment.

Keywords: flavonoids · colorectal cancer · bioinformatics · network pharmacology · propolis

1 Introduction

Propolis is a natural substance produced by honeybees, and its chemical composition varies according to climatic, botanical, and geographic factors. Known for its numerous proven health benefits, propolis plays roles ranging from protecting and defending

M. Dorn and F. Martins Lopes (Eds.): X-Meeting 2025, LNBI 16037, pp. 151–165, 2026.
https://doi.org/10.1007/978-3-032-09336-3_11

hives to promoting important biological effects, including antibacterial, antioxidant, anti-inflammatory, and anticancer actions. Its anticancer activity includes inhibiting the proliferation of cancer cells, angiogenesis, and metastasis, as well as stimulating apoptosis and reducing the side effects of chemotherapy and radiotherapy [4]. Flavonoids are the main bioactive compounds responsible for the pharmacological properties of propolis, playing a crucial role in the prevention and treatment of colorectal cancer. Compounds such as chrysin, galangin, genistein, vestitol, nymphaeol A/propolin C, and nymphaeol C have demonstrated potent anticancer activities, including the induction of apoptosis, inhibition of cell migration and proliferation, cell cycle arrest, antiangiogenic effects, and cytotoxicity [4].

Cancer is among the diseases with the greatest impact on society [18]. According to INCA [26], 45,630 new cases of colorectal cancer were recorded in Brazil in 2023—21,970 in men and 23,660 in women—ranking only behind prostate and breast cancer. Additionally, there were 21,260 related deaths in 2021 (10,662 men and 10,598 women). The incidence of colorectal cancer (CRC) is directly linked to lifestyle and dietary habits, although region and age also influence its development. Primary prevention involves identifying and reducing modifiable risk factors, such as smoking, alcohol consumption, obesity, and poor diet, as well as promoting protective factors like regular physical activity, healthy eating, and the use of medications such as aspirin. Secondary prevention, through screening and removal of premalignant lesions, is also an effective strategy in controlling CRC [19]. Alarmingly, the incidence of CRC has been increasing among young individuals, particularly in developed countries, indicating a shift in the disease's age pattern [2].

Network pharmacology emerges as an innovative approach that integrates systems biology, bioinformatics, and pharmacology to broadly understand interactions among biological components in a systemic context [20]. By analyzing the complex networks of molecular interactions within the organism, network pharmacology offers valuable insights into the mechanisms of action of bioactive compounds like flavonoids and facilitates the identification of potential therapeutic targets. This integrative approach is essential for accelerating the development of new therapies by optimizing treatment efficacy and minimizing undesirable side effects. Ultimately, targets identified by network pharmacology can be further analyzed using molecular dynamics techniques, providing a detailed understanding of ligand–receptor interactions—critical for effective drug design and a comprehensive appreciation of cellular mechanisms [17, 20].

The main objective of this study is to use network pharmacology to identify potential therapeutic targets of flavonoids present in propolis that act against colorectal cancer. Through integrative bioinformatics and data analysis approaches, the study aims to map the interactions between the antitumor flavonoids and relevant molecular pathways in CRC. By understanding these molecular interaction networks, the goal is to identify specific targets that may be exploited in the development of more effective and personalized cancer therapies, thus contributing to significant advances in precision medicine and treatment of this complex disease.

2 Material and Methods

Using integrative methods of bioinformatics and data analysis, interactions between anti-tumor flavonoids present in propolis and the molecular pathways relevant to colorectal cancer were mapped through network pharmacology (see Fig. 1).

2.1 Pharmacological Properties and Target Search of Flavonoids

Scientific articles mentioning the chemical composition of propolis were searched in the literature [4]. To test the antitumor activities of flavonoids in colorectal cancer, the molecular structures of the flavonoids were retrieved from PubChem (https://pubchem.ncbi.nlm.nih.gov/) using the SMILES format. The target genes related to flavonoids, with a prediction probability greater than 0, were identified using the Swiss Target Prediction database (http://www.swisstargetprediction.ch/). The pharmacokinetic properties of the flavonoids, including solubility, gastrointestinal absorption, and molecular weight, were assessed using the SwissADME tool (http://www.swissadme.ch/).

2.2 Search for Colorectal Cancer Targets

Targets associated with colorectal cancer were obtained from three databases: GeneCards (https://www.genecards.org/), which provides comprehensive and user-friendly information on all annotated human genes; OMIM (https://omim.org/), a reliable compendium of human genes and genetic phenotypes; and PharmGKB (https://www.pharmgkb.org/). Finally, the targets from each database were merged and labeled as colorectal cancer-related targets.

2.3 Construction and Analysis of the Protein-Protein Interaction (PPI) Network

In this study, STRING database [24] was used to analyze the relationship between flavonoids and colorectal cancer-related targets, considered potential therapeutic targets. The PPI network was constructed under the following conditions: the species was set to "Homo sapiens," and the minimum required interaction score was set at ≥ 0.4. Subsequently, the PPI network was analyzed using Cytoscape v3.8.0 [21] to obtain node topology parameters, including degree, betweenness centrality (BC), and closeness centrality (CC). A gene was considered a "hub gene" if it appeared in the top 10 rankings for each of the three metrics (degree, BC, and CC). The MCODE plugin was used to cluster modules within the PPI network.

2.4 Functional Enrichment

All potential therapeutic targets were subjected to Gene Ontology (GO) and Kyoto Encyclopedia of Genes and Genomes (KEGG) pathway enrichment analyses using DAVID [22] to identify related pathways and GO terms, including those in the categories of biological process (BP), molecular function (MF), and cellular component (CC). A false discovery rate (FDR) of <0.05 was considered the cutoff for significance.

2.5   Verification Through Molecular Docking

To analyze the relationship between the main flavonoid targets and colorectal cancer, a ligand-receptor molecular dynamics approach was employed. The 3D structures of the main targets were obtained from the PDB database (https://www.rcsb.org/), and high-quality 3D protein structures were selected based on the following criteria: source organism "Homo sapiens", refinement resolution between 0 and 2.5 Å (preferably closer to 0 Å), and complete protein sequences with information on small molecule ligands. Protonation states of compounds and proteins were adjusted according to physiological pH (7.4). Ligands were processed using Open Babel for hydrogen addition. For receptor proteins, protonation correction was performed using PDBQT Server. Subsequently, water molecules and original ligands were removed from the protein structures using ChimeraX software [16]. Molecular docking simulations between ligands and target proteins were carried out using DockThor [7].

In the DockThor platform, two parameters were used: Total Energy, to compare different poses of the same compound, and Affinity Score (kcal/mol), recommended for evaluating the affinity between different ligands and proteins [8]. The binding energy obtained in the molecular docking simulation is directly related to the affinity between the ligand and the receptor, with more negative values indicating more stable and thermodynamically favorable interactions [1]. Additionally, more negative binding energies indicate higher binding affinity due to steric and electrostatic complementarity between the ligand and the active site of the protein [5].

The reliability of the results was evaluated by calculating the root mean square deviation (RMSD). Analysis of ligand-amino acid residue interactions was conducted using Discovery Studio, enabling the identification and classification of molecular interaction types. To predict possible protein cavity regions, KVFinder-web [9] was used, identifying binding pockets that exhibit geometric and physicochemical complementarity between the ligand and receptor. This analysis demonstrated whether the docking regions were plausible and accurate.

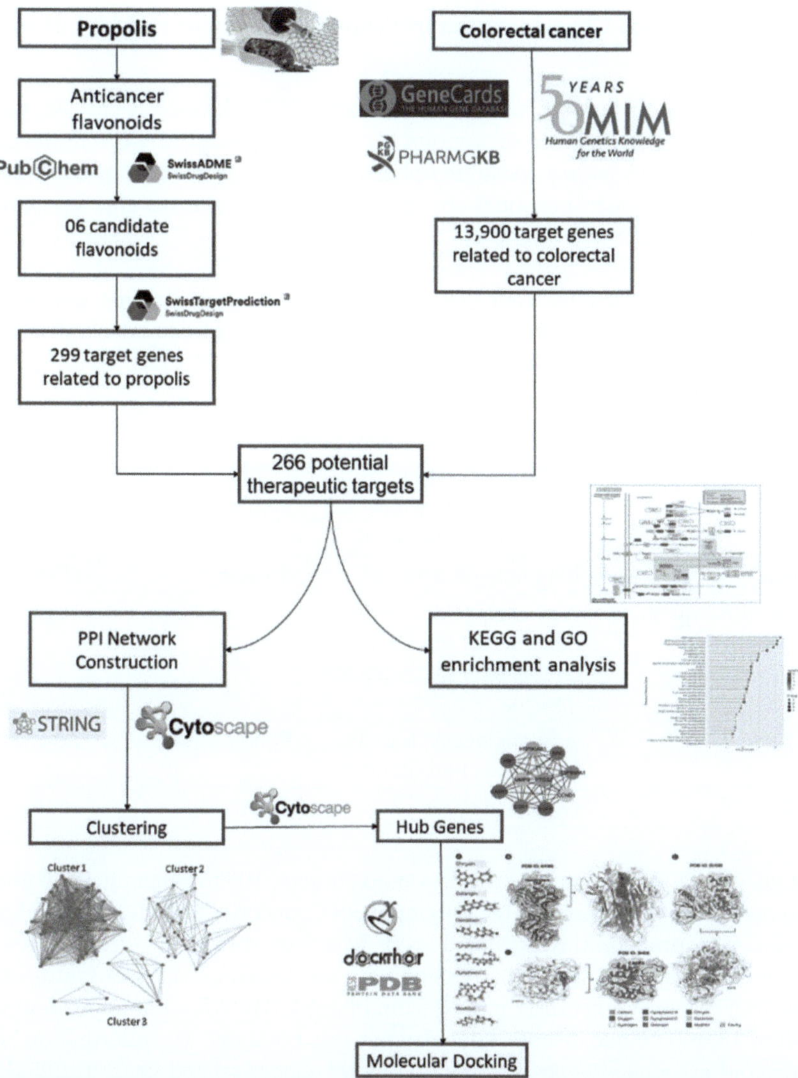

Fig. 1. Workflow for the network pharmacology-based investigation of propolis flavonoids against colorectal cancer. The methodology includes the selection of flavonoids, prediction of pharmacokinetic properties and target genes, identification of colorectal cancer-related targets, construction and analysis of the protein-protein interaction (PPI) network, functional enrichment analysis (GO and KEGG), and molecular docking validation of key targets.

3 Results and Discussion

To ensure transparency and reproducibility, all results from each stage of the analysis, including compound screening, target prediction, network construction, functional enrichment and molecular docking, are available in a publicly accessible repository on GitHub, at: https://github.com/alinecfelicio/XMeeting2025-Propolis-CLC.

3.1 Physicochemical Characteristics of Propolis Flavonoids and Identified Target Genes

Based on literature review, the molecular structures of the flavonoids chrysin, galangin, genistein, vestitol, nymphaeol A/propolin C, and nymphaeol C were retrieved from PubChem in SMILES format. Also, the pharmacokinetic properties of the flavonoids, including solubility, gastrointestinal absorption, and molecular weight, were evaluated using the SwissADME tool (Table 1).

Table 1. Bioactive flavonoids from propolis and their pharmacokinetic properties. The table summarizes the names, antitumor activities, solubility, and gastrointestinal absorption (GI absorption) predictions of the selected flavonoids.

Compound Name	Property	Solubility	GI absorption
Chrysin	Induction of apoptosis	Moderately soluble	High
Galangin	Induction of apoptosis and inhibition of migration	Soluble	High
Genistein	Inhibition of cell cycle	Soluble	High
Nymphaeol A/Propolin C	Anti-angiogenic activity, inhibition of proliferation inhibition of migration and invasion	Poorly soluble	High
Nymphaeol C	Anti-angiogenic activity, inhibition of proliferation	Poorly soluble	Low
Vestitol	Cytotoxic effect	Soluble	High

A total of 103 genes related to the flavonoid chrysin, 103 to galangin, 94 to genistein, 81 to nymphaeol A/propolin C, 104 to nymphaeol C, and 108 to vestitol were identified, with prediction probabilities greater than 0, based on the chemical structures of the compounds. In total, 329 genes associated with colorectal cancer were retrieved from OMIM, 13,570 from GeneCards, and 77 from PharmGKB. After removing duplicates, a final set of 13,900 unique disease-related genes was obtained. The intersection between the flavonoid-associated genes and the colorectal cancer-related genes resulted in 266 common genes, considered as potential therapeutic targets.

3.2 Protein-Protein Interaction (PPI) Network Analysis

The PPI network analysis revealed 266 nodes and 3,449 edges, with an average node degree of 25.9, indicating high connectivity among the proteins. Among the genes analyzed, 10 hub genes were identified: TNF, EGFR, CASP3, SRC, ESR1, HSP90AA1, PTGS2, HSP90AB1, MMP9, and CCND1. Moreover, these genes play essential roles by encoding proteins involved in crucial biological processes, such as regulation of inflammation (TNF and PTGS2), apoptosis (CASP3), extracellular matrix remodeling (MMP9), cell signaling (EGFR, SRC, and ESR1), cellular stress response (HSP90AA1 and HSP90AB1), and cell cycle regulation (CCND1). Given these functions, these genes are potentially relevant in the context of molecular mechanisms associated with diseases, including colorectal cancer.

PPI network clustering using the MCODE algorithm resulted in the formation of three distinct modules (Fig. 2), representing densely connected subnetworks. Within each cluster, hub genes were identified based on local topological parameters, mainly connectivity degree. A total of 47 hub genes were found in Cluster 1, 30 in Cluster 2, and 12 in Cluster 3. CCND1, CASP3, and PARP1 highlighted as the top functional targets in Cluster 1, being considered potential key targets in the context of colorectal cancer. For Cluster 2, the three main hub genes were SYK, PIK3CB and PIK2CD. For Cluster 3, the main hub gene was PLA2G4A.

3.3 Functional Enrichment of Potential Therapeutic Targets

To explore the biological functions and signaling pathways associated with the 266 common potential therapeutic targets between flavonoids and colorectal cancer, a functional enrichment analysis was performed. Principal biological pathways identified are highlighted in Fig. 2.

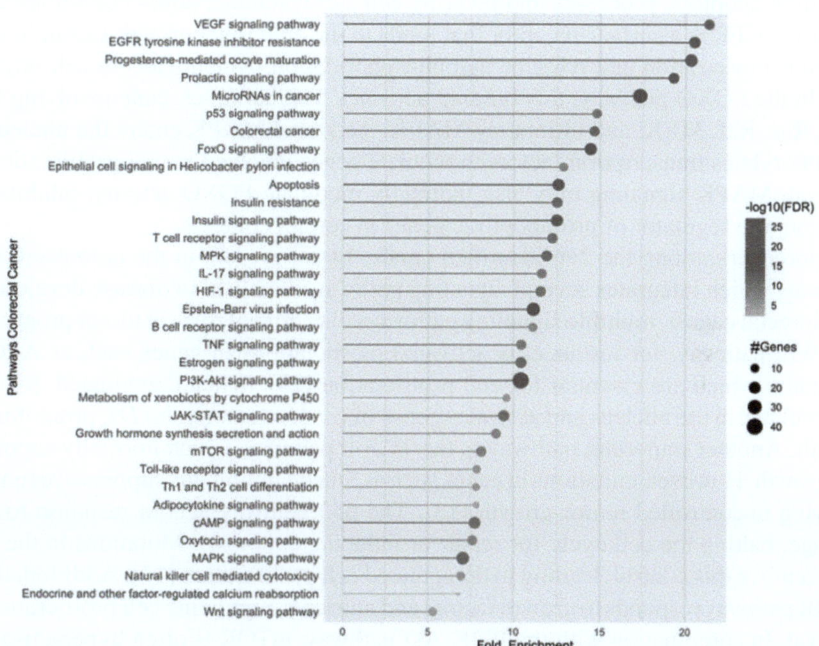

Fig. 2. Functional enrichment pathways from KEGG for the 266 common target genes between propolis flavonoids and colorectal cancer.

The PI3K/AKT pathway plays a fundamental role in cellular processes, and its dysregulation has been implicated in several types of cancer, including colorectal cancer [23]. Phosphoinositide 3-kinases (PI3Ks) are a large family of lipid enzymes capable of phosphorylating the 3'-OH group of phosphatidylinositols (PtdIns) at the plasma membrane [15]. Studies indicate that the PI3K-AKT pathway is hyperactivated in many human cancers, and its interaction with the FOXO signaling pathway plays a crucial role in regulating cell fate [12]. FOXO transcription factors are considered tumor suppressors due to their established functions in cell cycle arrest, apoptosis, senescence, differentiation, DNA damage repair, and elimination of reactive oxygen species [10]. Growth factors, such as insulin, are essential regulators of FOXO activity. Among the pathways that interact with FOXO, PI3K-AKT is the most relevant in oncological contexts, although other signaling pathways, such as JAK-STAT and MAPK, also interact with FOXO [3].

Among the 266 potential therapeutic targets associated with flavonoids and colorectal cancer, the receptors IGF1R and EGFR were highlighted. IGF1R binds to *insulin-like growth factor 1* (IGF1) at the plasma membrane. In the FOXO signaling pathway, IGF1 binding activates PI3K, generating the signaling molecule PIP3 (*phosphatidylinositol-3,4,5-trisphosphate*), which subsequently activates the kinase Akt. Akt phosphorylates the FOXO transcription factor, resulting in its inactivation. Growth factors signal the cell to promote proliferation, survival, differentiation, and growth. Since the PI3K-Akt pathway promotes cellular proliferation, activation of this pathway inactivates FOXO, inhibiting apoptotic processes and favoring cell survival under stress conditions. Additionally, EGFR is a surface receptor that binds to the epidermal growth factor, inducing receptor dimerization and tyrosine autophosphorylation, which leads to cell proliferation. In the FOXO pathway, this binding activates a signaling cascade involving Grb2, SOS, Ras, Raf, MEK, and ultimately MAPK. Activated MAPK enters the nucleus and phosphorylates transcription factors to regulate genes involved in cell proliferation and survival. MAPK signaling may also indirectly modulate FOXO activity, inhibiting its function as a regulator of pro-apoptotic genes in certain contexts.

Moreover, among the 266 identified genes, 14 are present in the colorectal cancer pathway, which integrates several signaling pathways involved in disease development. In colorectal cancer, multiple signaling pathways play crucial roles in tumor progression. The Wnt pathway, for instance, is activated by mutations in genes such as APC and β-catenin, which are essential for cell proliferation [25]. When deregulated, β-catenin accumulates in the nucleus and activates genes like *c-Myc* and *Cyclin D1*, promoting cell growth. Another important pathway is the TGF-β pathway, which normally suppresses cell growth. However, mutations in genes such as Smad4 inhibit this suppressive function, allowing uncontrolled tumor growth [13]. The p53 pathway acts in response to DNA damage, halting the cell cycle for repair or inducing apoptosis. Mutations in the TP53 gene remove this control, leading to deregulated cell proliferation [11]. Additionally, the mTOR pathway responds to growth factors and nutrients, regulating cell proliferation and survival. In combination with the PI3K-Akt pathway, mTOR is often hyperactivated in various tumors, contributing to excessive cell growth. Furthermore, the MAPK pathway, previously mentioned, is also involved in this process.

To further investigate the interactions among the identified genes, the interaction network was subjected to clustering analysis using the MCODE algorithm and all clusters functional enrichment was conducted. In Cluster 1, 85 significantly enriched terms related to biological processes (BP) were identified, among which the following is highlighted: positive regulation of DNA replication (GO:0045740, FDR: 0.0016), positive regulation of the apoptotic process (GO:0043065, FDR: 0.00288), cell surface receptor protein tyrosine kinase signaling pathway (GO:0007169, FDR: 0.0031), regulation of signal transduction by the p53 class mediator (GO:1901796, FDR: 0.0033), chromatin binding (GO:0003682, FDR: 0.0012), collagen receptor tyrosine kinase activity (GO:0038062, FDR: 0.0012) and 3-phosphoinositide-dependent protein kinase activity (GO:0004676, FDR: 0.0012).

In Cluster 2, 28 terms related to Biological Processes (BP) were identified, among which the following is highlighted: extracellular matrix disassembly (GO:0022617, FDR: 0.0011), regulation of cell population proliferation (GO:0042127, FDR: 0.0217), proteolysis (GO:0006508, FDR: 0.0239), B cell receptor signaling pathway (GO:0050853, FDR: 0.0451), positive regulation of cell migration (GO:0030335, FDR: 0.0132) and binding to signaling receptors (GO:0005102, FDR: 0.0051). Such molecular interactions are relevant in the regulation of oncogenic signaling pathways and the stability of cell cycle regulatory proteins. Cluster 3 presented 4 terms enriched in biological processes, including: linoleic acid metabolic process (GO:0043651, FDR: 0.0017), arachidonate secretion (GO:0050482, FDR: 0.0028), phospholipid metabolic process (GO:0006644, FDR: 0.0114) and cellular response to insulin stimulus (GO:0032869, FDR: 0.0278).

3.4   Molecular Docking Verification

The selected proteins were: TNF, with a degree of 129; EGFR, with a degree of 125; and CASP3, with a degree of 120. Among them, is highlighted the CASP3, as it not only ranks among the top 3 in the overall network but was also identified as the second main hub of Cluster 1 with a degree of 44, which reinforces its biological importance in the context of colorectal cancer. All previously selected compounds were used in the molecular docking analyses, including: Chrysin, Galangin, Genistein, Nymphaeol A/Propolin C, Nymphaeol C, and Vestitol. The goal was to predict the interaction between these ligands and the target receptors of colorectal cancer (CRC).

Based on the molecular docking tests, all analyzed flavonoids exhibited RMSD values equal to 0, indicating stable fitting in the predicted cavities of the target proteins. For the CASP3 protein (PDB ID: 3H0E), the flavonoid Nymphaeol A/Propolin C achieved the best binding energy (−8.543 kcal/mol), slightly higher than the value observed in the redocking of the co-crystallized ligand (−8.456 kcal/mol) (Fig. 3). Regarding the TNF protein (PDB ID: 6X86), the compound Nymphaeol C (−12.482 kcal/mol) presented the best binding energy results (Fig. 4), surpassing the co-crystallized ligand used in the redocking (−11.427 kcal/mol). For the EGFR protein (PDB ID: 5UGB), although all flavonoids also maintained an RMSD of 0, the compound Galangin stood out with a binding energy of −7.976 kcal/mol, followed closely by Chrysin (−7.927 kcal/mol) and Vestitol (−7.945 kcal/mol). These binding energies were less negative than the redocking value (−8.571 kcal/mol), indicating less favorable interactions (Fig. 5). Furthermore, the compounds Nymphaeol A/Propolin C and Nymphaeol C exhibited weaker chemical interactions, as indicated by the red bonds in Fig. 5. The interactions between the flavonoids and the target proteins CASP3, TNF, and EGFR, including the binding sites and predicted cavities, revealed that, although all proteins had suitable cavities for the ligands, the interactions were more favorable in the TNF and EGFR proteins.

In molecular fitting, besides energy, various types of interactions between amino acids play an essential role in the binding and stability of the formed complex. Among these interactions, hydrogen bonds stand out as crucial for the specificity of the binding between the drug and the protein's active site [6, 14]. Furthermore, van der Waals forces arise as weak and universal attractions between molecules, caused by changes in electron distribution, playing a complementary role in molecular interactions. The ionic interactions are stronger than hydrogen bonds, though weaker than covalent bonds [6]. All the results are available on GitHub.

The results of molecular docking of propolis' flavonoids and CASP3 were: **1) Chrysin:** Met28, Thr29, His88, Gly89, Glu90, Cys130, Tyr159 and Arg162; with − 7.761 kcal/mol; **2) Galangin:** Met28, Thr29, His88, Gly89, Glu90, Cys130 and Tyr159; with −7.794 kcal/mol; **3) Genistein:** Met28, Thr29, His88, Gly89, Glu90, Cys130 and Tyr159; with -7.596 kcal/mol; **4) Nymphaeol C:** His88, Glu90, Cys130, Tyr159, Trp161, Arg162 and Phe211, with −8.263 kcal/mol; **5) Vestitol:** Met28, His88, Glu90, Phe95, Cys130 and Tyr159; with −7.658 kcal/mol; The best energy binding value is represented in Fig. 3.

The intermolecular interaction and energy binding values between the protein TNF and the small molecules, excepting the best result that is represented in the Fig. 4 (Nymphaeol C), were: **1) Chrysin:** Ser3, Lys5, Leu40, Leu51, Ile129, Leu142, Ile149 and Leu151 with energy binding of −9.122 kcal/mol; **2) Galangin:** Leu51 and Tyr104 with −9.656 kcal/mol; **3) Genistein:** Leu40, Tyr42, Ser43, Leu51, Gly95, Ile149 and Leu151 with −9.661 kcal/mol; **4) Nymphaeol A:** Lys5, Leu40, Tyr42, Leu51, Tyr104, Tye125, Ter142, Leu142, Ile149 and Leu151 with −11.064 kcal/mol; **5) Vestitol:** Lys2, Val4, Lys5, Ile129, Ala130 and Leu131 with -8.059 kcal/mol;

The best result of energy binding with EGFR is represented in Fig. 5, referred to Vestitol. The others results of binding EGFR and propolis' flavonoids were: **1) Chrysin:** Cys101, Leu148 and Asp159 with −7.927 kcal/mol; **2) Galangin:** Lys51, Cys101, Leu148 and Asp159 with −7.976 kcal/mol; **3) Genistein:** Leu24, Val32, Lys51, Cys101, Asp104 and Asp159 with −7.532 kcal/mol; **4) Nymphaeol A:** Leu102, Leu118, Trp121, Cys122, Ile125, Met129, Leu132, Leu137, His139, Asp141, Leu142, Asn146, Val147, Leu148, Lys156, Ile157, Phe160, Ala163 and Leu211 with − 7.133 kcal/mol; **5) Nymphaeol C:** His77, Leu102, Cys122, Ile125, Met129, His139, Leu142, Ala143, Asp146, Val147, Val155, Ile157, Tyr204, Thr207, Val208 and Leu211 with -6.652 kcal/mol.

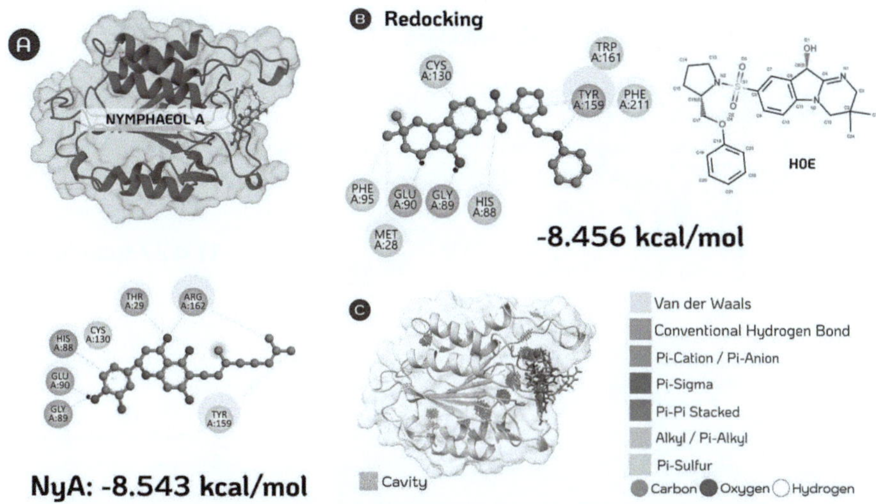

Fig. 3. Best molecular docking result of propolis' flavonoids and CASP3. Each letter indicates the binding results with the energy binding and the amino acids involved in the intermolecular interaction between the protein CASP3 and the small molecule. The legend explains the different types of intermolecular interactions using different colors; **A) Nymphaeol A**: Thr29, His88, Gly89, Glu90, Cys130, Tyr159, and Arg162; with −8.543 kcal/mol of energy binding; **B) Result of the redocking** between CASP3 and the original PDB ligand "H0E", with −8.456 kcal/mol. The amino acids involved in the interaction were Met28, His88, Gly89, Glu90, Phe95, Cys130, Tyr159, Trp161 and Phe211; **C) CASP3 had its cavity predicted** by KVFinder and is represented by a granulation effect in green color. The flavonoids are distinguished in the active site by many colors in the exact binding site after the molecular docking.

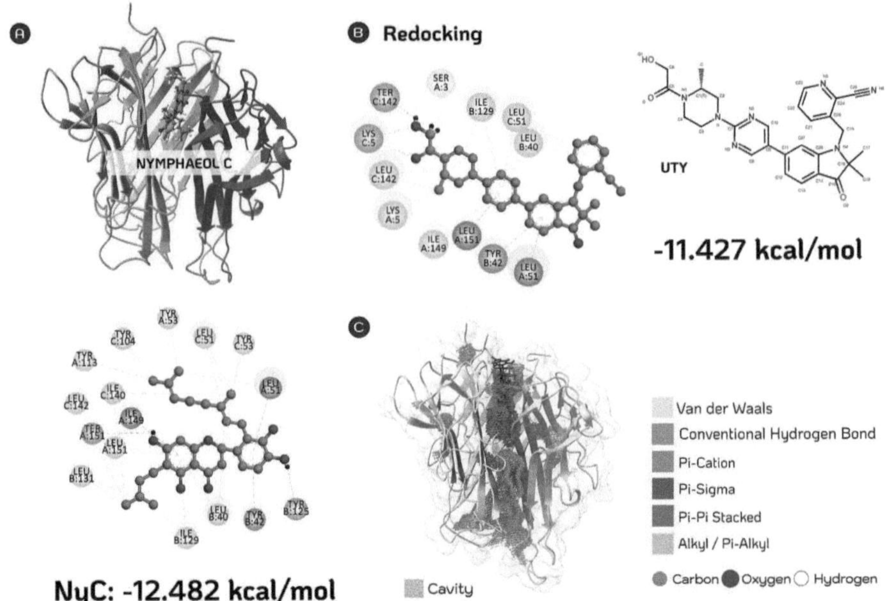

Fig. 4. Best molecular docking result of propolis' flavonoids and TNF. Each letter indicates the binding results with the energy binding and the amino acids involved in the intermolecular interaction between the protein TNF and the small molecule. The legend explains the different types of intermolecular interactions using different colors; **A) Nymphaeol C:** Leu40, Tyr42, Leu51, Tyr53, Tyr104, Tyr113, Tyr125, Ile129, Leu131, Ile140, Leu142, Ile149, Ter151 and Leu151; with −12.482 kcal/mol of energy binding; **B) Result of the redocking** between TNF and the original PDB ligand "UTY", with −11.427 kcal/mol. The amino acids involved in the interaction were Ser3, Lys5, Lys5, Leu 40, Tyr42, Leu51, Ile129, Ter142, Leu142, Ile14,9, and Leu151. **C) TNF had its cavity predicted** by KVFinder and is represented by a granulation effect in green color. The flavonoids are distinguished in the active site by many colors in the exact binding site after the molecular docking.

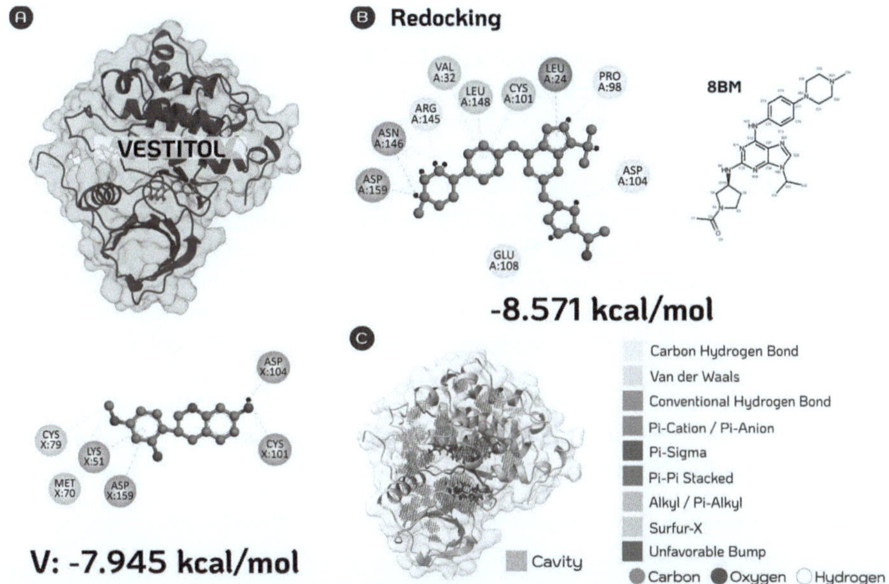

Fig. 5. Best Energy Binding value from Molecular Docking results of propolis' flavonoids and EGFR. Each letter indicates the binding results with the energy binding and the amino acids involved in the intermolecular interaction between the protein EGFR and the small molecule. The legend explains the different types of intermolecular interactions using different colors; **A) Vestitol**: Lys51, Met70, Cys79, Cys101, Asp104, and Asp159; with − 7.945 kcal/mol of energy binding; **B) Result of the redocking** between EGFR and the original PDB ligand "8BM", with − 11.427 kcal/mol, the best result. The amino acids involved in the interaction were Leu24, Val32, Pro98, Cys101, Asp104, Glu108, Arg145, Asn146, Leu148 and Asp159; **C) EGFR had its cavity predicted** by KVFinder and is represented by a granulation effect in green color. The flavonoids are distinguished in the active site by many colors in the exact binding site after the molecular docking.

4 Conclusion

Network pharmacology analyses enabled the identification of genes with high therapeutic potential present in the flavonoids from propolis against colorectal cancer. The analysis of the PPI interaction network, built from the 266 potential therapeutic genes, revealed high connectivity among proteins, resulting in the identification of 10 hub genes: TNF, EGFR, CASP3, SRC, ESR1, HSP90AA1, PTGS2, HSP90AB1, MMP9, and CCND1. Clustering of the PPI network resulted in three densely connected modules, with hub genes identified in each one. Molecular docking indicated strong interactions between flavonoids and the target proteins CASP3, TNF, and EGFR. Nymphaeol A/Propolin C and Nymphaeol C showed the best binding energies with CASP3 and TNF. Galangin, in turn, exhibited excellent interaction with EGFR, standing out as a potential therapeutic candidate. The development of colorectal cancer is driven by the dysregulation of several signaling pathways, such as Wnt, TGF-β, p53, PI3K-Akt, and MAPK, all contributing to tumorigenesis. In the molecular context of colorectal cancer, enrichment of signaling pathways critical for tumor progression was observed, including Wnt, TGF-β, p53, PI3K-Akt, MAPK, and FOXO. The latter plays an essential role in inducing apoptosis under cellular stress conditions and is often inactivated by activation of the PI3K-Akt pathway, thus promoting tumor cell survival and uncontrolled proliferation. Therefore, the analyzed flavonoids exhibit various antitumor properties, modulating oncogenic signaling pathways, inducing apoptosis, inhibiting cell migration and angiogenesis, and exerting cytotoxic effects. By interacting with therapeutic targets identified in the network analyses, these compounds may significantly contribute to the suppression of tumor progression and the induction of essential cellular responses, such as apoptosis. Future in vitro and in vivo investigations are warranted to further validate these findings and facilitate the development of novel drugs against colorectal cancer.

Acknowledgments. We'd like to thank São Francisco University for the institutional support. This study was financed in part by the Coordenação de Aperfeiçoamento de Pessoal de Nível Superior – Brasil (CAPES) – Finance Code 001.

Disclosure of Interests. The authors have no competing interests to declare.

References

1. Du, X., et al.: Insights into protein-ligand interactions: mechanisms, models, and methods. Int. J. Mol. Sci. **17**(2), 144 (2016). https://doi.org/10.3390/IJMS17020144
2. Eng, C., Hochster, H.: Early-onset colorectal cancer: the mystery remains. J. Natl. Cancer Inst. **113**(12), 1608–1610 (2021). https://doi.org/10.1093/JNCI/DJAB127
3. Farhan, M., et al.: FOXO signaling pathways as therapeutic targets in cancer. Int. J. Biol. Sci. **13**(7), 815 (2017). https://doi.org/10.7150/IJBS.20052
4. Forma, E., Bryś, M.: Anticancer activity of propolis and its compounds. Nutrients **13**(8), 2594 (2021). https://doi.org/10.3390/NU13082594
5. García-Ortegón, M., et al.: DOCKSTRING: easy molecular docking yields better benchmarks for ligand design. J. Chem. Inf. Model. **62**(15), 3486–3502 (2022). https://doi.org/10.1021/ACS.JCIM.1C01334/ASSET/IMAGES/LARGE/CI1C01334_0013.JPEG
6. Golan, D.E.: Princípios de Farmacologia - A Base Fisiopatológica da Farmacologia | Amazon.com.br. Guanabara Koogan, Rio de Janeiro (2014)
7. Guedes, I.A., et al.: DockThor-VS: a free platform for receptor-ligand virtual screening. J. Mol. Biol. **436**(17), 168548 (2024). https://doi.org/10.1016/J.JMB.2024.168548
8. Guedes, I.A., et al.: New machine learning and physics-based scoring functions for drug discovery. Sci. Rep. **11**(1), 1–19 (2021). https://doi.org/10.1038/s41598-021-82410-1
9. Guerra, J.V.S., et al.: KVFinder-web: a web-based application for detecting and characterizing biomolecular cavities. Nucleic Acids Res. **51**(W1), W289–W297 (2023). https://doi.org/10.1093/NAR/GKAD324
10. Jiramongkol, Y., Lam, E.W.F.: FOXO transcription factor family in cancer and metastasis. Cancer Metastasis Rev. **39**(3), 681–709 (2020). https://doi.org/10.1007/S10555-020-09883-W
11. Liebl, M.C., Hofmann, T.G.: The role of P53 signaling in colorectal cancer. Cancers (Basel) **13**(9), 2125 (2021). https://doi.org/10.3390/CANCERS13092125/S1
12. Lin, A., et al.: FoxO transcription factors promote AKT Ser473 phosphorylation and renal tumor growth in response to pharmacological inhibition of the PI3K-AKT pathway. Cancer Res. **74**(6), 1682 (2014). https://doi.org/10.1158/0008-5472.CAN-13-1729

13. Liu, A., et al.: PRMT5 methylating SMAD4 activates TGF-β signaling and promotes colorectal cancer metastasis. Oncogene **42**(19), 1572–1584 (2023). https://doi.org/10.1038/s41388-023-02674-x
14. Simmon, M.A.: Pharmacology: An Essential Textbook (2021)
15. Martini, M., et al.: PI3K/AKT signaling pathway and cancer: an updated review. Ann. Med. **46**(6), 372–383 (2014). https://doi.org/10.3109/07853890.2014.912836
16. Meng, E.C., et al.: UCSF ChimeraX: tools for structure building and analysis. Protein Sci. **32**(11), e4792 (2023). https://doi.org/10.1002/PRO.4792
17. Meng, X.-Y., et al.: Molecular docking: a powerful approach for structure-based drug discovery. Curr. Comput. Aided Drug Des. **7**(2), 146–157 (2011). https://doi.org/10.2174/157340911795677602
18. Rodríguez-García, C., et al.: Dietary flavonoids as cancer chemopreventive agents: an updated review of human studies. Antioxidants **8**(5), 137 (2019). https://doi.org/10.3390/ANTIOX8050137
19. Roshandel, G., et al.: Colorectal cancer: epidemiology, risk factors, and prevention. Cancers (Basel) **16**(8) (2024). https://doi.org/10.3390/CANCERS16081530
20. Shah, A., et al.: Network pharmacology and systems biology in drug discovery, pp. 231–252 (2023). https://doi.org/10.1007/978-981-99-1316-9_10
21. Shannon, P., et al.: Cytoscape: a software environment for integrated models of biomolecular interaction networks. Genome Res. **13**(11), 2498 (2003). https://doi.org/10.1101/GR.1239303
22. Sherman, B.T., et al.: DAVID: a web server for functional enrichment analysis and functional annotation of gene lists (2021 update). Nucleic Acids Res. **50**(W1), W216–W221 (2022). https://doi.org/10.1093/NAR/GKAC194
23. Swiechowski, R., et al.: Genetic insights into colorectal cancer: evaluating PI3K/AKT signaling pathway genes expression. Int. J. Mol. Sci. **25**(11), 5806 (2024). https://doi.org/10.3390/IJMS25115806
24. Szklarczyk, D., et al.: STRING v11: protein–protein association networks with increased coverage, supporting functional discovery in genome-wide experimental datasets. Nucleic Acids Res. **47**(D1), D607–D613 (2019). https://doi.org/10.1093/NAR/GKY1131
25. Zhao, H., et al.: WNT signaling in colorectal cancer: pathogenic role and therapeutic target. Mol. Cancer **21**(1), 1–34 (2022). https://doi.org/10.1186/S12943-022-01616-7
26. Estatísticas de câncer—Instituto Nacional de Câncer – INCA. https://www.gov.br/inca/pt-br/assuntos/cancer/numeros. Accessed 25 Apr 2025

BITSER: An Alignment-Free Approach for Feature Extraction and Classification of Viral Genomes

Lucas Costa Fuganti$^{(\boxtimes)}$, Matheus Henrique Pimenta-Zanon ,
and Fabricio Martins Lopes

Departamento Acadêmico de Computação (DACOM), Universidade Tecnológica
Federal do Paraná (UTFPR)- Campus Cornélio Procópio, Cornélio Procópio, Brazil
`lucascostafuganti@alunos.utfpr.edu.br`, `omatheuspimenta@outlook.com`,
`fabricio@utfpr.edu.br`

Abstract. The exponential growth of biological data, driven by high-throughput sequencing technologies, has created a pressing need for efficient and interpretable feature extraction methods in genomics. This study presents the BITSER method, a novel alignment-free approach for feature extraction and classification of biological sequences. Drawing inspiration from texture analysis techniques in computer vision, BITSER adapts the Local Binary Pattern (LBP) and its variants to extract histograms from sequences based on the electron-ion interaction potential (EIIP) of nucleotides. This method uses the raw FASTA sequences, avoiding the need for prior annotation or alignment, and offers a transparent and biologically meaningful feature representation. The BITSER was evaluated on SARS-CoV-2 and DENV viral genomes, achieving classification accuracies exceeding 99% across multiple classifiers by adopting different classification algorithms. Feature importance analysis enabled significant dimensionality reduction, preserving predictive power with only a few features per dataset. Compared to existing methods, BITSER demonstrated superior results, computational efficiency, and interpretability. These results underscore the method's robustness, scalability, and potential for broad application in large-scale genomic analysis.

Keywords: Genetic sequences · Classification · Feature extraction

1 Introduction

Biological data generation has increased exponentially due to high-throughput sequencing, particularly RNA-Seq [1]. Analyzing these vast datasets thoroughly offers opportunities to uncover novel insights into genetic information encoded within biological sequences [2–4]. Analyzing genome sequences is particularly important for advancing our understanding of genetic composition and variation [5].

Traditionally, alignment-based methods have been extensively employed to compare biological sequences in pairs or among multiple sequences. Various techniques and software tools have been developed, offering valuable applications

© The Author(s), under exclusive license to Springer Nature Switzerland AG 2026
M. Dorn and F. Martins Lopes (Eds.): X-Meeting 2025, LNBI 16037, pp. 166–180, 2026.
https://doi.org/10.1007/978-3-032-09336-3_12

across numerous areas of modern molecular biology. These include evolutionary studies and the prediction of secondary and tertiary structures, molecular functions, and intermolecular interactions [6]. However, alignment-based approaches exhibit some limitations when applied to highly divergent sequences or large-scale datasets, such as those encountered in viral datasets [7].

Alignment-free methods have emerged as a promising alternative, offering reduced computational complexity and enabling the efficient analysis of complete genomes. These methods are grounded in mathematical principles and incorporate concepts from several areas. They are highly adaptable and do not require prior knowledge of the sequences being analyzed. Instead, alignment-free approaches aim to identify discriminative patterns, which is particularly advantageous when analyzing highly mutable genomes, such as those of viruses [8].

A persistent challenge in biological data analysis is achieving accurate classification with fewer features while maintaining interpretability and efficiency, which are critical requirements for applications like clinical diagnostics. Despite advances in the field, there is still a high demand for efficient, explainable, and open-source computational tools to address the complexities of these analyses [9].

Feature extraction constitutes a fundamental component of computational analysis in biology, with the primary objective of identifying discriminative features that encapsulate critical sequence information. To address this task, several bioinformatics approaches has been developed, employing diverse methodological approaches to process and interpret biological data [10–18]. Despite their utility, a possible limitation of these approaches lies in their exclusive reliance on input data, without incorporating biological context. This restriction can affect the robustness and the generalization of such methods in different organisms and experimental conditions [19,20].

Feature extraction techniques from computer vision are entirely data-driven and do not consider external knowledge, achieving suitable results in pattern recognition tasks [21–28]. Inspired by these approaches, our study introduces a novel method for biological sequence classification that treats sequences as interpretable signals, similar to images. We extract features directly from raw nucleotide sequences in FASTA format by analyzing local variations in electron-ion interaction potential (EIIP), eliminating the need for prior alignment or annotation. The proposed approach can process thousands of viral genomes using standard personal computing resources. Moreover, it effectively identifies the most discriminative motifs associated with the classes under investigation. The experimental assessments on the SARS-CoV-2 and DENV viral genomes resulted in high classification accuracy and efficiency, indicating the suitability of the proposed method for classifying viral genomes.

2   Related Work

2.1   Texture Analysis

The concepts of Texture Unit and Texture Spectrum, proposed by L. Wang and D. He [21], offer a statistical approach to texture analysis. Texture Unit (TU) refers to a set of 9 pixels, obtained by a 3×3 sliding window over the image, with 1 central pixel and 8 neighboring pixels. The original work covered the concept of a Local Ternary Pattern (LTP), where each comparison of the central pixel in a neighborhood and each of its neighbors can take 1 of 3 different values. This work uses the Local Binary Pattern (LBP) version, where each comparison can take 1 of 2 values. In LBP, Texture Unit $TU = \{E_1, E_2, \ldots, E_8\}$, where E_i occupies the same position as pixel i, is defined as:

$$E_i = \begin{cases} 0 & \text{if } V_i < V_0 \\ 1 + V_0 & \text{if } V_i \geq V_0 \end{cases} \quad \text{for } i = 1, 2, \ldots, 8$$

where $V = \{V_0, V_1, \ldots, V_8\}$ being an array where V_0 represents the intensity value of the central pixel, and V_i represents the intensity value of neighboring pixel i.

The values of TU form an array, which can be represented by the Texture Unit Number (N_{TU}), which is calculated according to Eq. 1, where E_i is the element i of the Texture Unit array $TU = \{E_1, E_2, \ldots, E_8\}$. Using LBP, the combination allows for $2^8 = 256$ possible Texture Units.

$$N_{TU} = \sum_{i=1}^{8} 2^{(i-1)} E_i, \ N_{TU(B)} \in 0, 1, 2, \ldots, 255. \tag{1}$$

The 8 elements of the pixel neighborhood may be ordered differently, resulting in potentially different values for TU. Considering a clockwise order, the first element may be in any position from top-left (a) (commonly adopted) to middle-left (h), as shown in Fig. 1.

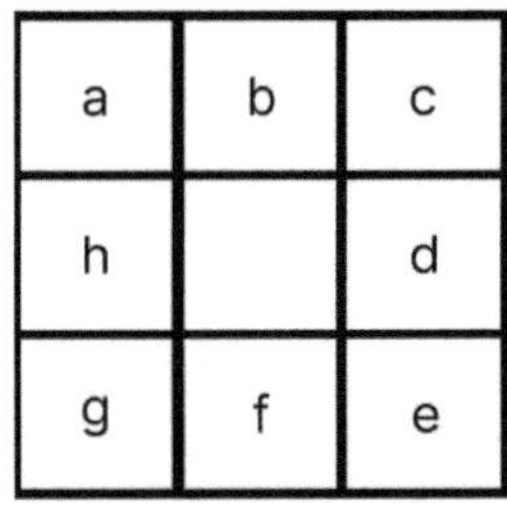

Fig. 1. Eight ordering ways of the Texture Unit elements [21].

Figure 2 shows an example of transforming a pixel neighborhood into N_{TU}.

Texture Spectrum is defined as the occurrence frequency function of all the Texture Units, with the abscissa indicating Texture Unit number N, and the ordinate representing its occurrence frequency. The defined 256 Texture Units can be represented as a histogram displaying such occurrences.

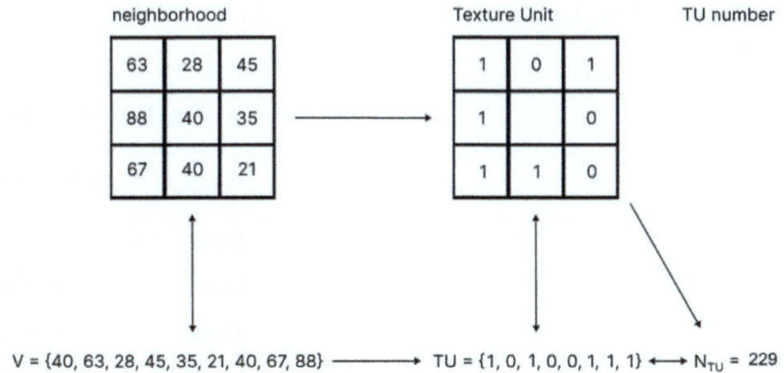

Fig. 2. Example of transforming a pixel neighborhood [21].

Texture features were also discussed by Wang and He [21], as additional features to aid in texture characterization and image classification. One such feature proposed is Black-White Symmetry (BWS), which can be calculated according to Eq. 2.

$$BWS = \left[1 - \frac{\sum_{i=0}^{126} |S(i) - S(128 + i)|}{\sum_{i=0}^{255} S(i)}\right] \cdot 100 \qquad (2)$$

where $S(i)$ represents the occurrence frequency of TU i, $i = 0, 1, 2, \ldots, 255$. BWS measures the symmetry of the Texture Spectrum's left half (0 to 126) and right half (128 to 255). A high BWS value can be understood as the intensity values of the original image remaining approximately the same when inverting the texture spectrum.

2.2 EIIP

Converting nucleotide or amino acid sequences into numerical sequences involves adopting a numerical conversion. The Electron-Ion Interaction Potential (EIIP) value represents the average energy states of all the valence electrons in nucleotides and amino acids. This representation was successfully applied using digital signal analysis techniques, including the Fourier transform [29]. The adopted EIIP values in this study are presented in Table 1.

Table 1. The Electron-Ion Interaction Potential (EIIP) Values for Nucleotides and Amino Acids [29].

Amino Acids

Amino acid	EIIP
Leu	0.0000
Ile	0.0000
Asn	0.0036
Gly	0.0050
Val	0.0057
Glu	0.0058
Pro	0.0198
His	0.0242
Lys	0.0371
Ala	0.0373
Tyr	0.0516
Trp	0.0548
Gln	0.0761
Met	0.0823
Ser	0.0829
Cys	0.0829
Thr	0.0941
Phe	0.0946
Arg	0.0959
Asp	0.1263

Nucleotides

Nucleotide	EIIP
A	0.1260
G	0.0806
T	0.1335
C	0.1340

3 Materials and Methods

3.1 Materials

The viral classes adopted in this study are summarized in Table 2, in which the corresponding number of samples used for training and testing is reported for each dataset. The SARS-CoV-2 sequences were retrieved from the NCBI database and encompass five variants of concern: Alpha, Beta, Delta, Gamma, and Omicron. The Dengue virus (DENV) dataset, obtained from the BV-BRC platform, comprises four distinct serotypes. Experiments were conducted on each dataset using a variety of classification algorithms.

3.2 Method

BITSER as a method proposes adapting the concepts of Local Ternary Pattern, Texture Unit, and Texture Spectrum [21] to the context of genetic sequences to

Table 2. Adopted datasets and their statistical measures

Dataset	Class	Training samples	Test samples	Validation samples
SARS-CoV-2	Alpha	700	300	70
	Beta	700	300	70
	Delta	700	300	70
	Gamma	700	300	70
	Omicron	700	300	70
DENV	Type 1	1800	771	180
	Type 2	1229	527	123
	Type 3	890	382	89
	Type 4	323	139	32

extract features. The Local Binary Pattern (LBP) [22] versions of the defined formulas were utilized.

The proposed Local Binary Pattern (LBP) algorithm variant constructs a histogram consisting of 256 bins. To adapt techniques from image processing, where pixel intensity values are utilized in calculations, to the context of genetic sequences, the Electron-Ion Interaction Potential (EIIP) values for nucleotides and amino acids, as defined in [29], were employed. The proposed approach, a sliding window, is applied over the genetic sequence, encompassing segments of 9 consecutive nucleotides or amino acids. In this configuration, the leftmost element is designated as the center, while the remaining 8 elements adjacent to it constitute the surrounding neighborhood. Figure 3 provides an overview of the BITSER methodology.

Figure 4 illustrates the sequential steps in transforming a genetic sequence into an LBP histogram. Additionally, Fig. 5 presents four representative examples of sequence segments, extracted from the sequence shown in Fig. 4, each being converted into its respective Texture Unit Number.

To further clarify the process of histogram bin computation, an interactive online tool was developed and is accessible online**[1]. This tool enables users to select between Local Ternary Pattern (LTP) and Local Binary Pattern (LBP) modes and to input any desired bin value corresponding to the respective histogram type. Upon selecting a specific input value, the tool computes the associated Texture Unit array that would produce the given bin. It generates illustrative examples, including a pixel neighborhood and a genetic sequence segment that would yield the same array. Additionally, it shows a table with the calculation steps described in Eq. 1.

Following the generation of the histogram, it becomes possible to compute additional features that further characterize each sequence. Among these features are the Black-White Symmetry (BWS), which assesses the similarity between the first and second halves of the histogram, and the Black-White Palindrome

---

[1] https://github.com/LCostaF/NTU_Calculator.

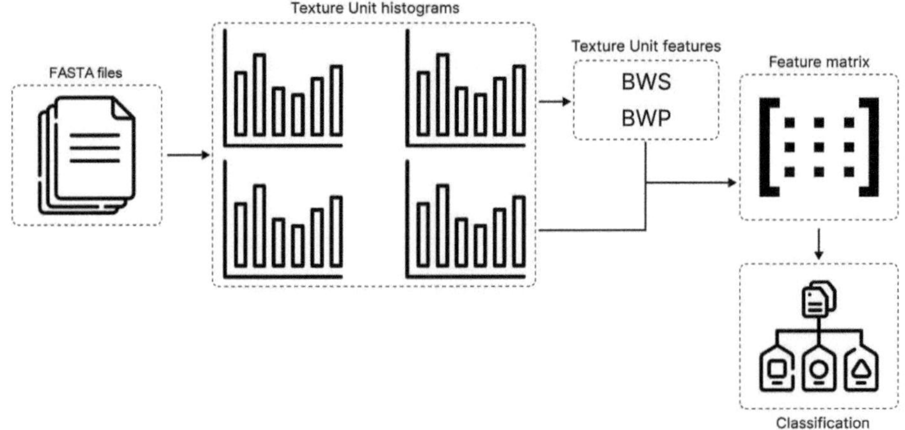

Fig. 3. Overview of the proposed methodology.

(BWP), a novel adaptation of BWS that evaluates the similarity between histogram positions equidistant from the central bin. The proposed definition of BWP is presented in Eq. 3.

$$BWP = \left[1 - \frac{\sum_{i=0}^{126} |S(i) - S(255 - i)|}{\sum_{i=0}^{255} S(i)}\right] \cdot 100 \tag{3}$$

The method can be applied to translated sequences (amino acid sequences) and untranslated sequences (nucleotide sequences). However, empirical analysis of the results did not reveal significant improvements when using translated sequences. Consequently, the decision was made to conduct the subsequent experiments using nucleotide sequences in this study.

4   Results and Discussion

To assess the effectiveness of the BITSER method, computational experiments were performed on viral genomes of the SARS-CoV-2 and DENV viruses, as outlined in Table 2. The evaluation process begins with an input directory containing FASTA files used to train the classification model. The model is constructed based on Texture Unit histograms and extracted features derived from the sequences in the training set. The same feature extraction procedure is then applied to a separate validation dataset, composed of sequences not included in the training set. The trained model subsequently serves as the basis for classifying the test data.

During the training step, 10-fold cross-validation was performed on the training data for each dataset. This validation process was repeated for all classifier types under consideration. Table 3 reports the resulting cross-validation accuracy scores. Although the classifiers yielded comparable performance, indicating

TTGTTGACCAGGGCCCTTTTTCTGTTGTACTACTGTGCAGTCAGATGAGCAGTGCAATATTAAAAGGGCATTGGCTGACAA

(a)

[0.1335, 0.1335, 0.0806, 0.1335, 0.1335, 0.0806, 0.1260, 0.1340, 0.1340, ... 0.1260]

(b)

(c)

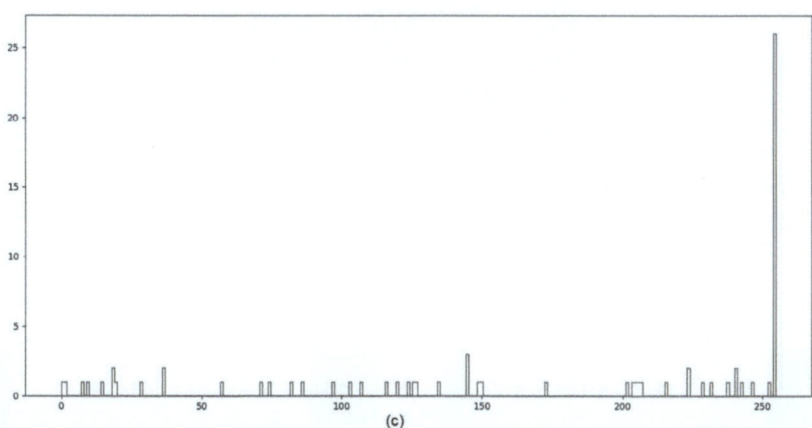

Fig. 4. Steps for obtaining a LBP histogram from a genetic sequence; (a) DNA sequence, (b) array of EIIP values respective to each nucleotide, (c) Texture Spectrum histogram.

<u>C</u>AATATTAA	<u>A</u>GTCAGATG
[0, 0, 0, 0, 0, 0, 0, 0]	[0, 1.126, 1.126, 1.126, 0, 1.126, 1.126, 0]
0	124
<u>T</u>AAAAGGGC	<u>G</u>GCTGACAA
[0, 0, 0, 0, 0, 0, 0, 1.1335]	[1.0806, 1.0806, 1.0806, 1.0806, 1.0806, 1.0806, 1.0806, 1.0806]
145	255

Fig. 5. Examples of sequence segments, their resulting Texture Unit array, and corresponding Texture Unit Number according to LBP. Underlined nucleotides represent the central value of each segment.

the suitability of the extracted features, the XGBoost (XGB) classifier demonstrated slightly superior results overall and was therefore selected for subsequent analyses.

Figures 6 and 7 show the confusion matrices for test executions over the SARS-CoV-2 and DENV datasets, respectively.

In both the cross-validation analysis and the evaluation of the trained models on the test datasets, the SARS-CoV-2 and DENV datasets exhibited accuracy values exceeding 99% on both validation and testing sets. The classification performance achieved by the proposed method on viral genomes, includ-

Table 3. Cross-validation results.

Dataset	Classifier type	Accuracy	Standard deviation
SARS-CoV-2	RF	99.9%	0.01%
	XGB	99.9%	0.01%
	SVM	99.9%	0.01%
	MLP	99.9%	0.02%
	Naive Bayes	99.6%	0.03%
DENV	RF	99.8%	0.02%
	XGB	99.8%	0.02%
	SVM	99.5%	0.03%
	MLP	99.5%	0.04%
	Naive Bayes	99.5%	0.04%

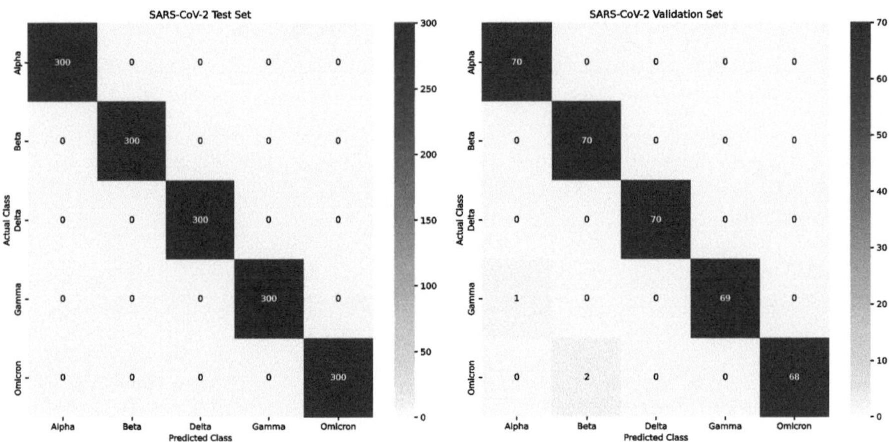

Fig. 6. Confusion matrices for SARS-CoV-2.

ing SARS-CoV-2 and DENV, is competitive with results previously reported in the literature. Methods such as CASTOR-KRFE [30] and KANALYZER [31] have demonstrated comparable accuracy; however, a notable drawback of these existing approaches lies in their high computational complexity, increased resource consumption, and limited interpretability. In contrast, the BITSER method offers a more efficient and explainable alternative for viral genome classification and a low computational complexity, allowing the proposed approach to handle a high volume of biological sequences.

To identify the most influential features contributing to the classification performance, feature importance analyses were conducted on both datasets, using the weight-based feature rankings for the XGB classifier [32]. Based on these analyses, and following additional testing using a reduced number of features, a subset of 9 features was selected for the SARS-CoV-2 dataset and 7 features

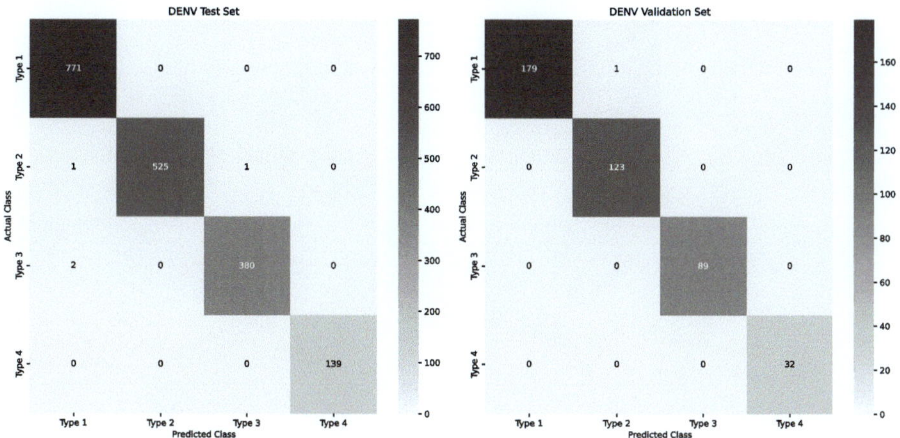

Fig. 7. Confusion matrices for DENV.

for the DENV dataset. Compared to the original set of 258, classification tests using only these selected features yielded comparable accuracy levels, indicating that the reduced feature sets preserved the model's predictive power.

Parallel coordinate plots depicting the relative importance of these features for each organism are presented in Figs. 8 and 9. In both figures, the features are ordered by importance. Tables 4 and 5 provide illustrative examples of subsequences that give rise to these features.

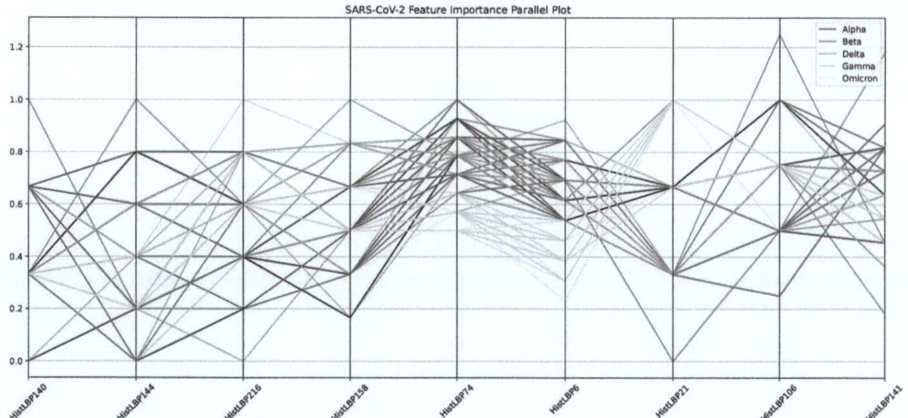

Fig. 8. Most important features for the SARS-CoV-2 dataset.

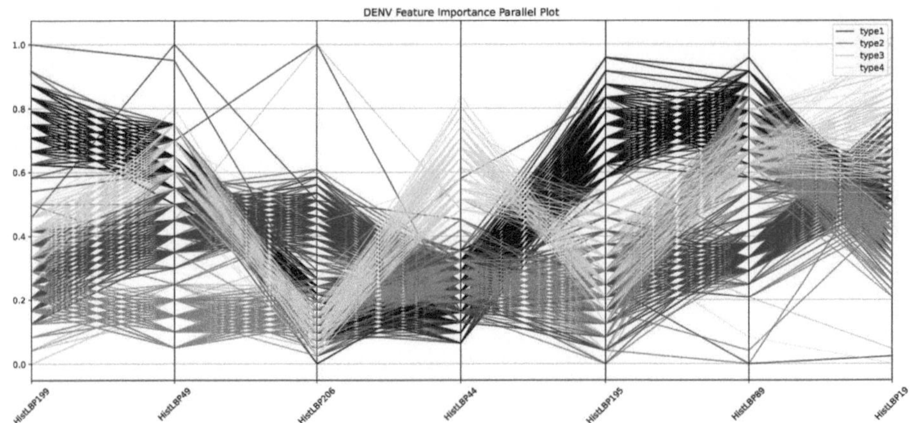

Fig. 9. Most important features for the DENV dataset.

Table 4. Most important Motifs (Features) for the SARS-CoV Dataset.

Histogram Bin	Subsequence Examples
Bin 140	TGATTAGGT, CAACCGTTC, AGGTTGGGA, TGATTAAAT, CGGCCGGAC
Bin 144	TAAAATAGC, CTTAGCTTC, CTATGCTAC, AGGGGCGGC, TGGAGCAAT
Bin 216	TGGACTATC, AGGGTAGTC, CAGTCCTCC, TAGGTCATC, CGAACCACC
Bin 158	AGATATGGT, CTCCCCGTC, CGCCCCAAC, TACCTTAAC, TGCCCTAAC
Bin 074	CTCGCGTCT, AGAGAGGAG, CGCTCTGCT, TGTGCGACA, TATGCAATG
Bin 006	TACCGGAAA, TATCGAAAA, AGACGGGGG, CGCCTATAG, CACCTTGTT
Bin 021	TTACGCAAA, TCATGTGGG, ACGTGCGGG, TTGCATGAA, CCACACAAT
Bin 106	TACGTGTTA, TGTACGCCG, TACGTATTA, AGTGCGTAG, CACGCGCCG
Bin 141	TTGCCGGAC, TCGCTAAAT, CCTCCTGGC, TTACTGGGT, CCGCCGATC

The results obtained from applying the proposed feature extraction methodology across various classification algorithms underscore the robustness and generalizability of the extracted features. These results demonstrate that high classification accuracy can be achieved independently of the classifier, thereby reducing algorithm-specific biases. Moreover, the ability to perform the classification task effectively using only a small subset of features further illustrates the method's capacity to capture highly discriminative information. This efficiency also facilitates the scalability of the proposed approach, enabling its application to large-scale genomic datasets, including millions of sequences, using standard personal computing resources.

Examining the parallel coordinate plots reveals specific histogram bins that exhibit clear class separability. For instance, in Fig. 8, the first four bins effectively distinguish between the four SARS-CoV-2 variants, while in Fig. 9, the first, fourth, and fifth bins show prominent separation among the four dengue virus serotypes. These observations reinforce the discriminatory strength of the

Table 5. Most important Motifs (Features) for the DENV Dataset.

Histogram Bin	Subsequence Examples
Bin 199	TCTCGAATT, TCCTGGGTT, CCCCAAACC, AACAGGGCA, TTCCAGATC
Bin 049	CCGGTCCTG, AAGGGACGG, TCAGACCGA, CCAGTCCTG, CCGTTCCAG
Bin 206	AGAACGGAC, TGCCCAATC, TGCTTGACT, AGAATGGTA, AGCTAGGCT
Bin 044	AGGACGTGG, CTTCCACTT, AGGAAGAGG, CGTCCTCGT, TGATTACGG
Bin 195	TCCGAGGCC, TTCGAAGTT, TCCGGAATC, ACAGGGGTC, CCCTTTACC
Bin 089	ATGGAAGAG, TTGATTGCA, TCAATTACA, CCAGCCTCT, TCAGTCGTG
Bin 019	AACGGTGGG, AAAGGTGGG, CCCAACGAG, TCTAGTAAA, AATGGCGGG

proposed features and indicate a low likelihood of overfitting, as the class separations are both evident and generalizable.

Additionally, it is possible to trace back the most informative bins to specific sequence motifs or subsequences. Representative examples of such subsequences are presented in Tables 4 and 5, with the full collection available via the online tool**[2]. This traceability contributes to the interpretability of the method, enabling biological insights into the genomic patterns underlying class distinctions.

5   Conclusion

In this work, BITSER is proposed as a new method for feature extraction, using EIIP values to represent nucleotide sequences, and adapting the LBP texture analysis technique to extract features from sequences in the form of a histogram, alongside the feature BWS, and the proposed feature BWP.

BITSER is alignment-free and based on the data, requiring only the input sequences. It offers interpretable results, leading to an understandable feature extraction process, and transparency in analyzing the results and identifying which features are used to recognize sequences.

The experiments were carried out over genomes of the viruses SARS-CoV-2 and DENV, with the proposed method having achieved classification accuracy superior to 99% considering both adopted datasets. Future work includes further testing the proposed method on more challenging organisms, such as HIV, and fine-tuning it for enhanced performance and computational efficiency.

BITSER method was implemented in open source and is available at GitHub: https://github.com/LCostaF/BITSER. The tool to obtain subsequences generated in each bin is available at: https://ntu-calculator.streamlit.app/.

Acknowledgments. This work was supported by national funds through the Coordenação de Aperfeiçoamento de Pessoal de Nível Superior (CAPES) - Finance Code 001, Fundação Araucária (Grant numbers 035/2019, 138/2021, and NAPI - BioinformÃątica), CNPq 440412/2022-6 and 408312/2023-8.

---

[2] https://github.com/LCostaF/NTU_Calculator.

Disclosure of Interests. The authors have no competing interests to declare that are relevant to the content of this article.

References

1. Corchete, L.A., Rojas, D E., Alonso-López, A., De Las Rivas, J., Gutiérrez, N.C., Burguillo, F.J.: Systematic comparison and assessment of RNA-SEQ procedures for gene expression quantitative analysis. Sci. Rep. **10**(1), 19737 (2020)
2. Costa-Silva, J., Domingues, D., Lopes, F.M.: RNA-Seq differential expression analysis: an extended review and a software tool. PLoS ONE **12**(12), e0190152 (2017)
3. De Pierri, C.R., et al.: Sweep: representing large biological sequences datasets in compact vectors. Sci. Rep. **10**(1), 91 (2020)
4. Costa-Silva, J., Domingues, D.S., Menotti, D., Hungria, M., Lopes, F.M.: Temporal progress of gene expression analysis with RNA-Seq data: a review on the relationship between computational methods. Comput. Struct. Biotechnol. J. **21**, 86–98 (2023)
5. Zheng, H., Talukder, A., Li, X., Hu, H.: A systematic evaluation of the computational tools for lncRNA identification. Briefings Bioinf. **22**(6), bbab285 (2021)
6. Thompson, J.D., Linard, B., Lecompte, O., Poch, O.: A comprehensive benchmark study of multiple sequence alignment methods: current challenges and future perspectives. PLoS ONE **6**(3), e18093 (2011)
7. Zielezinski, A., et al.: Benchmarking of alignment-free sequence comparison methods. Genome Biol. **20**, 1–18 (2019)
8. Zielezinski, A., Vinga, S., Almeida, J., Karlowski, W.M.: Alignment-free sequence comparison: benefits, applications, and tools. Genome Biol. **18**(1), 186 (2017). http://genomebiology.biomedcentral.com/articles/10.1186/s13059-017-1319-7
9. Adjeroh, D.A., et al.: Challenges in lncRNA biology: views and opinions. Non-Coding RNA **10**(4), 43 (2024)
10. Lopes, F.M., Martins, D.C., Jr., Barrera, J., Cesar, R.M., Jr.: A feature selection technique for inference of graphs from their known topological properties: revealing scale-free gene regulatory networks. Inf. Sci. **272**, 1–15 (2014)
11. Ito, E.A., Katahira, I., Vicente, F.F.D.R., Pereira, L.F.P., Lopes, F.M.: Basinet—biological sequences network: a case study on coding and non-coding RNAs identification. Nucleic Acids Res. **46**(16), e96–e96 (2018)
12. Bonidia, R.P., Domingues, D.S., Sanches, D.S., de Carvalho, A.C.: Mathfeature: feature extraction package for DNA, RNA and protein sequences based on mathematical descriptors. Briefings Bioinf. **23**(1), bbab434 (2022)
13. Breve, M.M., Lopes, F.M.: A simplified complex network-based approach to mRNA and nCRNA transcript classification. In: Advances in Bioinformatics and Computational Biology: 13th Brazilian Symposium on Bioinformatics, BSB,: São Paulo, Brazil, November 23–27, 2020, Proceedings 13. Springer, pp. 192–203 (2020)
14. de Souza Piotto, J.G., Lopes, F.M.: A feature extraction approach based on LBP operator and complex networks for face recognition. In: J.M.R.S., Papa, J.P., González Hidalgo, M. (eds.) Progress in Pattern Recognition, Image Analysis, Computer Vision, and Applications Tavares, pp. 440–450. Springer International Publishing, Cham (2021)
15. Pimenta-Zanon, M.H., De Souza, V.A., Hashimoto, R.F., Lopes, F.M.: Biological sequence analysis using complex networks and entropy maximization: a case study in SARS-CoV-2. In: Ambient Intelligence in Health Care: Proceedings of ICAIHC 2022, pp. 459–468. Springer (2022)

16. Chen, X.-G., Yang, X., Li, C., Lin, X., Zhang, W.: Non-coding RNA identification with pseudo RNA sequences and feature representation learning. Comput. Biol. Med. **165**, 107355 (2023)

17. Bueno de Souza, F., et al.: Resonant recognition model as a preprocessing technique for RNA classification. In: Guarda, T., Portela, F., Augusto, M.F. (eds.) Advanced Research in Technologies, Information, Innovation and Sustainability, pp. 3–17. Springer Nature Switzerland, Cham (2025)

18. Pimenta-Zanon, M.H., Kashiwabara, A.Y., Vanzela, A.L.L., Lopes, F.M.: GRAMEP: an alignment-free method based on the maximum entropy principle for identifying snps. BMC Bioinformatics **26**(1), 66 (2025)

19. Klapproth, C., Sen, R., Stadler, P.F., Findeiß, S., Fallmann, J.: Common features in lncRNA annotation and classification: a survey. Non-coding RNA **7**(4), 77 (2021)

20. Nie, Z., Gao, M., Jin, X., Rao, Y., Zhang, X.: MFPINC: prediction of plant ncRNAs based on multi-source feature fusion. BMC Genomics **25**(1), 531 (2024)

21. Wang, L., He, D.: A new statistical approach for texture analysis. Photogramm. Eng. Remote. Sens. **56**(1), 61–66 (1990)

22. Ojala, T., Pietikainen, M., Harwood, D.: Performance evaluation of texture measures with classification based on Kullback discrimination of distributions. In: Proceedings of 12th International Conference on Pattern Recognition, vol. 1, pp. 582–585. IEEE (1994)

23. Brilhador, A., Colonhezi, T.P., Bugatti, P.H., Lopes, F.M.: Combining texture and shape descriptors for bioimages classification: a case of study in ImageCLEF dataset. In: Iberoamerican Congress on Pattern Recognition, pp. 431–438. Springer (2013)

24. de Lima, G.V., Castilho, T.R., Bugatti, P.H., Saito, P.T., Lopes, F.M.: A complex network-based approach to the analysis and classification of images. In: Progress in Pattern Recognition, Image Analysis, Computer Vision, and Applications: 20th Iberoamerican Congress, CIARP,: Montevideo, Uruguay, November 9–12, 2015, Proceedings 20, pp. 322–330. Springer (2015)

25. Piotto, J.G.S., Lopes, F.M.: Combining surf descriptor and complex networks for face recognition. In: 2016 9th International Congress on Image and Signal Processing, BioMedical Engineering and Informatics (CISP-BMEI), pp. 275–279 (2016)

26. de Lima, G.V., Saito, P.T., Lopes, F.M., Bugatti, P.H.: Classification of texture based on bag-of-visual-words through complex networks. Expert Syst. Appl. **133**, 215–224 (2019)

27. de Souza Piotto, J.G., Lopes, F.M.: A feature extraction approach based on LBP operator and complex networks for face recognition. In: Progress in Pattern Recognition, Image Analysis, Computer Vision, and Applications: 25th Iberoamerican Congress, CIARP, Porto, Portugal, May 10–13, 2021, Revised Selected Papers 25, pp. 440–450. Springer (2021)

28. Pereira, D.F., Bugatti, P.H., Lopes, F.M., de Souza, A.L.S.M., Saito, P.T.M.: Assessing active learning strategies to improve the quality control of the soybean seed vigor. IEEE Trans. Industr. Electron. **68**(2), 1675–1683 (2021)

29. Cosic, I.: Macromolecular bioactivity: is it resonant interaction between macromolecules?-Theory and applications. IEEE Trans. Biomed. Eng. **41**(12), 1101–1114 (1994)

30. Lebatteux, D., et al.: Toward an alignment-free method for feature extraction and accurate classification of viral sequences. J. Comput. Biol. **26**(6), 519–535 (2019). https://www.liebertpub.com/doi/10.1089/cmb.2018.0239

31. Lebatteux, D., Soudeyns, H., Boucoiran, I., Gantt, S., Diallo, A.B.: KANALYZER: a method to identify variations of discriminative k-mers in genomic sequences. In: 2022 IEEE International Conference on Bioinformatics and Biomedicine (BIBM), pp. 757–762. IEEE (2022)
32. Ben Jabeur, S., Stef, N., Carmona, P.: Bankruptcy prediction using the XGBoost algorithm and variable importance feature engineering. Comput. Econ. **61**(2), 715–741 (2023)

Towards Fast Binding Affinity Scoring in Protein–Protein Complexes via Interatomic Contacts and Linear Regression

Ana Luísa Araújo Bastos[1], Rafael Pereira Lemos[1(✉)], Diego Mariano[1], Camila A. O. Yamada[2], Milenna M. Pirovani[1], and Raquel Cardoso de Melo-Minardi[1]

[1] Laboratory of Bioinformatics and Systems (LBS), Department of Computer Science, Universidade Federal de Minas Gerais, Belo Horizonte, Brazil
`rafaellemos@ufmg.br, raquelcm@dcc.ufmg.br`
[2] Laboratory for Macromolecular Biophysics - LBM, Department of Biochemistry and Immunology, Universidade Federal de Minas Gerais, Belo Horizonte, Brazil

Abstract. Protein-protein interactions (PPIs) are essential to understanding how proteins work together to perform most of the molecular processes that underlie life. However, capturing the structural and functional complexity of proteins, as well as their interactions, using computational representations remains an open challenge. In this study, we investigated the individual impact of contact types on binding affinity by constructing linear regression models based on interatomic contacts calculated with the COCαDA tool. A curated dataset comprising 81 protein–protein complexes was employed to systematically analyze ten categories of contacts, including both specific and nonspecific interactions. Our results emphasize the significance of polar-apolar contacts ($r = -0.55$), evaluated at the atomic level, in reducing the binding strength between protein-protein complexes, which corroborates previous findings in the literature. Additionally, hydrogen bonds demonstrated a notable contribution to binding stability, with a Pearson correlation of $r = -0.42$. The results presented here are an initial step towards establishing a scoring function based solely on contact calculations.

Keywords: Protein-protein Interactions · Interatomic Contacts · Binding Affinity · Linear Regression

1 Introduction

Weak interactions are non-covalent forces that stabilize the three-dimensional structure of proteins and mediate interactions with other molecules [1]. Contacts, typically detected using computational methods based on distance (*e.g.*,

A. L. A. Bastos and R. Pereira Lemos—These authors contributed equally to this work.

M. Dorn and F. Martins Lopes (Eds.): X-Meeting 2025, LNBI 16037, pp. 181–191, 2026.
https://doi.org/10.1007/978-3-032-09336-3_13

Euclidean distance) or geometric criteria (*e.g.*, Delaunay and Voronoi tessellations) [2], represent spatial relationships between atoms or residues within or between molecules [3].

It is essential to distinguish between "contacts," which are purely spatial proximities, and "interactions", which involve energetic contributions such as hydrophobic or electrostatic forces [3,4]. Although not every contact leads to an interaction, they are often prerequisites for biologically meaningful interactions. With this, physicochemical characteristics can be incorporated alongside spatial proximity, reducing the incidence of false positives in computational predictions. Some tools employ coarse-grained approaches, treating interactions at the residue level to minimize computational cost (reviewed in [3,5]).

Recently, the command-line tool COCαDA (Contact Optimization by Cα Distance Analysis) proposed a new efficient algorithm for calculating contacts at the atomic level [5]. The first version of COCαDA calculates seven types of contacts: Hydrogen and Disulfide Bond (HB and DB, respectively), Hydrophobic (HY), Repulsive (RE), Attractive (AT), Salt Bridge (SB), and Aromatic Stacking (AS). It also classifies contacts in protein structures into two types: INTRA, intramolecular contacts made between residues of the same protein chain, and INTER, intermolecular contacts made between different polypeptide chains.

Intermolecular contacts are crucial for characterizing protein-protein interactions (PPIs), which are fundamental to most biological processes, ranging from the regulation of essential functions such as cell signaling and immune response to DNA replication [6]. These interactions enable proteins and other macromolecules to act in a coordinated manner, forming functional networks that enhance the complexity and specificity of cellular responses.

Due to the significant importance of these kinds of interaction, several studies have sought to better understand and characterize these interactions using computational methods [7]. One example is the PRODIGY (PROtein binDIng enerGY prediction) tool [8,9], which predicts the binding affinity (BA) between two protein subunits based on their three-dimensional structures, typically obtained from Protein Data Bank (PDB) files. It estimates the binding free energy (ΔG) using models based on simple structural features of the protein-protein interface, such as the number of contacts calculated using a coarse-grained method, the binding energy, and the surface area of the directly interacting proteins.

In this context, the following questions were raised: 1) To what extent can we better understand the individual contribution of specific interatomic contacts to the overall BA of protein–protein complexes? 2) Can the prediction of BA be improved by using more accurate contact calculation methods, such as atomic-level contacts computed with COCαDA?

In this work, we used the interatomic contacts predicted by the COCαDA tool to predict the binding energy between protein-protein chains, along with three new types based on polarity and charge alone. We built a linear regression model using Orange Data Mining [10], in-house Python scripts, and the Scikit-learn library [11]. To evaluate our method, we collected protein complex data from the PDB and compared them with the results obtained in [8]. Our results highlight the importance of attractive contacts and hydrogen bonds in chain interactions, while also emphasizing the role of polar-apolar atom contacts in reducing the attraction force between structures.

2   Methods

2.1   Data Collection

We utilized the same list of 81 "reliable" protein-protein complexes from [8], which is derived from [12]. The data were downloaded from the PDB website in the legacy ".pdb" format, and the complex-forming chains were then filtered according to those described in [12] to avoid spurious contacts from other chain pairs.

2.2   Contact Definition and Calculation

COCαDA [5] uses definitions from [13,14] for distance-based interatomic contact calculations. Seven contact types are defined natively: HB, DB, HY, RE, AT, SB and AS. We then used an in-house modified version that includes three new types discussed in [8] (Table 1): a) Polar-apolar (PA), where polar atoms are those that perform hydrogen bonds (either donors or acceptors), and apolar atoms are those that perform hydrophobic interactions; b) Positive-apolar (PosA), where positive atoms are those that possess positive charges in neutral pH; and c) Negative-apolar (NegA), where negative atoms are those that possess negative charges in neutral pH. All three types use the 5.5Å distance cutoff previously defined.

Table 1. Summary of types, range and conditions for polar-apolar, positive-apolar and negative-apolar interatomic contacts. D_a = Euclidean distance between the atom pair.

Contact Type	Range (Å)	Condition (other than range)
Polar-Apolar	$0 \leq D_a \leq 5.5$	Polar + Apolar atoms
Positive-Apolar	$0 \leq D_a \leq 5.5$	Positive + Apolar atoms
Negative-Apolar	$0 \leq D_a \leq 5.5$	Negative + Apolar atoms

2.3   Model Construction

Linear regression models were initially built with Orange Data Mining [10]. No regularization parameters were used. The models were trained using a 10-fold cross-validation approach. To generate the scatter plots, the models were trained using each variable as an individual input. The following contact types were used as parameters for each input, regarding their absolute number in the interface:

HB, AT, RE, SB, HY, PA, PosA, and NegA. The input PDB ID and the experimentally obtained ΔG value were also included. Furthermore, the models were trained using different combinations of variables calculated by COCαDA. To validate the parameters used in the model presented here, correlation calculation experiments using inter-residue contacts proposed in the Prodigy paper [8] were reproduced using the parameters trained for the model proposed in this work. The same Pearson correlation was obtained for the combination of all inter-residue contacts (r = 0.59).

3   Results and Discussion

We first built a regressor to evaluate the representation capacity of the binding affinity of the contact types calculated by COCαDA. In the future, we intend to develop a scoring function to predict the binding energy between protein-protein complexes. Thus, we evaluated the Pearson correlation using each contact type individually.

Our results indicate that polar-apolar contacts yielded the highest Pearson correlation (r = −0.55). Next, the model built using only hydrogen bonds as input obtained an r = −0.42. The model built only with attractive contacts obtained an r = −0.22, while the model with repulsive contacts also obtained an r = −0.22. The salt bridge model obtained an r = −0.13, and the model with hydrophobic contacts r = −0.25. Finally, the model built with pairs of positively charged and nonpolar atoms obtained an r = −0.28, while the model built with pairs of negatively charged atoms obtained an r = −0.14 (Fig. 1).

The study by Vangone and Bonvin [8] considered contacts made at the residue level, obtaining the following results for each pair: charged/charged (r = −0.17), charged/polar (r = −0.26), charged/apolar (r = −0.45), polar/polar (r = −0.13), polar/apolar (r = −0.56), apolar/apolar (r = −0.34), hydrophilic/hydrophilic (r = −0.53), hydrophilic/hydrophobic (r = −0.34), and hydrophobic/hydrophilic (r = −0.05). It is important to emphasize that, considering only the impact of each variable, our results are comparable to the results obtained in [8]. However, while they combined multiple attributes related to contacts, interface characteristics, and free energy to achieve a higher overall correlation (r = −0.73), the focus of the present work is distinct. Rather than attempting to surpass the performance reported in their work, our primary goal is to evaluate the predictive potential of atomic-level contact calculations. The results presented here represent an initial step toward the development of a scoring function based solely on detailed interatomic contact analysis.

3.1   Evaluation of the Contribution of Individual Interatomic Contact Types on BA Values

In their study, Vangone and Bonvin [8] considered charges regardless of their sign, meaning that both positively and negatively charged residues were treated equally. To further detail our analysis, we decided to split the "charged-apolar"

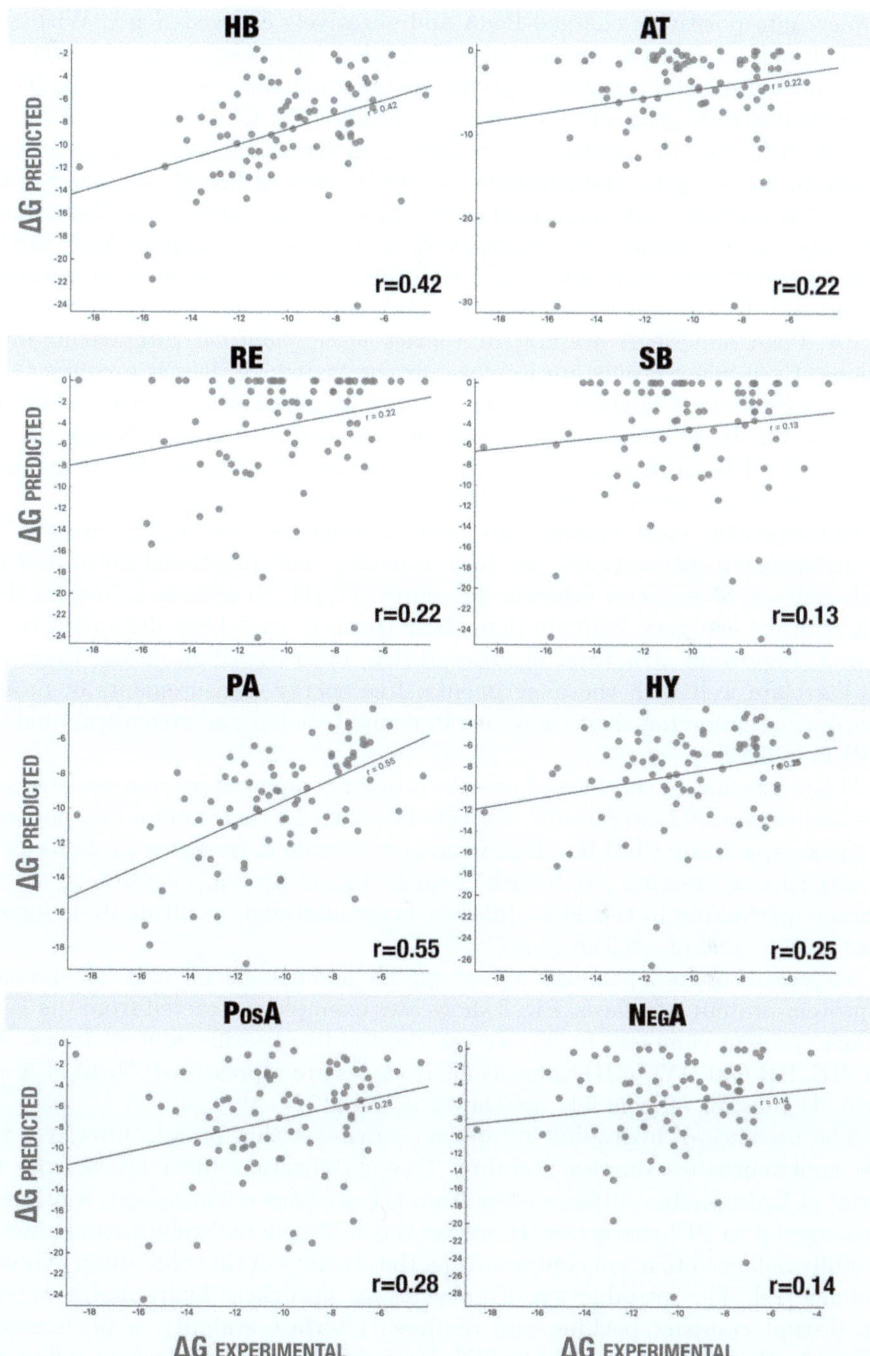

Fig. 1. Scatter plot of predicted vs. experimental binding affinities for each individual contact type. HB: Hydrogen Bond; AT: Attractive; RE: Repulsive; SB: Salt Bridge; HY: Hydrophobic; PA: Polar-Apolar; PosA: Positively Charged-Polar; and NegA: Negatively Charged-Polar. Pearson correlation (r) values are shown on the bottom right, and binding affinities are reported as absolute values in kcal/mol^{-1}.

contacts into positively charged-PosA and negatively charged-NegA. With this, we analyzed 10 different contact types, divided into two groups: specific contacts and nonspecific contacts. Specific contacts are those that pose significant energetic contributions, and are natively calculated by COCαDA: HB, DB, AT, RE, AS, SB, and HY. Nonspecific contacts, on the other hand, typically make no significant energetic contributions or effects, such as PA, PosA, and NegA.

No DB contacts were identified in the 81 complexes present in the dataset, and only 13 AS contacts were observed, so they were removed from further analysis. We then compared the eight remaining contact types according to their individual correlation with the experimental data (Fig. 1).

PA, PosA and NegA are not, in a strict sense, *bona-fide* interatomic interactions. Even when atoms are in close proximity (which defines a contact), no significant energetic contributions or effects take place. Rather, they arise primarily from dense steric packing and surface shape complementarity. In the context of PPIs, such contacts are largely governed by principles of maximal atomic close-packing, as previously described [15,16].

Consequently, these contacts are best classified as "nonspecific contacts" or "crystal-packing interactions," as they typically lack functional roles and are likely subject to negative selective pressures [17,18]. Nonetheless, despite their lack of direct energetic contribution, these contacts have been demonstrated to serve as important structural markers of BA. Their distribution and frequency can correlate well with the experimental free energy measurements of protein complexes, reinforcing their relevance in computational and structural analyses of PPIs [8,9,19].

When viewing the surface of protein-protein complexes, we can see how specific and nonspecific interatomic contacts take part on their interacting portions. In an example using PDB ID 1E6E (Fig. 2), the chain A (receptor protein) forms an extensive interacting patch with chain B (ligand protein), containing several contacts pertaining to the eight different types analyzed, resulting in an experimental ΔG value of $-8.3\,\mathrm{kcal/mol^{-1}}$.

To provide an in-depth view of how specific and nonspecific contacts manifest at protein-protein interfaces, Fig. 3 showcases examples extracted from the 1E6E protein–protein complex. In A), we can see the five specific contact types: AT, SB, RE, HB and HY; in B), nonspecific contacts are represented: NegA, PA and PosA. Details for all contacts are shown in Table 2.

The presence of hydrophobic (apolar) patches within protein interfaces further contributes to complex stability. This stabilization effect arises from the burial of hydrophobic surfaces away from the aqueous environment, a principle fundamental to PPI energetics. However, this hydrophobic stabilization must be carefully balanced to avoid compromising the stability of the individual, unbound proteins [19]. The introduction of polar atoms into these hydrophobic patches can disrupt compact packing and diminish interface stability, a phenomenon critical to the modulation of BAs [20]. Notably, PA contacts—which reflect the presence of polar atoms—have been found to correlate inversely with the BA [8]. Their occurrence appears largely incidental, a byproduct of steric surface packing

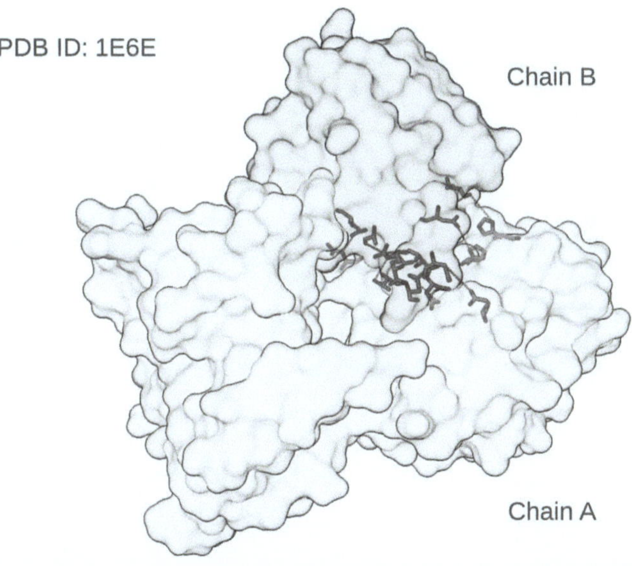

Fig. 2. Surface representation of the interface region with examples of specific and nonspecific interatomic contacts. The receptor (chain A) and the ligand (chain B) of the PBD ID 1E6E are shown as surfaces in cyan and magenta, respectively. The interacting residues are represented as sticks.

Table 2. Details of specific and nonspecific interatomic contacts identified in the interfacing region of the PDB ID 1E6E protein-protein complex. Atom nomenclature is Chain:Residue-Atom, and atom names follow the ones used in the PDB.

	Type	Atom 1	Atom 2	Distance (Å)
Specific	AT	A:28H-ND1	B:39D-OD2	5.27
	SB	A:24H-ND1	B:41D-OD2	3.84
	RE	A:382D-OD1	B:116E-OE2	5.55
	HB	A:378T-OG1	B:115R-NE	3.82
	HY	A:60N-CB	B:47E-CG	4.22
Nonspecific	NegA	A:353E-OE1	B:113D-CB	5.15
	PA	A:64T-CG2	B:45A-O	4.44
	PosA	A:381T-CG2	B:115R-CZ	4.50

rather than an optimized energetic feature, which may explain the evolutionary pressure to minimize such contacts.

Despite the general destabilizing role of polar contacts within hydrophobic interfaces, specific polar interactions, particularly hydrogen bonds (which are formed by polar atoms), are frequently observed even in tightly packed protein-protein interfaces [21,22]. Larsen and colleagues [23], in a study of 137 homod-

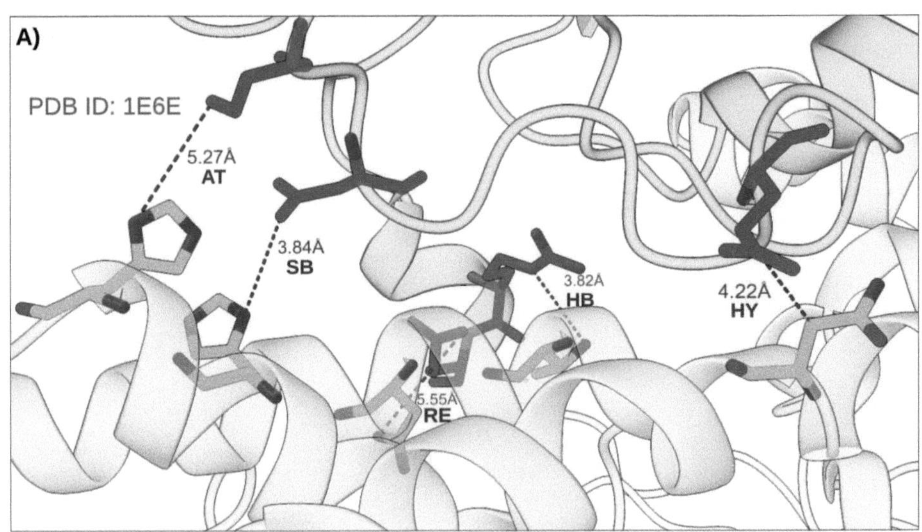

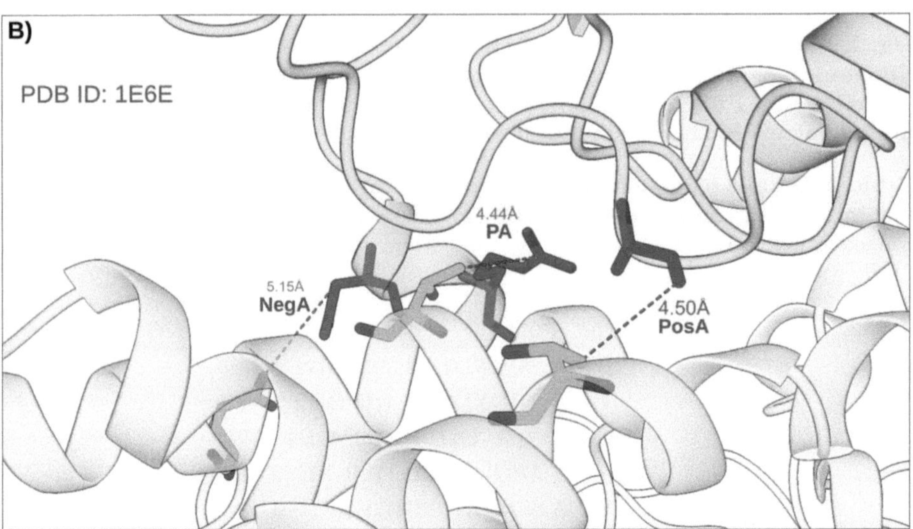

Fig. 3. Examples of interatomic contacts identified in the interfacing region of a protein-protein complex. For both figures, the same region of PDB ID 1E6E is shown. The receptor (chain A) and the ligand (chain B) are shown as cartoons in cyan and magenta, respectively. A) Specific contacts. AT: attractive contact between A:28H-ND1 and B:39D-OD2; SB: salt bridge between A:24H-ND1 and B:41D-OD2; RE: repulsive contact between A:382D-OD1 and B:116E-OE2; HB: hydrogen bond between A:378T-OG1 and B:115R-NE; HY: hydrophobic contact between A:60N-CB and B:47E-CG. B) Nonspecific contacts. NegA: negative-apolar contact between A:353E-OE1 and B:113D-CB; PA: positive-apolar contact between A:64T-CG2 and B:45A-O; PosA: positive-apolar contact between A:381T-CG2 and B:115R-CZ. Nomenclature is Chain:Residue-Atom, and atom names follow the ones used in the PDB. Distances between the atom pair, in angstroms, are highlighted for each contact.

imeric protein complexes, demonstrated that most of the interfaces contained numerous small hydrophobic patches interspersed with polar interactions and water molecules. This pattern underscores a complex architectural strategy: the overall interface maximizes hydrophobic stabilization while maintaining partial hydration, relying on a combination of localized hydrophobic contacts and hydrogen bonds [23,24]. This circumvents the need for complete desolvation, which is energetically costly, while preserving the structural integrity and flexibility of the proteins.

Such findings suggest that, while nonspecific contacts dominate the gross features of PPI interfaces, specific polar interactions are crucial in refining and stabilizing the binding landscape at a finer scale. Besides, structural and mutational analyses have revealed that networks of polar and charged residues—including hydrogen bonds and salt bridges—can contribute significantly to the stability of protein complexes, partially compensating for the energetic cost of desolvation [25].

4   Conclusions

In this study, we developed and evaluated a linear regression model based on interatomic contact types to predict the binding affinity of protein–protein complexes. Using the COCαDA tool, we systematically calculated a wide variety of contact types, including five types of specific contacts: hydrogen bonds, hydrophobic, attractive, repulsive, and salt bridge interactions; and three non-specific types: polar–apolar, negative-apolar, and positive-apolar.

Our results showed that polar–apolar contacts exhibited the strongest individual correlation with experimental binding affinities, followed by hydrogen bonds. These findings suggest that not only energetically significant interactions but also steric and surface packing effects play key roles in determining the stability of protein–protein interfaces.

We adopted linear regression for its interpretability and computational simplicity. However, we acknowledge that this approach assumes linearity and independence between variables, which may not fully capture the underlying complexity of protein–protein interactions. As a next step, we plan to explore machine learning approaches such as Random Forest and Neural Networks to better capture complex relationships and improve predictive performance.

In addition, future efforts will focus on incorporating additional structural features such as Buried Surface Area (BSA) and Non-Interacting Surface (NIS), which can provide valuable contributions. We also plan to expand the dataset to increase the robustness and generalizability of the model.

Overall, although this work represents an initial step, it provides new insights into the specific and nonspecific contributions to protein–protein binding and establishes a basis for the development of faster and more accurate scoring functions based on atomic-level contact analysis.

Acknowledgments. The authors thank the agencies: Coordenação de Aperfeiçoamento de Pessoal de Nível Superior—CAPES, Brazil; Fundação de Amparo à Pesquisa do Estado de Minas Gerais—FAPEMIG; and Conselho Nacional de Pesquisa e Desenvolvimento Científico e Tecnológico—CNPq. This study was financed in part by the Coordenação de Aperfeiçoamento de Pessoal de Nível Superior - Brasil (CAPES) - Finance Code 001.

Data Availibility Statement. The dataset used in this study was obtained in the Prodigy web tool, available at https://rascar.science.uu.nl/prodigy/dataset. PDB files were downloaded from the RCSB PDB website, available at https://www.rcsb.org. Supplementary files, containing the Orange session, input and output tables, are available at https://github.com/LBS-UFMG/binding_affinity_score_2025.

Disclosure of Interests. The authors have no competing interests to declare that are relevant to the content of this article.

References

1. Khatri, B., Majumder, P., Nagesh, J., Penmatsa, A., Chatterjee, J.: Increasing protein stability by engineering the n $\rightarrow$ π^* interaction at the β-turn. Chem. Sci. (2020)
2. Martins, P.M., Mayrink, V.D., de A. Silveira, S., da Silveira, C.H., de Lima, L.H.F., de Melo-Minardi, R.C.: How to compute protein residue contacts more accurately? In: Proceedings of the 33rd Annual ACM Symposium on Applied Computing. ACM, New York (2018)
3. da Silveira, C.H., et al.: Protein cutoff scanning: a comparative analysis of cutoff dependent and cutoff free methods for prospecting contacts in proteins. Proteins **74**(3), 727–743 (2009)
4. Godzik, A., Kolinski, A., Skolnick, J.: Topology fingerprint approach to the inverse protein folding problem. J. Mol. Biol. **227**(1), 227–238 (1992)
5. Lemos, R.P., Mariano, D., Silveira, S.A., de Melo-Minardi, R.C.: COCαDA - large-scale protein interatomic contact cutoff optimization by Cα distance matrices. In: Annals of the XVII Brazilian Symposium on Bioinformatics (BSB 2024), pp. 59–70. Brazilian Computer Society (SBC) (2024)
6. Greenblatt, J.F., Alberts, B.M., Krogan, N.J.: Discovery and significance of protein-protein interactions in health and disease. Cell **187**(23), 6501–6517 (2024)
7. Keskin, O., Tuncbag, N., Gursoy, A.: Predicting protein-protein interactions from the molecular to the proteome level. Chem. Rev. **116**(8), 4884–4909 (2016)
8. Vangone, A., Bonvin, A.M.: Contacts-based prediction of binding affinity in protein-protein complexes. Elife **4**, e07454 (2015)
9. Xue, L.C., Rodrigues, J.P., Kastritis, P.L., Bonvin, A.M., Vangone, A.: PRODIGY: a web server for predicting the binding affinity of protein-protein complexes. Bioinformatics **32**(23), 3676–3678 (2016)
10. Demšar, J., Zupan, B., Leban, G., Curk, T.: Orange: from experimental machine learning to interactive data mining. In: Boulicaut, J.-F., Esposito, F., Giannotti, F., Pedreschi, D. (eds.) PKDD 2004. LNCS (LNAI), vol. 3202, pp. 537–539. Springer, Heidelberg (2004). https://doi.org/10.1007/978-3-540-30116-5_58
11. Pedregosa, F., et al.: Scikit-learn: machine learning in Python. J. Mach. Learn. Res. **12**, 2825–2830 (2011)
12. Kastritis, P.L.: A structure-based benchmark for protein-protein binding affinity. Protein Sci. **20**(3), 482–491 (2011)

13. Sobolev, V., Sorokine, A., Prilusky, J., Abola, E.E., Edelman, M.: Automated analysis of interatomic contacts in proteins. Bioinformatics **15**(4), 327–332 (1999)
14. Fassio, A.V., Santos, L.H., Silveira, S.A., Ferreira, R.S., de Melo-Minardi, R.C.: nAPOLI: a graph-based strategy to detect and visualize conserved protein-ligand interactions in large-scale. IEEE/ACM Trans. Comp. Biol. Bioinf. **17**(4), 1317–1328 (2020). https://doi.org/10.1109/tcbb.2019.2892099
15. Chothia, C., Janin, J.: Principles of protein-protein recognition. Nature **256**(5520), 705–708 (1975)
16. Norel, R., Lin, S.L., Wolfson, H.J., Nussinov, R.: Shape complementarity at protein-protein interfaces. Biopolymers **34**(7), 933–940 (1994)
17. Janin, J.: Specific versus non-specific contacts in protein crystals. Nat. Struct. Biol. **4**(12), 973–974 (1997)
18. Prasad Bahadur, R., Chakrabarti, P., Rodier, F., Janin, J.: A dissection of specific and non-specific protein-protein interfaces. J. Mol. Biol. **336**(4), 943–955 (2004)
19. Tsai, C.J., Xu, D., Nussinov, R.: Protein folding via binding and vice versa. Fold Des. **3**(4), R71-80 (1998)
20. Tsai, C.J., Nussinov, R.: Hydrophobic folding units at protein-protein interfaces: implications to protein folding and to protein-protein association. Protein Sci. **6**(7), 1426–1437 (1997)
21. Xu, D., Tsai, C.J., Nussinov, R.: Hydrogen bonds and salt bridges across protein-protein interfaces. Protein Eng. Des. Sel. **10**(9), 999–1012 (1997)
22. Tam, J.Z., Palumbo, T., Miwa, J.M., Chen, B.Y.: Analysis of protein-protein interactions for intermolecular bond prediction. Molecules **27**(19), 6178 (2022)
23. Larsen, T.A., Olson, A.J., Goodsell, D.S.: Morphology of protein-protein interfaces. Structure **6**(4), 421–427 (1998)
24. Rego, N.B., Xi, E., Patel, A.J.: Identifying hydrophobic protein patches to inform protein interaction interfaces. Proc. Natl. Acad. Sci. U. S. A. **118**(6), e2018234118 (2021)
25. Sheinerman, F.B., Norel, R., Honig, B.: Electrostatic aspects of protein-protein interactions. Curr. Opin. Struct. Biol. **10**(2), 153–159 (2000)

Characterization of the Terpene Synthase Gene Family and its Role in Response to Water Deprivation in *Stylosanthes scabra*

Ramon da Silva de Souza, Ana Luíza Trajano Mangueira de Melo[(✉)], Manassés Daniel da Silva, Maria Luiza Carvalho Farias, Ana Maria Benko-Iseppon, and José Ribamar Costa Ferreira-Neto

Laboratório de Genética e Biotecnologia Vegetal, Departamento de Genética, Centro de Biociências, Universidade Federal de Pernambuco, Recife, Pernambuco, Brazil
analuiza.melo@ufpe.br

Abstract. Plants have evolutionarily developed multiple and complex defense mechanisms against abiotic stresses. Among these, the Terpene Synthase (TPS) gene family plays a pivotal role in the biosynthesis of terpenoids—key secondary metabolites involved in plant defense regulation and stress responses. Despite its significance, genomic characterization of this gene family in extremophile plant species, such as *Stylosanthes scabra*, remains absent from the literature. Thus, this study aimed to structurally characterize TPS genes in *S. scabra* and evaluate their root transcriptome expression profiles under 24-h water deprivation. A total of 42 TPS sequences with conserved domains were identified in the *S. scabra* reference genome. Phylogenetic analysis revealed five distinct subfamilies, with TPS-a and TPS-b being the most abundant. Regarding motif analysis, the catalytic DDxxD motif was conserved across all TPS subfamilies except TPS-c. In the root tissue of *S. scabra*, 12 TPS genes were found to be involved in the plant's response to 24-h water deprivation, with five showing downregulation and seven maintaining constitutive expression. This transcriptional response suggests a potential association with gibberellin signaling suppression as part of the plant's adaptive strategy to drought stress. Our findings enhance the understanding of TPS genes associated with the *S. scabra* genome, suggesting their potential role in the plant's high tolerance to water deficit. Additionally, this study provides a foundation for future research in plant biotechnology aimed at improving drought resilience.

Keywords: Abiotic stress · Fabaceae · Drought tolerance

1 Introduction

Climate change phenomena represent one of the primary factors affecting crop development and productivity, with far-reaching consequences for ecosystems, biodiversity, and global food security [1]. Among these, drought stands out as a major stressor that impairs plant growth and development [2], triggering molecular, biochemical, and physiological adaptations in response to the deleterious effects of prolonged water déficit [3].

© The Author(s), under exclusive license to Springer Nature Switzerland AG 2026
M. Dorn and F. Martins Lopes (Eds.): X-Meeting 2025, LNBI 16037, pp. 192–204, 2026.
https://doi.org/10.1007/978-3-032-09336-3_14

In this context, the Brazilian semi-arid region is characterized by periodic droughts and significant fluctuations in annual rainfall distribution [4].

Native plants inhabiting this region exhibit remarkable resilience, reflecting a rich genomic arsenal that enables adaptation to extreme environmental conditions [5]. Among these species, the genus *Stylosanthes* (Sw.) has been extensively studied since the 1970s [6] due to its exceptional adaptability to harsh environments, resistance to biotic and abiotic stresses,and notably high drought tolerance. Research has focused on identifying resistance genes with potential applications in crop improvement programs [7].

Throughout evolution, plants have developed sophisticated molecular defense mechanisms, including hormone-mediated responses involving jasmonic acid and salicylic acid, which play critical roles in counteracting herbivory and pathogen attacks [8]. Other key hormonal regulators, such as ethylene, abscisic acid (ABA), and gibberellins, modulate essential biological processes, including plant growth [9], leaf expansion, stomatal conductance [10], and leaf senescence [11], collectively enhancing plant survival under adverse environmental conditions [12].

Under stress, plants can induce the synthesis of secondary metabolites, notably terpenoids—one of the most diverse classes of natural compounds [13]. These molecules serve as precursors for monoterpenes (C10), sesquiterpenes (C15), and diterpenes (C20), derived from dimethylallyl diphosphate (DMAPP), geranyl diphosphate (GPP), and geranylgeranyl diphosphate (GGPP), respectively [14]. Beyond their role in hormone biosynthesis (e.g., ABA, gibberellins, and brassinosteroids), terpenoids contribute to photosynthetic pigments (chlorophylls, carotenoids) and molecular signaling under extreme environmental conditions, including drought [15, 16].

In this sense, Terpene synthase (TPS) constitute an important gene family, playing a crucial role in the biosyntheses of terpenoids. Studies on the TPS gene family have reported differential expression across plant species, suggesting its involvement in stress responses [17]. Notably, *TPS* genes exhibit downregulation under short- to medium-term abiotic stress [18], including water deprivation [19]. Tissue-specific expression patterns have also been observed, with roots showing pronounced downregulation under irrigation suppression, highlighting the spatial regulation of *TPS* in stress adaptation [20].

Despite these advances, the role of the *TPS* gene family in *S. scabra* remains unexplored particularly its contribution to abiotic stress resilience. Addressing this gap is crucial for elucidating the mechanistic basis of drought tolerance in this species. Here, we characterize the *TPS* genes in the *S. scabra* genome, performing structural genomic analysis and investigating their expression through root transcriptome libraries under water deprivation. This approach will lay the groundwork for future applications in plant biotechnology, such as the functional characterization of these genes and their influence on the molecular physiology of *S. scabra* in response to drought.

2 Materials and Methods

2.1 Structural Genomics Analysis

Mining and Identification of TPS Genes in Stylosanthes scabra

To obtain protein sequences, a BLASTp search (cut-off: e-value $< e^{-10}$) was performed using known *TPS* sequences from *Arabidopsis thaliana* and *Populus trichocarpa* (retrieved from the Phytozome database: phytozome.next.jgi.doe.gov) as queries against the *S. scabra* putative proteome. For further refinement, a Hidden Markov Model (HMM) was employed to identify conserved *TPS* domains, specifically: PF03936 (C- terminal domain) and PF01397 (N-terminal domain). These domains were screened using HMMER3, followed by validation through NCBI-CDD and Pfam to confirm the presence of characteristic TPS structural motifs.

Characteristics of TPS Genes

The genomic characteristics of TPS genes in *S. scabra* were determined using the Genestatsscript (https://gist.github.com/darencard/fcb32168c243b92734e85c5f8b5 9a1c3). The following parameters were analyzed: Transcript sequence length; Number of exons; Total exon sequence length; Number of introns; Total intron sequence length; Number of CDS segments; Total CDS sequence length; Number of 50 UTR sequences; Total 50 UTR sequence length; Number of 30 UTR sequences; Total 30 UTR sequence length [22].

Gene Structure, Conserved Motif Identification and Phylogenetic Analysis

Multiple alignment of TPS protein sequences from *S. scabra*, *A. thaliana*, and *Populus trichocarpa* was performed using MAFFT v.6 [23] and edited in MEGA v.7 [24]. A phylogenetic tree was constructed using the Neighbor-Joining (NJ) method with 1,000 bootstrap replications, and all other parameters were set to their default values. Conserved motifs of TPS proteins were analyzed using the MEME program, with the maximum number of predicted motifs set to 10 and other parameters kept as default. Gene structure diagrams and conserved motif maps were visualized using TBtools software v1.082 [22].

GO (Gene Ontology) and KEGG (Kyoto Encyclopedia of Genes and Genomes) Pathway Analysis

For the functional annotation of GO terms for SscTPS proteins, we utilizedthe PANNZER2 [54] prediction tool, which employs a statistical algorithm to identify overrepresented functions or categories within the input list. Subsequently, the genes of interest were analyzed for functional categories in KEGG pathways (Kyoto Encyclopedia of Genes and Genomes) using BlastKOALA (https://www.kegg.jp/blastkoala/).

2.2 Transcriptomic Analysis

Mining and Identification of SscTPS Genes in the S. scabra Transcriptome

Transcript sequences were obtained through a BLASTp search using ScTPS sequences identified in the putative proteome of *S. scabra* as queries against the translated root transcriptome of plants subjected to 24-h water deprivation. Additionally, two protein probes corresponding to specific domains of the terpene synthase family (PF01397 and PF03936, representing the N-terminal and C-terminal portions of TPS from the Pfam database) were employed. These domain sequences were retrieved by screening the genome using HMMER3 v.3.0 and subsequently validated through NCBI-CDD and Pfam databases to confirm TPS domain presence.

In Silico Differential Expression Analysis

Root transcriptome data from *S. scabra* plants subjected to 24-h water deprivation were generated using RNA-Seq technology at the Laboratory of Plant Genetics and

Biotechnology (LGBV). Detailed information regarding growth conditions, stress treatments, and library preparation can be found in the literature [7]. Transcript abundance estimation for each sample was performed using RSEM (RNA-Seq by Expectation–Maximization) v1.3.3 [58]. TPS transcript mining was performed based on Fold Change (FC) values calculated using EdgeR [25], with transcripts exhibiting Log2FC > 1, p-value < 0.05, and FDR < 0.05 considered differentially expressed. The resulting data were then clustered using CLUSTER v.3.0 software.

3 Results and Discussion

3.1 Identification of TPS Genes in the *S. scabra* Genome

A comprehensive analysis identified 42 TPS genes in the *S. scabra* genome, designated as SscTPS-1 to SscTPS-42. This number is notably higher than those reported in previous studies of other plant families, including Fabaceae [*Glycine max* (n = 23) [27], Brassicaceae [*A. thaliana* (n = 32) [28], Solanaceae [*Solanum lycopersicum* (n = 29) [29], and Apiaceae [*Apium graveolens* (n = 39) [30]. Such divergence in TPS gene copy numbers across species is expected and may reflect their distinct functional specializations in stress response mechanisms [18, 31].

Phylogenetic classification grouped these 42 TPS proteins into five subfamilies: TPS-a, TPS-b, TPS-c, TPS-e/f, and TPS-g, with 3 to 14 representatives per clade (Fig. 1). Among them, 39 proteins clustered as TPS class I, while SscTPS-4, SscTPS-18, and SscTPS-19 grouped with *AT4G02780* (a known TPS class II gene). Subfamily distribution was asymmetric, with TPS-e/f being the smallest group (n = 4)—fewer than in *Apium graveolens* (n = 6) [30] but more than in *Daucus carota* (n = 3) [32] or *Malus domestica* (n = 1).

Notably, TPS-b was the largest subfamily (n = 14), followed by TPS-a (n = 13) (Fig. 1). This expansion pattern aligns with observations in other species, such as *Cannabis sativa* [34], *Dendrobium officinale* [35], *P. trichocarpa* [36], and *Salvia splendens* [19], as well as legumes like *Glycine max* [27], though it contrasts with reports in *Medicago truncatula* [37]. Functionally, TPS-a, TPS-b, and TPS-c—the most conserved clades in angiosperms—are linked to the biosynthesis of sesquiterpenes, monoterpenes, and diterpenes, respectively [38]. These metabolites play pivotal roles in plant development, signaling, and growth, while also mediating ecological interactions under environmental stress [39]. Specifically, TPS-a members may drive the production of acyclic monoterpenes (e.g., limonene, linalool, and myrcene) [31], whereas other subfamilies contribute to drought-responsive adaptive mechanisms [31, 40].

3.2 Gene Structures and Conserved Protein Domains of SscTPS

Through analysis of SscTPS gene structures, we identified that 19 *loci* (45.2%) exhibited similar architectures, each containing 7 exons and 6 introns. Eight SscTPS genes (19.04%) possessed 6 exons and 5 introns. The remaining genes showed more variable organization: five (11.9%) contained fewer than 5 exons with corresponding intron variations, while nine (21.4%) displayed more complex structures with greater than 8 exons and associated intron patterns.

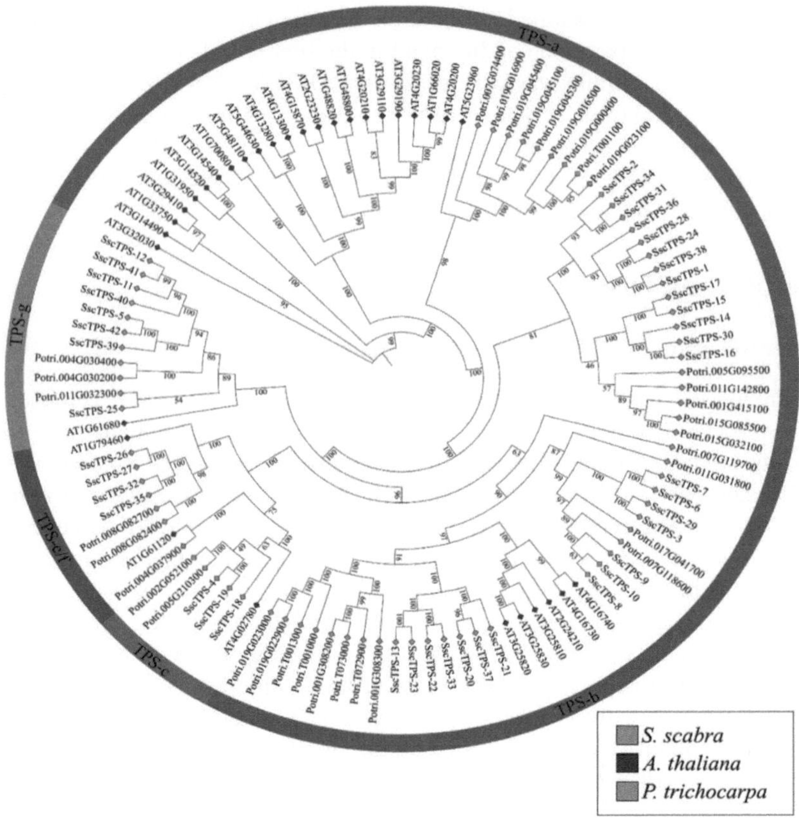

Fig. 1. Phylogenetic tree of 42 SscTPSs, AtTPSs, and 53 PotriTPSs. The tree was constructed using the Neighbor-Joining method. Red, dark green, sky blue, pink, and light green represent the TPS-a, TPS-b, TPS- c, TPS-e/f, and TPS-g subfamilies, respectively. (Color figure online)

Analysis of gene structures across TPS subfamilies revealed distinct organizational patterns. Members of the TPS-c, TPS-g, and TPS-e/f subfamilies exhibited similar genomic architectures, characterized by relatively long coding sequences (averaging 888 bp) containing 6 to 14 exons. In contrast, the TPS-a and TPS-b subfamilies showed more compact gene structures, with fewer exons ranging from 3 to 10. These findings demonstrate clear structural conservation within subfamilies while highlighting significant differences between them. The observed patterns align with previous reports for TPS genes in cotton (*Gossypium hirsutum*), suggesting these structural features may represent conserved evolutionary trends among divergent plant species [41]. The variation in exon number and gene length likely reflects functional specialization within the TPS gene family, with more complex structures potentially enabling greater regulatory complexity or enzymatic versatility, while compact forms may facilitate rapid expression responses to environmental stimuli [40].

The examination of highly conserved regions within the *S. scabra* genome revealed the presence of nine conserved motifs (Fig. 2). Among these, 39 sequences (92.9%) contained the characteristic DDxxD motif, distributed across all subfamilies except TPS-c, which showed notably low conservation. This pattern strongly suggests that the majority of identified SscTPS genes encode class I terpene synthases [55]. The absence of the DDxxD motif in TPS-c members aligns with the established functional properties of this class, as these proteins do not participate in prenyl diphosphate cleavage - a reaction specifically associated with the DDxxD motif [55, 56]. Instead, TPS-c proteins contain a distinct DXDD motif that plays a critical role in initiating protonation reactions characteristic of class II terpene synthases, serving as an essential component of their catalytic mechanism [19]. Previous studies have extensively characterized the functional significance of the DDxxD motif, demonstrating its crucial involvement in multiple catalytic processes. These include the initial ionization of isopentenyl diphosphate and dimethylallyl diphosphate substrates, coordination of water molecules and divalent metal ions, stabilization of the active site architecture, and ultimately the formation of various terpenoid compounds [13].

Additional analysis identified seven genes containing the NSE/DTE protein motif, exclusively present in the TPS-a, TPS-b, and TPS-e/f subfamilies. These motifs, along with DDxxD and RDR, perform essential functions in catalytic reactions and represent characteristic structural features of class I terpene synthases [55]. Notably, SscTPS sequences containing NSE/DTE motifs within the TPS-c and TPS-g clades exhibited significantly lower conservation levels, resulting in the complete loss of these regions in some cases (Fig. 2).

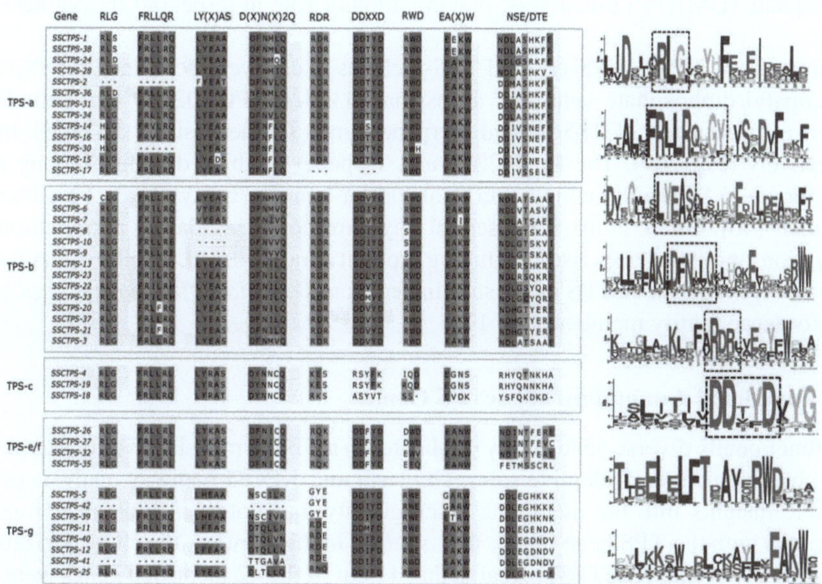

Fig. 2. Delimited sequence alignment of conserved amino acid motifs in terpene synthases from *the S. scabra* genome.

The limited conservation and incomplete understanding of the DDxx motif, along with other regions including LY(x)AS and EA(X)W, reflect the natural structural variability of these domains. As reported in rubber tree (*Hevea brasiliensis*) [42], these regions appear to participate in catalytic activities of TPS genes, despite their lower sequence conservation. The observed patterns in *S. scabra* align with emerging evidence that functional terpene synthases maintain essential catalytic cores while accommodating structural flexibility in ancillary domains - an evolutionary strategy that may enable metabolic diversification while preserving enzymatic activity under stress conditions [41, 42].

Additionally, the analysis revealed that only 39 of the 42 SscTPS genes showed potential kaurene synthase activity, directly linked to the presence of conserved DDxxD and NSE/DTE motifs. These motifs are essential for TPS catalytic activity, coordinating trinuclear magnesium clusters that facilitate substrate binding at the enzyme's active site [40, 42]. Their conservation suggests particular relevance for enzymatic function under stress conditions [43], especially water deficit [15, 16], enabling continuous production of defense and signaling terpenoids [44]. Thus, these motifs not only maintain catalytic activity under ideal conditions but may also contribute to *S. scabra's* adaptive responses [40, 42]. Furthermore, the Terpene_cyclase_plant_C1 (accession: cd00684) and Isoprenoid_Biosyn_C1 (accession: cd00385) domains, representing 66.7% and 9.5% of identified domains respectively, belong to the Isoprenoid_Biosyn_C1 superfamily (accession: cl00210) and were exclusively observed in TPS-a, TPS-b, and TPS-g clades. These domains are part of the trans-isoprenyl diphosphate synthase (IPPS) superfamily, responsible for synthesizing geranyl diphosphate (GPP), farnesyl diphosphates (FPP), and longer-chain products from isopentenyl diphosphate (IPP) and dimethylallyl diphosphate (DMAPP) precursors, playing a major role in terpenoid biosynthesis [42, 45].

In contrast, TPS-c, TPS-e/f, and TPS-g clades exclusively contained the PLN2592 (ent-copalyl diphosphate synthase, accession: cl33526), PLN02279 (ent-kaur-16-ene synthase, accession: cl31856), and Terpene_synth_C (accession: cl47853) motifs, respectively (Fig. 7D). The PLN02279 and Terpene_synth_C domains belong to the ent-kaurene (KS) family, which is crucial for ent-kaurene biosynthesis - a gibberellin precursor [46]. Gibberellins are essential phytohormones regulating germination, cell elongation, and stress responses, including drought conditions [9]. Similar domain distributions were reported in TPS genes scrutinized from *Paeonia suffruticosa*, *Oryza sativa*, and Rosaceae family members [15, 17].

3.3 Functional Annotation of SscTPS Genes

As a functionally diverse gene family implicated in the biosynthesis of various terpenoids with physiological and adaptive roles, GO term and KEGG pathway analysis provide valuable insights into the metabolic heterogeneity and potential biological functions associated with the TPS gene family in *S. scabra*. In this context, the characterization of *S. scabra* TPS genes (SscTPS) revealed that 41 out of the 42 identified genes were associated with 27 Gene Ontology (GO) terms, all belonging to the Biological Process (BP) category (Fig. 3). The remarkable biosynthetic versatility of these proteins suggests their crucial regulatory role in terpenoid synthesis, highlighting their functional importance in this metabolic pathway [30]. Functional prediction analysis confirmed that all identified TPS genes were involved in terpenoid-related processes, with specific classification into distinct terpene classes, validating the reliability of SscTPS identification.

Among the GO terms, "diterpene biosynthetic process" (GO:0016102) was predominant, with 41 SscTPS members associated. Other significant biological processes included "terpenoid metabolic process" (GO:0042214) and "monoterpene biosynthetic process" (GO:0043693) (Fig. 3A, B). The GO mapping analysis suggests SscTPS involvement in diverse plant developmental processes. These findings align with previous reports analyzing TPS transcripts in drought-tolerant *Pennisetum pedicellatum* (Trinap grass), where similar GO terms were associated with stress response, defense mechanisms, and secondary metabolite biosynthesis [47]. The KEGG pathway enrichment analysis identified 23 SscTPS genes associated with six distinct metabolic pathways (Fig. 3). Specifically, six genes (*SscTPS-3, -6, -7, -8, -9,* and *-29*) were mapped to the isoprene synthase pathway (K12742); five genes (*SscTPS-11, 12, - 25, -40,* and *-41*) to nerolidol synthase (K14175); and three genes each to ent-kaurene synthase (K04120: *SscTPS-4, -18, -19*), neryl diphosphate phosphatase (K24668: *SscTPS-5, - 39, -42*), and germacrene D synthase (K15803: *SscTPS-16, -17*) (Fig. 3C).

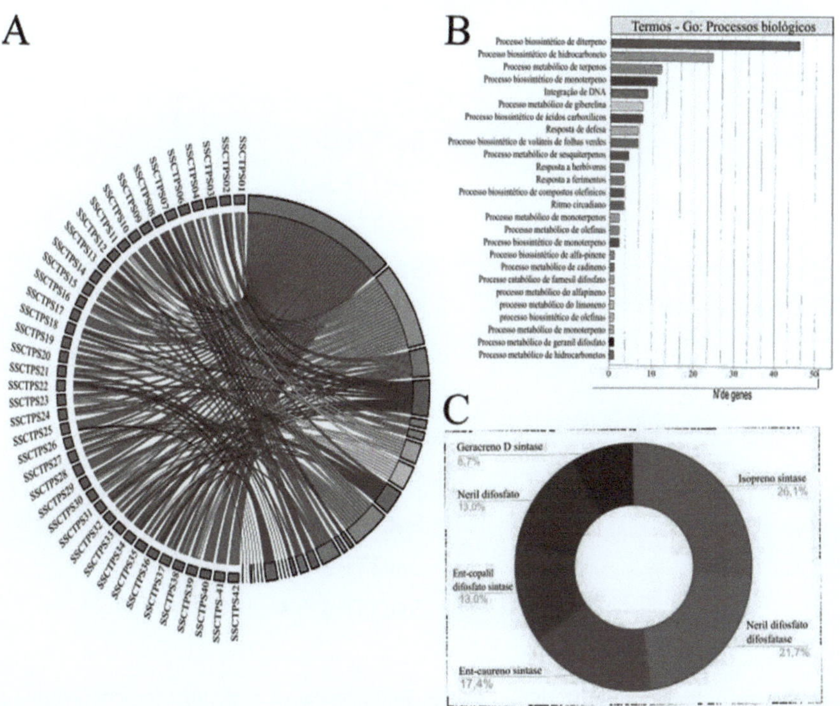

Fig. 3. Functional enrichment analysis of Gene Ontology (GO) and Kyoto Encyclopedia of Genes and Genomes (KEGG) pathways for differentially expressed genes: (A) GO term network for SscTPSs; (B) Bar plot of GO biological processes; (C) KEGG pathway doughnut chart.

The synthesis of compounds such as nerolidol synthase and ent-kaurene synthase is directly linked to phytohormone production, which plays key regulatory roles [18, 44]. These metabolites serve as critical intermediates in plant defense mechanisms against various stresses, including drought, herbivory, climatic fluctuations, and pathogen attacks [46, 48, 49].

3.4 Differential Expression of Terpene Synthase Genes in Response to Water Deprivation

To investigate TPS genes and their presence in the translated transcriptome of *S. scabra*, data were collected after 24 hours of water deprivation. As a result, 15 *SscTPS* genes were identified and renamed *SscTTPS*. These root transcriptome-derived *SscTTPS* genes were evaluated for differential expression under water stress conditions. The analysis revealed 12 differentially expressed TPS genes (*SscTTPS-1* to *SscTTPS-12*), with five showing downregulation (*SscTTPS-1*to *SscTTPS-5*) and seven maintaining constitutive expression (*SscTTPS-6* to *SscTTPS-12*) (Fig 4). This expression pattern suggests distinct regulatory mechanisms among *SscTTPS* members in response to water deficit, potentially reflecting their specialized roles in drought adaptation.

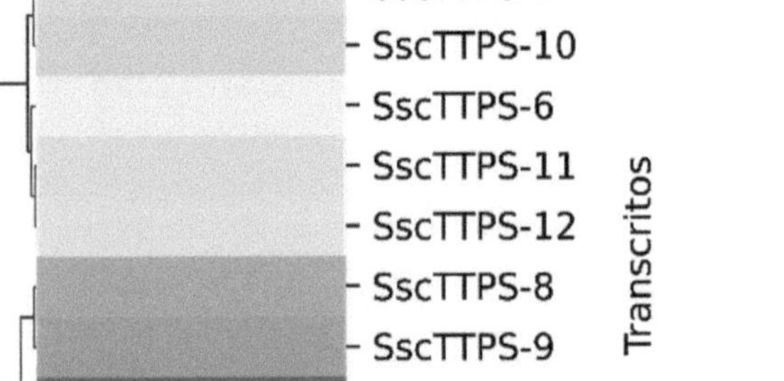

Fig. 4. Heatmap displaying differential expression patterns of *S. scabra* terpene synthase transcripts under water deprivation. Transcripts meeting the threshold criteria (Fold Change > 2, p-value < 0.05, and FDR < 0.05) are marked with asterisks (*)

The functional characterization of ScTTPs sequences revealed their participation in the diterpenoid biosynthetic process (GO:0016102), known to generate precursors for gibberellin (GA) production [18, 44]. As tetracyclic diterpenoid phytohormones, GAs regulates various plant developmental processes, though their synthesis is typically suppressed under osmotic stress [22, 50], potentially serving as drought response indicators [52].

The observed transcript repression may be attributed to the short stress exposure period. Previous studies in *Camelia sinensis* have demonstrated that TPS gene induction typically initiates only after 48 hours of water withholding [39], suggesting these molecular components may participate in later-stage plant defense responses. The downregulation of ScTTPs under water deficit conditions indicates their potential involvement in *S. scabra's* stress adaptation mechanisms. This pattern aligns with observations in *Bupleurum chinense* root transcriptomes, where water stress resulted in a greater number of downregulated than upregulated TPS genes [53]. Similar studies conducted with *Dendrobium catenatum* revealed that expression of the DcaPS-TPS genes under drought conditions was suppressed after more than 18 hours of stress exposure. These findings suggest these genes may undergo temporal modulation during water deficit [57]. These consistent findings across species demonstrate that acute water stress exerts an inhibitory effect on TPS gene expression, potentially representing a conserved earlyresponse mechanism in plants facing drought conditions.

4   Conclusion

Comprehensive genomic analysis of *Stylosanthes scabra* revealed a broad distribution of TPS genes encompassing all TPS subfamilies found in angiosperms. A total of 42 putative TPS genes were identified and classified into five distinct subfamilies, with TPS-b being the most abundant, comprising 14 representatives. Significant variation was observed across clades regarding intron-exon architecture. Among the conserved motifs analyzed, the catalytic DDxxD domain was present in all clades except TPS-c, where its conservation was limited. Functional annotation confirmed that all 42 genes encode proteins with terpene synthase activity. Transcriptome analysis demonstrated significant downregulation of SscTTPS genes following 24-h water deprivation, suggesting a potential association with gibberellin signaling suppression as part of the plant's adaptive response to drought stress.

This study provides the first systematic investigation of TPS gene distribution within the *Stylosanthes* genus (Sw.), establishing a genomic foundation for future biotechnological applications in agriculture. Further metabolomic approaches will be essential to elucidate the biosynthesis pathways of these secondary metabolites and their specific roles in plant defense mechanisms against abiotic stresses. The findings not only expand our understanding of terpenoid biosynthesis in drought-tolerant legumes but also highlight potential targets for crop improvement strategies aimed at enhancing stress resilience. The conserved DDxxD motif architecture, absent only in TPS-c members, reflects evolutionary patterns observed across angiosperms, while the distinct transcriptional response to water stress underscores the sophisticated regulatory mechanisms governing terpenoid metabolism in *S. scabra*.

Acknowledgments. The authors acknowledge the Fundação de Amparo à Pesquisa do Estado de Pernambuco (FACEPE) and Coordenação de Aperfeiçoamento de Pessoal de Nível Superior

(CAPES) for fellowships and financial support. The authors acknowledge the National Laboratory for Scientific Computing (LNCC), for providing high-performance computing resources through the Santos Dumont supercomputer, used to obtain the research results reported in this paper. The paper used Deepseek IA to perform the initial translation of the work from Portuguese to scientific English.

References

1. Shahzad, A., et al.: Nexus on climate change: agriculture and possible solution to cope future climate change stresses. Environ. Sci. Pollut. Res. **28**, 14211–14232 (2021)
2. Ahmadi, S.Z., Zahedi, B., Ghorbanpour, M., Mumivand, H.: Comparative morpho-physiological and biochemical responses of Capsicum annuum L. plants to multi-walled carbon nanotubes, fullerene C60 and graphene nanoplatelets exposure under water deficit stress. BMC Plant Biol. **24**, 116 (2024)
3. Spanic, V., Duvnjak, J., Hefer, D., D'Auria, J.C.: Changes in metabolites produced in wheat plants against water-deficit stress. Plants **14**, 10 (2025)
4. dos Santos, W.R., et al.: Can changes in land use in a semi-arid region of Brazil cause seasonal variation in energy partitioning and evapotranspiration? J. Environ. Manage. **367**, 121959 (2024)
5. Chandra, A.: Biotechnology of Stylosanthes. In: Jain, S.M., Dutta Gupta, S. (eds.) Biotechnology of Neglected and Underutilized Crops, pp. 217–241. Springer, Dordrecht (2013)
6. Reddy, R.S., et al.: Knowledge and adoption gaps of Stylosanthes seed production practices followed by farmers of Anantapur, Andhra Pradesh. Range Manage. Agroforestry **45**, 162–166 (2024)
7. Ferreira-Neto, J.R.C., et al.: Dehydration response in Stylosanthes scabra: transcriptional, biochemical, and physiological modulations. Physiol. Plant. **174**, e13821 (2022)
8. Sultana, R., et al.: Signaling and defence mechanism of jasmonic and salicylic acid response in pulse crops: role of WRKY transcription factors in stress response. J. Plant Growth Regul. **44**, 5–21 (2025)
9. Acharya, B.R., Gill, S.P., Kaundal, A., Sandhu, D.: Strategies for combating plant salinity stress: the potential of plant growth-promoting microorganisms. Front. Plant Sci. **15** (2024)
10. Pizzio, G.A., et al.: Basal ABA signaling balances transpiration and photosynthesis. Physiol. Plant. **176**, e14494 (2024)
11. Xing, J., et al.: Ethylene accelerates maize leaf senescence in response to nitrogen deficiency by regulating chlorophyll metabolism and autophagy. Crop J. **12**, 1391–1403 (2024)
12. Amist, N., Singh, N.B.: Chapter 11 - Regulatory role of strigolactones in abiotic stress tolerance. In: Bashri, G., Hayat, S., Bajguz, A. (eds.) Strigolactones, pp. 201–220. Academic Press (2024). https://doi.org/10.1016/B978-0-443-13521-7.00011-7
13. Jiang, L., et al.: An improved genome assembly of Chrysanthemum nankingense reveals expansion and functional diversification of terpene synthase gene family. BMC Genom. **25**, 593 (2024)
14. Kumar, Y., Khan, F., Rastogi, S., Shasany, A.K.: Genome-wide detection of terpene synthase genes in holy basil (Ocimum sanctum L.). PLOS One **13**, e0207097 (2018)
15. Sun, P., et al.: Composition diversity and expression specificity of the TPS gene family among 24 ficus species. Diversity **14**, 721 (2022)
16. Ma, S., et al.: Transcriptomic and physiological analysis of atractylodes chinensis in response to drought stress reveals the putative genes related to sesquiterpenoid biosynthesis. BMC Plant Biol. **24**, 91 (2024)

17. Ma, B., et al.: Functional analysis of PsHMGR1 and PsTPS1 related to floral terpenoids biosynthesis in tree peony. Int. J. Mol. Sci. **25**, 12247 (2024)
18. Zhou, F., Pichersky, E.: More is better: the diversity of terpene metabolism in plants. Curr. Opin. Plant Biol. **55**, 1–10 (2020)
19. Chen, Z., et al.: Genome-wide analysis of terpene synthase gene family in menthalongifolia and catalytic activity analysis of a single terpene synthase. Genes **12**, 518 (2021)
20. Li, C., Zha, W., Li, W., Wang, J., You, A.: Advances in the biosynthesis of terpenoids and their ecological functions in plant resistance. Int. J. Mol. Sci. **24**, 11561 (2023)
21. Hernández-López, J.A., Andrade, H.J., Barrios, M.: Agricultural drought assessment in dry zones of Tolima, Colombia, using an approach based on water balance and vegetation water stress. Sci. Total. Environ. **921**, 171144 (2024)
22. Chen, C., et al.: TBtools: an integrative toolkit developed for interactive analyses of big biological data. Mol. Plant **13**, 1194–1202 (2020)
23. Katoh, K., Toh, H.: Parallelization of the MAFFT multiple sequence alignment program. Bioinformatics **26**, 1899–1900 (2010)
24. Kumar, S., Stecher, G., Tamura, K.: MEGA7: molecular evolutionary genetics analysis version 7.0 for bigger datasets. Mol. Biol. Evol. **33**, 1870–1874 (2016)
25. Robinson, M.D., McCarthy, D.J., Smyth, G.K.: EdgeR: a Bioconductor package for differential expression analysis of digital gene expression data. Bioinformatics **26**, 139–140 (2010). https://doi.org/10.1093/bioinformatics/btp616
26. Saldanha, A.J.: Java treeview—extensible visualization of microarray data. Bioinformatics **20**, 3246–3248 (2004)
27. Liu, J., et al.: Genome-wide analysis of terpene synthases in soybean: functional characterization of GmTPS3. Gene **544**, 83–92 (2014)
28. Aubourg, S., Lecharny, A., Bohlmann, J.: Genomic analysis of the terpenoid synthase (AtTPS) gene family of Arabidopsis thaliana. Mol. Gen. Genom. **267**, 730–745 (2002)
29. Falara, V., et al.: The tomato terpene synthase gene family. Plant Physiol. **157**, 770–789 (2011)
30. Li, M., et al.: Genome-wide identification and analysis of terpene synthase (TPS) genes in celery reveals their regulatory roles in terpenoid biosynthesis. Front. Plant Sci. **13** (2022)
31. Lopes, J.M.L., et al.: Water stress modulates terpene biosynthesis and morphophysiology at different ploidal levels in Lippia alba (Mill.) N. E. Brown (Verbenaceae). Protoplasma **261**, 227–243 (2024)
32. Song, X., et al.: Deciphering the high-quality genome sequence of coriander that causes controversial feelings. Plant Biotechnol. J. **18**, 1444–1456 (2020)
33. Nieuwenhuizen, N.J., et al.: Functional genomics reveals that a compact terpene synthase gene family can account for terpene volatile production in apple. Plant Physiol. **161**, 787–804 (2013)
34. Allen, K.D., et al.: Genomic characterization of the complete terpene synthase gene family from Cannabis sativa. PLoS ONE **14**, e0222363 (2019)
35. Zhao, C., et al.: Functional characterization of a dendrobium officinale geraniol synthase DoGES1 involved in floral scent formation. Int. J. Mol. Sci. **21**, 7005 (2020)
36. Irmisch, S., Jiang, Y., Chen, F., Gershenzon, J., Köllner, T.G.: Terpene synthases and their contribution to herbivore-induced volatile emission in western balsam poplar (Populus trichocarpa). BMC Plant Biol. **14**, 270 (2014)
37. Parker, M.T., Zhong, Y., Dai, X., Wang, S., Zhao, P.: Comparative genomic and transcriptomic analysis of terpene synthases in Arabidopsis and Medicago. IET SystemsBiology **8**, 146–153 (2014)
38. Aqeel, U., Aftab, T., Khan, M.M.A., Naeem, M.: Regulation of essential oil in aromatic plants under changing environment. J. Appl. Res. Med. Aromatic Plants **32**, 100441 (2023)

39. Zhou, H.-C., Shamala, L.F., Yi, X.-K., Yan, Z., Wei, S.: Analysis of terpene synthase family genes in camellia sinensis with an emphasis on abiotic stress conditions. Sci. Rep. **10**, 933 (2020)
40. Chen, F., Tholl, D., Bohlmann, J., Pichersky, E.: The family of terpene synthases in plants: a mid-size family of genes for specialized metabolism that is highly diversified throughout the kingdom. Plant J. **66**, 212–229 (2011)
41. Zhang, C.-P., et al.: Genome-wide identification and characterization of terpene synthase genes in Gossypium hirsutum. Gene **828**, 146462 (2022)
42. Liang, J., et al.: In silico genome-wide mining and analysis of terpene synthase gene family in hevea brasiliensis. Biochem. Genet. **61**, 1185–1209 (2023)
43. Toffolatti, S.L., et al.: 16 - role of terpenes in plant defense to biotic stress. In: Jogaiah, S. (ed.) Biocontrol Agents and Secondary Metabolites, pp. 401–417. Woodhead Publishing (2021). https://doi.org/10.1016/B978-0-12-822919-4.00016-8
44. He, J., et al.: Cold stress regulates accumulation of flavonoids and terpenoids in plants by phytohormone, transcription process, functional enzyme, and epigenetics. Crit. Rev. Biotechnol. **43**, 680–697 (2023)
45. Drummond, L., et al.: High versatility of IPP and DMAPP methyltransferases enables synthesis of C6, C7 and C8 terpenoid building blocks. ChemBioChem **23**, e202200091 (2022)
46. Teng, Y., et al.: Genome-wide identification and expression analysis of ent-kaurene synthase-like gene family associated with abiotic stress in rice. Int. J. Mol. Sci. **25**, 5513 (2024)
47. Puttamadanayaka, S., et al.: Unravelling the molecular mechanism underlying drought stress tolerance in Dinanath (Pennisetum pedicellatum Trin.) grass via integrated transcriptomic and metabolomic analyses. BMC Plant Biol. **24**, 928 (2024)
48. Batish, D.R., Singh, H.P., Kohli, R.K., Kaur, S.: Eucalyptus essential oil as a natural pesticide. For. Ecol. Manage. **256**, 2166–2174 (2008)
49. Chan, W.-K., Tan, L.T.-H., Chan, K.-G., Lee, L.-H., Goh, B.-H.: Nerolidol: a sesquiterpene alcohol with multi-faceted pharmacological and biological activities. Molecules **21**, 529 (2016)
50. Shohat, H., et al.: Inhibition of gibberellin accumulation by water deficiency promotes fast and long-term 'drought avoidance' responses in tomato. New Phytol. **232**, 1985–1998 (2021)
51. Wang, Y., et al.: Transcriptome, miRNA, and degradome sequencing reveal the leaf stripe (Pyrenophora graminea) resistance genes in Tibetan hulless barley. BMC Plant Biol. **25**, 71 (2025)
52. Kittipornkul, P., et al.: The potential of proline as a key metabolite to design real-time plant water deficit and low-light stress detector in ornamental plants. Environ. Sci. Pollut. Res. **31**, 36152–36162 (2024)
53. Yang, L., Qiao, L., Su, X., Ji, B., Dong, C.: Drought Stress stimulates the terpenoid backbone and triterpenoid biosynthesis pathway to promote the synthesis of saikosaponin in bupleurum chinense DC. Roots. Molecules **27**, 5470 (2022)
54. Toronen, P., Medlar, A., Holm, L.: PANNZER2: a rapid functional annotation web server. Nucleic Acids Res. **46**, 84–88 (2018)
55. Sun, P., et al.: Composition diversity and expression specificity of the TPS gene family among 24 Ficus species. Diversity, **14**(9), 721 (2022)
56. Chen, Z., et al.: Genome-wide analysis of terpene synthase gene family in Mentha longifolia and catalytic activity analysis of a single terpene synthase. Genes, **12**, 518 (2021)
57. Zhan, X., Qian, Y., Mao, B.: Metabolic profiling of terpene diversity and the response of prenylsynthase-terpene synthase genes during biotic and abiotic stresses in dendrobium catenatum. Int. J. Mol. Sci. **23**(12), 6398 (2022)
58. Li, B., Dewey, C.N.: RSEM: accurate transcript quantification from RNA-Seq data with or without a reference genome. BMC Bioinform. **12**, 323 (2011). https://doi.org/10.1186/1471-2105-12-323

Protein Dimension DB: A Unified Protein Repository for Representation Learning and Functional Analysis

Pitágoras de Azevedo Alves Sobrinho[1,2]([✉]) [iD], Tetsu Sakamoto[1,2] [iD], and Wilfredo Blanco Figuerola[2,3] [iD]

[1] Digital Metropolis Institute, Federal University of Rio Grande do Norte, Natal, Brazil
`pitagoras.alves.104@ufrn.edu.br, tetsu@imd.ufrn.edu.br`
[2] Bioinformatics Postgraduate Program, Federal University of Rio Grande do Norte, Natal, Brazil
[3] State University of Rio Grande do Norte, Natal, Brazil

Abstract. Inspired by the success of large language models in areas like natural language processing, researchers have applied similar architectures, notably the Transformer, to protein sequences. Thanks to these developments, Protein Language Models (PLMs) have become important resources for diverse tasks such as predicting protein family, function, solubility, cellular location, molecular interactions and remote homology. However, the size of the best performing PLMs (which can be up to 15B parameters) requires substantial computational power. Protein Dimension DB addresses this critical bottleneck by providing a centralized, version-controlled resource of precomputed protein embeddings, experimentally validated molecular function annotations, and taxonomic encodings. The database integrates embeddings from seven state-of-the-art PLMs, including ProtT5, ESM2, and Ankh variants for all Swiss-Prot/ UniProt proteins. These models were compared by benchmarking molecular function prediction. Tests revealed that hybrid embeddings (e.g., Ankh Base + ProtT5) outperformed single-model approaches with minimal dimensionality increases. Taxonomic encodings further boosted performance by 2.9% AUPRC, demonstrating lineage-aware learning. By providing embeddings in Parquet format—a columnar storage optimized for machine learning workflows—the resource eliminates GPU-dependent preprocessing and reduces storage requirements. This enables immediate use in resource-constrained environments while maintaining backward compatibility through versioned releases. All datasets are freely accessible via Github and HuggingFace, with unified metadata enabling applications from functional annotation to evolutionary studies. Protein Dimension DB bridges the gap between cutting-edge PLMs and practical biological research, offering researchers standardized inputs for reproducible, multi-modal protein analysis.

Keywords: Database · Protein Language Models · Gene Ontology

M. Dorn and F. Martins Lopes (Eds.): X-Meeting 2025, LNBI 16037, pp. 205–213, 2026.
https://doi.org/10.1007/978-3-032-09336-3_15

1 Introduction

The representation and annotation of proteins presents one of the most fundamental challenges in modern bioinformatics, with far-reaching implications in biomedical research, evolutionary biology, and biotechnology. Although recent breakthroughs in protein structure prediction, particularly AlphaFold2 [1], have revolutionized our understanding of protein folding, these methods remain computationally prohibitive for many research groups, requiring specialized hardware and days of processing time for comprehensive analyses [2]. This computational bottleneck is particularly acute for studies with a large amount of novel proteins, where the need to process thousands of protein sequences makes structure-based approaches impractical.

Protein Language Models (PLMs) have emerged as a powerful alternative, offering the ability to capture structural and functional information directly from amino acid sequences [3]. Models like ProstT5 [4] and ESM-2 [5] can generate informative protein representations with just seconds of computation on standard hardware [7]. These numerical representations (embeddings) encode evolutionary patterns, physicochemical properties, and potential functional motifs, providing a rich foundation for downstream predictive tasks [6]. This efficiency makes them particularly valuable for large-scale comparative genomics studies, rapid annotation of newly sequenced proteins, analysis of organisms with limited structural data and resource-constrained research environments.

The UniProtKB [8] project generates a dataset with ProstT5 embeddings for all proteins in their "Swiss-Prot" subset. However, there is a lack of per-protein embedding datasets using other PLMs. Researchers must typically generate embeddings anew for each study, wasting computational resources and introducing unnecessary variability. This creates unnecessary barriers to their widespread adoption in biological research.

The most recent Critical Assessment of Protein Function Annotation (CAFA) [9] adopted NCBI taxonomic codes as one of its standard inputs, alongside protein sequences. Since then, several machine learning projects have used taxonomic unit encodings along with protein embeddings or structures [3,13], usually as "one-hot" encodings. Similarly to PLM embeddings, there is a lack of standardized taxon encodings available to the community.

This work has 3 main objectives:

- Enable researchers without access to high-end computing to use the encodings produced by the latest PLMs in their projects;
- To compare the capabilities of different PLMs;
- Measure how much strategies such as the combination of different PLMs and taxonomic information can improve molecular function prediction;

We approached these challenges with the creation of Protein Dimension DB, a resource which includes several datasets for the proteins in Swiss-Prot/Uniprot, such as PLM-based embeddings, numerical representations of taxonomy and experimentally confirmed gene ontology annotations.

The datasets in Protein Dimension DB were used to create molecular function prediction models, which were benchmarked. The Ankh family of models showed the highest performance. The tests also revealed that pairing medium-sized PLMs can provide the same level of performance as using the largest models and that taxonomic information can improve performance by up to 2%.

2   Building The Database

The data pipeline was implemented as a Nextflow pipeline. Data collection starts with obtaining the complete Swiss-Prot sequences dataset, which comprises the highest quality protein sequences of UniprotKB [8]. It accounted for a total of 569,059 proteins. The Gene Ontology Annotation (GOA) Database was downloaded and then filtered to exclude electronic annotations (IEA) and only keep annotations of Swiss-Prot proteins [10].

ProstT5 protein embeddings are downloaded from the UniprotKB database and converted from the original HDF5 format to Parquet format. Parquet format was used because its columnar storage design, which enables efficient compression and faster column-wise queries compared to row-based formats like HDF5 [11]. This is particularly beneficial for machine learning workflows, where selective access to specific columns and rows is common. This format was also adopted for the remaining datasets.

Differently from ProstT5 - Ankh and ESM2 embeddings were not available for all Swiss-Prot proteins. To address this, they were calculated locally. Ankh had two variants available: Base and Large. The ESM2 project had several different models: ESM2 T6, T12, T30, T33 and T36. Both PLM projects have Python APIs [5, 12], which we used to transform protein sequences into embeddings. The smaller models (ESM2 T6, T12, T30 and Ankh Base) showed good performance, but inference on the larger models (ESM2 T36 and Ankh Large) required several weeks of processing.

The NCBI taxon ID of each protein was also obtained from UniprotKB. The frequency of each taxa was counted and two sets were selected: The 128 and 256 most common taxa. They were treated as discrete categories and converted to "onehot" encodings.

3   Case Study: Benchmarking of Protein Molecular Function Classification

To evaluate the different protein representations and demonstrate the utility of Protein Dimension DB, we conducted a comprehensive benchmark evaluating different combinations of protein embeddings and taxonomic encodings for molecular function (MF) prediction. Using the experimentally validated GO annotations from GOA as ground truth, we trained a multi-label classifiers to predict MF terms, measuring performance via weighted AUPRC (prioritizing rare classes) and ROC AUC.

3.1 Protein and Molecular Function Sampling

First, we filtered the full list MF terms, keeping only those annotated at least 36 different proteins. This resulted in 1,487 MF terms. A total of 102,696 proteins (18% of Swiss-Prot) were annotated to at least one of those terms. Of these, 15% (15,577) was randomly selected for validation, 30% (30,808) for testing and 55% (56,311) for training.

We wanted to measure how these models perform not only on functions with a vast number of protein annotations, but also on functions with very few. Following this principle, we sorted the 1,487 trainable MF terms by their frequency. Then the first, middle and top 24 terms were selected. Combined, they made up a list of 72 MFs, which were used as classification targets.

3.2 Model Architecture

The classifier is a deep neural network (DNN). It was based on the architecture of the PROTGOAT model [3], due to its modular approach (Fig. 1). The model features separate modules for the different input features, whose last layers are connected by a concatenation layer, followed by a final Relu-activated dense layer and a Sigmoid-activated layer as output. Training used Adam optimizer and Binary Cross-Entropy as loss function. This design can be used to make classifiers with any list of input features, when properly optimized.

3.3 Optimization and Benchmarking

Metaparameter optimization was performed with random search over a uniform distribution, with each metaparameter having a minimum and maximum value (Table 1). Each feature had specific metaparameters (such as the dimensions of layers "Dense 1" and "Dense 2"), which were selected separatly.

Each generation of the optimization consisted of 120 random settings, made using the default minimum and maximum values. The features of the training proteins were used to train one model for each metaparameter setting. Then, the fitness of each model was calculated on the test proteins, by comparing the generated scores with the ground truth labels. Two metrics were calculated: ROC AUC Score and AUPRC Score, weighted to account for class imbalance. The fitness was the average of the two metrics: (ROC AUC + AUPRC)/2.

At the end of the generation, the 80 settings with best fitness were selected and the maximum and minimum range values of metaparameters was updated, using the minimum and maximum found in the best performing settings. This was done to gradually find better bounds metaparameter ranges for each feature.

After 4 generations, the setting with higher fitness was selected for validation. Validation was performed by predicting scores on the validation proteins, with weighted ROC AUC and AUPRC scores.

First, this metaheuristic algorithm was used to benchmark each individual PLM embedding as the single input feature. Subsequent analysis paired the top five best-performing PLMs (Ankh Large, Ankh Base, ESM2 T36, ProstT5 and

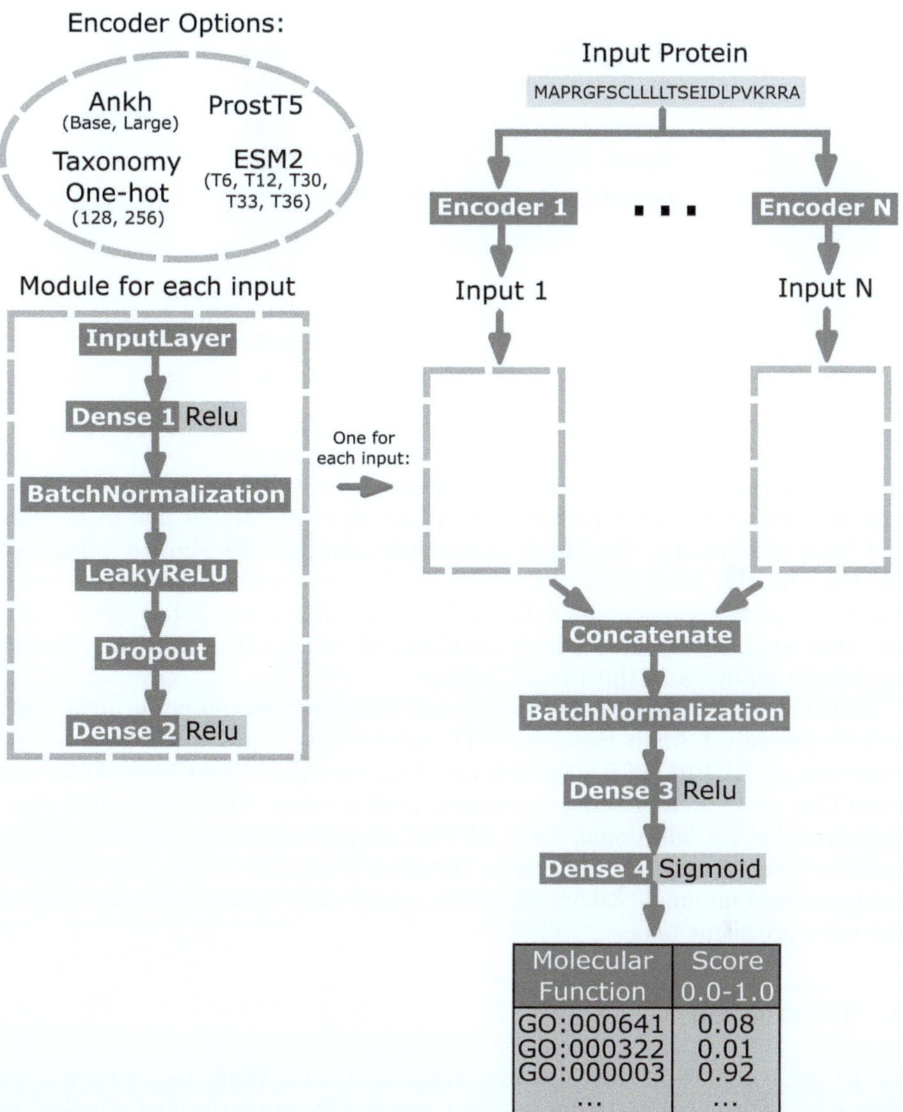

Fig. 1. Our implementation of the DNN architecture proposed by PROTGOAT [3]. The modular neural network architecture processes input features (such as protein embeddings and taxonomic encodings) through separate feature-specific branches. Each input type passes through two dense layers with batch normalization, LeakyReLU activation and dropout regularization. Intermediate representations are concatenated then refined through final dense layers (ReLU-activated) before sigmoid-activated output for multi-label molecular function prediction. This design enables flexible integration of heterogeneous biological data while mitigating overfitting through pathway-specific regularization.

Table 1. Metaparameter Ranges Used for Optimization

Metaparameter	Min.	Max.
"Dense 1" width	64	3600
"Dense 2" width	64	2048
"Dense 3" width	300	550
LeakyRELU Negative Slope	0.03	0.9
Dropout Rate	0.2	0.5
Patience	8	13
Epochs	38	48
Learning Rate	0.0006	0.00075
Batch Size	130	200

ESM2 T33) to identify optimal combinations of two different PLMs (Table 2). Combinations with lower performance PLMs were not tested due to hardware and time constraints. The three highest-performing pairs showed comparable results, with the Ankh Base + ProstT5 combination selected for further testing due to its more compact input dimensionality (1792 values total). This pairing was then augmented with onehot encodings of either 128 or 256 most frequent taxonomic groups as a third input feature.

Our benchmarking revealed several key insights. The top-performing configuration combined Ankh Base, ProstT5 embeddings, and 256-taxon encodings, achieving an AUPRC of 0.8006. This performance gain stems from Ankh's and ProstT5's protein embeddings combined performance, while taxonomic encodings provided an additional 2.9% AUPRC improvement over embedding-only models. Interestingly, the difference between using 128 versus 256 taxonomic groups proved minimal (<0.5% AUPRC), suggesting diminishing returns beyond the most prevalent taxa.

4   Discussion

Model size comparisons revealed important trade-offs. While larger ESM-2 variants (e.g., T36 with 2560 dimensions) marginally outperformed smaller ones (T6 with 320 dimensions), they required eight times the feature dimensionality. Notably, Ankh Large (1536 dimensions) surpassed ESM-2 T36 in AUPRC (0.7753 vs. 0.7641) despite its more compact representation. Model pairs showed higher performance when compared to single-model approaches. However, certain pairs like Ankh Large + ESM-2 T36 (4096 dimensions) demanded significantly more memory without delivering proportional performance gains.

The fact that the combination of embeddings from different PLMs (such as Ankh Base + ProtT5) outperform single models suggests that different models may capture complementary information about the protein that is relevant for predicting molecular function. Although it is difficult to specify exactly which

Table 2. Molecular Function Classification Benchmark

Input Features Used	Total Feature Length	AUPRC Score (W)	ROC AUC Score (W)	F1 Score (W)
TAXA 256 + Ankh Base + ProstT5	2048	0.8006	0.9094	0.7507
TAXA 128 + Ankh Base + ProstT5	1920	0.796	0.9051	0.7487
Ankh Base + ESM2 T33	2048	0.7802	0.8888	0.7283
Ankh Base + Ankh Large	2304	0.7796	0.8892	0.7317
Ankh Base + ProstT5	1792	0.778	0.8905	0.7289
Ankh Large + ProstT5	2560	0.7767	0.8913	0.7307
Ankh Large + ESM2 T36	4096	0.7765	0.8889	0.7252
Ankh Base + ESM2 T36	3328	0.776	0.8854	0.7266
Ankh Large	1536	0.7753	0.8889	0.7272
ESM2 T36 + ProstT5	3584	0.7722	0.8884	0.7195
Ankh Base	768	0.7718	0.8831	0.7238
Ankh Large + ESM2 T33	2816	0.7714	0.8851	0.7249
ESM2 T33 + ProstT5	2304	0.7704	0.8883	0.72
ESM2 T36	2560	0.7641	0.8824	0.7104
ESM2 T33 + ESM2 T36	3840	0.7636	0.8811	0.7143
ProstT5	1024	0.7604	0.8842	0.7142
ESM2 T33	1280	0.7583	0.8817	0.7075
ESM2 T30	640	0.7466	0.8765	0.6967
ESM2 T12	480	0.739	0.8707	0.6861
ESM2 T6	320	0.7162	0.8606	0.6638

The table presents Total Feature Length (sum of the lengths of all features used), Area Under the Precision-Recall Curve (AUPRC) Score, Area Under the Receiver Operating Characteristic Curve (ROC AUC) Score and F1 Score for all feature combinations tested. The AUPRC, ROC AUC and F1 metrics were calculated using the "weighted" averaging mode of the Scikit-Learn library [16], in order to address class imbalance.

features are described in the embedding space of each model, one can hypothesize that they learn different representations or prioritize different aspects of the sequence or structure that, when combined, provide a more complete view of the protein and its function.

For example, one model may be more effective in capturing local patterns important for binding sites or catalytic activity, while another may capture global or structural features important for subcellular localization or protein-protein interactions. ProtT5, for example, has been shown to capture aspects of protein structure impressively and to be effective in predicting variant effects [17].

The taxonomic encodings proved particularly valuable. According to Tiittanen et al. [15], taxonomic characteristics may improve classification because they allow models to generate different predictions for the same input sequence when the sequence occurs in different regions of the species taxonomy tree. However, Swiss-Prot contains a disproportional amount of sequences from *Homo sapiens* and model organisms. This represents an annotation bias, so results may not generalize equally well to proteins from underrepresented taxonomic groups.

5   Conclusions and Future Work

The results of the case study on molecular function prediction align with those of Vieira et al. [7], who concluded that medium-sized PLMs can achieve performance comparable to larger models while requiring substantially fewer computational resources. In addition, taxonomic input significantly improved function predictions.

These findings collectively demonstrate how precomputed features facilitate efficient experimentation with multi-modal inputs. By providing pre-generated embeddings from seven state-of-the-art PLMs, the database eliminates the need for researchers to perform resource-intensive computations, making advanced protein analysis accessible to groups without specialized hardware.

All molecular function annotations are filtered to exclude low-confidence predictions, ensuring that researchers work with reliable GO term assignments. This curation is particularly valuable given the noise present in many automated annotation pipelines [14].

Version-controlled releases in machine-learning-ready formats (Parquet) ensure consistency across studies, supporting the growing emphasis on reproducible research in computational biology. The datasets, which are currently in version 1.0, can be downloaded individually from the project page: https:// pentalpha.github.io/protein_dimension_db/. By making these resources freely available, we aim to accelerate discoveries across diverse areas of protein science, from basic biological research to applied biotechnology and drug discovery.

As the field continues to develop new PLM architectures and annotation strategies, this resource will serve as a foundation for integrating these advances into practical research workflows, helping to realize the full potential of machine learning in protein science.

Acknowledgments. We were able to generate the embeddings included in this database thanks to the computational infrastructure available in the Bioinformatics Multidisciplinary Environment (BioME), of the Federal University of Rio Grande do Norte.

Disclosure of Interests. The authors have no competing interests to declare that are relevant to the content of this article.

References

1. Jumper, J., Evans, R., Pritzel, A., et al.: Highly accurate protein structure prediction with AlphaFold. Nature **596**, 583–589 (2021). https://doi.org/10.1038/s41586-021-03819-2
2. Lee, C., Su, B.H., Tseng, Y.J.: Comparative studies of AlphaFold, RoseTTAFold and Modeller - a case study involving the use of G-protein-coupled receptors. Brief. Bioinform. **23**(5), bbac308 (2022)
3. Chua, Z.M., Rajesh, A., Sinha, S., Adams, P.D.: PROTGOAT: improved automated protein function predictions using protein language models. bioRxiv 2024.04.01.587572 (2024). https://doi.org/10.1101/2024.04.01.587572
4. Heinzinger, M., et al.: Bilingual language model for protein sequence and structure. NAR Genom. Bioinform. **6**(4), lqae150 (2024)
5. Lin, Z., et al.: Evolutionary-scale prediction of atomic-level protein structure with a language model. Science **379**(6637), 1123–1130 (2023). https://doi.org/10.1126/science.ade2574
6. Elnaggar, A., et al.: ProtTrans: toward understanding the language of life through self-supervised learning. IEEE Trans. Pattern Anal. Mach. Intell. **44**(10), 7112–7127 (2021). https://doi.org/10.1109/TPAMI.2021.3095381
7. Vieira, L.C., Handojo, M.L., Wilke, C.O.: Scaling down for efficiency: medium-sized protein language models perform well at transfer learning on realistic datasets. bioRxiv: the preprint server for biology, 2024.11.22.624936 (2025). https://doi.org/10.1101/2024.11.22.624936
8. Boutet, E., Lieberherr, D., Tognolli, M., Schneider, M., Bairoch, A.: UniProtKB/swiss-prot. In: Plant bioinformatics: methods and protocols, pp. 89–112. Humana Press, Totowa (2007). https://doi.org/10.1007/978-1-59745-535-0_4
9. Friedberg, I., Radivojac, P., De Paolis, C. et al.: CAFA 5 protein function prediction (2023). https://kaggle.com/competitions/cafa-5-protein-function-prediction
10. Huntley, R.P., et al.: The GOA database: gene ontology annotation updates for 2015. Nucleic Acids Res. **43**(D1), D1057–D1063 (2015). https://doi.org/10.1093/nar/gku1113
11. Vohra, D.: Apache Parquet. Practical Hadoop Ecosystem. Apress, Berkeley (2016). https://doi.org/10.1007/978-1-4842-2199-0_8
12. Elnaggar, A., et al.: Ankh: optimized protein language model unlocks general-purpose modelling. arXiv preprint arXiv:2301.06568 (2023)
13. Chervov, A., Vakhrushev, A., Fironov, S., Martignetti, L.: ProtBoost: protein function prediction with Py-Boost and graph neural networks–CAFA5 top2 solution. arXiv preprint arXiv:2412.04529 (2024)
14. Vu, T.T.D., Jung, J.: Protein function prediction with gene ontology: from traditional to deep learning models. PeerJ **9**, e12019 (2021). https://doi.org/10.7717/peerj.12019
15. Tiittanen, H., Holm, L., Törönen, P.: Optimizing InterProScan representation generates a surprisingly good protein function prediction method. bioRxiv (2022). https://doi.org/10.1101/2022.08.10.503467
16. Pedregosa, F., et al.: Scikit-learn: machine learning in Python. J. Mach. Learn. Res. **12**, 2825–2830 (2011)
17. Heinzinger, M.: How to speak protein? - representation learning for protein prediction. Doctoral dissertation. Technische Universität München (2022)

Forecasting Using SARIMAX Model and LSTM Approach for Arboviruses Using Exogenous Climatic Variables in Predicting Dengue Incidence

Claudia Stoeglehner Sahd[1], Elisângela Ap. da Silva Lizzi[1(✉)], Glaucia Maria Bressan[1], and Laurival Antonio Vilas-Boas[2]

[1] Mathematics Department, Graduate Program in Bioinformatics, Universidade Tecnológica Federal do Paraná - (UTFPR), Av. Alberto Carazzai, 1640, Cornélio Procópio, PR 86300-000, Brazil
`elisangelalizzi@utfpr.edu.br`

[2] General Biology Department, Graduate Program in Bioinformatics, Universidade Estadual de Londrina - (UEL), Campus Universitário, Londrina, PR, Brazil

Abstract. Dengue fever is a disease transmitted by the Aedes aegypti mosquito and has been a public health concern in tropical and subtropical regions. Its incidence is influenced by climatic factors, such as temperature and precipitation, which favor the development of the vector. This study aims to predict the incidence of dengue cases in the city of Londrina, Paraná, between 2013 and 2024, using predictive models based on time series analysis. Data on weekly dengue cases were obtained from the InfoDengue system and combined with climatic variables, such as temperature, humidity, and precipitation. The methodology includes the application of the time series model called Seasonal Autoregressive Integrated Moving Average with exogenous variables (SARIMAX), which incorporates climatic variables in the predictive process. In addition, Long Short-Term Memory (LSTM) recurrent neural networks were used as a comparative, aiming to explore the ability of neural networks to capture complex temporal patterns. The SARIMAX $(2,1,8)(1,1,1)52$ model includes the covariates and obtained the best fit with the minimum temperature, presenting an excellent fit to the data and good forecasting. On the other hand, LSTM neural networks, despite their greater complexity and deep learning capacity, demonstrated great potential to capture the temporal and seasonal variations of the disease, although with greater volatility in the predictions compared to SARIMAX, representing a significant advance for the improvement of dengue predictions. This study suggests that the SARIMAX model, integrated with climate variables, is an effective tool for predicting the evolution of dengue cases and can serve as a basis for the management and planning of preventive actions. In addition, it reinforces the importance of improving LSTM neural networks to improve the accuracy of predictions in highly complex scenarios, with direct implications for the control and prevention of dengue.

M. Dorn and F. Martins Lopes (Eds.): X-Meeting 2025, LNBI 16037, pp. 214–226, 2026.
https://doi.org/10.1007/978-3-032-09336-3_16

Keywords: Dengue · Time series analysis · Neural networks · Modeling predictive

1   Introduction

Dengue is defined as an arbovirus, transmitted predominantly by the *Aedes aegypti* mosquito, adapted to the urban environment of areas with high population density, which mainly affects tropical and subtropics of the world [23, 26, 30] and is responsible for putting more than four billion people at risk from these regions [21].

Representing one of the biggest challenges for public health systems, the disease is widely distributed wherever climatic conditions, such as high temperatures and humidity, favor the proliferation of the vector [12, 16]. Despite this, it is considered neglected due to limited attention in terms of public investments and policies, despite their significant impact on global health [8].

Brazil is the country with the highest number of dengue cases in the Americas. In 2023, the country recorded 2,376,522 cases of dengue, of which 1,051,773 (44.2%) were laboratory confirmed and 1,249 (0.05%) were classified as severe dengue [12, 22]. In 2024, Brazil continues to lead the number of cases, with 6,296,795 suspected cases, of which 3,040,736 were confirmed by a laboratory [16]. The high incidence in Brazil can be attributed to a combination of factors, including high population density, environmental conditions climates favorable to mosquito proliferation, circulation of multiple mosquito serotypes dengue virus and challenges in implementing large-scale vector control measures scale [5, 10, 20].

Particularly, the city of Londrina, in Paraná, has been facing the presence of dengue since the 1980s. Between 2015 and 2024, Londrina presented cyclical outbreaks of dengue, with emphasis on the 2019/2020 epidemic, when 32,245 cases and 29 deaths were confirmed, constituting one of the most critical periods in the city's history [27]. This increase was attributed to factors such as favorable climatic conditions for the *Aedes aegypti* vector, with high humidity and high temperatures, as well as the presence of different viral serotypes that circulated simultaneously in the region [6, 24].

To address this problem, mathematical and statistical models of time series [18] has been widely used to monitor and predict the incidence of dengue and other infectious diseases [2, 7, 15]. Dengue presents occurrence patterns that can be analyzed through statistical models, helping to understand its dynamics and implement strategies for control [9, 17, 25, 28]. These models provide a better understanding of the evolution of the disease, allowing predictions of the number of cases in periods subsequent to the series studied, which brings important assistance in decision-making in public political prevention and educational actions.

Faced with this problem, the objective of this work is to model the temporal evolution of the weekly number of reported dengue cases, using predictive models of temporal series such as SARIMAX, with the city of Londrina, PR, as a case study, for the notification period 2013 to 2024. Long Short-Term Memory (LSTM) recurrent neural networks were also used as a comparative model, aiming to explore the ability of neural networks to capture complex temporal patterns. Dengue case data monthly were obtained from the InfoDengue system, and combined with variables climatic factors, such as temperature and precipitation.

Therefore, this study addresses an important public health issue, particularly in relation to the control and prevention of diseases such as dengue, which affect thousands of people annually. The computational implementation of predictive models, with the potential for generating dashboards for surveillance rooms, facilitates not only the monitoring of dengue and other arboviruses but also enables a faster and more effective response by health authorities. By contributing to a deeper understanding of the temporal dynamics of these diseases, this study supports the development of more effective control and prevention strategies, ultimately improving the quality of life in communities exposed to the vector.

2   Materials and Methods

2.1   Study Design

This research is an ecological epidemiological study with a time series component, aiming to analyze the distribution of incident dengue cases in the city of Londrina, Paraná. The analysis was carried out using different modeling approaches and with time frames defined by epidemiological week, covering the years 2013 to 2024.

2.2   Data Acquisition

Data acquisition for this study was performed using InfoDengue, a platform developed by the Oswaldo Cruz Foundation (Fiocruz)[1] [5], which provides structured data on the incidence of dengue in national territory. During the preprocessing step, the dataset was filtered to include exclusively information related to the municipality of Londrina, Paraná, for the period 2013 to 2024.

In addition to the data on the incidence of dengue, the model was improved by incorporating climatic variables, such as temperature (average, minimum and maximum) and relative humidity of the air (average, minimum and maximum), also obtained from InfoDengue. Furthermore, precipitation data was acquired from the National Institute of Meteorology (INMET)[2].

Climate data, in turn, play a fundamental role in capturing potential relationships between environmental conditions and disease dynamics. The preprocessing step includes data standardization and consistency checks to ensure the integrity and comparability of variables. Additionally, organizing the data into

---

[1] Available in https://info.dengue.mat.br/.
[2] Available in: https://tempo.inmet.gov.br/TabelaEstacoes/83766.

weekly scales was essential to align the temporal format of both dependent and independent variables, allowing more robust and consistent analyzes. For reprodutibility access in: https://github.com/claudiasahd/SARIMAX_LSTM_ Dengue/tree/main.

2.3 Statistical Models

The statistical models employed in this study follow the methodology proposed by Box and Jenkins, which is based on the identification and adjustment of time series models to achieve the best fit to the analyzed data [3]. This methodological approach is particularly effective in incorporating seasonal components, making it well suited for modeling time series that present recurrent periodic peaks and declines over time.

Considering the seasonal nature of dengue incidence, this study adopted SARIMAX (Seasonal Autoregressive Integrated Moving Average with Exogenous Variables) models, configured with a 52-mweek seasonality, reflecting the well established seasonal patterns of the disease during year.

2.4 SARIMAX Model (Seasonal Autoregressive Integrated Moving Averages with Exogenous Variables)

The SARIMAX model is used to predict dengue cases considering the influence of variables exogenous climate factors, such as temperature, humidity and precipitation. SARIMAX requires not only the arguments p, d and q, but also requires another argument which is the periodicity of the seasonal cycle of arguments. According to [29], This modeling is expressed by:

$$\varphi_p(B)\Phi_P\left(B^S\right)\nabla^d\nabla_s^D Y_t = \beta x_t' + \theta_q(B)\Theta_Q\left(B^s\right)\varepsilon_t \tag{1}$$

In Equation (1), Y_t represents the time series of dengue cases at time t, while x_t' is the vector that includes exogenous input variables, such as temperature, humidity and precipitation. The term β is the coefficient associated with these exogenous variables. The notations $\varphi_p(B)$ and $\theta_q(B)$ represent the autoregressive and moving average polynomials, respectively, while $\Phi_P\left(B^S\right)$ and $\Theta_Q\left(B^s\right)$ capture the seasonal effects in the time series, considering the periodicity S. The differentiation operations ∇^d and ∇_s^D ensure stationarity in the series, where d represents the order of regular differentiation and D the order of seasonal differentiation. The variable ε_t denotes the model error, assumed to be white noise.

It is important to highlight that the choice of the SARIMAX model was motivated by the need to consider the variability of dengue cases influenced by climatic factors, such as temperature, humidity and precipitation, which were incorporated as exogenous covariates in the model. By adjusting the model, we aim to capture both the dynamics seasonality of dengue cases and the variations caused by climatic conditions.

Furthermore, the SARIMAX model allows forecasting based not only on the time series itself but also by considering the evolution of these exogenous variables over time, providing a more robust and sensitive approach to external factors that impact disease incidence. To compare and select the models, the Akaike Information Criterion (AIC) was employed [1], which assumes that the most appropriate model is the one with the lowest AIC value. This criterion considers the number of parameters in the model, favoring simpler models with fewer parameters while ensuring an adequate fit to the data.

The R software (version 4.2) was used for all data analyzes involving the SARIMAX model. The software was also employed to obtain results, including routines for describing the series, generating graphs, and estimating model coefficients, both with and without covariates. For the model with covariates, the Time Series Analysis (TSA) function library was utilized [4].

2.5   Recurrent Neural Networks (RNN)

Recurrent Neural Networks (RNN) have an architecture that allows the generation of a value of output based not only on current inputs, but also on information from previous steps. In this way, these networks are able to create more complex, which, although they increase the difficulty of training, increase significantly the variety of problems that can be solved using Machine Learning techniques [11,19].

The LSTM model stands out as an especially effective solution, particularly in scenarios in which long-term temporal dependencies are present, as in the case of time series associated with epidemic diseases such as dengue [13]. Moreover, LSTM is capable of integrating exogenous variables, such as climate conditions, which has a major impact on the evolution of epidemics [19]. The choice of this model to predict dengue cases in this study is justified by its ability to deal with the temporal complexity of data, considering both seasonal fluctuations and interactions with external factors.

In this study, the LSTM model was implemented with a clearly defined architecture and training configuration. The network consisted of a single recurrent layer with 50 LSTM units, followed by a dense (fully connected) output layer comprising one neuron responsible for producing the final prediction. Input data were reshaped into a three-dimensional format, as required by LSTM networks, with axes representing samples, time steps, and features. The LSTM layer employed the ReLU activation function, while the output layer used a linear activation, suitable for continuous value prediction in regression tasks. Training was performed over a maximum of 100 epochs with a batch size of 32. To avoid overfitting, early stopping was applied. Dropout regularization was not explicitly used, as the model demonstrated satisfactory convergence under these settings. This detailed configuration ensures reproducibility and meets the standards for rigorous model evaluation. Three LSTM models were developed with the same network architecture, consisting of two LSTM layers with 50 units each, followed by a dense output layer with a single neuron. The main difference among the models lies in the optimizer used: (i) SGD, with a learning rate of

0.01 and momentum of 0.9; (ii) RMSprop, with a learning rate of 0.001; and (iii) Adam, also with a learning rate of 0.001. The aim was to compare the network's performance under different optimization strategies and its ability to perform out-of-sample predictions.

The development of the LSTM model was conducted based on three core optimizers, widely used to adjust network weights neural networks: Adam (Adaptive Moment Estimation), RMSprop (Root Mean Square Propagation) and SGD (Stochastic Gradient Descent) [19]. Each optimizer has distinct characteristics that influence the speed and convergence of network training. Error metrics (RMSE, MAE and MAPE) were used to evaluate the performance of the models, with the objective of identifying the model that exhibited the best predictive performance for dengue cases. This comparison enabled the determination of the most efficient model configuration in terms of prediction accuracy [19]. Each optimizer has its own characteristics that influence the speed and convergence of network training, the weights of the neural networks were defined in three main layers, adjusted and interconnected with the last density layer. The computational implementation of the RNN was performed in Python, using the Colab environment, a cloud-based platform that offers processing systems, such as GPUs, essential for building and training complex models such as LSTM neural networks.

3   Results

The results show the construction and definition of the SARIMAX models with the covariates and the LSTM networks. At this first moment it is interesting to understand the mechanism generating the series, for this the autocorrelation graphs are illustrated.

Obtaining the autocorrelation function (ACF) and partial autocorrelation (PACF), it can be seen that there are autoregressive and moving average components that need to be considered to capture the serial component of the incidence data, as shown in Fig. 1. Furthermore, the series studied is non-stationary, therefore the integrated differentiation component for stabilizing the series is of order 1 in both the ARIMA component and the seasonal component.

Based on these criteria, it is plausible to incorporate components p=2 and q=8 in the SARIMAX modeling process. And the climate variables are added one by one to the X component to overcome the multicollinearity situation, as shown in Table 1.

Table 1 presents the results of the Akaike Information Criterion (AICc) for $SARIMAX(2, 1, 8)(1, 1, 1)_{52}$ models with different covariates (climatic variables) applied to dengue incidence in Londrina-PR in the period from 2013 to 2024. The parameters evaluated include: model quality measure, AIC, which indicates that the lower the value, the better the quality of the fit; coefficient of the covariate in the model in terms of the delay operators of the differentiated series; standard error of the estimate and mean absolute percentage error, MAPE (Mean Absolute Percentage Error), interpreted that the smaller, the better the fit of the model to the data.

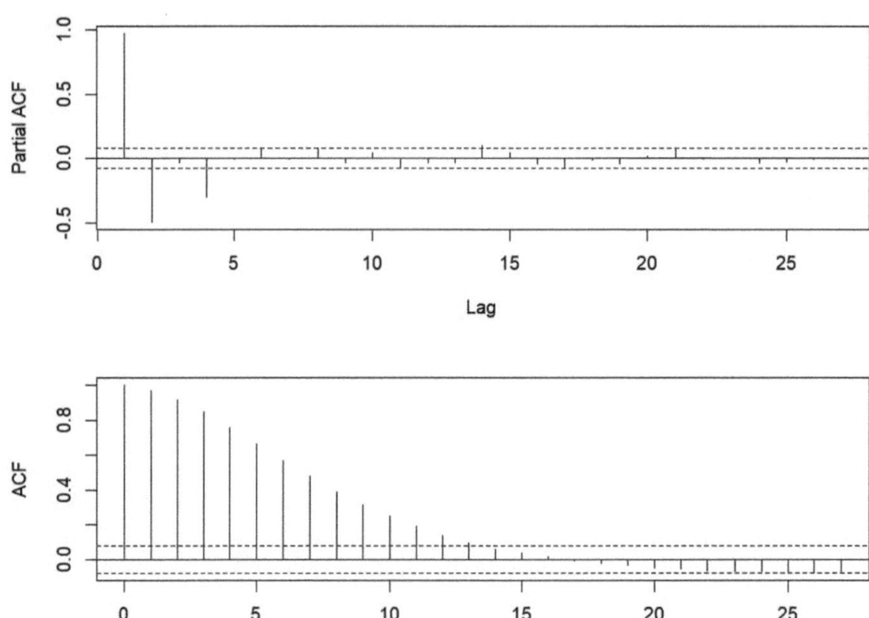

Fig. 1. Autocorrelation and partial autocorrelation of the dengue incidence time series

Table 1. SARIMAX models by covariates

Table - Akaike Information Criterion (AIC) considering SARIMAX $(2,1,8)(1,1,1)_{52}$ with different covariates, estimates, standard errors, and MAPE in Londrina, PR, 2013 to 2024.

Modelo	AICc	Estimate	Standard Error	MAPE
Minimum Temperature	8351.96	0.4246	0.7401	24.98%
Mean Temperature	8353.44	0.9099	1.6209	24.06%
Maximum Temperature	8354.79	0.4135	0.9856	23.55%
Minimum Humidity	8354.79	-0.4323	0.5926	23.29%
Mean Humidity	8354.66	-0.4452	0.9278	24.24%
Maximum Humidity	8354.69	-0.4335	0.4707	23.24%
Precipitation	8353.85	-0.0346	0.5094	24.77%

Source: Author's own work (2025)

The SARIMAX model with Minimum Temperature as a covariate presented the lowest AICc (8351.96), indicating the best fit among the models tested. The positive estimate (0.4246) suggests that higher minimum temperatures are associated with an increase in dengue incidence. Although the MAPE (24.98%) is not the lowest in the table, the combination of low AICc and statistical evidence reinforces the importance of this climate variable. The fit graph (Figure 2) demonstrates that the model adequately captured the seasonality and observed peaks, with random residuals (white noise), validating its applicability in this scenario in a satisfactory manner.

The LSTM neural network architecture is built with three main layers, suitable for time series prediction, where the network structure captures temporal dependencies, and the final density layer generates the desired prediction based on the structure of the previous layers. In terms of implemented optimizers, when using the Adam optimizer, the main difference is in the optimizer settings. Adam maintains two probabilistic moments (mean and variance) for each trainable parameter, which means it needs to store more information compared to the SGD and RMS optimizers. In other words, ADAM increases the number of optimizer settings because it maintains information (moments) for each trainable parameter. On the other hand, the SGD and RMS optimizers maintain less additional information, resulting in fewer optimizer settings. It is important to understand the difference between optimizers in compilation and memory usage, due to the computational complexity between different optimizers. Adam generally converges faster, but may consume more memory due to the additional probabilistic moments it maintains compared to RMS and SGD. In summary, the SARIMAX prediction follows a pattern close to the observed data, highlighting the model's ability to anticipate seasonal fluctuations, with a robust adjustment, especially in the part of the series that reflects the year 2020, when there was a spike in the number of cases due to the pandemic. The analysis of the model was essential to identify which variables most substantially influence the cases of the disease, and the SARIMAX model, with the minimum temperature as a covariate, proved to be the most effective for this study.

On the other hand, RNNs, specifically LSTM with different optimizers, have the advantage of dynamically learning the most complex temporal relationships, without being limited by probabilistic assumptions such as stationarity obtained in the integrated component, as in the SARIMA model. However, in this study, the SARIMAX adjustment was superior to the LSTM, as shown in Fig. 2, panel (a), since the incidence peaks were not profiled by the networks.

Table 2 presents the error metrics—RMSE, MAE, and MAPE—obtained from the evaluation of LSTM models trained with three distinct optimizers: Adam, RMSprop, and SGD. Each metric provides a complementary perspective on model performance: RMSE (Root Mean Squared Error) imposes a higher penalty on large prediction errors; MAE (Mean Absolute Error) estimates the average absolute deviations; and MAPE (Mean Absolute Percentage Error) assesses relative accuracy in percentage terms, facilitating interpretability of predictive performance.

Based on the results, the model trained with the Adam optimizer achieved the lowest RMSE (0.13) and MAE (0.07), suggesting higher precision in absolute terms. In contrast, SGD yielded the lowest MAPE (39.25%), indicating better

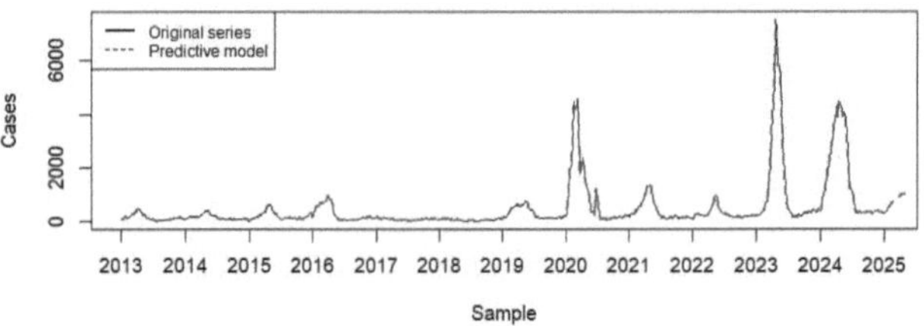

(a) Forecasting SARIMAX

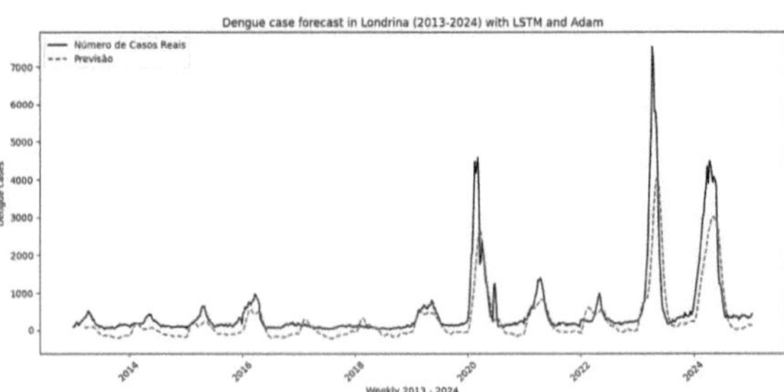

(b) Forecasting LSTM - ADAM optimizer

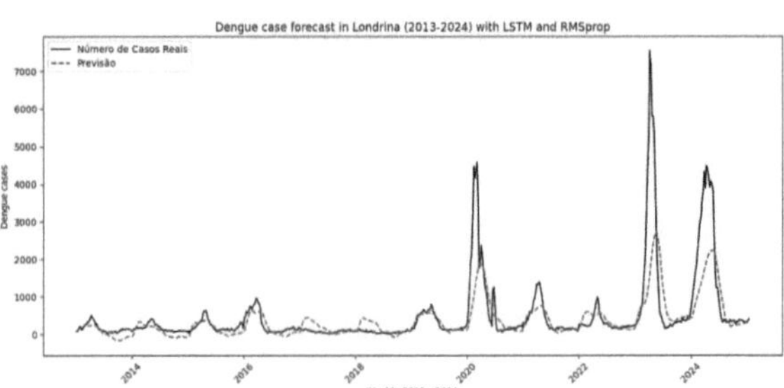

(c) Forecasting LSTM - RMS optimizer

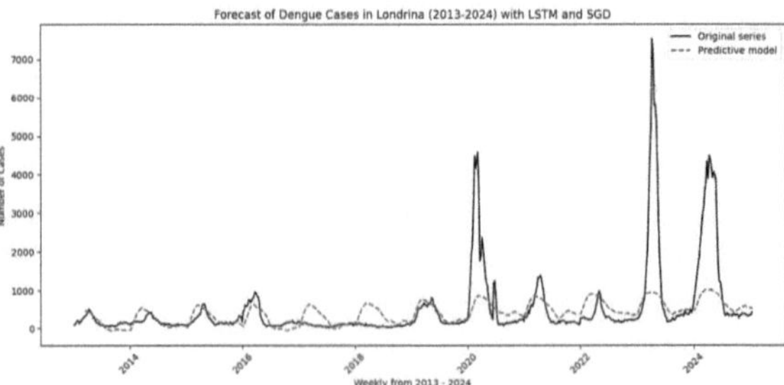

(d) Forecasting LSTM - SGD optimizer

Fig. 2. Adjustments of the forecasting models: SARIMAX and LSTM.

Table 2. Comparions LSTM metrics

Table 2 - Comparison of error metrics (RMSE, MAE e MAPE) by LSTM models with diferents optimizer (Adam, SGD e RMSprop) - Londrina, PR, 2013 a 2024.

Optimizer	RMSE	MAE	MAPE
Adam	0.13	0.07	45.11%
SGD	0.23	0.11	39.25%
RMSprop	0.16	0.10	104.11%

Source: Author's own work(2025)

relative performance compared to actual values, despite exhibiting higher RMSE and MAE. Meanwhile, the model trained with RMSprop showed the worst performance in MAPE (104.11%), reflecting greater instability in relative prediction accuracy. This comparative analysis demonstrates that the choice of optimizer significantly influences model performance, with Adam emerging as the most robust in terms of absolute error. The results indicate that the LSTM models with Adam and RMSprop optimizers performed well in forecasting dengue time series data, presenting a viable alternative to SARIMAX—particularly when accounting for data complexity and non-stationarity.

When adjusting the model, we sought to capture both the seasonal dynamics of dengue cases and the variations caused by weather conditions. Furthermore, the SARIMAX model allows forecasting to be performed not only based on the time series itself, but also on the evolution of these exogenous variables over time, providing a more robust forecast that is sensitive to external factors that impact the incidence of the disease. To adjust the LSTM (Long Short-Term Memory) networks, they were adjusted based on a weekly analysis of dengue cases, allowing us to capture variations and patterns in the incidence of the disease associated with weather variables, including humidity, temperature, and precipitation (Fig. 2, panel (b), (c) e (d). In this case, it is the ability of these methods to retain information, allowing the model to explore recurring structures of previous data over long periods and capture complex temporal patterns. This is particularly useful for time series that exhibit seasonal trends and long-term dependencies, as is the case with seasonal diseases such as dengue [14,15,19]. For the adjustment of LSTM (Long Short-Term Memory) networks, this choice is due to its structure, where information circulates between several layers, the LSTM neural network stands out especially in dynamic systems, in sequential data and in time series.

4   Discussion

Predictive modeling of dengue incidence using time series has proven to be a robust and effective approach for understanding the dynamics of this arbovirus disease, which is influenced by seasonal and regional factors. This methodology provides valuable support for the planning and implementation of public health policies, allowing peaks to be anticipated and resources to be allocated more strategically. Among the models applied, SARIMAX stood out for its ability to incorporate exogenous climate variables, such as temperature, humidity, and precipitation, which are crucial for capturing the influence of environmental factors on the proliferation of the Aedes aegypti vector, the main transmitter of dengue. This inclusion of external variables gives SARIMAX superiority over traditional models, such as SARIMA, which do not consider such factors and are limited to purely temporal analyses. Although SARIMAX presents stochastic and probabilistic performance, its accuracy in predicting seasonal periods of high incidence was remarkable, demonstrating its usefulness for epidemiological surveillance. However, the complex and non-linear nature of dengue dynamics suggests that complementary approaches, such as machine learning models, may be necessary to improve predictive accuracy, especially in scenarios with atypical peaks or abrupt changes in incidence patterns.

In this context, LSTM-type neural networks have emerged as a promising alternative, capable of capturing complex and non-linear temporal patterns. The comparison between the SARIMAX and LSTM models, using different optimizers (Adam, RMSprop and SGD), reinforced the superiority of SARIMAX in this scenario under study (city of Londrina), mainly due to its ability to integrate exogenous variables and provide more consistent predictions. However, when the Adam optimizer was applied to the LSTM, competitive results were observed, although still inferior to SARIMAX, especially during seasonal peaks, where the LSTM had difficulty capturing extreme variations.

The Adam optimizer allowed efficient learning, adjusting the predictions to the actual observed values. The LSTM model's ability to handle nonlinear data and its long-term dependencies was a differentiator compared to traditional models, which are often unable to capture the dynamic variations and volatility observed in dengue incidence time series. The inferior performance of the SGD optimizer, observed during epidemic peaks, corroborates the literature that highlights the vulnerability of this algorithm in time series with high volatility [14]. Despite its popularity for its simplicity and computational efficiency, SGD was unable to adequately adjust the model parameters during outbreaks, resulting in inaccurate predictions. This finding suggests that the choice of optimizer plays a crucial role in the accuracy of predictions, with Adam proving particularly effective in capturing the nuances of dengue time series. The results obtained with the SARIMAX and LSTM models have direct implications for epidemiological surveillance and dengue control. The use of robust predictive models can provide powerful tools to anticipate vector control interventions, allowing for more efficient allocation of resources and implementation of control measures before the number of cases reaches critical levels. In terms of limitations, the use of these models is linked to data quality. Underreporting of cases, unpredictable climate variations and the complexity of interactions between environmental and behavioral variables still represent challenges for modeling in arboviruses.

The integration of predictive models with epidemiological monitoring systems can result in dynamic predictive platforms capable of providing early warnings and contextual information to health managers, similar to InfoDengue[1] in Rio de Janeiro [5]. Finally, the evidence presented in this work reinforces the importance of predictive modeling not only as an analysis tool, but as a critical component in vector-borne disease control strategies. The application of statistical and machine learning methods in dengue forecasting has the potential to transform the way this and other endemic diseases are addressed, providing effective and informed solutions for health authorities.

5   Conclusion

It is concluded that the SARIMAX model, integrated with climate variables, is an effective tool for predicting the evolution of dengue cases and can serve as a basis for the management and planning of preventive actions. Furthermore, it reinforces the importance of improving LSTM neural networks to improve the accuracy of predictions in highly complex scenarios, with direct implications for the control and prevention of dengue.

References

1. Akaike, H.: Maximum likelihood identification of gaussian autoregressive moving average models. Biometrika **60**(2), 255–265 (1973)
2. AUNG, S.H., et al.: A SARIMA time series forecasting for dengue cases for reporting to Yangon region, Myanmar. J. Public Health Dev. **22**(1), 184–196 (2024)
3. Box, G.E.P., Jenkins, G.M., Reinsel, G.C.: Time Series Analysis: Forecasting and Control. Prentice-Hall Inc., New Jersey (1994)
4. Chan, K.S., Ripley, B., Chan, M.K.S., Chan, S.: Package 'tsa' (2022). R package version 1
5. Codeco, C.T., et al.: Fast expansion of dengue in brazil. Lancet Regional Health - Am. **12**, 100274 (2022)
6. De Almeida, D.S., et al.: Estudo da relação entre variáveis meteorológicas e ocorrência de casos de dengue em londrina – pr. Revista Brasileira De Geografia Física **14**(7), 3857–3866 (2022)
7. Dos Santos, T.R.: Uma comparação dos modelos sarima e estruturais para a previsão da incidência de dengue em belo horizonte, minas gerais. Rev. Brasileira Biometria **35**(1), 98–114 (2017)
8. Duvignaud, A., et al.: Epidemiology of travel-associated dengue from 2007 to 2022: a geosentinel analysis. J. Travel Med. (2024)
9. Rufino de Freitas, J., et al.: Modelo preditivo para o número de notificações de dengue na região metropolitana do recife-pe. Sigmae **8**(2), 584–595 (2019)
10. Geraldini, B., et al.: Influence of temperature and precipitation on dengue incidence in campinas, são paulo state, brazil (2013-2022). Rev. Soc. Brasileira Med. Trop. **57** (2024)
11. Guesmi, L., Fathallah, H., Menif, M.: Modulation format recognition using artificial neural networks for the next generation optical networks. In: Advanced Applications for Artificial Neural Networks, p. 11 (2018)

12. Gurgel-Gonçalves, R., Oliveira, W.K.D., Croda, J.: The greatest dengue epidemic in Brazil: Surveillance, prevention, and control. Rev. Soc. Brasileira Med. Trop. **57**, e00203–2024 (2024)
13. Hochreiter, S., Schmidhuber, J.: Long short-term memory. Neural Comput. **9**(1), 1–42 (1997)
14. Karasinghe, N., Peiris, S., Jayathilaka, R., Dharmasena, T.: Forecasting weekly dengue incidence in Sri Lanka: modified autoregressive integrated moving average modeling approach. PLoS ONE **19**(3), e0299953 (2024)
15. Lizzi, E.A.D.S., Pimenta-Zanon, M.H., Bressan, G.M., Sahd, C.S., Vilas-Boas, L.A.: Time series models for the description and forecasting of incident cases of dengue: a case study in londrina- Paraná. Contribuiciones Ciencias Soc. **17**, e13834 (2024)
16. Ly, H.: Dengue fever in the Americas. Virulence **15**(1) (2024)
17. Martinez, E.Z., Silva, E.A.S.D., Fabbro, A.L.D.: A SARIMA forecasting model to predict the number of cases of dengue in Campinas, state of São Paulo, Brazil. Rev. Soc. Brasileira Medicina Trop. **44**(4), 436–440 (2011)
18. Morettin, P.A., Toloi, C.M.: Análise de Séries Temporais—2a Edição Revista e Ampliada. ABE–Projeto Fisher, Editora Edgar Blücher (2006)
19. Nielsen, A.: Análise Prática de Séries Temporais: Predição com estatística e aprendizado de máquina. Alta Books (2021)
20. Nunes, P.C.G., et al.: 30 years of fatal dengue cases in Brazil: a review. BMC Public Health **19**(1), 329 (2019)
21. World Health Organization: Dengue and severe dengue (2021). https://www.who.int/news-room/fact-sheets/detail/dengue-and-severe-dengue. Accessed November 2024
22. World Health Organization: Disease outbreak news: Dengue – global situation (2024). https://www.who.int/emergencies/disease-outbreak-news/item/2024-DON518. Accessed November 2024
23. PAHO: Dengue (2004). https://www.paho.org/pt/topicos/dengue. Accessed November 2024
24. Paula-Shinobu, P.F., et al.: Uma abordagem geográfica da saúde na análise da distribuição de casos de dengue em londrina, paraná. Geosaberes **9**(17), 1–13 (2017)
25. Polwiang, S.: The time series seasonal patterns of dengue fever and associated weather variables in Bangkok (2003–2017). BMC Infect. Dis. **20**, 1–10 (2020)
26. Rodriguez-Roche, R., et al.: Virus evolution during a severe dengue epidemic in Cuba, 1997. Virology **334**, 154–159 (2005)
27. Secretaria de Saúde do Paraná: Boletins da dengue (2024). https://www.dengue.pr.gov.br/Pagina/Boletins-da-Dengue
28. Siqueira, I.S., et al.: A relação da incidência de casos de dengue com a precipitação na área urbana de belém-pa, 2007 a 2011, através de modelos multivariados de séries temporais. Rev. Brasileira Meteorologia **33**(2), 380–389 (2018)
29. Vagropoulos, S.I.e.a.: Comparison of SARIMAX, SARIMA, modified SARIMA and ANN-based models for short-term PV generation forecasting. In: 2016 IEEE International Energy Conference (ENERGYCON), pp. 1–6 (2016)
30. Wang, E., et al.: Evolutionary relationships of endemic/epidemic and sylvatic dengue viruses. J. Virol. **74**, 3227–3234 (2000)

Author Index

A

Albuquerque Pinto, Juliana Barreto   106
Antunes, Deborah   74
Araújo, Gabriel Freitas   45

B

Barra, Williams Fernandes   106
Bastos, Ana Luísa Araújo   181
Bastos, Fernanda Zettel   136
Beirão, Breno Castello Branco   136
Benko-Iseppon, Ana Maria   192
Bressan, Glaucia Maria   214

C

Caffarena, Ernesto R.   74
Castro, Mauro A. A.   62
Cavalheiro, Vitória Luisa   136

D

da Silva de Souza, Ramon   192
da Silva Lizzi, Elisângela Ap.   214
da Silva Mourão, Ronald Matheus   106
da Silva, Jéssica Manoelli Costa   106
da Silva, Manassés Daniel   192
da Silva, Valéria Cristiane Santos   106
de Araújo Junior, Helton Fabio Santos   122
de Assumpção, Paulo Pimentel   106
de Azevedo Alves Sobrinho, Pitágoras   205
de Carvalho, Lucas Miguel   151
de Melo Silva, Laryssa Bandeira   45
de Melo, Ana Luíza Trajano Mangueira   192
de Melo, Nicolly Clemente   151
de Melo-Minardi, Raquel Cardoso   181
de Queiroz, Artur Trancoso Lopo   122
de Souza Avelar da Costa, Daniel   106
Demachki, Samia   106
dos Anjos Adur, Mikaela   136

F

Farias, Maria Luiza Carvalho   192
Felicio, Aline Cristina   151
Ferreira-Neto, José Ribamar Costa   192
Figuerola, Wilfredo Blanco   205
Flores, Lorrana Verdi   30
Fuganti, Lucas Costa   166
Fukutani, Eduardo Rocha   122

G

Gonçalves, José Írahe Kasprzykowski   122

H

Haddi, Khalid   30

K

Kowalski, Thayne Woycinck   14

L

Lemos, Rafael Pereira   181
Lopes, Fabricio Martins   166

M

Maia, Giovana C. F.   90
Mariano, Diego   90, 181
Martins, Ingrid B. S.   74
Martins-Karl, Ana Luiza   1
Melo-Minardi, Raquel Cardoso de   90
Mendes Anaissi, Ana Karyssa   106
Monteiro, Ana Beatriz   30
Moreira, Fabiano Cordeiro   106
Mota, Tiago Feitosa   122
Moura, Patrícia   45

N
Neto, João Pacifico Bezerra   45

P
Paiva, Luciano Vilela   30
Peña, Samanda López   30
Pereira Lemos, Rafael   90
Pimenta-Zanon, Matheus Henrique   166
Pinto, Renan Terassi   30
Pirovani, Milenna M.   181
Puça, Maria Carolina   90

Q
Querne, Lana Bazan Peters   136
Quintanilha-Peixoto, Gabriel   1

R
Recamonde-Mendoza, Mariana   14
Reis, Matheus Henrique   74
Robertson, A. Gordon   62

S
Sahd, Claudia Stoeglehner   214
Sakamoto, Tetsu   205
Salazar, Yanka E. A. R.   90
Santos, Lucas Moraes dos   90
Shmulevich, Ilya   62
Sousa, Tais Nobrega de   90
Speggiorin, Laura Galant   14
Swanson, Nilus   62

T
Tercan, Bahar   62
Turquetti-Moraes, Dayana K.   1

V
Venancio, Thiago M.   1
Vilas-Boas, Laurival Antonio   214

Y
Yamada, Camila A. O.   181

MIX
Papier aus verantwortungsvollen Quellen
Paper from responsible sources
FSC® C105338

If you have any concerns about our products,
you can contact us on
ProductSafety@springernature.com

In case Publisher is established outside the EU,
the EU authorized representative is:
**Springer Nature Customer Service Center GmbH
Europaplatz 3, 69115 Heidelberg, Germany**

Printed by Libri Plureos GmbH
in Hamburg, Germany